D1523280

APULEIUS MADAURENSIS

Mediceus bibl. Laurentianae 68,2 (F): Apul. Met. 4,20 (89,15-92,21).

GRONINGEN COMMENTARIES ON APULEIUS

APULEIUS MADAURENSIS
METAMORPHOSES

Book IV 1-27
Text, Introduction and Commentary

B. L. HIJMANS Jr. – R. Th. VAN DER PAARDT
E. R. SMITS – R. E. H. WESTENDORP BOERMA
A. G. WESTERBRINK

GRONINGEN
BOUMA'S BOEKHUIS B.V. PUBLISHERS
1977

ISBN   90 6088 059 5

The publication of this book was made possible through a grant from the
Netherlands Organisation for the Advancement of Pure Research (Z.W.O.)

Printed in The Netherlands by Van Gorcum, Assen

PREFACE

During the spring of 1973 a group of Latinists at Groningen decided to publish a commentary in English on the Metamorphoses of Apuleius. We felt that for the time being certain books could be omitted since relatively recent commentaries on those exist, viz. book 1 (doctoral dissertation by Marg. Molt, Groningen 1938), book 2 (doctoral dissertation by B. J. de Jonge, Groningen 1941) both with a commentary in Latin; book 3, too, but with a commentary in English, was published as a Groningen dissertation (1971) by a member of our group, Dr. R. Th. van der Paardt. Of book 11 an edition with commentary has been announced by J. Gwyn Griffiths of Swansea, whereas Christine Harrauer wrote a commentary in German as a doctoral dissertation in Vienna (1973). She has been kind enough to provide us with a copy of her work.

We have undertaken the task, then, of writing commentaries on books 4-10 with this restriction that we shall defer the commentary on Amor and Psyche to the end[1]. In our opinion this section does not need a new commentary as urgently as the remainder, since several separate editions with commentaries are in existence; moreover the section requires time consuming preparation because of its special character and the large number of publications dealing with it. The entire project was announced in *Gnomon* 1973, p. 528 in order to forestall duplication[2].

We intend to publish as follows: the present volume contains *Met.* 4, 1-27; subsequently a volume will be published containing 6, 25-32 and the whole of book 7; next each of book 8, 9 and 10 will receive a volume (the last commentary on these sections is by G. F. Hildebrand, 1842). Finally we shall try our strength on Amor and Psyche.

We believe that our main emphasis must be an exegetical commentary and therefore give the Latin text of Helm's final Teubner edition with his page and line numbers. Indeed we have not attempted a new investigation of the MSS, since that seemed to be largely superfluous after the work of Helm, Robertson and Giarratano; but we do, in our commentary, consider critical problems and find we repeatedly differ from Helm's last edition[3] and, of course, even more from Robertson, whose

---

[1] This implies that we intend to prepare a new commentary on book 5 on which Dr. J. M. H. Fernhout had published his Groningen dissertation (Middelburg 1949).
[2] During the preparation of the present volume contact was established between our group and Mr. Alexander Scobie of the University of Wellington, New Zealand, who, unaware of our plans, was also preparing an English commentary on the whole of the *Metamorphoses*. In the meantime his first volume, containing a commentary on book 1, has appeared (Meisenheim am Glan 1975). With the greatest goodwill Mr. Scobie stated in a letter that he was not going to proceed beyond book 3.
[3] Departures from Helm's text have been listed separately.

collations are, it is true, accurate, but whose emendations are often open to question.

We work as follows: at the Classical Institute of the University of Groningen, we have gathered as complete a collection of publications on Apuleius as possible; the collections of the University Library and of the Buma Library at Leeuwarden have been made available on long term loans, xerox copies of periodical articles have been acquired and a card index has been arranged. It goes without saying that the material may be consulted by all interested. The participants in the project each attempt certain chapters, then assemble to criticize each other's work and in these discussions they try to achieve a consensus. The undersigned plays a supervisory role. We realize that it is a perilous undertaking to build a homogeneous commentary with five people of differing dispositions but we hope we have had some measure of success; in any case we like to state that we are working on the project with increasing pleasure — due no doubt to the stimulating effect of the internal discussions.

The English version was prepared by Dr. B. L. Hijmans Jr., but we are very grateful to Mrs. Philippa Goold M.A. who was kind enough to read through the entire manuscript and to correct the English where necessary and who, in addition, ferreted out a host of small and not so small errors. Miss Annette Harder undertook with great patience the tedious task of preparing the indices. We also thank the Dutch Organization for Pure Research (ZWO) which made the necessary grant to enable us to publish the work; we trust this invaluable organization will see its way clear to assist with subsequent volumes as well.

Thanks, too, are due to the Classical Department at Leiden for generously allowing Dr. R. Th. van der Paardt sufficient time to continue participating in the team after his appointment at Leiden University.

The librarians of the University Library at Groningen and the Buma Library at Leeuwarden may claim our gratitude for the long term loans of their collections of *Apuleiana*.

Similarly directors and staff of the Thesaurus Linguae Latinae at Munich are thanked for the readiness and accuracy with which they answered our questions and gave their assistance when we visited them.

Groningen, January 1976   R. E. H. Westendorp Boerma

CONTENTS

ABBREVIATIONS

A number of well known older editions and articles are referred to by author's name only: they may be found in the respective bibliographies of the commentaries the present volume is designed to continue. Volumes and articles mentioned in the bibliography of the present volume (pp. 000) have not been repeated here.

Aalto, *Untersuchungen* = P. A. Aalto, *Untersuchungen über das lateinische Gerundium und Gerundivum*, Helsinki 1949

André = J. André, *Étude sur les termes de couleur dans la langue latine*, Paris 1949

Apul.Gron. III = R. E. H. Westendorp Boerma and B. L. Hijmans Jr., *Apuleiana Groningana III*, *Mnemosyne* S. IV, 27 (1974), pp. 406-412

Armini 1928 = H. Armini, *Studia Apuleiana*, *Eranos* 26 (1928), pp. 273-339

Armini 1932 = H. Armini, *Till diskussionen om Apuleiustexten*, *Eranos* 30 (1932), pp. 49-92

Baehrens, *Synt.* = W. A. Baehrens, *Beiträge zur lateinischen Syntax*, *Philologus*, Supplementband 12 (1912)

Balsdon, *Roman Women* = J. P. V. D. Balsdon, *Roman Women*, Oxford 1962

Balsdon, *Life* = J. P. V. D. Balsdon, *Life and Leisure in Ancient Rome*, London etc. 1969

Baus, *Kranz* = K. Baus, *Der Kranz in Antike und Christentum*, Bonn 1940 (repr. 1965)

Becker = H. Becker, *Studia Apuleiana*, Diss. Köningsberg, Berlin 1879

Bernhard = M. Bernhard, *Der Stil des Apuleius von Madaura*, Stuttgart 1927 (repr. Amsterdam 1965)

Bétolaud = V. Bétolaud, *Apulée, Oeuvres Complètes*, Paris s.a.

Blomgren = S. Blomgren, *De sermone Ammiani Marcellini quaestiones variae*, Uppsala 1937

Bonnet = M. Bonnet, *Le latin de Grégoire de Tours*, Paris 1890

Burck = *Apuleius von Madaura. Metamorphosen oder Der goldene Esel*. Nach der Uebersetzung von August Rode (...) herausgegeben von Erich Burck, Berlin 1961

Callebat, *S.C.* = L. Callebat, *Sermo Cotidianus dans les Métamorphoses d'Apulée*, Caen 1968

Castiglioni 1931 = L. Castiglioni, *Apuleiana II*, *RIL* 64 (1931), pp. 475-489

Ciaffi = V. Ciaffi, *Petronio in Apuleio*, Torino 1960

Clouard = *Apulée. L'âne d'or ou les Métamorphoses*. Traduction nouvelle (...) par Henri Clouard, Paris s.a.

Corbett = P. E. Corbett, *The Roman Law of Marriage*, Oxford 1930

Curtius, *Eur. Lit.* = E. R. Curtius, *Europäische Literatur und lateinisches Mittelalter*, Bern ⁷1969

Dar.-Sagl. = C. R. Daremberg-E. Saglio, *Dictionnaire des Antiquités grecques et romaines*, 5 vols, Paris 1877-1919

Desertine = A. H. J. V. M. Desertine, *De Apulei studiis Plautinis*, Diss. Utrecht, Nijmegen 1898.

Eicke = W. Eicke, *Stilunterschiede in den Metamorphosen des Apuleius*, Diss. Göttingen 1956

Ernout, *Les Adj.* = A. Ernout, *Les adjectifs Latins en -osus et -ulentus*, Paris 1949

Ernout, *Philologica* = A. Ernout, *Philologica*, 3 vols. Paris 1946-1965

Ernout-Meillet = A. Ernout-A. Meillet, *Dictionnaire étymologique de la langue latine*, Paris 1951 ([4]1959-1960)

Ernout-Thomas = A. Ernout-F. Thomas, *Syntaxe latine*, Paris [2]1959

Feldbrugge = J. J. M. Feldbrugge, *Het schertsende karakter van Apuleius' Metamorphosen*, Diss. Nijmegen, Utrecht etc. 1938

Fernhout = J. M. H. Fernhout, *Ad Apulei Madaurensis Metamorphoseon librum quintum commentarius exegeticus*, Diss. Groningen, Middelburg 1949

Forcellini = A. Forcellini, *Lexicon totius Latinitatis* (...) Patavii 1965 (repr.)

Fraenkel, *Kolon u. Satz II* = Ed. Fraenkel, *Kleine Beiträge zur klassischen Philologie* I, Roma 1964, pp. 93-130

Friedländer, *SG* = L. Friedländer, *Darstellungen aus der Sittengeschichte Roms*, 2 vols., Leipzig [8]1910

Gargantini = L. Gargantini, *Ricerche intorno alla formazione dei temi nominali nelle Metamorfosi di Apuleio*, RIL 97 (1963), pp. 33-43

Gatscha = Fr. Gatscha, *Quaestionum Apuleianarum capita tria*, Diss. Wien 1898

GCA = Groningen Commentaries on Apuleius

vGeisau = J. von Geisau, *Syntaktische Graecismen bei Apuleius*, IF 36 (1916), pp. 70-98; pp. 242-287

Georges = K. E. Georges, *Ausführliches lateinisch-deutsches Handwörterbuch* (...) 8e (...) Aufl. von H. Georges, 2 Bde, Hannover etc. 1913-1918

Graur = A. Graur, *Quidam chez Apulée, Hommages à Marcel Renard* I, Bruxelles 1969, pp. 378-382

Hand, *Turs.* = F. Hand, *Tursellinus seu de particulis Latinis commentarii*, 4 vols., Leipzig 1829-1845 (repr. Amsterdam 1969)

Heine = R. Heine, *Untersuchungen zur Romanform der Metamorphosen des Apuleius von Madaura*, Diss. Göttingen 1962

Helm-Krenkel = *Apuleius. Metamorphosen oder der goldene Esel*. Lateinisch und deutsch von Rudolf Helm. Sechste (...) Auflage (...) von Werner Krenkel, Berlin 1970

Hofmann, *LU* = J. B. Hofmann, *Lateinische Umgangssprache*, Heidelberg [3]1951

Hoppe = H. Hoppe, *Syntax und Stil des Tertullian*, Leipzig 1903

Index Apul. = W. A. Oldfather-H. V. Canter-B. E. Perry, *Index Apuleianus*, Middletown 1934

de Jonge = B. J. de Jonge, *Ad Apulei Madaurensis Metamorphoseon librum secundum commentarius exegeticus*, Diss. Groningen 1941

Junghanns = P. Junghanns, *Die Erzählungstechnik von Apuleius' Metamorphosen und ihrer Vorlage*, Philologus, Supplementband 24 (1932)

K.St. = R. Kühner-C. Stegmann, *Ausführliche Grammatik der lateinischen Sprache*, Hannover 1912-1914

Latte, *RRG* = K. Latte, *Römische Religionsgeschichte*, München 1960

Lesky = A. Lesky, *Apuleius von Madaura und Lukios von Patrai, Gesammelte Schriften*, Bern 1966, pp. 549-578

Leumann-Hofmann = Stolz-Schmalz, *Lateinische Grammatik* (...) in fünfter Auflage (...) von Manu Leumann und Joh. Bapt. Hofmann, München 1928

LHSz = M. Leumann-J. B. Hofmann-A. Szantyr, *Lateinische Grammatik* II (Syntax und Stilistik), München 1965

Löfstedt, *Spätlat. Stud.* = E. Löfstedt, *Spätlateinische Studien*, Uppsala 1908

Löfstedt, *Per. Aeth.* = E. Löfstedt, *Philologischer Kommentar zur Peregrinatio Aetheriae*, Uppsala 1911 (repr. Darmstadt 1966)

Löfstedt, *Krit. Apol.* = E. Löfstedt, *Kritische Bemerkungen zu Tertullians Apologeticum*, Lund etc. 1918

Löfstedt, *Synt.* = E. Löfstedt, *Syntactica*, I Lund ²1942 (repr. 1956); II Lund 1933 (repr. 1956)

Löfstedt, *Verm. Stud.* = E. Löfstedt, *Vermischte Studien zur lateinischen Sprachkunde und Syntax*, Lund 1936

LS = Ch. T. Lewis-Ch. Short, *A Latin Dictionary*, Oxford 1879

LSJ = H. G. Liddell-R. Scott-H. Stuart Jones-R. McKenzie, *A Greek-English Lexicon*, Oxford 1958 (repr.)

Marquardt = J. Marquardt, *Privatleben der Römer*, Leipzig ²1886

Médan = P. Médan, *La latinité d'Apulée dans les Métamorphoses*, Thèse Paris 1925

Merkelbach = R. Merkelbach, *Roman und Mysterium in der Antike*, München etc. 1962

Möbitz = O. Möbitz, *Die Stellung des Verbums in den Schriften des Apuleius*, Glotta 13 (1924), pp. 116-126

Mohrmann, *Études* = Chr. Mohrmann, *Études sur le Latin des Chrétiens*, 3 vols., Roma 1961-1965

Molt = Marg.Molt, *Ad Apulei Madaurensis Metamorphoseon librum primum commentarius exegeticus*, Diss. Groningen 1938

Mommsen, *RStrR* = Th. Mommsen, *Römisches Strafrecht*, Leipzig 1899

Nachträge zu Otto = R. Häussler (Hrsgbr.), *Nachträge zu A. Otto, Sprichwörter und sprichwörtliche Redensarten der Römer*, Hildesheim 1968

Neue-Wagener = F. Neue-C. Wagener, *Formenlehre der lateinischen Sprache*, 3. Aufl., Leipzig 1892-1905

Neuenschwander = P. Neuenschwander, *Der bildliche Ausdruck des Apuleius von Madaura*, Diss. Zürich 1913

Norden, *Privatrecht* = F. Norden, *Apulejus von Madaura und das römische Privatrecht*, Leipzig etc. 1912

OLD = *Oxford Latin Dictionary*, Oxford 1968 —

Onians, *Origins* = R. B. Onians, *The Origins of European Thought about the Body, the Mind, the Soul, the World, Time and Fate*, Cambridge 1951

Opelt, *Schimpfwörter* = Ilona Opelt, *Die lateinischen Schimpfwörter und verwandte sprachliche Erscheinungen. Eine Typologie*, Heidelberg 1965

Otto, *Sprichw.* = A. Otto, *Die Sprichwörter und sprichwörtlichen Redensarten der Römer*, Leipzig 1890

vdP. = R. T. van der Paardt, *L. Apuleius Madaurensis. The Metamorphoses. A commentary on book III with text & introduction*, Amsterdam 1971

Pape-Benseler = W. Pape-G. E. Benseler, *Wörterbuch der griechischen Eigennamen*, 2Bde., Braunschweig 1884

Perry 1923 = B. E. Perry, *Some Aspects of the literary Art of Apuleius in the Metamorphoses*, *TAPA* 54 (1923), pp. 196-227

Perry, *Anc.Rom.* = B. E. Perry, *The Ancient Romances; A Literary-Historical Account of Their Origins*, Berkeley etc. 1967

R.E. = *Realencyclopädie der classischen Altertumswissenschaft*, Stuttgart 1894-

Riefstahl = H. Riefstahl, *Der Roman des Apuleius*, Frankfurt am Main 1938

Roscher = W. H. Roscher, *Ausführliches Lexikon der griechischen und römischen Mythologie*, Leipzig 1884-1937

Rossbach, *Unters.* = A. Rossbach, *Untersuchungen über die römische Ehe*, Stuttgart 1853

Ruiz de Elvira = A. Ruiz de Elvira, *Syntactica Apuleiana*, Emerita 22 (1954), pp. 99-136

Schrijnen-Mohrmann = J. Schrijnen-Chr. Mohrmann, *Studien zur Syntax der Briefe des hl. Cyprian*, 2 vols., Nijmegen 1936-1937

Scobie, *Aspects* = A. Scobie, *Aspects of the Ancient Romance and its Heritage*, Meisenheim am Glan 1969

Sommer = F. Sommer, *Handbuch der lateinischen Laut- und Formenlehre*, Heidelberg 1914

Strilciw = N. Strilciw, *De arte rhetorica in Apulei Metamorphosibus conspicua*, Eos 28 (1925), pp. 105-124

Svennung, *Oros.* = J. Svennung, *Orosiana. Syntaktische, semasiologische und kritische Studien zu Orosius*, Diss. Uppsala 1922

Svennung, *Pall.* = J. Svennung, *Untersuchungen zu Palladius und zur lateinischen Fach- und Volkssprache*, Lund 1935

Summers = R. Summers, *A Legal Commentary on the Metamorphoses of Apuleius*, Diss. Princeton 1967

ThLL = *Thesaurus Linguae Latinae*, Leipzig 1900-

Walde-Hofmann = A. Walde-J. B. Hofmann, *Lateinisches etymologisches Wörterbuch*, Heidelberg ²1938 (repr. 1966)

Walsh = P. G. Walsh, *The Roman Novel*, Cambridge 1970

Waszink = J. H. Waszink, *Quinti Septimi Florentis Tertulliani De Anima*. Edited with Introduction and Commentary, Amsterdam 1947

Wellek and Warren = R. Wellek-A. Warren, *Theory of Literature*, 3rd edition Harmondsworth 1963 (repr. 1973)

Weyman = C. Weyman, *Studien zu Apuleius und seinen Nachahmern*, SBAW München 1893 II, pp. 321-392

Wiman = G. Wiman, *Textkritiska Studier till Apuleius*, Diss. Göteborg 1927

Wissowa = G. Wissowa, *Religion und Kultus der Römer*, München ²1912

Wolterstorff = G. Wolterstorff, *Artikelbedeutung von ille bei Apuleius*, Glotta 8 (1917), pp. 197-226

BIBLIOGRAPHY

For the bibliography up to 1971 the reader is referred to the Groningen dissertations by M. Molt (Groningen 1938), B. J. de Jonge (Groningen 1941), J. M. H. Fernhout (Middelburg 1949) and R. T. van der Paardt (Amsterdam 1971). Since van der Paardt's commentary on the third book of the Metamorphoses the following bibliographical survey, text, translation, commentaries and studies appeared (with some titles omitted by van der Paardt):

Bibliographical survey:

C. C. Schlam, *The Scholarship on Apuleius since 1938, CW* 64 (1971), pp. 285-309

Text (with translation):

P. Scazzoso, *Apuleio. Metamorfosi*, Milano 1971

Translation:

Amor und Psyche, Lat. Text nach Metamorphoseon libri XI ed. R. Helm, übers. von R. Jachmann, mit einem Nachwort *Das Märchen Amor und Psyche von Apuleius*, von E. G. Schmidt & einem Nachwort *Die Fresken zu Amor und Psyche von Moritz von Schwind*, von G. Claussnitzer, Leipzig 1972

Commentaries:

Chr. Harrauer, *Kommentar zum Isisbuch des Apuleius*, diss. Wien (dactylogr.) 1973
A. Scobie, *Apuleius Metamorphoses (Asinus Aureus) I, A Commentary*, Meisenheim am Glan 1975
J.-C. Fredouille, *Apulée, Métamorphoses. Livre XI*, (Collection Érasme) Paris 1975
J. Gwyn Griffiths, *Apuleius of Madauros, The Isis-Book (Metamorphoses, Book XI)*, edited with an introduction, translation and commentary (Etudes préliminaires aux religions orientales dans l'empire romain, tome 39), Leiden 1975

Studies:

M. von Albrecht, *Meister römischer Prosa von Cato bis Apuleius*, Heidelberg 1971, pp. 197-206
L. Alfonsi, *Ancora subductisupercilicarptores, Aevum* 46 (1972), p. 115
J. Amat, *Sur quelques aspects de l'esthétique baroque dans les Métamorphoses d'Apulée, REA* 74 (1972), pp. 107-152
F. Amoroso, *Apuleio, Metam. 5, 20. Sulcato itinere regressus, Pan* 2 (1974), pp. 67-70
J. Beaujeu, *Apulée helléniste*, Résumé: *REL* 46 (1968), pp. 11-13
J. Beaujeu, *Sérieux et frivolité au IIe siècle de notre ère: Apulée, BAGB* 4, 1 (1975), pp. 83-97
J. Bergman, *Decem illis diebus. Zum Sinn der Enthaltsamkeit bei den Mysterienweihen im Isisbuch des Apuleius*, Studia G. Widengren oblata, Leiden 1972, I, pp. 332-346
G. Bianco, *La fonte greca delle metamorfosi di Apuleio*, Brescia 1971
R. K. Bohm, *The Isis Episode in Apuleius, CJ* 68 (1973), pp. 228-231
L. Callebat, *Sermo cotidianus dans les Métamorphoses d'Apulée, IL* 22 (1970), pp. 32-35

U. Carratello, *Apuleio uomo e romanziere, Argentea aetas, in memoriam E. V. Marmorale, Univ. di Genova Pubbl. Ist. di Filol. class.* 37 (1973), pp. 189-218

E. Cizek, *La diversité des structures dans le roman antique, Studii Clasice* 15 (1973), pp. 115-124

W. Clarysse, *De inleiding van Apuleius' Amor en Psyche (Metam. IV, 28-29). Een stilistisch onderzoek, Kleio* 2 (1972), pp. 34-43

M. Cruz Marin Ceballos, *La religión de Isis en "Las Metamórfosis" de Apuleyo, Habis* 4 (1973), pp. 127-179

G. C. Drake, *Candidus. A unifying theme in Apuleius' Metamorphoses, CJ* 64 (1968), pp. 102-109

G. C. Drake, *Lucius' business in the Metamorphoses of Apuleius, Papers on Lang. and Lit. V*, Carbondale, Ill. Southern Illinois Univ. 1969, pp. 339-361

Ph. Dust, *Apuleius, Metamorphoses 4, 24, 5, CJ* 63 (1968), pp. 266-267

J. Englert & T. Long, *Functions of Hair in Apuleius' Metamorphoses, CJ* 68 (1973), pp. 236-239

N. Fick, *Du palais d'Eros à la robe olympienne de Lucius, REL* 47 (1969), pp. 378-396

N. Fick, *La symbolique végétale dans les Métamorphoses d'Apulée, Latomus* 30 (1971), pp. 328-344

H. Fliedner, *Amor und Cupido. Untersuchungen über den römischen Liebesgott*, Meisenheim am Glan 1974, pp. 68-81

M. L. von Franz, *A Psychological Interpretation of the Golden Ass of Apuleius*, Zürich 1970

J. G. Griffith, *Apuleius, Metamorphoses VI, 29, 3, Hermes* 96 (1968-1969), p. 762

P. Grimal, *Le calame égyptien d'Apulée, REA* 73 (1971), pp. 343-355

J. Gwyn Griffiths, *Luna and Ceres, CPh* 63 (1968), pp. 143-154

J. Hani, *L' 'âne d'or' d'Apulée et l'Egypte, RPh* 47 (1973), pp. 274-280

L. Herrmann, *Styx et auctor adulterinus dans le conte de Psyché, AC* 39 (1970), pp. 78-87

L. Herrmann, *Lucius de Patras et les trois romans de l'âne, AC* 41 (1972), pp. 573-599

B. L. Hijmans & R. E. H. Westendorp Boerma, *Apuleius Met. IV, 1 (74, 16): Levigatos or Levatos?, Mnemosyne* S. IV, 26 (1973), pp. 396-397

B. L. Hijmans & R. Th. van der Paardt, *Love's Labour ... Een Psychanalyse, Hermeneus* 47 (1975), pp. 147-160

F. E. Hoevels, *Wer ist die Regina Coeli des Apuleius, Hermes* 102 (1974), pp. 346-352

H. G. Ingenkamp, *Thelyphron. Zu Apuleius Metamorphosen II, 20 ff., RhM* 115 (1972), pp. 337-342

Ph. B. Katz, *The myth of Psyche, Arethusa* 9 (1976), pp. 111-118

B. Kenny, *The reader's Role in the Golden Ass, Arethusa* 7 (1974), pp. 187-209

K. Kerényi, *Der antike Roman*, Darmstadt 1971, pp. 51-55

H. Krämer, *Die Isisformel des Apuleius (Met. XI, 23, 7), eine Anmerkung zur Methode der Mysterienforschung, W & D* 12 (1973), pp. 91-104

G. Kranz, *Amor und Psyche. Metamorphose eines Mythos bei C. S. Lewis, Arcadia* 4 (1969), pp. 285-299

H. Krautter, *Philologische Methode und humanistische Existenz. Filippo Beroaldo und sein Kommentar zum goldenen Esel des Apuleius*, München 1971

S. Lilja, *Odour sensations in the Roman Novel, Arctos* 7 (1972), pp. 31-45

G. Lopez, *Apuleius, Met. 7, 9, 1 e l'ὀξύμωρον, GIF* N.S. 1 (1970), pp. 86-91

L. A. MacKay, *Two Notes on Apuleius' Metamorphoses, CPh* 67 (1972), p. 55

J. P. Mahé, *Quelques remarques sur la religion des Métamorphoses a'Apulée et les doctrines gnostiques contemporaines, RSR* 46 (1972) pp. 1-19

T. Mantero, *Amore e Psiche. Struttura di una "Fabia di magia"*, Genova 1973

T. Mantero, *L'isola di Psiche, Atti Accad. ligure di Sc. e Lett.* (Genova) 29 (1972), pp. 3-17

T. Mantero, *La psiche apuleiana ed i giuramenti d'amore, Maia* 26 (1974), pp. 127-139

L. Marchese, *Le metamorfosi di Apuleio, ALGP* 7-8 (1970-1971), pp. 249-254

A. Marchetta *L'uso di quamquam, quamvis, licet, etsi e tamen in Apuleio, AFLC* 33, 2 (1970)

R. Martin, *Le sens de l'expression asinus aureus et la signification du roman apuléien*, *REL* 48 (1970), pp. 332-354

R. Martin, *De Plutarque à Apulée. Le sens de l'expression asinus aureus*, *REG* 83 (1970), p. xix

H. J. Mason, *Lucius at Corinth*, *Phoenix* 25 (1971), pp. 160-165

H. J. Mette, *Neugier und Neuzeit. Ein unzeitgemässes Problem*, *A &A* 16 (1970), pp. 1-11

W. R. Nethercut, *Apuleius' literary Art. Resonance and depth in the Metamorphoses*, *CJ* 64 (1968), pp. 110-119

W. R. Nethercut, *Apuleius' Metamorphoses. The journey*, *Agon* 3 (1969), pp. 97-134

J. D. Order, *Isaic Elements in the Metamorphoses of Apuleius*, Diss. Vanderbilt Univ. Nashville, Tenn. 1971 (summary in *DA* 32 (1971) 2661 A)

R. Th. van der Paardt, *Asinina (Apuleius, Shakespeare, Couperus)*, *Hermeneus* 46 (1974/1975), pp. 335-338

R. Th. van der Paardt, *Bataafse Ezels en een Vlaams staartje*, *Hermeneus* 48 (1976), pp. 33-45

B. E. Perry, *Who was Lucius of Patrae?*, *CJ* 64 (1968), pp. 97-101

H. Ponci, *L'humanisme d'Apulée*, *BAGB* 1969, pp. 437-442

M. Ruch, *Psyché et les quatre vertus cardinales (Apulée, Mét. VI, 10-21)*, *IL* 23 (1971), pp. 171-176

A. Ruiz de Elvira, *Mito y Novella*, *CFC* 5 (1973), pp. 15-52

G. N. Sandy, *Comparative Study of Apuleius' Metamorphoses and other Prose Fiction of Antiquity*, Diss. Ohio State Univ. Columbus 1968 (summary in *DA* 30 (1969) 702 A-703 A)

G. N. Sandy, *Knowledge and Curiosity in Apuleius' Metamorphoses*, *Latomus* 31 (1972), pp. 179-183

G. N. Sandy, *Foreshadowing and Suspense in Apuleius' Metamorphoses*, *CJ* 68 (1973), pp. 232-235

G. N. Sandy, *Serviles voluptates in Apuleius' Metamorphoses*, *Phoenix* 28 (1974), pp. 234-244

C. C. Schlam, *The Structure of the Metamorphoses of Apuleius*, Diss. Columbia Univ. New York 1968 (summary in *DA* 30 (1969) 703 A)

C. C. Schlam, *The Curiosity of the Golden Ass*, *CJ* 64 (1968), pp. 120-125

C. C. Schlam, *Platonica in the Metamorphoses of Apuleius*, *TAPhA* 101 (1970), pp. 477-487

A. Scobie, *The dating of the earliest printed Spanish and French translations of Apuleius' Metamorphoses*, *The Library*. Transactions of the Bibliographical Soc. 27 London Bibliographical Soc. 1972 pp. 236-237

A. Scobie, *More Essays on the Ancient Romance and its Heritage*, Meisenheim am Glan 1973

A. Scobie, *Notes on Walter Anderson's "Märchen von Eselmenschen"*, *Fabula* 15 (1974), pp. 222-231

M. Simon, *Apulée et le christianisme*, Mélanges (...) Puech, Paris 1974, pp. 299-305

W. S. Smith, *Lucius of Corinth and Apuleius of Madaura. A Study of the narrative Technique of the Metamorphoses of Apuleius*, Diss. Yale Univ. New Haven 1968 (summary in *DA* 29 (1969) 3990 A)

W. S. Smith, *The narrative Voice in Apuleius' Metamorphoses*, *TAPhA* 103 (1972), pp. 513-534

E. R. Smits, *Ad Apul. Met. IV, 8 (80, 15-16)*, *Mnemosyne* S. IV, 27 (1974), p. 417

S. Stabryla, *The Functions of the Tale of Cupid and Psyche in the Structure of the Metamorphoses of Apuleius*, *Eos* 61 (1973), pp. 261-272

F. G. Stockin, *Sequence of thought and motivation in the Metamorphoses of Apuleius*, Diss. Univ. of Illinois 1954 (summary in *DA* 14 (1954) 824)

R. G. Summers, *A legal commentary on the Metamorphoses of Apuleius*, Diss. Princeton Univ. 1967 (summary in *DA* 28 (1968) 3164 A)

R. G. Summers, *Roman Justice and Apuleius' Metamorphoses*, *TAPhA* 101 (1970), pp. 511-531

R. G. Summers, *Apuleius Iuridicus, Historia* 21 (1972), pp. 120-126

R. G. Summers, *A Note on the Date of the Golden Ass, AJPh* 94 (1973), pp. 375-383

J. H. Tatum, *Thematic Aspects of the Tales in Apuleius' Metamorphoses*, Diss. Princeton Univ. 1969 (summary in *DA* 31 (1970) 739 A)

J. H. Tatum, *The Tales in Apuleius' Metamorphoses, TAPhA* 100 (1969), pp. 487-527

J. H. Tatum, *Apuleius and Metamorphosis, AJPh* 93 (1972), pp. 306-313

R. Thibau, *Les Métamorphoses d'Apulée et la Théorie Platonicienne de l'Erôs, Stud. Phil. Gand.* 3 (1965), pp. 89-144

H. van Thiel, *Der Eselsroman*, 2 vols., (Zetemata 54, 1 and 2) München 1971-1972

I. Trencsényi-Waldapfel, *Das Rosenmotiv ausserhalb des Eselsromans, Beiträge zur alten Geschichte und deren Nachleben.* Festschrift für Franz Altheim zum 6.10.1968, hrsg. von R. Stiehl und H. E. Stier, I, Berlin 1969, pp. 512-517

J. M. Walker, *The Satyricon, the Golden Ass and the Spanish golden Age picaresque Novel*, Diss. Brigham Young Univ. Provo Utah 1971 (summary in *DA* 32 (1971) 3288 A)

P. G. Walsh, *Was Lucius a Roman?, CJ* 63 (1968), pp. 264-265

Ph. Ward, *Apuleius on Trial at Sabratha*, New York 1969[2]

R. E. H. Westendorp Boerma & B. L. Hijmans, *Apuleiana Groningana III, Mnemosyne* S. IV, 27 (1974), pp. 406-412

A. Wlosok, *Römischer Religions- und Gottesbegriff in heidnischer und christlicher Zeit, A&A* 16 (1970), pp. 39-53

C. S. Wright, *"No art at all": a note on the proemium of Apuleius' Metamorphoses, CPh* 68 (1973), pp. 217-219

J. R. G. Wright, *Folk-tale and literary technique in Cupid and Psyche, CQ* 21 (1971), pp. 272-284

INTRODUCTION

The structure of book IV

The present volume contains a commentary on *Met.* 4, 1-27, that is to say it takes as its boundaries two dividing points of dissimilar character, the second being a natural dividing point in the narrative structure, chosen so as not to disrupt the tale of Amor and Psyche, the other the formal point of division between books 3 and 4[1]. The latter represents a break in the narrative, but a much less deep one than the breaks before and after the center piece.

a. The center piece of the *Met.*, the tale of Amor and Psyche, starts at 4, 28, ends at 6, 24, and is set in a frame[2] as a story told by an old woman to a young girl. The old woman is housekeeper to a band of robbers who have kidnapped the young girl Charite. The activities of this band, as observed by Lucius, the ass, form the material of 3, 28-4, 27 and 6, 25-7, 14[3]. In the second half of that frame the central figure is Haemus-Tlepolemus, who tells his story (7, 5-8) and captures Charite's captors (7, 8-13). In the first half the report of one group of robbers concerning three events, involving the loss of three colleagues, forms the main section: 4, 8-21.[4] The section is framed by a dinner, which is preceded by the robbers' arrival with their captive pack-animal, Lucius, and followed by their departure and return with the captive Charite:

3, 24   Lucius' metamorphosis
3, 28   Lucius' capture by robbers (group 1)

---

[1] For the book-division see Junghanns p. 126 n. 13 (cf. Helm-Krenkel p. 33); Junghanns is of the opinion that Apuleius carefully marks the end of a book as a resting point. Where a night intervenes J.'s point is, of course, well taken; but he is quite right also at the beginning of bk 4 where the journey is formally resumed after the painful decision, at the end of bk 3, not to eat the *rosae uirgines* of 73, 24, but to chew his *frena* instead (unless he is eating *faena*, cf. however comm. on 76, 9 and vdP. p. 207).
[2] For inserted tales in Greek and Roman prose fiction in general see Sandy, *Comp. St.*, pp. 118 ff.
[3] It is to be noted that of the characters who play important parts in these sections of the work not one survives. In most cases a reason may be assigned, but a further reason, beyond the ostensible one, is more easily divined in some cases than in others. See also Schlam, *Structure*, p. 42, Tatum, *Aspects*, p. 142.
[4] The three tales (on the triad see below note 18) illustrate in miniature the robbers' episode as a whole (cf. also Haemus' story). They have a balance in the magical warning tales, Amor and Psyche, the adultery stories. See Tatum's discussion, *Aspects*, pp. 27 f. who argues that content rather than form characterizes these stories.

Lucius' stay with the robbers is, of course, only a part of the series of experiences he undergoes before his metamorphosis is reversed, but if those experiences may be divided into things that happen to him person- ally and those that happen to others but are observed by him (whether he sees them or hears of them), examples of both kinds of experience are included in the present section (4,1-27). Amor and Psyche, the only section of the *Met.* formally presented as a 'mere' tale (quite possibly an indication that it is to be taken as more than a mere tale!) is included through the presence of its introduction in 4, 27; the rest of 4, 1-27 consists of events experienced or witnessed by the narrators.

b. Book 4, then, starts between Lucius' second[3] and third attempts at freeing himself from his asinine form. The second attempt had been abandoned because of a *consilium longe salubrius* at 3, 29 (74, 1-2), which at once introduces a whole set of further adventures for the ass and emphasizes the fact that for all his asininity he has retained his human intelligence — a fact that had been made explicit first at 3, 26 (71, 6 ff.) then at 74, 11 f., 75, 12-15 and 78,16 f. and is referred to once again at 4, 6 (78,20 ff.) at the beginning of the frame round the robbers' tales. The passage (4, 1-5) between the *consilium salubre* and the frame which begins at 4, 6 is essentially taken up by a continuation of the process of adjust- ment (or perhaps taming!),[4] a process in which an attempted escape through suicide (ch. 2-3)[5] and the vicarious death of his fellow-ass (ch. 5) play a major role. The attempted suicide by eating oleander is

---

[1] Stabryla argues p. 268 that the Charite and Psyche stories show 'a chain-like structure consisting of the elements of a similar emotional value'.
[2] Tatum, *Aspects*, p. 138 suggests that the speech of Haemus in bk 7 is a parody on the robbers' stories.
[3] The first attempt had been prevented by Lucius' slave (3, 27), see vdP. p. 193 n. 1, Junghanns p. 51, vThiel I p. 97.
[4] See Schlam, *Structure*, p. 51 on the ironic 'training' 10, 17 (249, 26).
[5] W. S. Smith Jr, *Lucius*, pp. 45 ff. compares the situation of Psyche at 136,16 ff.

2

prevented by the *hortulanus* whose vegetable patch Lucius had laid waste[1]. The death of the other ass — who dies because he does what Lucius had in mind doing himself — results in Lucius' submission to his fate, at least temporarily. He now appears to take some pride in his role as an observer. (Of course the narrating subject and the experiencing subject sometimes coincide, sometimes alternate: at 4,6 we get a clear glimpse of the literary artist behind the (human) ass).

It does not do to regard ch. 1-5 as little more than part of the frame for the robbers' tales (as Scobie seems to do, *More Essays*, p. 73). In relating the continuation of the metamorphosis and its peculiar dangers (the start of a series of adventures which continue first at 6, 25, again at 7, 15,[2] once more at 8, 15) they have very much of a function of their own. The actual frame takes up ch. 6-8 and falls into

a. the description of the den (ch. 6),
b. the arrival of the first group of robbers with the ass (and horse) and the introduction of the old housekeeper (ch. 7),
c. the arrival of the second group of robbers (larger than the first)[3] just in time for dinner.[4] They are provoked into giving a report of their activities (ch. 8).

This last section of the frame has its corresponding element at ch. 22; in that same chapter the *anus* also plays a role, and the robbers start on their next trip, but the description of the den and its surrounding scenery is not picked up again (unless one wishes to press 92, 12 *riuulo proximo* into rather too heavy a service). The provocation, however, is formally marked as a frame by a verbal reminiscence: *sarcinis istis, quas aduexistis* 80, 24 = *istas quas uidetis praedas adueximus* 91, 8. A similar referential function may be attributed to 80, 14 *strepitu cantilant* = 91, 11 *canticis quibusdam Marti deo blanditi*. The enclosed report,[5] given by a single narrator, presents three distinct events:

---

[1] If there is 'Motiventsprechung' with 3, 27, there is also a climactic element in the three attempts: 1. Lucius is almost beaten to death but is saved by the arrival of the robbers; 2. Lucius wisely refrains from eating roses, in order to save his life; 3. Lucius is almost beaten to death and *thereby* is prevented from committing suicide. See also Junghanns p. 57 n. 85. Schlam, *Structure*, p. 39 feels that 3, 29-4, 5 "presents the principal motifs" of the middle section of the *Met.* He also insists, quite rightly, on the pervasive, and usually perverse, role of Fortuna; *ibid.* and, more specifically, pp. 120 ff.; for the beginning of bk 4 pp. 131 f. A more general discussion of intervention by Fortune in ancient prose fiction in Sandy, *Comp. St.*, pp. 126 ff., in the *Met.* pp. 132 f. See also Tatum, *Aspects*, p. 91 n. 174, Heine pp. 137 ff.
[2] This passage is marked by a further reference to roses; cf. vThiel I, p. 99.
[3] Both groups have booty.
[4] The traditional time for telling one's story (see comm. on 80, 14-16).
[5] On the question whether this report may be classified as a series of *fabulae* see Junghanns (p. 122, n. 5), who feels that they constitute an amplification ("Erweiterung"); Bernhard pp. 259 ff. says that all insets ('Einlagen') function as "Erweiterung". Their various terms need to be evaluated against their respective interpretations of the genesis of the *Met.* More interesting for our purposes is Tatum's remark, *Aspects*, pp. 5 f. and n. 10, that in almost all cases some formal

ch. 9-11 The attack on the house of Chryseros at Thebes and the demise of Lamachus (suicide).

ch. 12 Alcimus' attempt to rob an old woman of her meager possessions, apparently still in the same city, and his death by being pushed out of the window.

ch. 13-21 The attempt to defraud Demochares of his wealth by disguising Thrasyleon as a bear. Thrasyleon's death through a spear-cast.

Schlam remarks with a great deal of perception that "the emphasis on daring trickery connects the three robber stories closely with the 'Charite complex' in which Tlepolemus after freeing Charite by a clever ruse falls victim to the guile of Thrasyllus" (*Structure* p. 41).

It has been thought that the third of these stories formed no part of the original from which Apuleius' *Met.* derives. The most important arguments for this opinion[1] are the following:

1. The story is full of inconsistencies, improbabilities and lacunae, e.g. many bears die in the streets, and one of them is then openly removed by a set of unrecognized robbers; Thrasyleon kills by means of an unexplained sword and without noise; his victims are never discovered; a slave wakes up for no apparent reason; a supposedly precious bear is attacked and killed rather than hunted and caught.

2. The story shows none of the wit or irony of the other two.

3. Its main elements are duplicated elsewhere.

4. The story is excessively long.

The argumentation involves the question of Apuleius' sources and the use he made of them. We are for the moment, however, more interested in the structure of book 4, and in that context the last argument should be dealt with first. It seems that within the *Met.* uneven lengths of insets are the rule rather than the exception, and it would be very hard to prove that the length of this particular story shows awkward handling in comparison with a "Vorlage". "Motiventsprechungen" are more frequent in Apuleius than in the *Epitome*, but they are not lacking in the latter (Junghanns p. 172 n. 93). That the story shows none of the wit of the other stories is demonstrably incorrect (see comm. on 82, 22; 85, 13; 85, 17; 85, 26; 86, 8; 87, 1-2; 88, 10; 89, 9; 90, 15; 90, 22; 91, 1; 91, 4, not an exhaustive list, since it becomes tedious always to explain the joke[2]).

It may well be that at least some of the inconsistencies and supposed lacunae — there are quite a few in the stories of Lamachus and Alcimus — are functional. Thus the apparent difficulty of Thrasyleon's handling a sword at 88,7 ff. may be due to a foreshortened narrator's perspective (see comm. *ad loc.*). Scobie has pointed out that the element of *épater le bourgeois*, the element of *thaumazein* and of paradox in the *Met.* is very

---

designation appears, as here (81, 13) *res ipsa denique fidem sermoni meo dabit.* See also *ibid.* p. 24 n. 54 on *denique.*

[1] See Perry (1923) pp. 219 f.; vThiel I pp. 105 f.

[2] There is no "Vorlage" for the name Thrasyleon, hence its humour may actually have to be assigned to Apuleius himself...

4

important (*Aspects* pp. 43 ff.) and notes (p. 51) that *nouitas* occurs in the middle of the story of Thrasyleon (87, 1). It may function there as a kind of key word.

If, then, it may be argued on the grounds mentioned that the story did not belong to the "Vorlage" — and it is at the very least doubtful that the arguments show anything of the kind — the same arguments may be used to show that the story is fully integrated in Apuleius' artistic unity.[1] This, too, is the opinion of Walsh, who notes (pp. 148 ff.) *variatio* in the structure of the *Met.* as a whole, and who feels that the robber-stories as a group represent a comic element[2] balanced against the romantic episode of Amor and Psyche. In keeping with this theory he maintains that all three of the robbers' exploits were inserted by Apuleius himself[3]. He opposes Lesky, who argues (pp. 555 ff.) that the "Vorlage" must have had at least some robbers' exploit[4] on the grounds 1) that the *Onos* speaks of λόγος πολὺς ἐν τῷ συμποσίῳ (ch. 21), 2) that a second group of robbers appears, 3) that the expression οἰωνὸς οὐκ ἀγαθός (*Onos* 22, cf. *Met.* 147,22) must refer to something in the "Vorlage" that may serve as a reason for the robbers to call the ass a bird of ill omen. Indeed, Lesky feels that it was precisely the Demochares story that figured in the "Vorlage" since *Onos* 21 also mentions booty.

Closing a frame usually takes less space than opening it. At ch. 22 the robbers once again drink and sing, and the ass and horse, who at the start of ch. 7 had been tied at the entrance of the cave, are now fed by the old woman whom the robbers had shouted at when first entering.

While feeding[5] Lucius observes the departure of the robbers *in Lemures reformati*. The robbers return after daybreak with the captivating captive Charite, whose parents they believe will pay sufficient ransom[6] (ch. 23). Charite's lamentations, suicidal inclination (94, 7 f.) and story take up chapters 24-26, her frightening, and perhaps ominous, dream with the old woman's soothing reaction ch. 27. The tale of Amor and Psyche (ch. 28 ff.) is presented as the direct result of that soothing reaction.

c. The time span[7] of the section of bk 4 up to the tale of Amor and

[1] See also comm. on 88, 2-3 (typology of the robbers).
[2] On the farcical aspect see Walsh p. 158.
[3] On the importance of triads see e.g. Junghanns pp. 156 ff., Lesky p. 562, Schlam, *Structure*, pp. 10, 42 ff., 63, vThiel I p. 98.
[4] Schlam, *Structure*, p. 8 agrees.
[5] Once again Lucius emphasizes his essential difference from his horse; he eats bread (cf. ch. 1, Lucius in the vegetable patch).
[6] No attempt to collect the ransom is mentioned.
[7] There are, of course, many kinds of time, and if the narrated time of the section in question is short, narrated time in the subordinate robbers' tales is much longer. Narrating time, however, is of equal, if not greater importance and should be measured by the (uneven) speed at which it flows by; see von Albrecht p. 198. vThiel's estimate of Apuleius' results in this respect shows (e.g. I p. 16) a disapproval of the function of the author's rhetoric: non laetatur lector doctus ... (see however I p. 21).

5

Psyche is very short. The book starts in the middle of the day; if we are right in our commentary, ch. 4 speaks of the afternoon. The dinner that takes place must take a little time: the robbers fall asleep (though not the ass — unlike the robbers he has not had any wine). They wake up *nocte promota* (92, 3) while the ass continues eating till early morning (92, 11); Lucius then drinks from a stream and the robbers return with Charite, who soon falls asleep, wakes up immediately, cries once more and is told the tale of Amor and Psyche. At most, then, a time span of 24 hours during which the ass — who after all is our observer — does not sleep at all. In the *Onos* on the other hand, the robbers return with the girl τρισὶν δὲ ὕστερον ἡμέραις μεσούσης σχεδὸν τῆς νυκτός (22, 1). It is likely, then, that Apuleius' version differs in this respect from the "Vorlage". In this connection it is to be noted that the sequence of days is fairly strictly accounted for in the first part of the *Met.* (see Schlam, *Structure*, pp. 35 ff.) but becomes much vaguer from bk 4 onwards (Schlam, *Structure*, pp. 44 f.). The unsatisfactory time sequence of bk 4 itself in some way forms the transition — a necessary transition since bks 1-10 are to cover a year from one rose-studded spring to the next.

NOTE TO THE TEXT

Generally we have followed Helm's text, as printed in his latest Teubner-edition (³1931, reprinted with Addenda and Corrigenda 1955). In the following places, however, we have chosen a different reading:

Our text	Helm's text
74, 16 leuatos F corr.	leuigatos F
75, 6 protectus F	frutectis Philomathes
75, 22 felices beatae F	felices ⟨et⟩ beatae ς
76, 12 posterioribus F	posteriorum ς
77, 25 scilicet Oudendorp	se F
77, 26 in mortuum F corr.	in ⟨modum⟩ mortui Colvius
78, 23 perobliqua Nolte	per obliqua F
79, 6-7 commoda F	commodae Helm
79, 11 quo F	qua ς
80, 15 ⟨ti⟩tuban⟨t⟩ibus Smits	cenan⟨t⟩ibus Helm
81, 15 sed[d]um Wiman	[sed dum] Salmasius
81, 16 popularium Pricaeus	populari⟨s⟩ ς
82, 10 patibulum F	patibul⟨at⟩um Scaliger
82, 22 religionis F	re[li]gionis ς
83, 9 † eum † F	tamen ς
83, 10 abducere ς	adducere F
84, 9 diffissa Beroaldus	diffusa F
84, 23 confixilis F	confixiles Leo
84, 24 sublic⟨i⟩as Westendorp Boerma	sublic⟨i⟩ae Philomathes
85, 1 forensis F	forinsecus Nic. Heinsius
86, 28 ut ipse habebat † F	ut ipse habebat F
87, 8 bestia[m] iret, iubet vdPaardt	bestiam [iret iubet] Lütjohann
88, 22 uigilassent F	⟨e⟩uigilassent Stewech
89, 1 scilicet diuinitus F	scilicet ⟨uel⟩ diuinitus Helm
91, 1 peribit Stewech	periuit F
91, 7 asperae F	asper⟨itat⟩e Scaliger
91, 14 sali⟨ar⟩es scilicet cenas se ⟨esse⟩ crederet vdPaardt	sali⟨ar⟩es se cenas ⟨cenare⟩ crederet Helm
91, 15-17 see Appendix III	
92, 4 armati F	arma⟨ti, par⟩tim φ in margine
92, 13 ultra anxii F	ultra ⟨modum⟩ anxii Haupt
92, 16 gladiis, totis manibus F	gladiis ⟨totis⟩, totis manibus Einar Löfstedt
92, 21 speluncam uerbisque F	speluncam ⟨ducunt⟩ uerbisque Haupt
93, 16 incerta F	incerto Beroaldus
93, 20 tendore φ	tundore F
94, 1 recussa longeque F	recussa…longeque Lütjohann
94, 16 manuque F	manu⟨m⟩que F corr.
95, 9 gladiatorum impetus F	gladiatorum ⟨fit⟩ impetus Helm
96, 14 uexatum iri Beroaldus	uiam datum iri Helm

TEXT

LIBER IV

H 74 1   Diem ferme circa medium, cum iam flagrantia solis caleretur, in pago quodam apud notos ac familiares latro- 10 nibus senes deuertimus. Sic enim primus aditus et sermo prolixus et oscula mutua quamuis asino sentire praesta- bant. Nam et rebus eos quibusdam dorso meo depromptis munerabantur et secretis gannitibus, quod essent latro- cinio partae, uidebantur indicare. Iamque nos omni sar- 15 cina leuatos in pratum proximum passim libero pastui tradidere nec me cum asino uel equo meo conpascuus coetus attinere potuit adhuc insolitum alioquin prandere faenum. Sed plane pone stabulum prospectum hortulum 19

H 75 iam fame perditus fidenter inuado et quamuis crudis ho- 1 leribus, adfatim tamen uentrem sagino deosque compre- catus omnes cuncta prospectabam loca, sicubi forte con- terminis in ⟨h⟩ortulis candens repperirem rosarium. Nam et ipsa solitudo iam mihi bonam fiduciam tribuebat, si 5 deuius et protectus absconditus sumpto remedio de iu- menti quadripedis incuruo ‖ gradu rursum erectus in ho- minem inspectante nullo resurgerem.

2   Ergo igitur cum in isto cogitationis salo fluctuarem, aliquanto longius uideo frondosi nemoris conuallem um- 10 brosam, cuius inter uarias herbulas et laetissima uirecta fulgentium rosarum mineus color renidebat. Iamque apud mea non usquequaque ferina praecordia Veneris et Gra- tiarum lucum illum arbitrabar, cuius inter opaca secreta floris genialis regius nitor relucebat. Tunc inuocato hilaro 15 atque prospero Euentu cursu me concito pro*ri*pio, ut her- cule ipse sentirem non asinum me, uerum etiam equum currulem nimio uelocitatis e⟨f⟩fectum. Sed agilis atque praeclarus ille conatus fortunae me⟨ae⟩ scaeuitatem anteire non potuit. Iam enim loco proximus non illas rosas te- 20 neras et amoenas, madidas diuini roris et nectaris, quas rubi felices beatae spinae generant, ac ne conuallem quidem usquam nisi tantum ripae fluuialis marginem densis arboribus septam uideo. Hae arbores in lauri faciem pro- lixe foliatae pariunt in modum floris [in] odori porrectos 25

H 76 caliculos modice punicantes, quos equidem fraglantis mi- 1 nime rurest⟨r⟩i uocabulo uulgus indoctum rosas laureas

3   appellant quarumque cuncto pecori cibus letalis est. Tali-

9

bus fatis implicitus etiam ipsam salutem recusans sponte
illud uenenum rosarium sumere gestiebam. Sed dum cunc- 5
tanter accedo decerpere, iuuenis quidam, ut mihi uideba-
tur, hortulanus, cuius omnia prorsus holera uastaueram,
tanto damno cognito cum grandi baculo furens decurrit
adreptumque me totum plagis obtundit adusque uitae
ipsius periculum, nisi tandem sapienter alioquin ipse mihi 10
tulissem auxilium. Nam lumbis eleuatis in altum, pedum
posterioribus calcibus iactatis in eum crebriter, iam mul-
cato grauiter atque iacente contra procliue montis attigui
fuga me liberaui. Sed ilico mulier quaepiam, uxor eius
scilicet, simul eum prostratum et semianimem ex edito 15
despexit, ululabili cum plangore ad eum statim prosilit,
ut sui uidelicet miseratione mihi praesens crearet exitium.
Cuncti enim ‖ pagani fletibus eius exciti statim conclamant
canes atque, ad me laniandum rabie perciti ferrent im-
petum, passim cohortantur. Tunc igitur procul dubio iam 20
morti proximus, cum uiderem canes et modo magnos et
numero multos et ursis ac leonibus ad conpugnandum
idoneos in me conuocatos exasperari, e re nata capto con-
silio fugam desino ac me retrorsus celeri gradu rursum in
stabulum, quo deuerteramus, recipio. At illi canibus iam 25
H 77 aegre cohibitis adreptum me loro quam ualido ad an- 1
sulam quandam destinatum rursum caedendo confecissent
profecto, nisi dolore plagarum aluus artata crudisque illis
oleribus abundans et lubrico fluxu saucia fimo fistulatim
excusso quosdam extremi liquoris aspergine, alios putore 5
nidoris faetidi a meis iam quassis scapulis abegisset.

4   Ne⟨c⟩ mora, cum iam in meridiem prono iubare rur-
sum nos ac praecipue me longe grauius onustum produ-
cunt illi latrones stabulo. Iamque confecta bona parte
itineris et uiae spatio defectus et sarcinae pondere de- 10
pressus ictibusque fustium fatigatus atque etiam ungulis
extritis iam claudus et titubans riuulum quendam ser-
pentis leniter aquae propter insistens subtilem occasionem
feliciter nactus cogitabam totum memet flexis scite cruri-
bus pronum abicere, certus atque obstinatus nullis uer- 15
beribus ad ingrediundum exsurgere, immo etiam paratus
non fusti tantum, sed machaera perfossus occumbere. Rebar
enim iam me prorsus exanimatum ac debilem | mereri
causariam missionem, certe latrones partim inpatientia
morae, partim studio festinatae fugae dorsi mei sarcinam 20
duobus ceteris iumentis distributuros meque in altioris
5 uindictae uicem lupis et uulturiis praedam relicturos. Sed
tam bellum consilium meum praeuertit sors deterrima.
Namque ille alius asinus diuinato et antecapto meo cogi-
tatu statim scilicet mentita lassitudine cum rebus totis ‖ 25

offudit[ur] iacensque in mortuum non fustibus, non 26
H 78 stimulis ac ne cauda et auribus cruribusque undique 1
uersum eleuatis temptauit exsurgere, quoad tandem
postumae spei fatigati secumque conlocuti, ne tam
diu mortuo, immo uero lapideo asino seruientes fugam
morarentur, sarcinis eius mihi equoque distributis destricto 5
gladio poplites eius totos amputant ac paululum a uia
retractum per altissimum praeceps in uallem proximam
etiam nunc spirantem praecipitant. Tunc ego miseri com-
militonis fortunam cogitans statui iam dolis abiectis et
fraudibus asinum me bonae frugi dominis exhibere. Nam 10
et secum eos animaduerteram conloquentes, quod in pro-
ximo nobis esset habenda mansio et totius uiae finis quieta
eorumque esset sedes illa et habitatio. Clementi denique
transmisso cliuulo peruenimus ad locum destinatum, ubi
rebus totis exsolutis atque intus conditis iam pondere 15
liberatus lassitudinem uice lauacri puluer⟨e⟩is uolutatibus
digerebam.

6   Res ac tempus ipsum locorum speluncaeque illius,
⟨quam⟩ latrones inhabita⟨ba⟩nt, descriptionem exponere
flagitat. Nam et meum simul periclitabor ingenium, et 20
faxo uos quoque, an mente etiam sensuque fuerim asinus,
sedulo sentiatis. Mons horridus siluestribusque frondibus
umbrosus et in primis altus fuit. Huius perobliqua de-
uexa, qua saxis asperrimis et ob id inaccessis cingitur,
conualles lacunosae cauaeque nimium spinetis aggeratae 25
et quaqua uersus repositae naturalem tutelam praebentes
ambiebant. De summo uertice fons afluens bullis in-
H 79 gentibus scaturribat perque prona delapsus euomebat un- 1
das argenteas iamque riuulis pluribus dispersus ac ualles
illas agminibus stagnantibus inrigans in modum stipati
maris uel ignaui fluminis cuncta cohibebat. Insurgit spe-
luncae, qua margines montanae desinunt, | turris ardua; 5
caulae firmae solidis cratibus, ‖ ouili stabulationi com-
moda, porrectis undique lateribus ante fores exigui
tramitis uice structi parietis attenduntur. Ea tu bono
certe meo periculo latronum dixeris atria. Nec iuxta
quicquam quam parua casula cannulis temere contecta, 10
quo speculatores e numero latronum, ut postea comperi,
sorte ducti noctibus excubabant.

7   Ibi cum singuli derepsissent stipatis artubus, nobis
ante ipsas fores loro ualido destinatis anum quandam
curuatam graui senio, cui soli salus atque tutela tot nu- 15
mero iuuenum commissa uidebatur, sic infesti compellant:
'Etiamne tu, busti cadauer extremum et uitae dedecus
primum et Orci fastidium solum, sic nobis otiosa domi
residens lusitabis nec nostris tam magnis tamque pericu-

losis laboribus solacium de tam sera refectione tribues? 20
Quae diebus ac noctibus nil quicquam rei quam merum
saeu⟨i⟩enti uentri tuo soles auditer ingurgitare.'

Tremens ad haec et stridenti uocula pauida sic anus:
'A*t* uobis, fortissimi *fi*delissimique mei hospitatores iuuenes,
adfatim cuncta suaui sapore percocta pulmenta praesto 25
sunt, panis numerosus, uinum probe calicibus exfricatis

H 80 affluenter immissum et ex more calida tumultuario la- 1
uacro uestro praeparata.'

In fine sermonis huius statim sese deuestiunt nuda-
tique et flammae largissimae uapore recreati calidaque
perfusi et oleo peruncti mensas dapibus largiter instructas 5

8 accumbunt. Commodum *cu*buerant et ecce quid*a*m longe
plures numero iuuenes adueniunt alii, quos incunctanter
adaeque latrones arbitrarere. Nam et ipsi praedas aure-
orum argentariorum⟨*que*⟩ nummorum ac uasculorum ue-
stisque sericae et intextae filis aureis inuehebant. Hi[i] 10
simili lauacro refoti inter toros sociorum sese reponunt,
tunc *s*orte ducti ministerium faciunt. Estur ac potatur
incondite, pulmentis aceruatim, panibus aggeratim, poculis
agminatim ingestis. Clamore ludunt, strepitu cantilant, ‖
conuiciis iocantur, ac iam cetera semiferis Lapithis ⟨*ti-*⟩ 15
*tu*ban⟨*t*⟩ibus Centaurisque similia. Tunc inter eos unus, qui
robore ceteros antistabat: 'Nos quidem', inquit, | 'Milonis
Hypatini domum fortiter expugnauimus. Praeter tantam
fortunae copiam, quam nostra uirtute nacti sumus, et in-
columi numero castra nostra petiuimus et, si quid ad rem 20
facit, octo pedibus auctiores remeauimus. At uos, qui
Boeotias urbes adpetistis, ipso duce uestro fortissimo La-
macho deminuti debilem numerum reduxistis, cuius salutem
merito sarcinis istis, quas aduexistis, omnibus antetulerim. 24

H 81 Sed illum quidem utcumque nimia uirtus sua peremit, 1
inter inclitos reges ac duces proeliorum tanti uiri me-
moria celebrabitur. Enim *u*os bonae frugi latrones inter
furta parua atque seruilia timidule per balneas et aniles
cellulas reptantes scrutariam facitis.' 5

9 Suscipit unus ex illo posteriore numero: 'Tune solus
ignoras longe faciliores ad expugnandum domus esse
maiores? Quippe quod, licet numerosa familia latis de-
uersetur aedibus, tamen quisque magis suae saluti quam
domini consulat opibus. Frugi autem et solitarii homines 10
fortunam paruam uel certe satis amplam dissimulanter ob-
tectam protegunt acrius et sanguinis sui periculo muniunt.
Res ipsa denique fidem sermoni meo dabit. Vix enim
Thebas ⟨*h*⟩eptap*y*los accessimus: quod est huic disciplinae 15
primarium studium, sed[d]um sedulo fortunas inquire-
bamus popularium; nec nos denique latuit Chryseros

quidam nummularius copiosae pecuniae dominus, qui metu
officiorum ac munerum publicorum magnis artibus magnam
dissimulabat opulentiam. Denique solus ac solitarius
parua, se⟨d⟩ satis munita domuncula contentus, pannosus 20
alioquin ac sordidus, aureos folles incubabat. Ergo placuit
ad hunc primum ferremus aditum, ut contempta pugna
manus unicae nullo negotio cunctis opibus otiose potire-
10 *mur*. Nec mora, cum noctis initio foribus eius praesto-
lamur, quas neque subleuare neque dimouere ac ne per- 25
fringere ‖ quidem nobis uidebatur, ne ualuarum sonus
H 82 cunctam uiciniam nostro suscitaret exitio. Tunc itaque 1
sublimis ille uexillarius noster Lamachus specta[ta]tae
uirtutis suae fiducia, qua claui immittendae foramen
patebat, sensim inmissa manu | claustrum euellere gestie-
bat. Sed dudum scilicet omnium bipedum nequissimus 5
Chryseros uigilans et singula rerum sentiens, lenem gra-
dum et obnixum silentium tolerans paulatim adrepit
grandique clauo manum ducis nostri repente nisu fortis-
simo ad [h]ostii tabulam offigit et exitiabili nexu pati-
bulum relinquens gurgustioli sui tectum ascendit 10
atque inde contentissima uoce clamitans rogansque uicinos
et unum quemque proprio nomine ciens et salutis com-
munis admonens diffamat incendio repentino domum suam
possideri. Sic unus quisque proximi periculi confinio
11 territus suppetiatum decurrunt anxii. Tunc nos in anci- 15
piti periculo constituti uel opprimendi nostri uel deserendi
socii remedium e re nata ualidum eo uolente comminisci-
mus. Antesignani nostri partem, qua manus umerum
subit, ictu per articulum medium tem⟨p⟩erato prorsus
abscidimus atque ibi brachio relicto, multis laciniis offulto 20
uulnere, ne stillae sanguinis uestigium proderent, ceterum
Lama*ch*um raptim reportamus. Ac dum trepidi reli-
gionis urguemur graui tumultu et instantis periculi metu
terremur ad fugam nec uel sequi propere uel remanere
tuto potest uir sublimis animi uirtutisque praecipuus, 25
multis nos adfatibus multisque precibus querens adhorta-
tur per dexteram Martis, per fidem sacramenti, bonum
commilitonem cruciatu simul et captiuitate liberaremus.
Cur enim manui, quae rapere et iu⟨gu⟩lare sola posset,
fortem latronem superuiuere? Sat se beatum, qui manu 30
H 83 socia uolens occumberet. Cumque nulli nostrum spontale 1
parricidium suadens persuadere posset, manu reliqua
sumptum gladium suum diuque deosculatum per medium ‖
pectus ictu fortissimo transadigit. Tunc nos magnanimi
ducis uigore uenerato corpus reliquum ues[ti]te lintea 5
diligenter conuolutum mari celandum commisimus. Et
nunc iacet noster Lamachus elemento toto sepultus.

12   Et ille quidem dignum uirtutibus suis uitae terminum
posuit. Enim uero Alcimus sollertibus coeptis †eum† saeuum
Fortunae nutum non potuit abducere. Qui cum dormientis 10
anus perfracto tuguriolo conscendisset cubiculum superius
iamque protinus oblisis faucibus interstinguere eam de-
buisset, prius maluit rerum singula | per latiorem fene-
stram forinsecus nobis scilicet rapienda dispergere. Cum-
que iam cuncta rerum nauiter emolitus nec toro quidem 15
aniculae quiescentis parcere uellet eaque lectulo suo de-
uoluta uestem stragulam subductam scilicet iactare simi-
liter destinaret, genibus eius profusa sic nequissima illa
deprecatur: "Quid, oro, fili, paupertinas pannosasque rescu-
las miserrimae anus donas uicinis diuitibus, quorum haec 20
fenestra domum prospicit?" Quo sermone, callido deceptus
astu et uera quae dicta sunt credens Alcimus uerens
scilicet, ne et ea, quae prius miserat, quaeque postea
mi⟨s⟩surus foret, non sociis suis, sed in alienos lares 24

H 84 iam certus erroris abiceret, suspendit se fenestra sagaciter 1
perspecturus omnia, praesertim domus attiguae, quam dixerat
illa, fortunas arbitraturus. Quod eum strenue quidem, ⟨s⟩et
satis inprouide conantem senile illud facinus, quanquam
inualido, repentino tamen et inopinato pulsu nutantem ac 5
pendulum et in prospectu alioquin attonitum praeceps
inegit. Qui praeter altitudinem nimiam super quendam
etiam uastissimum lapidem propter iacentem decidens per-
fracta diffi⟨s⟩saque crate costarum riuos sanguinis uomens
imitus narratisque nobis, quae gesta sunt, non diu cru- 10
ciatus uitam euasit. Quem prioris exemplo sepulturae
traditum bonum secutorem Lamacho dedimus. |

13   Tunc orbitati⟨s⟩ duplici plaga petiti iamque Thebanis
conatibus abnuentes Plataeas proximam conscendimus ciui-
tatem. Ibi famam celebrem super quo[n]dam Demochare 15
munus edituro gladiatorium deprehendimus. Nam uir et
genere primarius et opibus plurimus et liberalitate prae-
cipuus digno fortunae suae splendore publicas uoluptates
instruebat. Quis tantus ingenii, qui⟨s⟩ facundiae, qui
singulas species apparatus multiiugi uerbis idoneis posset 20
explicare? Gladiatores isti famosae manus, uenatores illi
probatae pernicitatis, alibi noxii perdita securitate — suis
epulis bestiarum saginas — instruentes confixilis machinae
sublic⟨i⟩as turres tabularum nexibus, ad instar cir-
cumforaneae domus, floridae picturae, decora futurae uena- 25
tionis receptacula. Qui praeterea numerus, | quae facies

H 85 ferarum! Nam praecipuo studio forensis etiam aduexerat 1
generosa illa damnatorum capitum funera. Sed prae⟨ter⟩
ceteram speciosi muneris sup[p]ellectilem totis utcumque
patrimonii uiribus immanis ursae comparabat numerum

copiosum. Nam praeter domesticis uenationibus captas, 5
praeter largis emptionibus partas amicorum etiam dona-
tionibus uariis certatim oblata⟨s⟩ tutela sumptuosa solli-
14 cite nutrieba[n]t. Nec ille tam clarus tamque splendidus
publicae uoluptatis apparatus Inuidiae noxios effugit
oculos. Nam diutina captiuitate fatigatae simul et aestiua 10
flagrantia maceratae, pigra etiam sessione languidae, re-
pentina correptae pestilentia paene ad nullum rediuere
numerum. Passim per plateas plurimas cerneres iacere
semiuiuorum corporum ferina naufragia. Tunc uulgus
ignobile, quos inculta pauperies sine delectu ciborum 15
tenuato uentri cogit sordentia supplementa et dapes gra-
tuitas conquirere, passim iacentes epulas accurrunt. Tunc
e re nata suptile consilium ego et iste Babulus tale com-
miniscimur. Vnam, quae ceteris sarcina corporis ⟨p⟩rae‖-
ualebat, quasi cibo parandam portamus ad nostrum re- 20
ceptaculum eiusque probe nudatum carnibus corium ser-
uatis sollerter totis *u*nguibus, ipso etiam bestiae capite
adusque confinium ceruicis solido relicto tergus omne
rasura studiosa tenuamus et minuto cinere perspersum
soli siccandum tradimus. Ac dum caelestis uaporis flam- 25
mis examurgatu*r*, nos interdum pulpis eius ualenter sagi-
H 86 nantes sic instanti militiae disponimus sacramentum, ut 1
unus e numero nostro, non qui corporis adeo, sed animi
robore ceteris antistaret, atque is in primis uoluntarius,
pelle illa contectus ursae subiret effigiem domumque
Democharis inlatus per opportuna noctis silentia nobis 5
15 ianuae faciles praestaret aditus. Nec paucos fortissimi
collegii sollers species ad munus obe[di]*u*ndum adrexerat.
Quorum prae ceteris Thrasyleon factionis optione delectus
ancipitis machinae subi*u*it aleam. Iamque habili corio et
mollitie tractabili uultu sereno sese recondit. Tunc te|nui 10
sarcimine summas oras eius adaequamus et iuncturae
rimam, licet gracilem, setae circumfluentis densitate sae-
pimus, ad ipsum confinium gulae, qua ceruix bestiae
fuerat execta, Thrasyleonis caput subire cogimus paruisque
respiratui circa nares et oculos datis foraminibus fortissi- 15
mum socium nostrum prorsus bestiam factum inmittimus
caueae modico prae[de]stinatae pretio, quam constanti
uigore festinus inrepsit ipse. Ad hunc modum prioribus
16 inchoatis sic ad reliqua fallaciae pergimus. Sciscitati
nomen cuiusdam Nicanoris, qui genere Thracio proditus 20
ius amicitiae summum cum illo Demochare colebat, litteras
adfi⟨n⟩gimus, ut uenationis suae primitias bonus amicus
uideretur ornando muneri[s] dedicasse. Iamque prouecta
uespera abusi praesidio tenebrarum Thrasyleonis caueam
Demochari cum litteris illis adulterinis offerimus; qui 25

15

miratus bestiae magnitudinem suique contubernalis oppor-
tuna liberalitate laetatus iubet nobis protinus gaudii sui
gerulis decem aureos, ut ipse habebat†, e suis loculis ‖ 28
H 87 adnumerari. Tunc, ut nouitas consueuit ad repentinas 1
uisiones animos hominum pellere, multi numero mirabundi
bestiam confluebant, quorum satis callenter curiosos aspectus
Thrasyleon noster impetu minaci frequenter inhibebat;
consonaque ciuium uoce satis felix ac beatus Demochares 5
ille saepe celebratus, quod post tantam cladem ferarum
nouo prouentu quoquo modo fortunae resisteret, iubet
noualibus suis confestim bestia[m] iret, iubet summa cum
diligentia reportari. Sed suscipiens ego:

17   "Caueas", inquam, "domine, fraglantia solis et itineris 10
spatio fatigatam coetui multarum et, ut audio, non recte
ualentium committere ferarum. Quin potius domus tuae
patulum ac perflabilem locum, immo et lacu aliquo con-
terminum refrigerantemque prospicis? An ignoras hoc genus
bestiae lucos consitos et specus roridos et fontes amoenos 15
semper incubare?"

Talibus monitis Demochares perterritus numerumque
perditorum secum recensens non difficulter adsensus, ut
ex arbitrio nostro caueam locaremus, facile permisit. "Sed
et nos", inquam, "ipsi parati sumus hic ibidem pro cauea 20
ista excubare noctes, ut aestus et uexationis incommodo
bestiae fatigatae et cibum tempestiuum et potum solitum
accuratius offeramus."

"Nihil indigemus labore isto uestro", respondit ille,
"iam paene tota familia per diutinam consuetudinem nu- 25
triendis ursis exercitata est."

18   Post haec ualefacto discessimus et portam ciuitatis
egressi monumentum quoddam conspicamur procul a uia
remoto et abdito loco positum. Ibi capulos carie et uetu- 29
H 88 state semitectos, quis inhabitabant puluerei et iam cine- 1
rosi mortui, passim ad futurae praedae receptacula rese-
ramus et ex disciplina sectae seruato noctis inlunio tem-
pore, quo somnus obuius impetu primo corda mortalium
ualidius inuadit ac premit, cohortem nostram gladiis ar- 5
matam ante ipsas fores Democharis uelut expilationis
uadimonium sistimus. Nec setius Thrasyleon examus⟨s⟩im
capto ‖ noctis latrocinali momento prorepit cauea statim-
que custodes, qui propter sopiti quiescebant, omnes ad
unum, mox etiam ianitorem ipsum gladio conficit clauique 10
subtracta fores ianuae repandit nobisque prompte con-
uolantibus et domus alueo receptis demonstrat horreum,
ubi uespera sagaciter argentum copiosum recondi uiderat.
Quo protinus perfracto confertae manus uiolentia, iubeo
singulos commilitonum asportare quantum quisque poterat 15

auri uel argenti et in illis aedibus fidelissimorum mor-
tuorum occultare propere rursumque concito gradu recur-
renti⟨s⟩ sarcinas iterare; quod enim ex usu foret omnium,
me solum resistentem pro domus limine cuncta rerum
exploraturum sollicite, dum redirent. Nam et facies ursae 20
mediis aedibus discurren*tis* ad proterrendos, siqui de
familia forte uigilassent, uidebatur opportuna. Quis
enim, quamuis fortis et intrepidus, immani forma tant*ae*
bestiae noctu praesertim uisitata non se ad fugam statim
concitaret, non obdito cellae pessulo pauens et trepidus 25

19 sese cohiberet? His omnibus salubri consilio recte dispo-
sitis occurrit scaeuus euentus. Namque dum reduces socios
nostros suspensus opperior, quidam seruulum st⟨r⟩epitu[s] 28

H 89 scilicet diuinitus inquietus proserpit leniter uisaque 1
bestia, qua꞉ libere discurrens totis aedibus commeabat,
premens obnixum silentium uestigium suum replicat et
utcumque cunc|tis in domo uisa pronuntiat. Nec mora,
cum numerosae familiae frequentia domus tota completur. 5
Taedis, lucernis, cereis, sebaciis et ceteris nocturni luminis
instrumentis clarescunt tenebrae. Nec inermis quisquam
de tanta copia processit, sed singuli fustibus, lanceis, de-
strictis denique gladiis armati muniunt adit*us*. Nec secus
canes etiam uenaticos auritos illos et horricomes ad com- 10

20 primendam bestiam cohortantur. Tunc ego sensim gliscente
adhuc illo tumultu retrogradi fuga domo facesso, sed plane
Thrasyleonem mire canibus repugnantem, latens pone
ianuam ipse, prospicio. Quamquam enim uitae metas
ultimas obiret, non ‖ tamen sui nostrique uel pristinae 15
uirtutis oblitus iam fa⟨u⟩cibus ipsis hiantis Cerberi re-
luctabat. Scaenam denique, quam sponte sumpserat, cum
anima retinens nunc fugiens, nunc resistens uariis cor-
poris sui schemis ac motibus tandem domo prolapsus est.
Nec tamen, quamuis publica potitus libertate, salutem 20
fuga quaerere potuit. Quippe cuncti canes de proximo
angiportu satis feri satisque copiosi uenaticis illis, qui
commodum domo similiter insequentes processerant, se
ommisce[u]nt agminatim. Miserum funestumque spectamen 24

H 90 aspexi, Thrasyleonem nostrum cateruis canum saeuientium 1
cinctum atque obsessum multisque numero morsibus lania-
tum. Denique tanti doloris impatiens populi circumfluentis
turbelis immisceor et in quo solo poteram celatum auxi-
lium bono ferre commilitoni, sic indaginis principes 5
dehortabar: "O grande", inquam, "et extremum flagitium,

21 magnam et uere pretiosam perdimus bestiam." Nec tamen
nostri sermonis artes infelicissimo profuerunt iuueni; quippe
quidam procurrens e domo procerus et ualidus incunctanter
lanceam mediis iniecit ursae praecordiis nec secus alius 10

et ecce plurimi, iam timore discusso, certatim gladios
etiam de proximo conger*unt*. Enimuero Thrasyleon egre-
gium decus nostrae factionis tandem immortalitate digno
illo spiritu expugnato magis quam patientia neque cla-
more ac ne ululatu quidem fidem sacramenti | prodidit, 15
sed iam morsibus laceratus ferroque laniatus obnixo
mugitu et ferino fremitu praesentem casu⟨*m*⟩ generoso
uigore tolerans gloriam sibi reseruauit, uitam fato reddidit.
Tanto tamen terrore tantaque formidine coetum illum tur-
bauerat, ut usque diluculum, immo et in multum diem 20
nemo quisquam fuerit ausus quamuis iacentem bestiam
uel digito contingere, nisi tandem pigre ac timide quidam
lanius paulo fidentior utero bestiae resecto ursae magni-
ficum despoliauit latronem. Sic etiam Thrasyleon nobis 24
H 91 periuit, sed a gloria non peribit. Confestim itaque con- 1
strictis ‖ sarcinis illis, quas nobis seruauerant fideles mor-
tui, Plataeae terminos concito gradu deserentes istud apud
nostros animos identidem reputabamus merito nullam
fidem in uita nostra repperiri, quod ad manis iam et 5
mortuos odio perfidiae nostrae demigrarit. Sic onere
uecturae simul et asperae uiae toti fatigati tribus co-
mitum desideratis istas quas uidetis praedas adueximus.'
22   Post istum sermonis terminum poculis aureis memo-
riae defunctorum commilitonum uino mero libant, dehinc 10
canticis quibusdam Marti deo blanditi paululum con-
quiescunt. Enim nobis anus illa recens ordeum adfatim
et sine ulla mensura largita est, ut equus quidem meus
tanta copia et quidem solus potitus sali⟨*ar*⟩‖es scilicet ce-
nas se ⟨*esse*⟩ crederet. Ego uero, numquam alias hordeo 15
*ci*ba*t*us, *c*um minutatim et diutina co*qu*itatione iuru-
lentum   semper   esserim,   rimatus   angulum,   quo
H 92 panes reliquiae totius multitud⟨*in*⟩is congestae fuerant, 1
fauces diutina fame saucias et araneantes ualenter exerceo.
Et ecce nocte promota latrones expergiti castra commo-
uent instructique uarie, partim gladiis armati[m] in
Lemures reformat⟨*i*⟩ concito se gradu proripiunt. Nec 5
me tamen instanter ac fortiter manducantem uel somnus
imminens impedire potuit. Et quamquam prius, cum
essem Lucius, unico uel secundo pane contentus mensa
decederem, tunc uentri tam profundo seruiens | iam ferme
tertium qualum rumigabam. Huic me operi attonitum 10
23 clara lux oppressit. Tandem itaque asinali uerecundia
ductus aegerrime tamen digrediens riuulo proximo sitim
lenio. Nec mora, cum latrones ultra anxii atque
solliciti remeant, nullam quidem prorsus sarcinam uel
omnino, licet uilem, laciniam ferentes, sed tantum gladiis, 15
totis manibus, immo factionis suae cunctis uiribus

unicam uirginem fil[i]o liberalem et, ut matronatus eius
indicabat, summatem re[li]gionis, puellam mehercules et
asino tali concupiscendam, maerentem et crines cum ueste
sua lacerantem aduehebant. Eam simul intra speluncam 20
uerbisque quae dolebat minora fa‖cientes sic
adloquuntur: 'Tu quidem salutis et pudicitiae secura breuem
patientiam nostro compendio tribue, quos ad istam sectam
paupertatis necessitas adegit. Parentes autem tui de 24

H 93 tanto suarum diuitiarum cumulo, quamquam satis cupidi, 1
tamen sine mora parabunt scilicet idoneam sui sanguinis
redemptionem.'

24 His et his similibus blateratis necquicquam dolor se-
datur puellae. Quidni? Quae inter genua sua deposito 5
capite sine modo flebat. At illi intro uocatae anui prae-
cipiunt, adsidens eam blando, quantum posset, solaretur
alloquio, seque ad sectae sueta conferunt. Nec tamen
puella quiuit ullis aniculae sermonibus ab inceptis fletibus
auocari, sed a⟨l⟩tius eiulans sese et assiduis singultibus 10
ilia quatiens mihi etiam lacrimas excussit. Ac sic: 'An
ego', inquit, 'misera, tali domo, tanta familia, tam cari⟨s⟩
uernulis, tam sanctis parentibus desolata et infelicis ra-
pinae praeda et mancipium effecta inque isto saxeo car-
cere seruiliter clausa et omnibus deliciis, quis innata atque 15
innutrita sum, priuata sub incerta salutis et carni-
ficinae lani[g]ena inter tot ac tales latrones et horrendum
gladiatorum populum uel fletum desinere uel omnino
uiuere potero?'

Lamentata sic et animi dolore et faucium tendore et 20
corporis lassitudine iam fatigata marcentes oculos demisit
25 ad soporem. At commodum coniuerat nec diu, cum re-
H 94 pente lymphatico ritu so‖mno recussa longeque 1
uehementius adflictare sese et pectus etiam palmis infestis
tundere et faciem illam luculentam uerberare incipit et
aniculae, quanquam instantissime causas noui et instaurati
maeroris requirenti, sic adsuspirans altius infit: 'Em nunc 5
certe, nunc maxime funditus perii, nunc spei salutiferae
renuntiaui. Laqueus aut gladius aut certe praecipitium
procul dubio capessendum est.'

Ad haec anus iratior dicere eam saeuiore iam uultu
iubebat, quid, malum,‖fleret uel quid repente postliminio 10
pressae quietis lamentationes licentiosas refricaret. 'Ni-
mirum', inquit, 'tanto compendio tuae redemptionis de-
fraudare iuuenes meos destinas? Quod si pergis ulterius,
iam faxo lacrimis istis, quas parui pendere latrones con-
suerunt, insuper habitis uiua exurare.' 15
26 Tali puella sermone deterrita manuque eius exoscu-
lata: 'Parce', inquit, 'mi parens, et durissimo casui meo

19

pietatis humanae memor subsiste paululum. Nec enim, ut reor, aeuo longiore maturatae tibi in ista sancta canitie miseratio prorsus exaruit. Specta denique scaenam meae 20 calamitatis. Speciosus adolescens inter suos principal*is*, quem filium publicum omnis sibi ciuitas co*o*ptauit, meus alioquin consobrinus, tantulo triennio maior in aetate, qui mecum primis ab annis nutritus et adultus indiuiduo contubernio domusculae, immo uero cubiculi torique, sanctae 25 caritatis adfectione mutuo mihi pigneratus uotisque nuptia-

H 95 libus pacto iugali pridem destinatus, consensu parentum 1 tabulis etiam maritus nuncupatus, ad nuptias officio frequenti cognatorum et adfinium stipatus templis et aedibus publicis uictimas immolabat; domus tota lauris obsita, taedis lucida constrepebat hymenaeum; tunc me gremio 5 suo mater infelix tolerans mundo nuptiali decenter ornabat mellitisque sauiis crebriter ingestis iam spe⟨m⟩ futura⟨m⟩ liberorum uotis anxiis propagabat, cum inruptionis subitae gladiatorum impetus ad belli faciem saeuiens, nudis et infe*s*tis mucronibus coruscans: non caedi, non 10 rapinae manus adferunt, | sed denso conglo*b*atoque cuneo cubiculum nostrum inuadunt protinus. Nec ullo de familiaribus nostris repugnante ac ne tantillum quidem resistente misera⟨m⟩, exanimem saeuo pauore, trepido de medio matris gremio rapuere. Sic ad instar Attidis uel 15

27 Protesilai dispectae disturbataeque nuptiae. Sed ecce saeuissimo somnio mihi nunc etiam redintegratur, immo uero cumulatur ‖ infortunium meum; nam uisa sum mihi de domo, de thalamo, de cubiculo, de toro denique ipso uiolenter extracta per solitudines auias infortunatissimi 20 mariti nomen inuocare eumque, ut primum meis amplexibus uiduatus est, adhuc ungentis madidum, coronis floridum consequi uestigio me pedibus fugientem alienis. Vtque clamore percito formonsae raptum uxoris conquerens populi testatur auxilium, quidam de latronibus importunae 25

H 96 persecutionis indignatione permotus saxo grandi pro pedi- 1 bus a*d*repto misellum iuuenem maritum meum percussum interemit. Talis aspectus atrocitate perterrita somno funesto pauens excussa sum.'

Tunc fletibus eius adsuspirans anus sic incipit: 'Bono 5 animo esto, mi erilis, nec uanis somniorum figmentis terreare. Nam praeter quod diurnae quietis imagines falsae perhibentur, tunc etiam nocturnae uisiones contrarios euentus nonnumquam pronuntiant. Denique flere et uapulare et nonnumquam iugulari lucrosum prosperum- 10 que prouentum nuntiant, contra ridere et mellitis dulciolis uentrem saginare uel in uoluptatem ueneriam conuenire tristitiae animi, languori corporis damni⟨s⟩que ceteris

uexatum iri praedicabant. Sed ego te narrationibus
lepidis anilibusque fabulis protinus auocabo', et incipit: 15

CHAPTER I

After he has reluctantly let go a chance of release (3,29), the ass arrives at a village where he takes the opportunity first to fill his empty stomach, then to look for another rose.

74, 9-10 Diem ferme circa medium, cum iam flagrantia solis caleretur: "About the middle of the day, more or less, when it was already getting hot because of the blazing sun..."

The time indicator in Apuleius' narrative technique here seems to function as a level plain or valley between two rather steep emotional rises, the first of which consists in the temptation by the *rosae uirgines* of 3,29 (73,24) the second in the threat of the *rosae laureae* of 4,2 (76,2). Books 2, 3, 7, 8, 10 similarly start with indications of time, judiciously varied.

diem ferme circa medium: for the hyperbaton see (e.g.) Bernhard p. 24. Cf. 8,30 (201,6); *Onos* 17,2: ἐπεὶ δὲ ἦν αὐτὸ <τὸ> μέσον τῆς ἡμέρας. According to the statistics of ThLL (V, col. 1024) Apuleius has *dies* 37 times as masc., 24 as fem. No rational division can be found; cf. 9,30 (225,17) *diem ferme circa mediam*, vdP. p. 124.

cum iam flagrantia solis caleretur: *caleret'* F (= *caleretur*) produces both good sense and a good clausula. The reading *caleret* was last accepted by Oudendorp as an emendation of *calerent*, the "scripta lectio". Robertson and Frassinetti report it as the ς reading. The impersonal passive is very common in Apuleius, e.g. 101,7 *maeretur, fletur, lamentatur diebus plusculis*; 5,15 (115,3) *psallitur...sonatur...cantatur*; even such forms as *pluitur, ningitur, Fl.* 2 (2,15); LHSz p. 288 give a number of instances of an impersonal used in describing weather conditions. For *caleretur* see Pl. *Capt.* 80 with Lindsay *ad loc.* and *Truc.* 65 with Enk *ad loc.* See also Desertine p. 77, Callebat, *S.C.*, p. 495.

flagrantiā: in Apuleius confined to the heat of the sun; adverbial expressions, redundant with the verb, are discussed by Bernhard p. 178. See, on the spelling, Appendix II.

74, 10-11 in pago quodam apud notos ac familiares latronibus senes deuertimus: "we stopped at a village, at the house of elderly people known to and on friendly terms with the robbers".

Oudendorp saw and resolved two questions: *apud* (mss.) or *ad* (Pricaeus), *diu-* (edd.) or *deu.* (mss.); Callebat, *S.C.*, p. 197 adds a third by remarking that *in pago quodam* is not immediately dependent on *deuertimus* but must be seen as a more general adverbial of place. Though it is not possible to prove him wrong, it should be pointed out that not only does the construction with *apud* have its parallel (2, 3 (26, 24) *ut non apud te deuertar*) but so also does the construction with *in* +abl. (9, 2 (204, 9-10) *cubiculum in quo mei domini deuertebant*; 10, 1 (236, 23-24) *nec in stabulo sed in domo cuiusdam decurionis deuertimus*).

An ἀπὸ κοινοῦ construction should therefore be considered. It would seem that 9, 2 (204, 9-10), a passage not mentioned by Callebat, *S.C.*, p. 197, goes a long way towards disproving his attempts to explain away the ablatives at 4, 1 ("indication de locale générale") and 10, 1 ("le terme du mouvement après un verbe au parfait"). See also below on 4, 3 (76, 25).

deuertimus: probably present tense; *Index Apul.* treats the form as a perfect; cf. however *Onos* 17,2: καταλύομεν.

Sic enim primus aditus et sermo prolixus et oscula mutua 74, 11-13
quamuis asino sentire praestabant: "For so the first encounter and the torrent of talk and the exchange of kisses gave me to understand, ass though I was." First the overwhelming impression of familiarity, then, with *nam...indicare*, more detailed observations of the relationship that exists between the robbers and the *pagani*. P. A. MacKay, *G&R* 10 (1963), p. 150, briefly notices the "curious picture of a bandit society".

primus aditus et sermo prolixus et oscula mutua: polysyndetic tricolon with the first two members in chiastic arrangement; some alliteration. See Bernhard p. 35.

primus aditus: F's original (?) *primos* is without value; cf. Hor. *S.* I, 9, 56 *difficiles aditus primos habet*.

sermo prolixus: there is no end to the talking; the ὕστερον πρότερον with *oscula mutua* coupled with the polysyndeton *et ... et* is functional in creating an impression of simultaneity in all this meeting, kissing, talking. See vdP. p. 179 on *prolixus*.

quamuis asino: the emphasis on the human intelligence in the animal form is a central element in Apuleius' technique; cf. Feldbrugge p. 47; Heine p. 302 and note 1. See below on 4, 2 (75, 13), Introd. p. 2. For the frequency of this type of construction see Médan pp. 236 ff.

sentire praestabant: *praestare* with infinitive also in Tert. *Herm.* 8 (135, 4 and 5) *et nemo qui praestat de suo uti, non in hoc superior est eo, cui praestat uti*; Chrysol. *Serm.* 147, *PL* 52 (col. 595 A) *coelestis regni praestat esse participem*. See Waszink p. 530; *Apul. Gron. III*, pp. 406 f. LHSz p. 345 regard the construction as analogous to *dare* with inf. For the function of the sentence cf. 7, 1 (154, 7-8) *sic enim mutuae salutationis officium indicabat*.

Nam et rebus eos quibusdam dorso meo depromptis munera- 74, 13-15
bantur et secretis gannitibus, quod essent latrocinio par-
tae, uidebantur indicare: "For they unpacked some things from my back and gave them to them, and seemed to indicate in a confidential chatter that they had been obtained by robbery."

23

The slightly disjunctive *et ... et* serve to distinguish between the more animal impression (*dorso meo*) and the more human observation (*secretis gannitibus*).

secretis: followed by *uidebantur* this word acquires the force of 'secretive' rather than 'secret'. Cf. Tac. *Dial.* 14, 2 *num parum tempestiuus... interueni secretum consilium*.

gannitibus: the basic meaning is 'yelping', here possibly more in general 'chattering' (though 'whispering' would fit the context even better). Cf. 2, 15 (37, 12) and De Jonge *ad loc.* (erotic context); 6, 27 (149,21): soft words to calm the excited animal. Callebat, *S.C.*, p. 404 translates "chuchotements". See also vdP. p. 152.

quod essent latrocinio partae: for *quod* + subj. in o.o. in general cf. Löfstedt, *Per. Aeth.*, pp. 116 ff.; LHSz pp. 576 f. (with literature); vdP. p. 50 on 3, 4 (55, 9) *quod sit innocens persuadere* (vdP.'s ref. to Callebat, *S.C.*, p. 319 should read pp. 338-339); also vdP. p. 109.

74, 15-17 **Iamque nos omni sarcina leuatos in pratum proximum passim libero pastui tradidere:** "And presently they relieved us of all the luggage and let us into the nearest meadow to feed freely far and wide". Our attention is directed back to the animal. With *libero* we receive the first hint of raised hope again.

leuatos: F has *leuigatos*, corrected to *leuatos* (*leuigatos* with the addition of *-uatos* in the margin for good measure). φ has *leuigatos* but *leuatos* occurs in ς. Editors are divided. If *leuigatos* is to be read it should have *ĕ*, not *ē* as at 1, 2 (3, 8). The verb with *ĕ* does not occur until the 4th cent. (e.g. Greg. M. *Ep.* 7, 75 *ipsum leuigantes pondus sollicitudinis*), but even then there is no instance of *lĕuigare* with accusative and ablative as we have here. The reasons for our choice of *leuatos* have been set out more fully in *Mnemosyne* S. IV, 26 (1973), pp. 396 f.

pratum proximum passim libero pastui: the alliterating series consists of two sets of two-member groups, the second of which is broken by an adjective. Interruptions of an alliterating series are neither uncommon nor confined to small particles (Bernhard p. 222); cf. 97, 10-12 *sic immensum procedit in dies opinio, sic insulas iam proxumas et terrae plusculum prouinciasque plurimas fama porrecta peruagatur* (three series: *pr-pl* and *p* of which *pr* and *pl* are both interlocking and interrupted by elements other than small particles). For the functionality see on 74, 19.

74, 17-18 **nec me cum asino uel equo meo conpascuus coetus attinere potuit:** "but communal pasturage with an ass or my own horse could not hold my interest." The animals had not struck a very welcoming attitude towards their master in his new shape (3, 26 (71, 22)). Note the ironic flavour given to the sentence by *meo* (cf. *meus* 71, 22) and enhanced by the alliteration *cum...conpascuus coetus*.

nec: the adversative usage (= *nec tamen*); similarly 85, 8; cf. e.g.

24

Sal. *Jug.* 88, 4; Liv. 3, 55,1; 5, 12, 5; see LHSz p. 481 with literature; the related usage of *ac, atque* etc. vdP. pp. 40 f. For the parataxis with change of subject see Bernhard p. 48.

conpascuus coetus: a bold expression; normally *conpascuus* qualifies *ager* and the like ("shared by the farmers", "common"; cf. the name of the Dutch village Emmercompascuum); Apuleius here uses it to qualify the animals that share the same pasture, but he does so indirectly by indulging his taste for abstracts and construing the adjective with *coetus*, itself not very common for a gathering of animals (see 87, 11 and comm. *ad loc.*; cf. Cic. *Fin.* 2,109 *congregatione aliae* (*bestiae*) *coetum quodam modo ciuitatis imitantur*).

attinere: 'captivate' (rather than 'capture'; cf. Pl. *Mil.* 1327; Sal. *Iug.* 108, 3; Fronto p. 253, 6 N (= 43, 2 vdH).

adhuc insolitum alioquin prandere faenum: "apart from my 74, 18-19
being as yet unaccustomed to dining on grass." *Alioquin* places the phrase in a somewhat ironic contrast with the preceding one; see also comm. on 76, 11.

Participles with *adhuc* are common in Apuleius (Bernhard p. 126 f.). For the position of *alioquin* immediately after the participle or adjective see Bernhard p. 30; vdP. p. 52.

faenum: in the sense of undried grass, cf. Plin. *Nat.* 2, 211 *in Crustumino natum fenum ibi noxium, extra salubre est*; Vegetius, *Mulomed.* 2, 53, 6 *faenum uiride adponis*; Vet.lat. *gen.* 1, 11 *fructicet terra herbam faeni* (Vulg.: *herbam uirentem*); 3, 29 (74, 7) would provide a parallel if the reading *faena* were tenable against the onslaught of Gruter and his followers; see vdP. *ad loc.*

Sed plane pone stabulum prospectum hortulum iam fame 74, 19-75,1
perditus fidenter inuado: "But being by now quite famished, I boldly break into a vegetable garden that is plainly to be seen behind the shed". The double alliteration may be functional (see Bernhard p. 221 on 11, 19 (280, 21 f.): "Ausgerechnet eine Reihe von mit p beginnenden Leckerbissen werden dem Esel von seinem Herrn vorgesetzt"). Note also the double homoeoteleuton.

plane...prospectum: the adverb is not uncommonly separated from the word it qualifies; see vdP. on 3, 27 (72, 16) *temere...positum*. Callebat, *S.C.*, p. 537 takes *plane pone* together ("just behind"). *Plane*, of course, also qualifies other adverbs elsewhere in the *Met.* (e.g. 9, 40 (234, 2) *plane identidem*) but not *pone*; it is, on the other hand linked with *prospicere* at 89, 12-14 *sed plane Thrasyleonem mire canibus repugnantem, latens pone ianuam ipse prospicio*, cf. comm. *ad loc.* The garden was lying there "in full view behind the shed".

et quamuis crudis holeribus, adfatim tamen uentrem sagino: 75, 1-2

25

"and though these were but raw vegetables, I liberally load my stomach with them." Raw cabbage and carrots hardly constitute a fit meal for gentleman Lucius, but the ass needs to fill up. Besides *crudis* the words *adfatim* and *sagino* underscore the animal aspect and create a contrast with *deosque comprecatus* etc.

adfatim: "amply", "sufficiently"; if the etymology (*fatiscere, fatigare*) is still felt, "to the point of tiring". On adverbs in *-tim* see Callebat, *S.C.*, pp. 475 ff.; vdP. p. 34. The word is found in use with verbs of feeding and otherwise from Livius Andronicus (*com.* 4) onwards. Cf. e.g. 10, 13 (246, 22) *oblatis ego diuinitus dapibus adfatim saginabar. Saginare* ("to stuff", "to fatten") is as suggestive of the farm as of the luxurious habits of high class dinner tables as described with such gusto by Seneca, e.g. *Ben.* 4, 13, 1... *cibis potionibusque intra hortorum latebram corpora ignauia pallentia saginare*.

75, 2-4   deosque comprecatus omnes cuncta prospectabam loca, sicubi forte conterminis in hortulis candens repperirem rosarium: "and with a prayer to all the gods I looked around over the whole place to see if perhaps I could find a glowing rosebush in the adjoining gardens". This second half of the sentence is concerned with Lucius' spiritual hunger as the first was concerned with the ass's stomach; the contrast is accompanied by a change in tense, see Bernhard p. 152 (an example of *variatio*); see also Callebat, *S.C.*, p. 427; vdP. p. 101. The juxtaposition of *omnes* and *cuncta* is by no means the only remarkable element in the phrasing here. There is also the mirrored word order (noun, verb, adjective; adjective, verb, noun); if we omit *-que*, the two halves *deos...omnes* and *cuncta...loca* have an identical number of syllables both times arranged 2-4-2 (several similar arrangements have been noted elsewhere, see index *s.v.* 'colometry').

sicubi: see Leumann-Hofmann pp. 289, 766; LHSz p. 651 wrongly exclude the interrogative use. Médan p. 98: '*si* introduit une proposition interrogative comme chez les comiques, Properce et Horace'. Callebat, *S.C.*, pp. 355 f. regards it as belonging to the *sermo cotidianus*.

candens...rosarium: F's *scandens* cannot be defended. The basic meaning of *candens* is 'glowing', see J. André pp. 31 f.

The colour-content is fixed by 75, 12 *mineus*; cf. *candens* used of gold coins 9, 18 (216, 24); Hor. *S.* 2, 6, 103 *rubro ubi cocco/tincta super lectos canderet uestis eburnos*. See also below on 75, 12 *fulgentium*.

75, 4-8   Nam et ipsa solitudo iam mihi bonam fiduciam tribuebat, si deuius et protectus absconditus sumpto remedio de iumenti quadripedis incuruo gradu rursum erectus in hominem inspectante nullo resurgerem: "For also the very solitude gave me considerable confidence to see if, away from the road and screened, hidden even, I could take the medicine and, from the bent-over

26

gait of a quadruped rise up erect into the stance of a man, without anyone watching": the motivation for the further rise in spirits announced in the previous phrase.

et: i.e. over and above his full stomach, we presume.

fiducia...si: cf. Médan p. 98; Callebat, *S.C.*, p. 356 speaks of "une nuance d'éventualité subsistant dans la proposition introduite par *si*". See also *sicubi* (above 75, 3).

deuius et protectus absconditus: thus the mss. With some exceptions scholars have preferred *frutectis* (Philomathes' conjecture, not Elmen-horst's as Helm thought). This introduces a new element into the text for which there is no warrant other than distrust of an *asyndeton bimembre*. A similar distrust has caused Helm to introduce *et* below 75, 22. See, however, Blomgren, p. 5 n. 1 who, after Kronenberg, Wiman, Armini, defends the mss. reading; further parallels in *Mnemosyne*, S. IV, 27 (1974), pp. 407 ff.

de iumenti quadrupedis incuruo gradu rursum erectus... resurgerem: Bernhard p. 46 mentions Apuleius' penchant for repeating the meaning of the main verb in a "redundant" participle. The heaped up pleonasms (Bernhard p. 175) may be functional in so far as the words are descriptive of Lucius' longing reflections (cf. 75, 9 *in isto cogitationis salo*).

Oudendorp quotes Lact. *Opif.* 8. See for the topos (man's erect stature distinguishes him from the animals) e.g. Ov. *Met.* 1, 84 ff. *pronaque cum spectent animalia cetera terram/ os homini sublime dedit caelumque uidere/ iussit et erectos ad sidera tollere uultus*. Bömer *ad loc.* provides a wealth of parallels, as does Mayor on Juv. 15, 147.

in hominem: ἀπὸ κοινοῦ with *erectus* and *resurgerem*. Waszink on Tert. *An.* 35,6 explains *resurgere in hominem* as "to recover his human body", and compares for this sense of *homo* 7, 15 (165, 14) *asino meo* and several further instances.

inspectante nullo: the motivation at 3, 29 (74, 2-5) *ne, si rursum asino remoto prodirem in Lucium, euidens exitium inter manus latronum offen-derem uel artis magicae suspectione uel indicii futuri criminatione*; cf. vdP. *ad loc.*; Vallette compares 11, 6 (270, 21 ff.) where Isis promises Lucius immunity on this very score. Chr. Harrauer, commenting on the latter passage (p. 38), speaks of the competition between religion and its perversion, magic.

CHAPTER II

Hope and disappointment...

75, 9 Ergo igitur cum in isto cogitationis salo fluctuarem: "And so, as I floated on that sea of thought...". The imagery occurs also at 9, 19 (217, 3) *miroque mentis salo et cogitationum dissensione*, with the difference that here the subject floats, there he is tossed to and fro between two distinct thoughts. Wherever Apuleius uses it, the imagery symbolizes upheaval and sorrow or anxiety: *Soc.* 12 (20, 5) (*deos*)... *igitur et misereri et indignari et angi et laetari omnemque humani animi faciem pati, simili motu cordis et salo mentis ad omnes cogitationum aestus fluctuare, quae omnes turbelae tempestatesque procul a deorum caelestium tranquillitate exulant.* (The passage is quoted by August. *C.D.* 9, 3). See also *Met.* 5, 21 (119, 10); 7, 4 (156,19); 11, 29 (290, 14). Where the metaphor occurs in connection with *cogitationes* this word appears almost to have the sense of "emotions". In addition the metaphor occurs with several more specific emotions, e.g. love: *Apol.* 31 (38, 1) *ab aestibus fretorum ad aestus amorum* (cf. Pi. *fr.* 123,4 Snell: ὃς μὴ πόθῳ κυμαίνεται); anger: Verg. *A.* 4, 532 and 564 (see Pease *ad loc.*); care or sorrow: Catul. 64, 62 (see Fordyce *ad loc.*). Cf. Prud. *Ham.* 278 *mens fragilis facili uitiorum fluctuat aestu.* See also the interesting note in Hesychius: σάλος· φροντίς, ταραχή, κλύδων, καὶ ἡ τῆς θαλάσσης κλύδωνος κίνησις. On Apuleius' use of water imagery in de scribing psychological states see Neuenschwander pp. 92 f.; for water imagery in general see Bernhard p. 201.

ergo igitur: on the duplication of synonymous conjunctions see Médan pp. 360 f. More fully Bernhard p. 173 under g; vdP. p. 144 collects the literature. See also 11, 5 (270, 5) and Chr. Harrauer *ad loc.*

in isto cogitationis salo fluctuarem: ironic contrast with the prosaic *ergo igitur*. Apuleius' imitation of the poets often acquires the flavour of a parody. See vdP. p. 65.

75, 10 aliquanto longius uideo frondosi nemoris conuallem umbrosam, cuius inter uarias herbulas et laetissima uirecta fulgentium rosarum mineus color renidebat: "... I saw, a little farther away, a valley full of the shade of a leafy wood. Among its variegated little plants and rich shrubbery there gleamed the reddish colour of blazing roses." If we compare the description of this pleasant spot with the *locus amoenus* as defined by Curtius, *Eur. Lit.*, pp. 202 ff., a stream or spring is lacking among the items required to qualify for the latter. Descriptions of a similar *locus amoenus* occur on several occasions when the ass hopes to reach his rose. The most closely related is perhaps the passage in the parallel situation at 3, 29 (73, 22 ff.) *hortulum quendam prospexi satis amoenum, in quo praeter ceteras gratas herbulas rosae uirgines matutino rore florebant.*

At 7, 15 the expectation of immediate delivery is more remote, but still we read (165, 11): *ueris initio pratis herbantibus rosas utique reperturus aliquas.* On the other hand, 10,29 (260,8 ff.) is explicit: ... *quod uer in ipso ortu iam gemmulis floridis cuncta depingeret et iam purpureo nitore prata uestiret et commodum dirrupto spineo tegmine spirantes cinnameos odores promicarent rosae, quae me priori meo Lucio redderent.* Here the rose is a last ray of hope for escape from an impossible situation. *Loci amoeni* also at 8, 4 (178, 25), 8, 18 (191, 19 f.) and the man-made pleasure spot of 10, 30 (261, 5). Cf. Cic. *Tusc.* 1, 28, 69 who quotes the following lines (ascribed to Ennius, *Eumenides*, by Ribbeck, Vahlen, Warmington, omitted by Jocelyn): *caelum nitescere, arbores frondescere,/ uites laetificae pampinis pubescere,/ rami bacarum ubertate incuruescere,/ segetes largiri fruges, florere omnia,/ fontes scatere, herbis prata convestirier.* And, almost six centuries later, Prud. *Cath.* 3, 101: *tunc per amoena uirecta iubet/ frondicomis habitare locis,/ uer ubi perpetuum redolet/ prataque multicolora latex/ quadrifluo celer amne rigat.* See also comm. on ch. 6.

frondosi nemoris conuallem umbrosam: note the chiastic arrangement, further strengthened by the assonance *frondosi... umbrosam.*

frondosi nemoris: cf. 8, 4 (178, 25) *frondosum tumulum ramorumque densis tegminibus umbrosum*; 8, 18 (191, 19) *nemus proceris arboribus consitum.*

conuallem umbrosam: cf. 6, 3 (130, 26) *inter subsitae conuallis sublucidum lucum*; the element of shade is strengthened by *opaca* below (75, 14).

cuius inter uarias herbulas et laetissima uirecta fulgentium rosarum mineus color: four adjective-plus-noun groups, arranged in two pairs, the first pair linked by *et*, the second pair asyndetic.

uarias herbulas: cf. 3, 29 (73, 24) *gratas herbulas*; 10, 30 (261, 7).

laetissima uirecta: cf. 8, 18 (191, 20) *pratentibus uirectis*; 10, 30 (261, 5) *consitus uirectis et uiuis arboribus.* See also Verg. *A.* 6,638 (cf. Prud. *Cath.* 3, 101 quoted above).

fulgentium rosarum mineus color: it should be observed that the operative group is left to the end in order to enhance the element of tension. The *rosae uirgines* of the previous occasion occupy a comparable place in the sentence (73 ,24).

fulgentium: once again the roses are fiery; cf. 11, 13 (276, 1) *coronam quae rosis amoenis intexta fulgurabat,* and below (75, 15) *floris genialis regius nitor.* Also 10, 29 (260, 11) ... *promicarent rosae, quae me priori meo Lucio redderent,* though in the latter instance *promicare* may refer more to the prominence of the flowers on their bushes, cf. 3,21 (68,10).

It may be possible to link the shining quality of the rose in these instances with the function it has in Lucius' metamorphosis and, therefore, the central place it acquires in the ass's imagination. Whether the fact that Fotis at 2, 16 (37, 19) and Venus at 6, 11 (136, 7) are decked with roses has special significance in this context remains to be seen. See Chr. Harrauer on 11, 6 (270, 13) *roseam... coronam*, who forges a link as follows (p. 37): "vergeblich versuchte Lucius öfter an das ihm von Photis versprochene Heilmittel (3, 25, 3), die Rose, die Blume der Venus und des Kosmos (Philostr. mai. imag. 1, 2, 4), zu kommen; nun wird es ihm, in Form eines Rosenkranzes, von Isis, der wahren Venus, der Herrin des Kosmos, versprochen". On the symbolic functions of the rose in Western literature, see Barbara Seward, *The Symbolic Rose*, New York 1960; see also below on 75, 15 *floris genialis*.

mineus: "reddish"; see Gargantini p. 35 concerning the suffix; N. Vels Heijn, *Kleurnamen en kleurbegrippen bij de Romeinen*, Diss. Utrecht 1951, p. 44, André pp. 117 f., on the colour. Plin. *Nat.* 35, 45 speaks of *fulgorem minii*.

75, 12-15 Iamque apud mea non usquequaque ferina praecordia Veneris et Gratiarum lucum illum arbitrabar, cuius inter opaca secreta floris genialis regius nitor relucebat: "And in my not altogether beastly breast I now thought it a grove of Venus and the Graces, within whose shaded recesses shone the joyous flower's royal sheen." Lucius' imagination, ass though he is, takes the characteristic direction of Venus. In almost any moralistic interpretation of the novel Venus and the animal figure belong together. Here they are playfully contrasted.

apud...praecordia: cf. 91, 3 *apud nostros animos*; see Callebat, *S.C.*, p. 216 for several further instances.

usquequaque: used in the sense of *prorsus*, see Callebat, *S.C.*, pp. 539 f.

non usquequaque ferina praecordia: the motif of the ass who is not quite an ass; vdP. on 3, 26 (71, 6) speaks of a mere device of the author; we should note, however, that the device is integrated in the structure of the novel, both in the plot (e.g. at 6, 29 (151, 12) where the struggle between Lucius and Charite leads to their recapture by the robbers) and in the comic element: Heine pp. 301 f. notes that the "Aufhebung der Naturordnung" in a human ass gradually loses some of its grotesqueness and changes into a "Vehikel vordergründiger Komik". In a moralistic interpretation of the novel it would be precisely the question whether what is designated as 'human' is worthy of the name.

For the contrast between the ass's body and the human *ingenium* see Introd. p. 2; 78, 20-22; see also Junghanns p. 62 and note 91; Lesky p. 576; vThiel I (p. 181 n. 47 and p. 185) refers to the ass who carries a divine image (i.e. the statue of a god). Cf. Helm-Krenkel, *Einf.* p. 20.

Veneris et Gratiarum lucum: cf. 2, 8 (32, 3-4); Venus is combined with the Graces from Homer onwards: *Il.* 5, 338, *Od.* 8, 364, *h.Ven.* 61; cf. e.g. Pi. *P.* 6, 2 and *Pae.* 6, 2 f. See Radt on the latter passage; Hor. *Carm.* 3, 21,21 f.; Serv. on Verg. *A.* 1, 720.

Gratiarum: see Pi. *O.* 9, 27; Ov. *Fast.* 5, 209 ff. (garden of Flora), in

30

particular line 219: *protinus accedunt Charites* and Bömer *ad loc.*

floris genialis regius nitor: chiastic construction, see on 75, 22.

floris genialis: see Médan p. 154: the word *genialis* is used in the enlarged sense of "beau", "joyeux"; cf. ThLL *s.v.* 1807, 83 with a reference to *genius* in the sense of *uenustas* (*ibid.* 1839, 47).

The passages in which the rose is merely associated with Venus (in Apuleius e.g. *Met.* 6, 11 (136, 7)) are much more numerous than those in which the rose is expressly said to be sacred to her, yet the latter are not lacking altogether. Pausanias describes a sanctuary of the Graces in Elis (6,24, 6-7): ἔστι δὲ καὶ Χάρισιν ἱερὸν καὶ ξόανα ἐπίχρυσα τὰ ἐς ἐσθῆτα, πρόσωπα δὲ καὶ χεῖρες καὶ πόδες λίθου λευκοῦ· ἔχουσι δὲ ἡ μὲν αὐτῶν ῥόδον, ἀστράγαλον δὲ ἡ μέση, καὶ ἡ τρίτη κλῶνα οὐ μέγαν μυρσίνης. ἔχειν δὲ αὐτὰς ἐπὶ τοιῷδε εἰκάζοι τις ἂν τὰ εἰρημένα, ῥόδον μὲν καὶ μυρσίνην Ἀφροδίτης τε ἱερὰ εἶναι καὶ οἰκεῖα τῷ ἐς Ἄδωνιν λόγῳ, Χάριτας δὲ Ἀφροδίτῃ μάλιστα <φίλας> εἶναι θεῶν· ἀστράγαλον δὲ μειρακίων τε καὶ παρθένων κτλ. And in the Latin Anthology (86, I 1 p. 120 f. Buecheler-Riese) Amor complains: *Unde rosae, mater, coeperunt esse nocentes?| Unde tui flores pugnant latentibus armis?* On the other hand Aphrodite has used a rose perfume from *Il.* 23, 186 onwards (thereby creating the problem *quapropter idem poeta rosam non norit, oleum ex rosa norit,* Gel. 14, 6). The rose is sometimes said to have originated from the blood of Venus herself (e.g. *Anth. Lat.* 85, I 1 p. 120 Buecheler-Riese), sometimes from the blood of Adonis (Bion, *Idyll.* I 64, cf. Servius on *Ecl.* 10, 18). Cypris' abode is scattered with roses in Sappho (*fr.* 2,6 βρόδοισι δὲ παῖς ὁ χῶρος / ἐσκίαστ') as well as in *Anth. Lat.* 86 (referred to above) a poem which starts with the line *Hortus erat Veneris, roseis circumdatus herbis.* A mine of information is to be found in Ch. Joret, *La rose dans l'antiquité et au moyen age, histoire, légendes et symbolisme,* Paris 1892.

regius nitor: the combination is not found elsewhere. Oudendorp mentions but does not adopt the conjecture *egregius,* for which in fact there is no need; cf. Pl. *Mil.* 10: *forma regia.* For *nitor* in the sense of colour cf. Lucr. 2, 817 ff.; Prop. 2, 18, 24.

Tunc inuocato hilaro atque prospero Euentu cursu me con-   75, 15-18
cito proripio, ut hercule ipse sentirem non asinum me,
uerum etiam equum currulem nimio uelocitatis effectum.
"Then calling on happy and favourable Outcome I launched myself into a fast gallop so that, by Hercules, I felt myself to be no longer an ass but changed by this excess of speed into a chariot-horse." The climax of the situation is given a thoroughly Apuleian nuance in the human ass's obvious pride in his equine achievement. Note the double homoeoteleuton in the first half of the period. For a similar '*equitas*' see 6, 28 (149, 24).

hilaro atque prospero Euentu: cf. 11, 28 (290, 3) *spiritu fauentis Euentus.* Chr. Harrauer *ad loc.* speaks of the νοῦς of God which the Initiate has absorbed; she omits this passage in which we have a reference to a well known divinity *Euentus,* more usually *Bonus Euentus.* References in

31

ThLL *s.v.* 1019, 56 ff.; cf. *R.E.* III 715 ff.; Suppl. III 446 f., G. Wissowa, *Religion u. Kultus d. Römer*, München ²1912, p. 267 (*Handbuch* V 5). The replacement volume, Latte, *RRG*, omits all reference to this divinity.

Without a qualifying adjective he occurs in Donatus on *A.* 7, 498 *deum quem debemus accipere nisi Euentum, qui humanos actus aut inplet aut deserit?* Cf. Claudianus *De bello Gild.* 1, 250; *In Eutrop.* 2, 489. The noun is often combined with *prosper*: e.g. Liv. 22, 23, 3 *laeto uerius dixerim quam prospero euentu pugnatum*. For a hostile *euentus* (or *Euentus*) see 88, 26-27; Heine p. 139.

hilaro: Médan (p. 176) lists *hilarus* (against *hilaris*) as an instance of *sermo cotidianus*. This is doubtful. W. A. Baehrens, *Sprachlicher Kommentar zur vulgärlateinischen Appendix Probi*, Halle 1922, p. 108 and ThLL *s.v.*, 2786, show that *hilarus* is the older form, but one which continues to be used by Cicero, Seneca and others, though *hilaris* gains the upper hand. Callebat does not mention *hilarus*; cf. vdP. p. 93.

cursu me concito proripio: cf. 8, 13 (187, 7-8) *cursu furioso proripit se*; 10, 35 (265, 29) *iam cursu me celerrimo proripio*. Similar pleonasms (an adjective added to a noun which is in itself redundant) are listed in Bernhard p. 178. The ass's lack of restraint is to be contrasted with his attitude when the rose is finally granted him in 11, 12 (275, 22 f.): *nec tamen gaudio subitario commotus inclementi me cursu proripui, uerens scilicet, ne repentino quadripedis impetu religionis quietus turbaretur ordo...*, where the alliteration of *c* appears once again.

equum currulem: a horse fit to participate in chariot races (ἵππος δρομεύς), cf. 9, 9 (209, 11) *cohibita equorum curr[ic]uli rabie*; (φ reads *curriculi* but the margin shows *curuli* in the same hand). Fest. p. 49M (= 43 L) *currules equi quadrigales*; Amm. 20, 8, 13 *equos praebebo currules Hispanos*. The distinction between *currulis* and *curulis* is not entirely clear. *Currulis* referring without doubt and exclusively to chariots occurs regularly from the 2nd century A.D. onwards (e.g. Fronto 218, 10 vdH. *curruli strepitu*; Min. Fel. 37, 11 *in ludis currulibus*). *Curulis* with reference to chariots e.g. in Liv. 24, 18, 10 *curulium equorum* (processional horses), Aug. *Anc.* 1, 21 *tris egi curulis triumphos* (= τρὶς ἐφ' ἅρματος), cf. Suet. *Aug.* 22. OLD sees *currulis ⟨ currus* as a late formation and questions the derivation *curulis ⟨ currus* referring to a possible Etruscan origin, which Walde-Hofman regard as improbable.

nimio uelocitatis: Petschenig's correction is certain. Cf. 3, 28 (73, 2) *opulentiae nimiae nimio*; 7, 23 (171, 16) *nimio libidinis*; vdP. p. 199; vGeisau p. 261 ff.

effectum: thus Rohde (*RhM*, 40 (1885) pp. 66-113) against the mss. *refectum*, followed by all modern editors. In Apuleius *reficere* and *refectus* always refer to the restoration of health or recovery from fatigue, or even feasting the eyes (10, 29 (260, 19) *oculos patente porta spectaculi prospectu gratissimo reficiens*). Nor is it easy to find a passage elsewhere in which *reficere* means "change into" or "replace by". In an absolute sense it means "replace" in Verg. *G.* 3, 69 ff: *semper erunt, quarum mutari corpora malis: |semper enim refice ac, ne post amissa requiras,|anteueni*

et subolem armento sortire quotannis. See also vdP. p. 93 on *refingere*
and p. 174 on *reformare* (cf. Callebat, *S.C.*, p. 153).

Sed agilis atque praeclarus ille conatus fortunae meae 75, 18-20
scaeuitatem anteire non potuit: "But that nimble and splendid
attempt of mine could not outstrip my fortune's perversity". Note the
humorous effect of the chiastic construction in which *agilis atque prae-*
clarus ille conatus continues the idea in *equum currulem* of the previous
sentence, whereas *fortunae meae scaeuitatem* takes us back to *asinum*.
The result is that the anticlimax which *sed* announces is postponed for
another five words. See also Feldbrugge pp. 48 f. on the humour of the
passage.

agilis atque praeclarus: *Met.* 6, 10 (135, 24) uses *agiles* of ants, Amm.
17, 13, 9 has *equitum…turmis agilibus*. Feldbrugge p. 48 is right in re-
marking that *praeclarus* is regularly used in an ironic sense; cf. e.g. 3, 26
(71, 22) where Lucius first joins his horse in the stable and speaks of
praeclarus ille uector meus. Not ironic: 96, 20.

fortunae meae scaeuitatem: the necessary correction from *me* to *meae*
was made by a corrector in F. All parallels in Apuleius support the
meaning "perversity" for *scaeuitas*: 3, 14 (62, 15), cf. vdP. pp. 108 f.;
7, 3 (156, 15) *sed quid ego pluribus de Fortunae scaeuitate conqueror,*
[quan] quam nec istud puduit me cum meo famulo meoque uectore illo equo
factum conseruum atque coniugem; 9, 10 (210, 3). Cf. Vallette p. 7 n. 2 on
the adjective *scaeuus* ("lefthanded", "awkward", "perverse") and its
relationship with *saeuus* ("cruel"). Oudendorp capitalizes *Fortunae*,
perhaps correctly: certainly the word is to be contrasted with *hilaro atque*
prospero Euentu above.

anteire continues the humorous imagery of the race between the chariot
horse and lefthanded, awkward, perverse Fortune, i.e. the ass-as-a-horse
racing his asinine fate.

Iam enim loco proximus non illas rosas teneras et amoenas, 75, 20-24
madidas diuini roris et nectaris, quas rubi felices beatae
spinae generant, ac ne conuallem quidem usquam nisi
tantum ripae fluuialis marginem densis arboribus septam
uideo. "For when I got close to the place I saw, not the tender and
pleasant roses I was expecting, moist with a divine dew and nectar, which
shrubs abundant, blessed thornbushes produce, nor even an enclosed
valley anywhere, but only the rim of the riverbank boarded with dense
trees". The ass's disappointment is painted the more vividly in that it
starts with a mirage-like dissolution of the *locus amoenus,* of which
several elements return in the description of the flowers, shrubs, valley,
not seen by Lucius.

teneras et amoenas, madidas…: the asyndeton has an almost explicative
force. Several types of *asyndeton bimembre* have been mentioned above

33

on 75, 6. Cf. 81, 19-20: *denique solus ac solitarius, parua sed satis munita domuncula contentus.*

madidas: nowhere else in Latin literature is *madidus* construed with the genitive; see Médan p. 37; K.St. II 1 p. 441; LHSz p. 77 treat it as an analogy with *plenus, refertus* and the like. ThLL *s.v.*, 37, refers to Prud. *Perist.* 10, 363 *uapor uincens... auras madentes Persicorum aromatum.*

rubi felices beatae spinae: Helm (1955), Vitali, Scazzoso, retain *et*, notwithstanding the objections of Blomgren (p. 5 n. 4), Castiglioni (1931) and Robertson. Bernhard in listing (p. 32) this instance under those chiasmi that have their adjectives enclosed by nouns appears to accept *et*. It has, however, all the earmarks of a "Verschlimmbesserung". Gruter's conjecture *felicis*, (mistakenly attributed to Koziol by Helm) was approved by Koziol and adopted by vdVliet, but is equally unnecessary: there is an element of climax in the oxymoron *beatae spinae*, all the more bitterly ironic, since those rose thorns are not there. On the use of oxymoron in Apuleius see G. Lopez *GIF* 22 (1970) pp. 86-91; Strilciw p. 118.

ac ne conuallem quidem: Oudendorp reads *ac*, but mentions several editors who retained *at*. It is difficult, however, to find a satisfactory parallel for the combination *at ne...quidem*, nor is a contrast required so much as an escalating element.

ripae fluuialis marginem: *ripa* and *margo* are here synonymous; a similar redundancy in e.g. 5, 27 (124, 20) *per saxa cautium membris iactatis.* Further instances in Médan p. 362; Fernhout p. 33 on 5, 3 (105, 15) *hominum nemo.*

arboribus: "shrubs" rather than "trees", see the comments on the next sentence.

septam: the trend towards monophthongization is treated by Sommer p. 71.

75,24-76,3 Hae arbores in lauri faciem prolixe foliatae pariunt in modum floris [in]odori porrectos caliculos modice punicantes, quos equidem fraglantis minime rurest⟨r⟩i uocabulo uulgus indoctum rosas laureas appellant quarumque cuncto pecori cibus letalis est: "These laurel-like trees with their rich foliage produce displays of pale red blossoms like the scented flower, which, though they have no fragrance whatever, the uneducated people call by the country name, laurel-roses. To eat these is lethal to all livestock". For a moment the attention shifts away from the ass and the trees are looked at with an almost botanical interest. The last clause of the sentence however — *in cauda uenenum* — prepares us for the shift back and the utter dejection of the next sentence.

hae arbores: the plant described is the oleander (*Nerium Oleander L.*); cf. V. Hehn-O. Schrader, *Kulturpflanzen und Haustiere*, Berlin [8]1911, pp. 416-420. Plin. *Nat.* 16, 79 gives a description which tallies very well both with the one in Dioscorides *Mat. Med.* 4, 82 (cf. also Isidorus *Etym.* 17,

34

7, 54) and with the one we have here: *rhododendron, ut nomine apparet, a Graecis uenit; alii nerium uocarunt, alii rhododaphnen, sempiternum fronde, rosae similitudine, caulibus fruticosum. Iumentis caprisque et ouibus uenenum est, idem homini contra serpentium uenena remedio.* Cf. 21, 77; 24, 90. Dioscorides adds φύεται ἐν παραδείσοις καὶ παραθαλασσίοις τόποις καὶ παρὰ ποταμοῖς.. Palladius 1, 35, 9 mentions the use of its leaves against mice. Sprengel on Dioscorides *Mat. Med.* 4, 82 doubts whether this is the plant referred to in Strabo 15, 2, 7 (722). M. Rikli, *Das Pflanzenkleid der Mittelmeerländer*, Bern 1943-8, vol. I p. 186 describes the oleander's geographical dissemination, confirms its toxic quality ("sehr giftig") and its predilection for river banks: "zur Blütezeit verraten lange, intensiv rosarote Streifen schon aus weiter Ferne den Verlauf der Flusztäler" (on the southern slopes of the Sierra Morena).

in lauri faciem: cf. Hehn-Schrader p. 223. Though the ancients knew several types of laurel, probably the *Laurus nobilis L.* is meant. A clear picture of its foliage may be found in Elfriede Abbe, *The Plants of Virgil's Georgics*, Ithaca 1965, pp. 94-95. For *in faciem* + gen. cf. 3, 29 (74, 6 f.).

in modum floris odori: this reading appears in the tradition as a correction (ς) and is defended by Oudendorp with verve and reason. Even so Gaselee reads *inodori*. Robertson, followed by Brandt-Ehlers, prints *in⟨odori⟩ modum floris [inodori]*. The advantage of his conjecture lies in its implicit explanation of the appearance in the text of an unnecessary *in*. It is, however, also possible that a corrector or scribe who knew the oleander to be almost scentless referred the phrase directly to its flower and changed *odori* to *inodori*, a hypercorrection which was then caught by one of his later colleagues. There is no reason to delete *odori* altogether as vThiel suggests should be done. The basic difficulty lies in the fact that the phrase occurs at all: it is not easy to see how the oleander produces cuplike blooms "in the manner of a fragrant flower", or, if we wish to combine the phrase with *porrectos* "cup-like blooms that stick out like a fragrant flower". The problem disappears if we take *floris odori* to refer to the real rose and translate "in the manner of *the* fragrant flower".

porrectos caliculos: *porrectos* can be taken in three different ways, either as referring to the shape of the flowers ("elongated", thus Vallette, Grimal, Helm, Schwartz) or as referring to their position (on long stems, thus Butler), or in the sense of "spread out", "displayed". Cf. Ov. *Pont.* 3, 1, 13: *nec tibi pampineas autumnus porrigit uuas.*

modice punicantes: the neologism *punicans* also 1, 6 (6, 8) and 3, 1 (52, 6). See vdP. p. 23. André p. 228 gives a large number of similar colour names in participle form; cf. *ibid.* p. 385 for several colour-names that occur in Apuleius only.

equidem: vdP. pp. 192 f.

fraglantis minime: before Gruter *minime* was commonly only taken with *rurestri*. Oudendorp salutes Gruter's innovation as a real advance but continues to print a comma after *fragrantis*. The word group forms a strong contrast with *floris odori* above and has a slightly concessive connotation in view of the element *rosas* in the popular name. The form *fragl-* alternates with *fragr-*, cf. Callebat, *S.C.*, p. 129; De Jonge on 2, 8 (32, 5) *cinnama fraglans*; see also Appendix II.

rurest⟨r⟩i uocabulo: F reads *ruresti*. The correction was made in ς; Helm notes in the *Add. et Corr.* "fortasse recte", comparing 8, 6 (181, 6) where the same situation occurs. The material made available by the ThLL at Munich provides no further support for forms without *r*. Two instances of *rurestis* in one manuscript probably are too shallow a foundation on which to start a life in the lexica. On the question *rurester/rurestris* see Neue-Wagener II³, p. 20.

uocabulo is used both in the sense of the name of a species and as a proper name; for the latter see Nipperdey-Andresen on Tac. *Ann.* 12, 66, 2; Goodyear on Tac. *Ann.* 1, 8, 3; Röver-Till on Tac. *Ann.* 12, 27 with literature. Oudendorp tells us the name is a "rustic" one because the plant is neither a laurel nor a rose.

uulgus indoctum: Apuleius himself took an interest in plants and trees, witness the titles *De medicinalibus* (*fr.* 14), *De arboribus* (*fr.* 16).

rosas laureas: cf. *Onos* 17, 2 ῥοδοδάφνη, Corp. Gloss. II 428, 35 *lauriandrum*, It. oleandro, Fr. laurier-rose, Germ. Lorbeerrose. We suspect the name was close to being regarded as a single word even in Apuleius' time.

appellant: see, for the plural with a collective singular subject, Callebat, *S.C.*, p. 336.

cuncto pecori cibus letalis: on the toxic quality of the plant see the note on *hae arbores* above. Rikli notes that even camels succumb to the poison.

CHAPTER III

The chapter starts with the ass's death-wish, and subsequently involves him in three situations likely to cause his death, from which respectively he extricates himself by force, by prudence and by taking extreme measures.

76, 3-5

Talibus fatis implicitus etiam ipsam salutem recusans sponte illud uenenum rosarium sumere gestiebam: "Enmeshed in this fatal coil, rejecting even life itself, I was quite ready to take this rose-poison".

A similar description of the situation occurs at 10, 13 (246, 1) *At ego tunc temporis talibus fatorum fluctibus uolutabar.* The image may be clarified by comparison with 11, 25 (286, 26) *fatorum... inextricabiliter contorta...licia* (see Chr. Harrauer *ad loc.* on *licium* in magical practice), but whether *implicitus* implies a conscious use of the rope or tying metaphor remains somewhat doubtful. At 3, 19 (66, 10) we read *quo me tantis angoribus implicasti* (cf. Cic. *Tusc.* 5, 3; Amm. 20, 4, 13), at 10, 9 (243, 21) *morbi inextricabilis ueterno uehementer implicitus* (cf. e.g. Lucr. 6, 1232), at 5, 20 (118, 18) *exordio somni prementis implicitus*; in all these passages the sense "enveloping" fits as well or better. *Fata* as the agents occur here only, but see Verg. *A.* 11, 108 *quaenam uos tanto fortuna... implicuit bello.* For metaphors involving noose and shackles see Neuenschwander p. 51; *ibid.* p. 41. See also Onians, *Origins*, pp. 310 f. For metaphors of envelopment it is not easy to find literature (the notion appears not to be indexed in V. Pöschl, H. Gärtner, W. Heyke, *Bibliographie zur antiken Bildersprache*, Heidelberg 1964).

etiam ipsam salutem recusans: the psychology is convincing: the ass has gone from highest hope to deepest despair.

illud uenenum rosarium: the choice of adjective produces the connotation not only of the false but of the real rose; but the expression also contains the word *illud* indicating this death-producing, rather than that salutary variety. For the various connotations of *uenenum* see Ch. S. Rayment *CB* 35 (1959) pp. 49-53. The adjective *rosarius* is a neologism possibly formed by Apuleius himself. Cf. vdP. pp. 191, 210.

sumere gestiebam: see vdP. p. 107 on the connotation of *gestire* ("ready to take", rather than "itching to take").

76, 5-11

Sed dum cunctanter accedo decerpere, iuuenis quidam, ut mihi uidebatur, hortulanus, cuius omnia prorsus holera uastaueram, tanto damno cognito cum grandi baculo furens decurrit adreptumque me totum plagis obtundit adusque uitae ipsius periculum, nisi tandem sapienter alioquin ipse mihi tulissem auxilium: "But as I cautiously approached to pick the flower, a young man – as I supposed the small-time gardener, all of whose vegetables I had ruined – realizing the enormous damage came running down in a rage with a huge stick, grabbed me and covered me all over with blows to the point of endangering my very life, had I not, wisely enough, at last rendered some aid to myself".

sed: once again the conjunction marks a turning point in the tides of fortune as well as mood. See the note on 75, 18 above; see also, for a similar use of *aber*, Horst Steinmetz, *aber bij Kafka*, Leiden 1971, pp. 8 ff.

dum cunctanter accedo decerpere: the alliteration seems to mark the hesitation. Final infinitives occur regularly in Apuleius, see Médan p. 76, LHSz pp. 344 f. The absence of a pronoun object in this and similar cases is noted by Bernhard pp. 159 f.

iuuenis quidam: Graur argues that in many cases the force of *quidam* has become that of an indefinite article. Thus below (77, 1-2) *ad ansulam quandam destinatum*; cf. 8, 30 (201, 10) *me renudatum ac de quadam quercu destinatum*; also e.g. 90, 22; 95, 25.

hortulanus: in view of its derivation from *hortulus*, the word may carry a connotation of poverty. Cf. 9, 31 (226, 24) *pauperculus quidam hortulanus*. Médan p. 107 collects the passages in which the neologism occurs. See e.g. Macr. 3, 18, 11; 7, 3, 20. According to Callebat, *S.C.*, p. 28 the word belongs to the *sermo cotidianus*.

cuius omnia prorsus holera uastaueram: see above 75, 2 *adfatim ... uentrem sagino*, a major disaster in view of the poverty implicit in *hortulus* and *hortulanus*. For the position of the adverb between adjective and noun see Bernhard p. 30.

tanto damno cognito: some of the humour of the passage lies in the solemn note taken of two major aspects of the ass's crime (committed for dear life: *iam fame perditus* 75, 1), viz. commission and discovery, before the third, punishment (the aspect needed to carry the story further), can be embarked upon.

cum grandi baculo: Médan p. 63 notes the use of *cum* in the sense of "armed with", common also in classical Latin, cf. e.g. Cic. *S. Rosc.* 32: *etiamne ad subsellia cum ferro atque telis uenistis...*

grandi: the stick is huge and fearsome, cf. 7, 18 (168, 10) *fusti grandissimo* and 82, 8 *grandique clauo*. On the question whether *grandis* takes over the function(s) of *magnus* see Löfstedt, *Synt.* II, pp. 339 f., H. L. W. Nelson, *Petronius en zijn "vulgair" Latijn* I, Alphen a/d Rijn 1947, p. 119, A. Castellano, *Una lotta di parole; magnus e grandis*, *AGI* pp. 148-171. Callebat, *S.C.*, p. 407 rightly remarks that in the *Met.* the adjective always has "un élément de pittoresque présentant l'objet non pas dans sa dimension objective exacte mais dans celle, élargie, de la personne intéressée".

furens decurrit: the position of the participle causes a slight hyperbaton.

As a result the participle itself gains some extra force. See also Heine p. 244. The verb *decurrit* (present tense, cf. *obtundit*) indicates that the *hortulanus* is busy on the hillside when he notices the ass down by the river, where the *rosa laurea* is growing. Apparently his wife is with him, cf. 76, 15-16 *ex edito despexit*.

adreptumque me totum plagis obtundit: F reads *abreptumque*, but the necessary correction occurs in ç. For the confusion of the verbs *abripio/ adripio* in the mss. see vdP. pp. 59 f. The gardener probably catches the ass by the *frena* he was chewing at the end of the previous book (if the correction is right). Médan p. 182 treats *obtundit* as a word from the *sermo cotidianus*, Callebat, *S.C.*, p. 518 thinks of a comic background; of course the entire situation is closely related to comedy.

adusque uitae ipsius periculum: the addition of *ipsius* underscores the contrast with *ipsam salutem recusans* above (76, 4).

nisi tandem … tulissem: the apodosis of the unreal condition is contained in the words *uitae … periculum* (differently Ruiz de Elvira p. 123).

sapienter alioquin: Callebat, *S.C.*, p. 463 notes that *alioquin* is used elsewhere as well to mark parentheses, not unlike *scilicet* (cf. 76, 15 below); both adverbs "marquent nettement l'intervention de l'auteur dans le récit", *ibid.* p. 459). See also comm. on 74, 18.

Nam lumbis eleuatis in altum, pedum posterioribus calci- 76, 11-14
bus iactatis in eum crebriter, iam mulcato grauiter atque
iacente contra procliue montis attigui fuga me liberaui:
"For raising my back-side aloft, I rained blows on him with my back-hooves, and when he lay badly bruised on the adjoining slope, I escaped by flight".

The three asyndetically juxtaposed (cf. Bernhard p. 56) abl. abs. constructions give successively preparation, performance and result of the first of the two actions of the sentence. The constructions consist respectively of three, four, and five words. All three are followed by elements of further precision also of increasing length, but of equal unimportance for the basic story: *in altum*, *in eum crebriter* and *contra procliue montis attigui*. The slight oddity in the sentence is caused by the unconcern with which *mulcato* is placed near *in eum*. It is not easy to see, however, how a different participle construction could be fitted in instead of the third abl. abs. Cf. Callebat, *S.C.*, p. 321, vdP. p. 97. For the ellipsis of *eo* with the third abl. abs. see Bernhard p. 45. Pricaeus compares 7, 16 (166, 16 ff.) *hic, elatis in altum uastis pectoribus arduus capite et sublimis uertice primoribus in me pugillatur ungulis*. We note the contrast between the dignified stallion and the rather less dignified ass. (The second stallion also uses his hindfeet but the word *uelitatur* indicates a swift-running skirmish, not lifted hind-quarters.)

For the expression *in altum* instead of *alte* see Bernhard p. 107.

pedum posterioribus calcibus: Oudendorp changes ("cum membra-
nis d'Orvillianis") *posterioribus* to *posteriorum* with the rhetorical question
"suntne ergo pedum et priores calces?" Hildebrand points out that
hypallage is a frequent phenomenon in Apuleius. Eyssenhardt, vdVliet,
Médan (p. 348), Bernhard p. 215 (but p. 45 n. 2 he reads *posteriorum*),
Armini 1932 pp. 73 f. follow Hildebrand, all other editors follow Ouden-
dorp, presumably because of 6, 27 (149, 9) *incussis in eam posteriorum
pedum calcibus*. Note the difference in word order. Apuleius allows small
changes in otherwise identical expressions elsewhere as well, e.g. 74, 9
diem ferme circa medium and 9, 30 (225, 17) *diem ferme circa mediam*.
The hypallage moreover is rather less striking than e.g. 9, 11 (210, 21)
lucubrabant peruigilem farinam. Though the 2 + 2 arrangement of *pedum
posteriorum calcibus iactatis* may seem attractive, it cannot carry weight
against the ms. reading. Cf. also 7, 16 (166, 18 f.) *primoribus … calcibus*;
9, 1 (202, 26 f.) *me proripio totis pedibus, ad tutelam salutis crebris calcibus
uelitatus*. The meanings "hoof" and "kick" are not altogether sharply
distinguished.

   crebriter: see vdP. p. 119. The Thesaurus shows that the word is con-
fined to Vitruvius (4×), Apuleius (4×) and Diom. gramm. (1, 477, 5).

   iacente contra procliue montis attigui: see on 75,18 *nimio uelocitatis*.
   attigui cf. 84, 2; 97, 4; 6, 12 (137, 17). The word occurs for the first time
in Fron. *agrim*. p. 11 Lachmann (*attiguis possessoribus*). See Callebat,
S.C., p. 163.

Sed ilico mulier quaepiam, uxor eius scilicet, simul eum
prostratum et semianimem ex edito despexit, ululabili cum
plangore ad eum statim prosilit, ut sui uidelicet misera-
tione mihi praesens crearet exitium: "But at once some woman
— his wife no doubt — as soon as she saw him from the hill-top lying
half-dead, immediately leaped wailing and howling towards him, ob-
viously intending, by arousing pity for herself, to cause an immediate
end to me".

   Apuleius himself adds the character of the gardener's wife since the
Onos states expressly that it is the gardener who calls for the dogs:
(18, 3) ὁ δὲ ἐπειδὴ εἶδεν δρόμῳ ἀπιόντα, ἀνέκραγε λῦσαι τοὺς κύνας ἐπ' ἐμοί.
The addition exemplifies Apuleius' technique of building up to a high
point, then to deflate by the introduction of a new, so far unmentioned,
aspect or circumstance. See also above on 75, 18 ff.; the converse at
76, 5. Perry (1923, pp. 201 f.) uses the present passage to support his im-
pression that Apuleius particularly likes to describe female characters.
See also Stockin pp. 72 f.

   ilico … statim: Médan p. 364 quotes these adverbs as an instance of
juxtaposed synonyms. So also ThLL *s.v*. "per pleonasmum". See also
11, 18 (280, 11-15) *confestim … ilico*. The redundancy however, is func-
tional, for although both adverbs logically qualify *prosilit, ilico* psycho-

logically contrasts the disaster this woman tries to produce with the good fortune promised by *liberaui* at the end of the previous sentence. For the etymology and history of *ilico* see Ernout, *Philologica* I, pp. 125 ff.; his survey of occurrence (pp. 128 f.) is now out of date (see ThLL).

uxor eius scilicet: for the parenthesis see above on 76, 10. Note the almost redundant effect of *eius...eum...ad eum*.

ex edito despexit: see above on 76, 8 *furens decurrit*. Bernhard p. 107 gives a number of parallels for sing. neuter with prep. instead of adverb.

ululabili cum plangore: as a result of the activities of a later hand F presents *eiulabili*, for the earlier reading *ululabili*; cf. 5, 7 (108, 13) *uocis ululabilis*, 10, 5 (240, 7) *ululabili clamore*. Gargantini expresses the value of the suffix as *ululatu plenus* p. 34). Cf. Amm. 24, 1, 7. In Apuleius *plangor* always denotes a wailing noise rather than breast-beating; cf. 3, 8 (57, 22); 9, 31 (226, 18-19); in the plural 5, 5 (107, 2); 7, 26 (174, 15); 9, 30 (226, 8).

ut sui uidelicet miseratione mihi praesens crearet exitium: the humorous effect of the final clause is created by the projection of the ass's fears into the woman's aims. We almost have a rare case of inverted pathetic fallacy. The parenthesis *sui uidelicet miseratione* (Callebat, S.C., p. 463) is rather less obvious than the ones mentioned above (76, 10); *uidelicet* (in the *Met.* only here) has an ironic flavour.

For *sui...miseratione* two main interpretations are current, "by arousing pity for herself" (thus Butler, Vallette, Rode-Burck, Brandt-Ehlers, Carlesi) and "by her lamentations" (thus Adlington-Gaselee, Lindsay, Schwartz, Helm). The second of these suffers from the lack of parallels for the meaning "lamentation". In all eight other cases Apuleius uses *miseratio* in the sense of pity, and in particular the pity one hopes to arouse for oneself in others. It is not until Jul. Val. *res gest. Alex.* 2, 34 that one comes across a clear case of *miseratio*=lamentation. *Sui*, on the other hand, may not count against the second interpretation: see K. St. I pp. 598-599. A certain contrast between *sui* and *mihi* is evident, as is the contrast between *miseratione* and *exitium*, if we choose the first interpretation, but in addition we have a piece of subtly (?) ironic psychology in the woman arousing pity for herself while (or since) her husband is lying there half-dead.

praesens crearet exitium: Pricaeus compares 5, 5 (106, 21 f.) *tibi uero summum creabis exitium*. See also Cic. *Deiot.* 16: *propter metum praesentis exiti*. For *praesens* see Callebat, S.C., p. 291; G. Pascucci, *Consens, praesens, absens, SIFC* 33 (1961) pp. 1-61.

Cuncti enim pagani fletibus eius exciti statim conclamant _{76, 18-20} canes atque, ad me laniandum rabie perciti ferrent impetum, passim cohortantur: "For stirred by her weeping all the villagers at once called out their dogs and on all sides urged them on to attack me in a frenzy of rage and tear me to pieces".

The word *cuncti* may seem an exaggeration to us, but would not be regarded as such by anyone acquainted with the life of an ancient village. For the poetic plural *fletibus* see vdP. p. 66. Bernhard pp. 101 f. collects a large number of similar abstract plurals.

statim conclamant canes: cf. 2, 27 (47, 22) *conclamant ignem* "they call for fire"; see vdP. p. 195 on a different sense of *conclamare*.

ad me...ferrent impetum...cohortantur: cf. Médan p. 87, Bernhard pp. 51 f. for the ellipsis of *ut*; vdP. p. 35 gives some parallels and literature for the irregular sequence of tenses, in which an imperfect subjunctive depends on a historic present.

rabie perciti: "aroused by rage"; in view of *cohortantur* an obvious prolepsis. The description of the dogs (see comm. on 76, 21 f.) is clearly affected by the narrator's fear and the apparent lack of logic may well be intended as a characteristic of that fear. Note also the rhyme with *fletibus...exciti* in the previous line. Médan p. 184 lists *percitus* under the heading "langue familière". See Heine p. 149 on the hyperbolic savagery.

ferrent impetum: for the sense "to make an attack" ThLL gives only one parallel: Amm. 29, 5, 30 *arbitrata in se impetum agminum ferri complurium.*

76, 20-23   Tunc igitur procul dubio iam morti proximus, cum uiderem canes et modo magnos et numero multos et ursis ac leonibus ad conpugnandum idoneos in me conuocatos exasperari...: "At that point, then, being by now certainly in imminent danger of death, when I saw that the dogs which had been set upon me had their hackles up — huge in size and many in number and fit to fight bears and lions as they were..."

procul dubio: Médan p. 184 treats the expression as archaic. The preposition *procul* + abl. is, in Apuleius, confined to this combination. See Callebat, *S.C.*, p. 210. Doubtless the expression has a solemn ring in view of the nearness of death, both here and in the other passages in which it occurs: 94, 8 *laqueus aut gladius aut certe praecipitium procul dubio capessendum est; 7, 26 (174, 5); 8, 13 (187, 8).*

cum uiderem canes...exasperari: for the word-order see Bernhard p. 16: it is most often verbs with an infinitive following that acquire a position at the head of the subordinate clause. For *exasperari* cf. 8, 17 (190, 16); 8, 25 (197, 8).

et modo magnos et numero multos et ursis ac leonibus ad conpugnandum idoneos: the exaggeration is expressed in the very length of the cola which show respectively 5, 6 and 16 syllables. Bernhard p. 71 speaks of an "anisokolisches Trikolon" and notes a crescendo. Robertson's tentative suggestion *modulo* is to be rejected, since *numerosa responsio* alone should carry no weight against the ms. reading. See vdP. p. 185. Rohde reads *mole*, but *modo* gives a perfectly satisfactory sense: *modus* = size is listed in ThLL s.v. col. 1258, 49 "specialiter de animantium corporibus". Cf. Luc. 9, 804 *nondum stante modo crescens fugere cadauer*, and Gel. 6, 22, 4 (a portly gentleman) *cuius corpus in tam immodicum modum luxuriasset*

42

exuberassetque. For *numero multos* see comm. on 79, 15 f. and 90, 2. The description of the fierce dogs shows all the characteristics of a topos. Compare the descriptions in 8, 17 (190, 12 ff.): *canes rabidos et immanes et quibusuis lupis et ursis saeuiores...praeter genuinam ferocitatem tumultu suorum exasperati* and 9, 36 (230, 19 ff.) *canes pastoricios uillaticos feros atque immanes, adsuetos abiecta per agros essitare cadauera.* There, too, the dogs are at once *signo...pastorum incensi* and *furiosa rabie conciti.* The motif also occurs at *Onos* 18 and in Xenophon of Ephesus (*Eph.* 4, 6, 4) where the dogs that are to devour Anthia ἦσαν ... Αἰγύπτιοι, καὶ τὰ ἄλλα μεγάλοι καὶ ὀφθῆναι φοβεροί.

ursis ac leonibus ad conpugnandum idoneos: ThLL *s.v. compugno* col. 2169, 73 takes *ursis* etc. with *idoneos* and *ad conpugnandum* absolutely, quoting as the first instance of *compugnare* + dat. Hil. *in Matth.* 5, 14. This is no doubt correct, as otherwise we would have here the only instance of *idoneus ad* in the *Met.*, whereas the dative construction also occurs 9, 39 (233, 21): *rebus amplioribus idoneus.* See Scobie, *Aspects*, p. 50 n. 60.

conpugnare is *hapax legomenon* in Apuleius.

..e re nata capto consilio fugam desino ac me retrorsus celeri gradu rursum in stabulum, quo deuerteramus, recipio: "...I matched my plan to the circumstances, gave up my flight and, making an about-face, withdrew at speed, back into the stable where we had made our halt".

e re nata capto consilio: cf. 85, 18 *e re nata suptile consilium...comminiscimur.* Callebat, *S.C.*, p. 207 quotes Donatus on Ter. *Ad.* 295 *e re nata, sic proprie dicimus de iis quae contra uoluntatem nostram acciderunt.* The definition is quite apt for the various passages in which Apuleius uses the expression: 82, 17; 5, 8 (109, 12); 9, 6 (207, 4). See also Dziatzko-Kauer on the Terence passage quoted above.

fugam desino: cf. e.g. 93, 18 *fletum desinere*; 8, 25 (197, 8) *emptionem desineret.* Médan p. 31 regards the (not uncommon) construction as poetic, Callebat, *S.C.*, p. 179 as belonging to the *sermo familiaris.* Both are right.

ac me retrorsus celeri gradu rursum in stabulum...recipio: compare 3, 12 (61, 12) *qui domum rursum reuerterim*, and vdP. p. 98 *ad loc.*, Verg. *A.* 3, 690 *talia monstrabat relegens errata retrorsus/ litora Achaemenides* where Servius notes: *retrorsus — quasi a fine ad caput retexens*, which aptly describes the function of the word in our passage. The adverb *retrorsus* occurs at 9, 10 (210, 9) *eos retrorsus abducunt*, the adjective at 2, 6 (30, 10) *saepe retrorsa respiciens substitit.* (The latter passage used to be much discussed, see Oudendorp p. 101, unnecessarily: for the adjective cf. Plin. *Nat.* 9, 99 *cancri in pauore et retrorsi pari uelocitate redeunt*; 26, 93 *retrorsa manu.*) The juxtaposition of *me retrorsus* argues the adverb here.

quo deuerteramus: cf. above 74, 10-11 *in pago quodam...deuertimus.* Callebat, *S.C.*, p. 197 regards *quo* as the ablative of the pronoun, and this is not impossible if one compares Cic. *Verr.* 3, 75 *cum...locus...quo deuerteretur datus esset*; *Font.* 19 *si qui Cobiomago…deuerterentur*. On the other hand Liv. 26, 11, 10 (*Coelius Romam euntem ab Ereto deuertisse eo Hannibalem tradit*) construes the word with an adverb. See also LHSz p. 277 on the confusion between *ubi* and *quo*. (ThLL also gives Seneca *Ep.* 48, 8 *quo deuerteris* but both Hense and Reynolds read *diuerteris*.) See also the note on 79, 11.

76, 25-77,6 At illi canibus iam aegre cohibitis adreptum me loro quam ualido ad ansulam quandam destinatum rursum caedendo confecissent profecto, nisi dolore plagarum aluus artata crudisque illis oleribus abundans et lubrico fluxu saucia fimo fistulatim excusso quosdam extremi liquoris aspergine, alios putore nidoris faetidi a meis iam quassis scapulis abegisset: "But the villagers, restraining their dogs with difficulty, took hold of me and tied me with a very stout thong to a ring. And once again they would certainly have beaten me to death had not my belly, contracted by the pain of the blows and overflowing with those raw vegetables and sick with diarrhoea, through the sudden emission of a jetstream of ordure, removed some by spraying them with this fluid to end all fluids, others by the rotten reek and stench, from my already battered haunches".

canibus iam aegre cohibitis: the description of the dogs' fierceness continues to the very point of their dismissal; so did the description of the *locus amoenus* in the previous chapter continue right into its disappearance (75, 20-24).

adreptum me: see comm. on 76, 9.

loro quam ualido: see Callebat, *S.C.*, pp. 531 f. and 538 on *quam* used to reinforce adverbs and adjectives; for the history of this usage see vdP. p. 55 and the literature mentioned there. See also LHSz p. 164 ("oft seit Apuleius").

ad ansulam quandam destinatum: for the diminutive *ansula* see Médan p. 145, Callebat, *S.C.*, p. 31. OLD gives "hook or staple" for this passage, Callebat "anneau". At 11, 4 (269, 7) Apuleius uses the word in the sense of "handle".

quandam: see comm. on 76, 6 *iuuenis quidam*.

destinatum: see Marg. Molt p. 77 on 1, 13 (12, 7) *membris…destinatis*.

nisi dolore…abegisset: the scatological clincher occurs also, though more simply, in the *Onos* 18, 5; cf. Feldbrugge p. 49. See also 7, 28 (176, 9 ff.) *…donec solo, quod restabat, nisus praesidio liquida fimo strictim egesta faciem atque oculos eius confoedassem*. Callebat, *S.C.*, p. 456 treats the passage under the heading "alliance de réalisme-préciosité".

crudisque…et: Bernhard pp. 82 f. collects numerous passages of this type of *variatio*.

lubrico fluxu saucia: *fluxus* in this sense occurs only in Apuleius' generation; see Callebat, *S.C.*, p. 27, who quotes Fronto 72, 7 N (= vdH 65, 21) *alui fluxus constitit*.

44

fimo fistulatim excusso: the alliteration with *fluxu* may deserve the adjective "studied"; *fistulatim* is a neologism possibly with an archaic connotation, see Médan p. 125; Bernard p. 140; vdP. p. 39.

excusso has the connotation of violent discharge, cf. Tac. *Hist.* 4, 23 *excussa ballistis saxa.* The closest parallel is found in Aur. *acut. pass. lib.* 3, 17, 165 *stercus per eam partem excutitur* (ThLL *s.v. excutio* col. 1311, 84).

quosdam extremi liquoris aspergine, alios putore nidoris faetidi: the word-order is mildly chiastic. Bernhard p. 95 mentions the *variatio* in the words *quosdam...alios* under the heading anantapodoton. See for *quosdam* Graur p. 380.

putor is a slightly archaic word (Médan p. 172) and thus provides a precious element in a realistic scene (see comm. on 77, 3).

nidoris faetidi: "foul-smelling vapour". *Nidor* may refer to a mist or vapour (e.g. Lucr. 6, 987 *nidores odores*) as well as its smell. The olfactory aspect refers to an acrid smell (e.g. burning hair *Met.* 3, 18 (65, 18); Verg. *A.* 12, 301 etc.). Médan regards the word as poetic (p. 190), but it occurs e.g. in Cicero (*Pis.* 13) and Pliny the Elder (28, 230; 35, 175).

abegisset: thus a medieval emendation (ç); *abegisse* F. Hildebrand and Koziol (p. 221) defend the anacoluthon, Bernhard p. 94 accepts Helm's emended text as in all the other cases of apparent anacoluthon: 3, 18 (65, 22); 7, 21 (170, 2); 9, 8 (208, 19 ff.); 10, 23 (255, 1); vdP. (pp. 140 f.) rejects all emendations at 65, 22 f. Some restoration seems advisable at 170, 2, but Helm himself (1956) accepts the anacoluthon at 208, 19. At 255, 1 the addition ⟨*cum uideret*⟩ seems almost as disturbing as acceptance of the anacoluthon. Anacoluthon also occurs at 95, 21 (see comm. *ad loc.*). We do not feel therefore that the appearance of an anacoluthon as such is sufficient reason to emend the text. In the present case, however, the confusion *abegissē* vs. *abegisset* is readily explained in view of the distance of *aluus*. Hence the old emendation should be accepted.

CHAPTER IV

The relief occasioned by the bowel movement does not last: a different and heavier load is awaiting Lucius.

77, 7-9 **Nec mora, cum iam in meridiem prono iubare rursum nos ac praecipue me longe grauius onustum producunt illi latrones stabulo**: "Immediately after this, when the sun was already beginning to set, those robbers took us from the stable; we were much more heavily loaded, I in particular".

For *nec mora cum* see vdP. p. 29; for other expressions suggesting speed see Junghanns p. 52 n. 74, Heine pp. 178 ff., vThiel I p. 20, n. 56.

VdP.'s remark (p. 93), "rapidity is the most characteristic feature", refers (or should refer) to time narrated, not time of narration. (For the use of this terminology see E. Lämmert, *Bauformen des Erzählens*, Stuttgart ⁵1972, pp. 23, 32.

iam in meridiem prono iubare has created difficulties; Helm-Krenkel p. 404 formulate the problem as follows: "Die Ueberlieferung *meridiem* widerspricht der Logik (*prono*) und dem Zusammenhang (4, 1, 1)." Since 1955 Helm therefore reads *in metam diei prono iubare*, but this conjecture, however splendid, has not met with the approval of others.[1] Helm's arguments are valid only if *meridies* means 'noon' or 'south'. (Thus ThLL *s.v.*; P. Grimal, *Romans grecs et latins*, Paris 1958, p. 202; outside the *Met.* Apuleius uses the word only in this sense). Hildebrand suggested the possibility that *meridies* in Apuleius "non ipsum significat diem medium, ubi calor vehementissimus est, sed tempus promeridianum." Vallette agrees and adds (*ad loc.*): "par un glissement analogue à celui qui nous fait donner le nom de matinée à une représentation qui commence dans le courant de l'après-midi". This explanation is accepted by Augello p. 122, n. 1. The translation is found, without comment, e.g. in Lindsay and Scazzoso. Indeed how can we maintain the meaning "noon" in 6, 12 (137, 13) *sed dum meridies solis sedauerit uaporem*? And how in 2, 11 (33, 24) *commodum meridies accesserat*, if this phrase is immediately followed by (34, 8) *diem ceterum lauacro ac dein cenae dedimus*? And is there a need, then, for a conjecture at 9, 22 (219, 27) where the tradition has *ergo igitur meridie propinquante*? It seems, therefore, that the reading of the (more important) mss. is not inexplicable, but the expression is affected. As elsewhere with indications of time in the *Met.* (see vdP. pp. 23 f.) Apuleius parodies the epic poets, in particular their use of metonymy (*iubar* instead of *sol* is very rare outside poetry). The main effect is contrast: after the scatological fun of ch. 3 we sojourn for a little while in a higher realm to

---

[1] vThiel follows Oudendorp in deleting *in meridiem* as a gloss.

return immediately afterwards to an ass full of self-pity (accentuated by the assonance of *u* and *o*).

For *longe* as a replacement of *multo* see K.St. II, 2 p. 463, LHSz p. 136.

According to Médan p. 217 *illi* is used "exactement au sens de l'article en français", but this theory, first defended by Wolterstorff, has been refuted by Löfstedt, *Synt.* I², pp. 361 ff. *Illi* here has a pejorative sense; see Callebat, *S.C.*, p. 277.

Iamque confecta bona parte itineris et uiae spatio defectus et sarcinae pondere depressus ictibusque fustium fatigatus atque etiam ungulis extritis iam claudus et titubans riuulum quendam serpentis leniter aquae propter insistens subtilem occasionem feliciter nactus cogitabam totum memet flexis scite cruribus pronum abicere...: "When a good part of the road had already been travelled and I was worn out by the long journey and dog-tired because of the heavy load and the repeated cudgelling, and even, since my hooves were worn, lame already and limping, I stopped at a little stream with gently running water: having happily obtained this fine opportunity I was planning to bend my legs cunningly and throw my whole body headlong..."

iamque confecta bona parte itineris: cf. 6, 18 (141, 25 f.) *iamque confecta bona parte mortiferae uiae*; 8, 30 (210, 7) *bonaque itineris parte...transacta. Bonus* in the sense of *magnus* occurs in this combination only, but the combination occurs in all genres of Latin literature. See Wilkins on Cic. *de Orat.* 2, 3, 14.

defectus: cf. 6, 1 (129, 8 f.) *gradum, quem defectum prorsus adsiduis laboribus spes incitabat*; 9, 9 (209, 2 f.) *sed adsiduis interrogationibus argumenti satietate iam defecti.*

et sarcinae pondere depressus ictibusque fustium fatigatus: the cudgelling is "audible" in the alliteration and assonance, which are even more clearly marked in the chiastic arrangement. The misery increases along with the number of syllables and culminates in the following *ungulis extritis*, which also occurs in 8, 23 (195, 15 f.). Médan's remark (p. 179) to the effect that *exterere* belongs to archaic language is, as a generalization, incorrect, though it is true that, used of parts of the body, it occurs elsewhere only in Pl. *Cist.* 408 *cum extritis talis* (if that reading is correct; see E. Fraenkel, *Das Original der Cistellaria des Plautus, Philologus* 87 (1932) p. 118).

quendam = *aliquem*; see comm. on 76, 6.

serpentis leniter aquae: the water's gentle running provides for Lucius a painful contrast with his own limping! Note the hyperbaton.

propter: if we take it as a preposition (with Hildebrand, H. Koziol, *Der Stil des L. Apuleius*, Wien 1872, pp. 338 f., *Index Apul. s.v. propter*, ThLL *s.v. insistere*) we have an instance of anastrophe here, a phenomenon which Bernhard (pp. 28 ff.) has shown does not occur elsewhere in the *Met.* See Oudendorp *ad loc.*, de Jonge on 2, 23 (44, 8), Becker p. 46.

47

subtilem occasionem: Oudendorp respectfully mentions Heinsius' *labilem* for *subtilem*, but Hildebrand correctly interprets: "*subtilis* est *occasio*, quae callido se praebet et opportuna est" (enallage).

cogitabam: for *cogitare = consilium inire* or *uelle* cf. 8, 25 (197, 7) *cogitabam subito uelut lymphaticus exilire*.

memet: for the suffix *-met*, which occurs a dozen times in the *Met.*, see Neue-Wagener II³, pp. 362 ff. (a rich collection of material); E. Norden on Verg. *A*. 6, 505 regards the suffix as an archaism, an opinion that is invalidated by G. B. A. Fletcher's collection of material: *The suffix -met in post-Vergilian poetry*, *Hermes* 94 (1966) pp. 254 ff.

scite: Feldbrugge (p. 49) is right in mentioning the ironic effect of *scite*, an aspect that is lacking in the *Onos*.

77, 15-17 certus atque obstinatus nullis uerberibus ad ingrediundum exsurgere, immo etiam paratus non fusti tantum, sed machaera perfossus occumbere: "irrevocably resolved not to get up and go on for any lashes, nay, even ready to die pierced by the sword, not merely by the cudgel". The emotion is accentuated by a climax and a zeugma. *Certus* is found with infinitive from Verg. *A*. 4, 564, in prose from Tac. *Ann*. 4, 57 onwards; *obstinatus* with infinitive occurs a few times in Livy. The latter also uses the combination *certum atque obstinatum est* (2, 15, 5), but in that passage *obstinatum* obviously is still a past participle. See Callebat, *S.C.*, p. 316 (*certus*), p. 310 (*obstinatus*).

Robertson's conjecture (adopted by Scazzoso, who incomprehensibly places a comma after *tantum*): *non fusti tantum ⟨percussus⟩ sed machaera perfossus occumbere* unjustifiably removes a functional zeugma (φ on the other hand has *percussus* instead of *perfossus*).

More interesting because of their heuristic value are vdVliet's: *non fusti tantum ⟨resistere⟩, sed ⟨ne⟩ machaera perfossus occumbere*, and Desertine's: *non fusti sed tantum machaera perfossus occumbere* (p. 134). Both are trying to eliminate the contradiction that exists between the present passage and the developments in the next chapter in which Lucius, upon seeing what happens to obstinate asses, decides to make the best of the circumstances: *tunc ego miseri commilitonis fortunam cogitans statui ...asinum me bonae frugi dominis exhibere* (78, 8-10). Of the conjectures mentioned Desertine's doubtless merits the greater attention. Another possibility would be to read: *non fusti tantum, sed ⟨ne⟩ machaera perfossus occumbere*, in which *non tantum* is used in the sense of *non tantum non* (see LHSz p. 519). If we retain the tradition we must accept that Lucius in our passage has a great deal more in mind than finally, when confronted with hard reality, he decides to perform — something which is not out of character for an *asinus humano ingenio*.

77, 17-19 Rebar enim iam me prorsus exanimatum ac debilem mereri causariam missionem: "For I felt that, utterly exhausted and feeble as I was, I finally deserved a discharge for reasons of health."

For *prorsus/prorsum* see vdP. p. 32; for *debilem, ibid.* p. 195.

Roman military law knows several types of *missio*. In *dig.* 49, 16, 13, 3 we read: *missionum generales causae sunt tres: honesta, causaria, ignominiosa. Honesta est, quae tempore militiae impleto datur; causaria, cum quis uitio animi uel corporis minus idoneus militiae renuntiatur; ignominiosa causa est, cum quis propter delictum sacramento soluitur.* The definition originates in Macer *De re militari* 2 and is also found in *dig.* 3, 2, 2, 2, where Ulpian is quoted; in addition to the reasons given by Macer Ulpian mentions a fourth: *est et quartum genus missionis, si quis euitandorum munerum causa militiam subisset. Causarius* is the term used for an invalid soldier: cf. Liv. 6, 6, 14 *tertius exercitus ex causariis senioribusque a Lucio Quinctio scribatur.* For *causa* in the sense of *morbus* see Kirby Flower Smith on Tib. 1, 8, 51.

Apuleius' witty use of this technical term is imitated in *Gaeomemphionis Cantaliensis Satyricon* (1628)[1], cap. 229: *uerum ego cum missionem causariam ficto corporis languore impetrassem.* For military metaphors in the *Met.* see Neuenschwander pp. 66-72; Médan pp. 254-257; Bernhard pp. 195-197; Helm-Krenkel, Einf. p. 23; see also Appendix I.

certe latrones partim inpatientia morae, partim studio 77, 19-22
festinatae fugae dorsi mei sarcinam duobus ceteris iumentis distributuros meque in altioris uindictae uicem lupis et uulturiis praedam relicturos: "that surely the robbers, partly because they would brook no delay, partly because they wished to make a fast escape, would distribute my back's burden among the two other pack-animals and that as a further punishment they would leave me a prey to wolves and vultures".

partim...partim: the structure of the anaphoric dicolon is clever: 3 words of 10 syllables in all are, asyndetically, followed by 4 words of 11 syllables in all, with numerous alliterations. Oudendorp and Gatscha p. 145 cite, as a parallel for *fugam festinare*, Verg. *A.* 4, 574 f. *deus aethere missus ab alto/festinare fugam tortos incidere funis/ecce iterum instimulat.* For imitations of Vergil in the *Met.* see vdP. p. 65.

in...uicem in Apuleius may mean either "in the manner of", "as" or "instead of"; see Callebat, *S.C.*, p. 232, who opts for the second sense.

altior uindicta has no parallels, but *altior = grauior* occurs 98, 6 f. *fremens altius*; 10, 3 (238, 4) *altius agitata.*

The sentence as a whole (*rebar enim...relicturos*) shows four dicola (see Bernhard pp. 57 f.). A comparison with *Onos* 19, 3 is instructive: ᾠήθην γὰρ ὅτι πάντως ἡττώμενοι τὰ μὲν ἐμὰ σκεύη διανεμοῦσιν τῷ τε ἵππῳ καὶ τῷ ἡμιόνῳ, ἐμὲ δὲ αὐτοῦ ἐάσουσιν κεῖσθαι τοῖς λύκοις.

---

[1] More imitations of Apuleius are mentioned in the edition of this work by Juliette Desjardins, Leiden 1972, pp. 59 ff.

CHAPTER V

Soon all hope is lost: the other ass does what Lucius had wanted to do and the results are fearful. Lucius adapts himself to his role.

77, 22-23 Sed tam bellum consilium meum praeuertit sors deterrima: "But this fine plan of mine was upset by a most evil fate".

Sed is, as often in Apuleius, the introduction to the anticlimax; see comm. on 76, 5. The position of the subject (with chiasmus) is functional in this respect; cf. Bernhard p. 19.

Sors, Fatum and *Fortuna* are synonyms "für den blossen unberechenbaren Zufall, für Geschick oder für ein starres unabänderliches Schicksal" (Heine p. 137; see also Helm-Krenkel, Einf. p. 30). Cf. *Onos* 19 ἀλλά τις δαίμων βάσκανος... με περιήνεγκεν, obviously less subtle.

77, 24-26 Namque ille alius asinus diuinato et antecapto meo cogitatu statim scilicet mentita lassitudine cum rebus totis offunditur: "For that other ass guessed my plan and at once beat me to it: from exhaustion (simulated, of course) he threw himself down, load and all".

Most editors read with Helm: *statim se mentita lassitudine...offudit. Offudit* is Bursian's conjecture for *offuditur* (F) and *offunditur* (φ). If we side with Eyssenhardt in retaining *offunditur* (*offuditur* is of course senseless, for the absence of *n* cf. e.g. 86, 22) we gain a present tense which parallels πίπτει of the corresponding passage in the *Onos*, but are left with an impossible *se*. Oudendorp, however, had long ago proposed to read *scilicet* for *se*, *scilicet* often being abbreviated *sc*. (see also vdP. p. 194). Doubtless this is correct, for without *scilicet* Apuleius would commit an error of perspective: to use the terminology of F. K. Stanzel (*Typische Formen des Romans*, Göttingen ⁶1972), an "auktoriale Erzählsituation" ("Olympian" point of view) instead of an "Ich-Erzählsituation" ("I" point of view).

ille: not a definite article (Wolterstorff p. 223), but "rappelle ici un terme déjà cité et possède un caractère emphatique marqué pour désigner l'âne devenu instrument du destin" (Callebat, *S.C.*, p. 281).

alius: used in the sense of *alter*; cf. Médan p. 221, Callebat, *S.C.*, p. 286, LHSz p. 207.

cogitatus is here used in the sense of *consilium*; there are no earlier instances; cf. 8, 25 (197, 9 f.) *praeuenit cogitatum meum emptor anxius* and also *cogitare=consilium inire* at 77, 14.

For passive *mentiri* cf. 5, 26 (123, 20) *mentito nomine* and further instances mentioned in Helm's critical apparatus. Other deponent verbs used with passive meaning are discussed by Callebat, *S.C.*, p. 297 f. For *totus=omnis* see vdP. p. 121.

iacensque in mortuum: this reading of the second hand in F is most probably correct, though all modern editors, with the exception of Frassinetti, accept Colvius' conjecture *in modum mortui*. However, *in identitatis* or *in praedicativum* is by no means an unknown phenomenon in Apuleius; cf. 3, 24 (70, 9) *in auem similem gestiebam*; 6, 29 (151, 10) *Iupiter mugiuit in bouem*. Parallels also occur in Petr. 62, 10 *in laruam intraui*; Schol. Juv. 2, 147 *Nero...pugnauit in gladiatorem*; August. *C.D.* 20, 19 *dicimus 'sedet in amicum', id est 'uelut amicus'*. See Médan p. 69; Pepe, *GIF* 12(1959) p. 317; Frassinetti, *Athenaeum* 38 (1960) p. 121; Callebat, *S.C.*, p. 230; LHSz p. 275; vdP. pp. 178 f. (further literature *ibid.*, n. 1).

non fustibus, non stimulis ac ne cauda et auribus cruribusque undique uersum eleuatis temptauit exsurgere: "no cudgels, no goads, not even being pulled on all sides by tail, ears and legs could make him try to get up".

The sentence starts with an asyndetic anaphora; the swift series of assonances (*u/i*, then *au*, *u/i* again, then *e/a*, as well as *f*, *st*, *c...*, *c...*, *qu...*, *qu...*, *t...*, *t...*, *t...*) provides a counterpart in sound of the ill-treatment of the ass, and this is matched by the variation in syntax (instrumental abl. followed by absolute abl.). See Bernhard p. 85 on "Neigung zur Abwechslung".
ne = ne...quidem: see vdP. p. 62

postumae spei fatigati: Graves rightly translates "realizing that the case was hopeless", but how does one explain the phrase? The expression is very affected and it comes as a surprise that only one scholar has tried a conjecture, viz. vdVliet: ⟨*fatigati et*⟩ *postumae spei frustrati*. Vallette (p. 10, n. 1) explains: "Le génitif *postumae spei* peut être rapproché de *animi* à valeur locale ou limitative". It is more likely, however, that vGeisau (p. 250) is right in explaining *postumae spei* as a *gen. causae* (or *relationis*), analogous to the construction of *fessus* or *fastidiosus* (Médan p. 39). Cf. Verg. *A.* 1, 178 *fessi rerum*; Sil. 2, 234 *fessi...salutis*; Stat. *Theb.* 3, 395 *fessum bellique uiaeque*. See K.St. II, 1 p. 444.
Postuma spes is usually explained as *ultima spes* (ThLL), but, as often, Apuleius is playing with a legal term. Cf. 6, 30 (152, 16 f.) *cenam, quam postuma diligentia praeparauerat infelix anicula*, where *postuma diligentia* does not mean "with extreme care" (LS s.v.), but "in ihrer über den Tod hinauswirkenden Fürsorge" (Helm), as Wowerus ("remanserat, tamquam postuma diligentia parata"), Oudendorp and Forcellini also used to interpret. *Postuma spes*, then, is an expectation to be fulfilled only after someone's death. See also Norden, *Privatrecht* p. 147.

77, 26

77,26-
78,2

78,3

51

78,3 secum...conlocuti: "after consulting each other". Apuleius does not use *secum* in the sense of *inter se* in his other works; see vdP p. 54 f.

78, 3-5 ne tam diu mortuo, immo uero lapideo asino seruientes fugam morarentur: "so as not to delay their flight so long to look after a dead, or even petrified, ass". Several translators take *tam diu* with *mortuo*, e.g. Helm: "einem längst schon toten ... Esel zuliebe", but in that case the robbers' exertions are incomprehensible.

Bernhard p. 211 mentions *lapideus* among the words that add to the "poetische Kolorit des Autors". In this (figurative) sense it occurs before Apuleius not only in Plaut. *Truc.* 818, but in Enn. *Scaen.* 139.

The use of the verb *seruire* is certainly functional here: the robbers do not relish the reversal of roles which would make them subordinate to the ass. See also Feldbrugge p. 50 on the comical aspect of the expression.

78,5 destricto: *districto* is preferred by Helm, Eyssenhardt, Giarratano-Frassinetti, Terzaghi, Vitali, vThiel, *Index Apul.*; *destricto* by Oudendorp, Hildebrand, vdVliet, Robertson, Brandt-Ehlers, Scazzoso, ThLL and (apparently) OLD. In view of the confusion between the two verbs in the *codices* in general, and the confusion between *e* and *i* in our *codices* in particular (see Helm Praef. *Fl.* p. XLIV), *destricto* seems to be the correct reading.

78, 6-8 paululum a uia retractum per altissimum praeceps in uallem proximam etiam nunc spirantem praecipitant: "they dragged him a little distance away from the road and threw him, still breathing, down a very deep, sheer rock-face into the nearest valley". The robbers' cruelty will come down upon their own heads; cf. 7, 13 (164, 9 f.) *ipsos* (sc. *latrones*) *partim constrictos, uti fuerant, prouolutosque in proximas rupinas praecipites dedere, alios uero suis sibi gladiis obtruncatos reliquere*.

The predicative sense of *praeceps* in the passage just quoted need not argue an adverbial use in our passage; that explanation found e.g. in Helm, Brandt-Ehlers and the *Index Apul. s.v.* disturbs both the symmetry and the chiastic arrangement.

For *praeceps* as a noun cf. Juv. 10, 107 *praeceps inmane*. Note the paronomasia (with etymological link; see Bernhard p. 229, F. Westermann, *Archaïsche en archaïstische woordkunst*, diss. Amsterdam, Nijmegen etc. 1939, p. 126) and the functional alliteration of *p* and *r*. See Callebat, *S.C.*, p. 451 on the absent *eum*.

78, 8-9 miseri commilitonis fortunam: "the fate of my poor comrade-in-arms" (cf. Lindsay: "the fate of my fellow campaigner in misery"). A similar metaphor at 9, 13 (212, 11) *iam de meo iumentario contubernio*

52

quid .... *memorem?* See Neuenschwander p. 68; Bernhard p. 196; Appendix I to the present work.

Vallette (p. 10, n. 2) remarks that in this passage Apuleius reverses his usual tendency and is "plus banal et moins expressif" than the author of the *Onos* 19, 7 who has Lucius say about the ass: τὸν δὲ ἄθλιον κοινωνὸν καὶ τῆς αἰχμαλωσίας καὶ τῆς ἀχθοφορίας. The stylistic simplification in Apuleius has a good reason: Apuleius characterises the other ass as more malevolent than the *Onos* does: there is no mention of *mentita lassitudo* in the *Onos!* Or perhaps it is better to say that in Apuleius Lucius is so self-centred that he interprets all actions by others that happen to be unfavourable for him as deliberately harmful.

asinum...bonae frugi: "a good ass", cf. 81, 3 ff. *uos bonae frugi latro-*   78, 10
nes inter furta parua...scrutariam facitis; 5, 29 (126, 14 f.) *honesta... haec et natalibus nostris bonaeque tuae frugi congruentia.* The expression clearly has the mark of *Umgangssprache* (see Médan p. 176, Callebat, *S.C.*, p. 468) and occurs very frequently in Plautus, see Enk ad Pl. *Mer.* 521. Its counterpart is lacking in the *Onos*; see also comm. on 77, 15-17.

nam et secum eos animaduerteram conloquentes, quod in   78, 10-12
proximo nobis esset habenda mansio: "for I had also heard them saying to each other that we should be making a halt nearby". Concerning *secum* see above on 78, 3; for *conloquentes quod* + subj. on 74, 14; for *in proximo* see Bernhard p. 107.

Mansio is here used in an abstract sense, *mansionem habere* hence is a periphrasis for *manere*; cf. Cass. *Var.* 8, 32, 4 *cum mansionem supradictus Nymphadius habuisset.* See Gargantini p. 39 on Apuleius' preference for abstracts in *-io*. The development of *mansio* (later the word equals *deuersorium*) is briefly sketched by Löfstedt, *Per. Aeth.*, p. 76; Waszink p. 549.

et totius uiae finis quieta eorumque esset sedes illa et ha-   78, 12-13
bitatio: "and that this would mean a quiet end to the entire journey, for there was their settlement and home". The words *totius uiae finis quieta* are grouped as a chiasmus both with respect to the parts of speech and the number of syllables.

The gender of *finis* is remarkable. Elsewhere in the *Met.* it is, as usual, masculine[1]. *Finis* is feminine in Lucretius (almost always, see Bailey on 1, 107), and often in Vergil (cf. Maguinness on Verg. *A.* 12, 793: "in cases where the context enables us to determine the gender, the singular of *finis* is in Virgil nearly as often feminine as masculine"). Aulus Gellius gives an interesting "explanation" of the phenomenon (13, 21, 12); commenting on Verg. *A.* 2, 554 *haec finis Priami fatorum*

---

[1] Fem. also *Pl.* 1,5 (87,9) and *Mun.* 19 (156,5).

he remarks: *si mutes 'haec' et 'hic finis' dicas, durum atque absonum erit respuentque aures quod mutaueris. Sicut illud contra eiusdem Vergilii insuauius facias, si mutes*

quem das finem, rex magne, laborum?[1]

Nam si ita dicas: 'quam das finem', iniucundum nescio quo pacto et laxiorem uocis sonum feceris.

Gellius' theory is not entirely convincing: in *Verg. A.* 10, 116 we read *hic finis fandi*. A different explanation is found in Leumann-Hofmann p. 368: "Der Feminin-gebrauch von *finis* hat seinen Ausgang genommen von Wendungen, wie *qua (hac, ea) fini*, die zunächst bedeuteten: 'soweit (wobei hier) eine Grenze ist'".

-que has explicative force, see vdP. p. 34. Concerning *illa* cf. Callebat, *S.C.*, p. 279: "Apulée place volontiers ce pronom entre deux membres de phrase pour déterminer deux mots ou deux groupes de mots."

habitatio (used only here in the *Met.*) has the concrete sense of *domus*, *casa*. Usually it is employed in an abstract sense, as is the case in the one other passage in which Apuleius employs the word, *Apol.* 72 (81, 6).

78, 13-14   clementi denique transmisso cliuulo: "when, then, we had negotiated a friendly little hill". In view of Lucius' double load, *clemens...cliuulus* must be ironic; cf. Junghanns p. 62, Callebat, *S.C.*, p. 374. It is quite possible to translate *denique* as "finally", but the sense of *ergo*, *igitur*, usual in Apuleius, perhaps fits the context better. (Neither Marg. Helbers-Molt, *De vocabuli*, "denique" apud Apuleium usu, *Mnemosyne* S. III, 11 (1943), pp. 129-132, nor Callebat, *S.C.*, p. 325 list it in this sense, see vdP. p. 42.)

78, 16-17   lassitudinem uice lauacri puluereis uolutatibus digerebam: "I attempted to cast out my fatigue through rolling in the dust by way of a bath". Ever since Helm I, Pricaeus' conjecture *puluereis* has been accepted in the text (F has *pulueris*, which would have to be explained as a kind of objective genitive). Not only may we compare Tert. *Pall.* 4, 1, where we also find a *puluerea uolutatio*, but this rather bold phrase also finds parallels in such expressions as *auxilium rosarium* and *ientaculum ambulatorium*. See vdP. p. 191.

Hildebrand remarks: "lavari enim et pulvere volutari equis maxime conducere putant equisones, praescribuntque medici equarii." Cf. X. *Oec.* 11, 18 ἐπειδὰν δὲ ταῦτα γένηται, ὁ παῖς ἐξαλίσας τὸν ἵππον οἴκαδε ἀπάγει. Ar. *Nu.* 32 ἄπαγε τὸν ἵππον ἐξαλίσας οἴκαδε; Suda s.v. ἐξαλίσας: ἐκκυλισθῆναι ποιήσας εἰς τὴν κόνιν. The spot where the horse — but also other animals — may roll in the dust is called in Greek ἀλινδήθρα (cf. Ar. *Ra.* 904a), in Latin *uolutabrum*.

The *Onos* has no counterpart of the dust bath. In Apuleius there is an

[1] Verg. *A.* 1, 241.

54

obvious contrast between Lucius' adapting himself to his ass's role and the pride with which, in the next chapter, he will demonstrate that he has retained his *ingenium humanum*.

digerere is a technical term from the realm of medicine, see Médan p. 258.

CHAPTER VI

Ecphrasis: description of the robbers' cave.

78, 18-22 Res ac tempus ipsum locorum speluncaeque illius, quam latrones inhabitabant, descriptionem exponere flagitat. Nam et meum simul periclitabor ingenium, et faxo uos quoque, an mente etiam sensuque fuerim asinus, sedulo sentiatis: "The subject and the point in time demand that I should give a description of the area and that cave which the robbers inhabited. For I shall both put my literary skill to the test and, at the same time, contrive that you gain a clear insight into the question whether I was an ass in thought and perception as well as in body".

The text of the first sentence contains a number of problems:

1) Robertson reads: *speluncaeque quam illi latrones inhabitabant*, for which he refers back to 77, 9 *me...producunt illi latrones stabulo*. Doubtless he is right in drawing our attention to the fact that the use of *illius* needs explaining; his emendation, however, is unnecessary, see below.

2) Robertson mentions the following possibility in his critical apparatus: *speluncaeque illi ubi latrones* (cf. Petschenig: *speluncaeque illius ubi latrones*); in these attempts *quam* is put in doubt. This relative has been added in F by a later hand and it is striking because it makes *inhabitare* a transitive verb, though at 88, 1 it is used intransitively[1]: *capulos..., quis inhabitabant puluerei et iam cinerosi mortui*. Apart from *ubi*, one might consider *quibus* (Kronenberg) or *quis*, and *qua* presents another possibility. However, in view of the fact that *inhabitare* is regularly transitive from Plin. *Nat.* 5, 1 onwards, it seems best to retain *quam*.

3) The imperfect *inhabitabant* is a correction of the vulgate (ς). F has the present which has been adopted by Eyssenhardt only. The correction appears right for reasons of palaeography (cf. the difficulties in 96, 14) and narrative technique, see below.

4) A plural *flagitant* occurs in ς, is adopted by vdVliet and mentioned by Médan p. 77. That *flagitat* is correct, however, is confirmed by Cic. *Fam.* 14, 21 *res tempusque postulat*; cf. also *Att.* 2, 25, 2 *ualde te exspecto... neque ego magis quam ipsa res et tempus poscit*. The infinitive *exponere* dependent on *flagitat* is discussed by Médan p. 77, Callebat, *S.C.*, p. 309, LHSz p. 346; on *descriptionem exponere* for *describere* see Bernhard p. 184.

This introduction to the subsequent description is a traditional formula also found at 9, 32 (226, 26-28): *res ipsa mihi poscere uidetur, ut huius quoque seruiti mei disciplinam exponam*. It occurs especially in

---

[1] This is the only comparable instance in Apuleius, for the non-Apuleian Ascl. 38 (78, 13) *dii caelestes inhabitant summa caelestia* of course cannot count as such.

historians: cf. Sal. *Jug.* 17, 1 *res postulare uidetur Africae situm paucis exponere*; *ibid.* 95, 2 *sed quoniam nos tanti uiri res admonuit, idoneum uisum est de natura cultuque eius paucis dicere*; id. *Cat.* 5, 9 *res ipsa hortari uidetur ... supra repetere*; Caes. *Gal.* 6, 11, 1 *quoniam ad hunc locum peruentum est, non alienum esse uidetur de Galliae Germaniaeque moribus ... proponere.* See also J. F. D'Alton, *Roman Literary Theory and Criticism*, London etc. 1931, pp. 507 f.

Concerning the contrast *ingenium-corpus asininum* see comm. on 75, 12 ff. and 78, 16.

an does not introduce here a direct question, *pace* Médan p. 97; *an... fuerim sentiatis* is on the contrary an instance of the extension of the use of *an* in indirect questions. The closest parallel is found in Sen. *Ep.* 58, 32 *itaque de isto feremus sententiam, an oporteat fastidire senectutis extrema*. See Callebat, *S.C.*, p. 354, LHSz p. 542; instances from St. Cyprian in Schrijnen-Mohrmann II, pp. 128 f.

Médan p. 362 is quite mistaken in regarding *mente...sensuque* as synonyms (and their use as an "inutile jeu de style"). In this combination *mens*[1] refers to the understanding, *sensus* to perception. Cf. Cic. *Orat.* 2, 8 *quod neque oculis neque auribus neque ullo sensu percipi potest, cogitatione tantum et mente complectimur*; August. *C.D.* 20, 2 *manifestabitur quam iusto iudicio Dei fiat ut...paene omnia iusta iudicia Dei lateant sensus mentesque mortalium*.

The introduction to the ecphrasis is interesting from the point of view of narrative technique as well. See B. Romberg, *Studies in the narrative technique of the first-person novel*, Stockholm 1962, p. 133: "In this instant, the narrative recedes into the background, and the narrator himself steps into the foreground with reflections on his rôle as narrator, not as main character. After thus establishing direct contact with the reader[2] outside the framework of his narrative, he further emphasizes this contact by generously endowing the reader with the responsibility of assessing his narrative talent." See also Eicke p. 89.

This, too, is the explanation of the use of *illius* with *speluncae*; though the cave has not been mentioned earlier nor is known outside the world of this novel, it is of course known to the narrator Lucius. An example from a contemporary (admittedly "personal") novel: Anna Blaman, De verliezers, Amsterdam,[10]1973. One of the protagonists of the novel, Louis Kostiaan, is hit by "een zenuwachtig hol gevoel. Dat had hij trouwens veel vroeger, in zijn jongensjaren, ook al gekend. Op *dat* schoolreisje bijvoorbeeld, op *die* excursie naar *die* koekjesfabriek." The reader has not been made aware of these things before. This point of view also increases the likelihood of the imperfect *inhabitabant*(ς).

---

[1] *Mens = animus* in Seneca: see G. Maurach, *Der Bau von Senecas Epistulae Morales*, Heidelberg 1970, p. 107, n. 116. In Lucretius also *mens* and *animus* are often equivalent, see Bailey on Lucr. 3, 94.

[2] The reader is apostrophized both in the plural (as here) and in the singular (see comm. on 79, 8-9). See Heine p. 220, n. 3.

78, 22-23 Mons horridus siluestribusque frondibus umbrosus et in primis altus fuit: "The reader must imagine a mountain, wild, shaded by its forests' foliage and exceptionally high". A sonorous sentence: alliteration of *r*, assonance of *i* and *u*, some rhyme. For the position of the adjectives see Bernhard p. 22; *frondes* is a poetic plural, see Médan p. 265. See Callebat, *S.C.*, p. 430 on the perfect *fuit* (after the imperfect *inhabitabant*).

78, 23-27 Huius perobliqua deuexa, qua saxis asperrimis et ob id inaccessis cingitur, conualles lacunosae cauaeque nimium spinetis aggeratae et quaqua uersus repositae naturalem tutelam praebentes ambiebant: "Its very steep slopes, where it was encircled by jagged and hence inaccessible rocks were surrounded by valleys which, being full of gullies, deep, covered with a profusion of thornbushes and stretching in all directions, offered a natural protection". *perobliqua* written as one word is an emendation by Nolte (*Philologus* 21 (1864), p. 674 without comment) that solves two difficulties: the curious usage of *per* and the intransitive use of *ambire*, which occurs neither elsewhere in Apuleius nor in other authors (in itself this is no uncommon phenomenon, see Médan pp. 8 f.). *perobliquus* is further supported by a) the superlatives (or equivalent expressions) in the description of the mountain and b) Apuleius' predilection for the prefix *per* (see *Index Apul.*).

deuexum also occurs at 103, 3 *per deuexa rupis excelsae*; it is no "mot de la langue postérieure" (Médan p. 201) for it is found as a noun from Caes. *Gal.* 7, 88, 1 onwards. For the use of *ob id*, see Bernhard p. 182, Callebat, *S.C.*, p. 419. According to Médan p. 159, Lewis-Short, Georges and OLD, *lacunosae* here means "full of ponds, waterholes"; the other dictionaries and Ernout, *Les adj.*, p. 22 keep to the usual sense of "full of gullies". The meaning "full of ponds" is evidently postulated because of 9, 9 (209, 5) (*uiam*) *lacunosis incilibus uoraginosam*, but it is doubtful whether even there *lacunosus* has that meaning. By means of punctuation Oudendorp and Hildebrand indicate that they wish to take *nimium* ("exceedingly", "very") with *cauae*. This is possible, cf. 10, 5 (240, 27 f.) *uxoris dilectae nimium*, but the symmetry of the qualifiers of *conualles* (note the asyndeton) is more attractive if we take *nimium* with *aggeratae*. For this position of the adverb, see vdP. p. 195.

The reading *repositae* has been convincingly defended by Oudendorp and Hildebrand (they explain *conualles quaqua uersus repositae* as "convalles in longum et procul iacentes circumcirca"). Cf. Verg. *A.* 3, 364 *terras...repostas, ibid.* 6, 59. The conjectures by vdVliet: *opsitae* (Helm mistakenly gives *obsitae* in his *app. crit.*), Heinsius: *veprosae* (Robertson mistakenly attributes this conjecture to Helm) and Robertson: *uepre obsitae* (?) therefore are superfluous. For the conjugation of *ambire* see Sommer p. 538.

58

De summo uertice fons afluens bullis ingentibus scaturri- 78, 27-79,1
bat: "From the highest peak there flowed a spring abounding in huge
bubbles". It is not necessary to follow Bernhard (p. 175) in regarding
summus uertex as a pleonasm. *Afluens* is the reading in F; it is accepted
by Helm, Gaselee, Giarratano, Terzaghi, Vitali and Scazzoso; the other
editors read, with ς, *affluens*, Nolte (cited above on 78, 23-27) proposed
effluens. With B. Dombart, *N.J.* 115 (1877), pp. 341 ff. (who gives many
examples of the use of the verb and who is unacceptably brushed aside
in Robertson's *crit. app.* with a mere *"uix recte def."*; ThLL and OLD are
more positive) we are of the opinion that *afluens* is right. The translation
given above seems better than "flowing from" or "overflowing" which
would imply that *bullis ingentibus* qualifies *scaturribat*. For the form
scaturribat instead of *scaturriebat* cf. 7, 4 (156, 22) *parturibam;* 10, 14
(247, 2 f.); 10, 23 (255, 6). See Médan p. 6, Neue-Wagener III, pp. 317 ff.
The description of the *fons* finds a parallel in Plin. *Nat.* 31, 8, 12 *fontem...
plurimis bullis stellantem (v.l. stillantem)*. Eicke p. 90 compares Curt.
Ruf. 3, 1.

perque prona delapsus euomebat undas argenteas: "and 79, 1-2
pouring down the slopes it threw up silvery waves". For the substantive
use of *pronus (prona = deuexa* is not mentioned in the dictionaries) cf.
5, 7 (108, 13) *per prona delapso*; 7, 24 (172, 18) *per...prona...deuolutus.
Argenteus* has poetic connotations, see Bernhard p. 211.

iamque riuulis pluribus dispersus ac ualles illas agminibus 79, 2-4
stagnantibus inrigans in modum stipati maris uel ignaui
fluminis cuncta cohibebat: "and then branched out into numerous
rills and irrigated those valleys with a stagnant inundation enclosing
everything in the manner of a swollen sea or a slow river". A sentence
with a strong poetic flavour, produced by word-order, alliteration,
assonance and oxymoron, as well as the connotations of the nouns used.
    illas: not a definite article but a reference to the *conualles* mentioned
earlier (78, 25); *agminibus stagnantibus* is oxymoron, especially if looked
at etymologically; *agmen* has poetic connotations; Eicke, p. 84 refers to
Ennius *Ann.* 175 *per amoenam urbem leni fluit agmine flumen*. See also
Beaujeu on *Mun.* 23 (159, 7) *aquarum agminibus*. Concerning *stagnare*
Hildebrand remarks: "de rivulis dicitur, qui ignavi maris instar vallem
lente circumfluunt, quia effluere nequeunt, sed recentibus agminibus
semper moventur."
    Instead of *stipati* scholars have proposed to read *sopiti* (Pricaeus),
strati (Wasse) and *stupidi* (Oudendorp); the latter interpreted *stipatus*
as either *stagnans* or *congelatus*. Butler and Lindsay translate "land-
locked", Adlington-Gaselee "enclosed", Médan p. 163 prefers "calme,
paisible"; Vallette, followed by Grimal, translates *in modum stipati maris*
as "comme une mer fermée" and Helm offers an enigmatic "wie in einem
ganzen Meer". For the meaning "swollen" cf. Solinus 32, 10 *stipato...*

flumine (the Nile) and 37, 1 *stipatus conuenis aquis* (the Euphrates). The adjective *ignauus* is poetic as well: see Médan p. 194 (his ref. Lucr. 5, 442 should read Luc. 5, 442: *ignaua...stagna tacentis aquae*).

Though *cuncta* is taken with *agmina* by some translators, Oudendorp's interpretation is doubtless right: "Per *cuncta* vero intellige non *agmina*, sed antra et omnia illa descripta latronum loca, quae undique angebant, sive includebant et *continebant* hae aquae". *Cohibere* is used in the sense of *circumcludere*, cf. 11, 2 (267, 14) *terrae...claustra cohibens*.

79, 4-8 Insurgit speluncae, qua margines montanae desinunt, turris ardua; caulae firmae solidis cratibus ouili stabulatione commoda porrectis undique lateribus ante fores exigui tramitis uice structi parietis attenduntur: "Above the cave, where the mountain's edges end, a high tower rises. In front of the entrance, a short narrow path, there is a sturdy fence, suitable as a sheep-pen with its close-woven wattle, which runs like a wall, with projections on all sides". The passage has been transmitted badly (cf. Hildebrand: "hic locus omnium est difficillimus, nec probam adhuc sententiam eius interpretes poterant efficere"), but Lütjohann pp. 497 f. has, by and large, given the correct interpretation. In particular his proposal to punctuate heavily after *ardua* (previous editors punctuated after *lateribus*) meant an appreciable gain.

For *insurgere* with dative ("rise up above") cf. Verg. *A.* 8, 233 f. *stabat acuta silex.../speluncae dorso insurgens*.

For *qua=ubi* see Svennung, *Pall.* p. 615. In later Latin adverbs denoting direction, place whence and place whither are confused. Thus *undique* in the present sentence means "everywhere" and *quo* (79, 11) "where". See Médan pp. 55 ff., LHSz pp. 652 f. The object of the *turris ardua* is not clear, since the *casula* to be mentioned later on serves as a look-out.

margines montanae: just like in 2, 4 (27, 21) and 75, 23, the gender of *margo* is feminine; cf. Eicke p. 85: "Masculinum ist es dagegen durchweg bei den besseren (!) Autoren". See also Neue-Wagener [3]I, p. 975.

caulae firmae is Lütjohann's emendation of *caule firmas* (F). The noun *caula* which occurs almost exclusively in the plural and is rare at that, according to Callebat, *S.C.*, p. 48 belongs to the category of "le réalisme familier". Eicke, p. 88 suspects a Vergil reminiscence; cf. Verg. *A.* 9, 59 f. *ac ueluti pleno lupus insidiatus ouili /cum fremit ad caulas*.

Editors generally read with Helm *ouili stabulationi*[1] *commodae* rather than the ms. tradition also printed above which is followed only by Giarratano and Scazzoso (Lütjohann, too, wished to retain this reading; in the ThLL it is to be found *s.v. commodus*). Frassinetti on the other hand prints *ouili stabulatione commodae* (probably a printer's error: cf. *crit. app.* "stabulatione F, em. Oud."). As an abl. qual. (according to Hildebrand abl. abs.) however the ms. reading is quite conceivable.

[1] First proposed by Oudendorp.

According to LS the adjective *ouilis* occurs as early as Cato *R.R.* 39, 1, but there it is obviously the noun *ouile* we are dealing with. However, it is no neologism (Médan p. 118 and Eicke pp. 85 f.), for the adj. *ouilis* occurs in Varro *RR* 2, 1, 18 *pecori...ouili*.

ante fores exigui tramitis: "in front of the entrance, viz. an *exiguus* (probably referring to both length and width) *trames*". This interpretation of *tramitis* (Lütjohann's emendation for F's *tramites*; Fulvius proposed *ramices*, Oudendorp *termites*) as an explicative genitive is the more attractive, though Lütjohann's interpretation appears to be not impossible; he translates "vor der Thür des eigentlichen Höhlenganges" and compares for this sense of *trames* Ovid *Met.* 10, 53 and Stat. *Theb.* 6 (read 2), 49. A door, however, is nowhere mentioned.

For *attendi* in the sense of "extend", see 6, 11 (136, 17 f.) *nemus, quod fluuio praeterluenti ripisque longis attenditur*. There the verb is construed with a dative; ThLL offers no parallels for the absolute use.

Ea tu bono certe meo periculo latronum dixeris atria: 79, 8-9 "This you may call — and I promise to take the blame — the robbers' atrium". Once again the reader (here singular, cf. *uos* at 78, 21) is addressed emphatically. For *bono...meo periculo* see Callebat, *S.C.*, p. 86. The fenced in area may be compared with an *atrium*, since the latter may be regarded as *pars domus prior* (see Gel. 16, 5, 2 and Marquardt p. 228, n. 1). The plural *atria* is also used in the ecphrasis at 2, 4 where the house of Byrrhena is described (see de Jonge *ad loc.*). Cf. Helm-Krenkel p. 404: "Um das Spaszige zu empfinden, vergleiche man die Schilderung des Atriums im Hause der Byrrhena...mit der hiesigen Darstellung"; Burck Anm. p. 225: "Wir haben hier eine Art Gegenstück zu der Ekphrasis am Anfang des 2. Buches."

parua casula cannulis temere contecta: "a small hut, roughly 79, 10 covered with reeds". The ass has indeed great powers of observation! For the diminutives see vdP. p. 100. *Cannula*, exceedingly rare, may be an Apuleian neologism (Médan pp. 134, 145 and Eicke p. 85); see, however, Vitr. 2, 1, 5, where *cannula* has been restored *per coniecturam*.

quo speculatores e numero latronum, ut postea comperi, 79, 11-12 **sorte ducti noctibus excubabant:** "where, as I discovered later, watchers, chosen by lot from the robbers' number, kept guard by night".

The narrator's perspective is maintained through the addition of *ut postea comperi*. Generally *qua* is read with Oudendorp, but with Baehrens, *Synt.*, p. 493 Giarratano-Frassinetti wish to retain F's *quo*. In view of 2, 1 (24, 20-21) *Thessaliae loca..., quo artis magicae natiua cantamina... celebrentur* (Helm *qua*), 10, 12 (245, 13) *sepulchrum quo corpus pueri depositum iacebat* (according to Helm, *Ph. W.*, 50 (1930) p. 507 *quo* in this passage is to be explained as *in quo*) and, in general, the frequent interchange in later Latin of *quo* and *ubi* (see comm. on 76, 25) they appear to be right. Cf. also the subsequent *ibi* used in the sense of *eo* (see e.g. Löfstedt, *Per. Aeth.*, p. 182). For the abl. of extent of time in *noctibus* see comm. on 79, 21.

Eicke, p. 91 remarks with respect to this *descriptio locorum*: "Zwei Wesenszüge des apuleianischen Erzählungsstils vereinigen sich in diesem in malerischer Vordergründigkeit gegebenen Gesamtbild: das Streben nach Anschaulichkeit und die Neigung zum Atmosphärischen." We have no difficulty in agreeing with the later remark: the wild mountainside is not just described for its own sake but also serves as a 'background' for the robber stories and the 'fairytale' of Amor and Psyche, in which a *turris praealta* plays an important part (6, 17 ff.). Whether Apuleius aimed at descriptive clarity remains to be seen: according to many scholars he did not succeed if that was his aim. Thus Vallette p. 11, n. 1 remarks: "Ses descriptions manquent souvent de clarté, tant par l'abus des détails que par l'accumulation de certaines constructions ... dont la valeur devient difficile à saisir". In view of the rhetors' express prescript that clarity is to be aimed at in an ecphrasis (see D'Alton p. 507) one should here think of authorial irony underlined by the pretentious introduction.

That the chapter is to be taken as a parody is also the opinion of Eva Keuls in *Une cible de la satire: le "locus amoenus"*, LEC 42 (1974) pp. 265 ff. She points out that the *clemens cliuulus* (78, 13 f.) is suddenly transformed into a huge and wild mountain: "Les contradictions de ce morceau de parodie sont intentionnelles et visent un effet comique: elles veulent ridiculiser une convention littéraire".

CHAPTER VII

The robbers enter the cave. Conversation with an old woman.

Ibi cum singuli derepsissent stipatis artubus, nobis ante 79, 13-16
ipsas fores loro ualido destinatis anum quandam curuatam
graui senio, cui soli salus atque tutela tot numero iuuenum
commissa uidebatur, sic infesti compellant: "When one by one
the robbers had crept doubled-up down into the cave (they had tied us
with a strong strap right at the entrance), they spoke to an old woman,
bent with extreme age, who seemed to have been entrusted all alone with
the well-being and care of all these men, and they threatened as follows":
The entrance clearly is low and narrow, as appears also from *exigui
tramitis* (79, 7 f.), but not long: the ass outside is able to follow the events
inside very well indeed. Moreover, he has excellent hearing, *auribus
grandissimis praeditus* (9, 15 (214, 18)). Surprisingly Perry (1923, p. 202)
remarks: "In order to insert the tale of Cupid and Psyche within the
hearing of the ass, Apuleius makes him remain in (sic!) the cave listening
to the old woman...". *Ibi* is used here in the sense of *eo*; see comm. on 79,
11. The reading in F and φ *direpsissent* is wrong. *Direpere* does not occur
according to ThLL, whereas *e* and *i* are often interchanged in the mss;
see comm. on 78, 5.

stipatis artubus: cf. Luc. 4, 781 f. *non arma mouendi | iam locus est
pressis, stipataque membra teruntur.* For the spelling *-ubus* see Sommer p.
393 and Neue-Wagener I³ pp. 553 ff.

nobis ante ipsas fores destinatis: Apuleius gives variety by using abl.
abs. in combination with a subordinate clause. See Bernhard p. 43.

anum: the old woman is not characterized as unsympathetically as
Junghanns (p. 60, n. 89) intimates by calling her "die hässliche, säufe-
rische böse Räuberwirtschafterin", though he relents a little later (p. 66,
n. 96). She is afraid of the robbers (79, 23), willing to be of service:
dinner is ready, as it is at 6, 30 (152, 16). She demonstrates her faithful-
ness to the robbers at 94, 12 and 6, 27 (149, 5). The robbers on the other
hand call her names (79, 17 f.), do not react when their accusations are
shown to be incorrect and, when she appears to have hanged herself at 6,
30 (152, 14) they throw her with supreme indifference into a canyon.
The old woman tries to console Charite (93, 9), gets angry, but allows
herself to be mollified (96, 5). In addition she is friendly towards Lucius
(91, 12) by providing barley in abundance, but she does try at 6, 27
(149, 5) to prevent his flight. Lucius says hardly anything unfavourable
about her in book 4 (her *uocula stridula* may well be due to fear) but at
6, 25 (147, 3) she is *delira et temulenta* (the exaggerated picture perhaps

serves to create a contrast with the Amor and Psyche story; see Heine p. 182 on this change of mood). The fact that Lucius has little to say later in the old woman's favour is understandable since then she alone blocks his freedom. Finally some pity may be heard in the words *infelix anicula* at 6, 30 (152, 17). All in all she is sketched as a type from comedy. See also the slapstick-like scene at 6, 27.

For *quandam* see comm. on 76, 6

curuatam graui senio: similar expressions are to be found in Tac. *Ann.* I, 34, 3 *curuata senio membra*; Ter. *Eu.* 336; Ov. *Ars* 2, 670; id. *Met.* 9, 435.

salus atque tutela: the common combination *salutem committere* causes *tutela* to be linked with the same verb, though *tutelam permittere* is more usual. The combination with *committere* also occurs in Lucius Ampelius (29, 1) who may have been Apuleius' contemporary: (*Populus Romanus*) ... *tutelam sui consulibus praetoribus tribunis plebis commisit*. For the redundancy in *tot numero iuuenum* see Strilciw p. 116; Bernhard p. 177; vdP. p. 46; see also comm. on 76, 22.

79, 17-20 "Etiamne tu, busti cadauer extremum et uitae dedecus primum et Orci fastidium solum, sic nobis otiosa domi residens lusitabis nec nostris tam magnis tamque periculosis laboribus solacium de tam sera refectione tribues? quae diebus ac noctibus nil quicquam rei quam merum saeu⟨i⟩enti uentri tuo soles auditer ingurgitare": "Well, you last stiff of the pyre, you number one disgrace to life, Death's only reject, are you sitting here at home enjoying yourself with nothing to do? Aren't you going to comfort us with late-night refreshment after all our dangerous labours? You don't do a single thing, day or night, but guzzle strong drink down into that ravening belly of yours." The scene is strongly reminiscent of comedy, The *Onos* (20) has διὰ τί οὕτως καθέζει καὶ οὐ παρασκευάζεις ἄριστον; See Vallette's remark (p. 12, n. 1) that Apuleius intended to sketch a general type of robber full of cynicism and bluster by giving him individual traits.

The invective is cunningly chosen and artfully structured. The tricolon consists of syntactically equivalent elements of 8, 7 and 8 syllables; each colon ends in an identical clausula, which reinforces the effect.

Etiamne underscores "le caractère pressant d'une demande ou l'impatience d'une interrogation" (Callebat, *S.C.*, p. 92); cf. Pl. *Mos.* 522 *sed tu, etiamne astas nec quae dico optemperas?* and *ibid.* 937.

extremum...primum...solum: the meaning of the first of these three qualifiers is not very clear; possibly it was chosen for mere contrast with *primum*.

busti cadauer extremum: see for invective and similar phenomena Ilona Opelt, *Die lateinischen Schimpfwörter und verwandte sprachliche Erscheinungen*, Heidelberg 1965. For the present expression cf. Pl. *Ps.* 412 *ex hoc sepulcro uetere uiginti minas/ ecfodiam* (Pseudolus referring to old Simo), Mart. 3, 93, 23 where old *Vetustilla* is called *cadauer* and 10, 90, 2 where

64

Ligeia is termed *busti cineres*. *Cadauer* is used as invective also in politics, e.g. Cic. *Pis.* 33, 82; *ibid.* 9, 19; Claud. in Eutrop. 1, 147. Cf. furthermore Apul. *Met.* 6, 26 (148, 21 f.) *an custodiam anus semimortuae formidabis?* A *praeco* is called *cadauer* at 8, 25 (196, 23). In Greek a similar term of abuse occurs, see e.g. Ar. *Lys.* 372 ὦ τύμβ᾽ and v. Leeuwen *ad loc.*

uitae dedecus primum: Desertine (p. 107) cites Pl. *As.* 892 *capuli decus*, cf. 9, 26 (222, 14) *uniuersi sexus grande dedecus.*

Orci fastidium solum: old age often is a reason for *fastidium*, cf. e.g. Tac. *Hist.* 1, 7 *ipsa aetas Galbae irrisui ac fastidio erat assuetis iuuentae Neronis* and ThLL *s.v.* Here the notion is transferred to the person. Desertine (p. 107) compares Pl. *Ps.* 795 f. *quin ob eam rem Orcus recipere ad se hunc noluit/ ut esset hic qui mortuis cenam coquat.*

sic: with the construction of the main clause we may compare 9, 5 (206, 14) *sicine uacuus et otiosus insinuatis manibus ambulabis mihi nec obito consueto labore uitae nostrae prospicies et aliquid cibatui parabis?*

lusitabis belongs to the *sermo cotidianus*; see Médan p. 181, Bernhard p. 133, Callebat, *S.C.,* p. 516. The twice repeated *tam* creates a rhetorical effect increasing the emphasis of the question. *Tantus* is replaced by *tam magnus* in cases of particular emphasis: LHSz p. 206. Apuleius does this a number of times; cf. e.g. 6, 32 (154, 2 f.) *quam (sententiam) meis tam magnis auribus accipiens.* Löfstedt, *Per. Aeth.,* p. 72 f. notes that *magnus* occurs only four times in the *Peregrinatio*, three times in the combination *tam magnus* and once in a bible quotation. He points out that *magnus* is replaced by such words as *grandis* and *ingens.* See also his *Synt.* II p. 339 f. where he remarks that Petronius has *tam magnus* with some frequency (9×). See also comm. on 76, 5-11. The expression is preserved in romance languages: Spanish tamaño; Portuguese tamanho etc. See also V. Väänänen, *Introduction au Latin vulgaire*, Paris 1963, p. 81.

A passage of considerable interest is found at 10, 22 (253, 12 ff.) ... *reputans, quem ad modum tantis tamque magnis cruribus possem delicatam matronam inscendere.* To begin with we find, apart from this *tam*, another five instances in the passage: 14 f. *tam lucida tamque tenera ...membra*, 17 *tam amplo ore tamque enormi*, and 19 *tam uastum genitale.* Furthermore we note that once again *tam magnus* has taken over the original meaning of *tantus*; moreover *tantus* is used here in the sense of *tot.* See LHSz p. 206, Svennung, *Oros.* pp. 75 f. and Callebat, *S.C.,* p. 289, who quotes 6, 10 (135, 16) *sic assignato tantorum seminum cumulo.* Most translators miss the point, e.g. Helm-Krenkel "mit so mächtigen und grossen Beinen", Carlesi "con delle gambe cosi grandi e grosse", Adlington-Gaselee "with my huge and great legs" and others. The Frenchman Vallette translates correctly "avec tant et de si grandes jambes": the ass must have some place for his legs to go.... (the point is well illustrated by Hans Erni's sketches in the Rode-Rüdiger translation pp. 446 and 449).

For the periphrasis *solacium... tribues* see vdP. pp. 50 and 72; for instrumental *de* vdP. pp. 72 and 154, to the literature mentioned there add Waszink p. 119.

refectione: Fernhout on 5, 5 (107, 7) is right to explain (against Médan p. 159) "omnia, quibuscumque homines recreari solent". Whereas in the parallel quoted by him (8, 19 (192, 3)) the preceding words are summarized in *refectio*, here dinner and bath are anticipated (79, 25 ff.).

diebus ac noctibus is an abl. of extent of time; see Callebat, *S.C.*, p. 193. The combination occurs from Seneca onwards (ThLL *s.v.*); cf. e.g. Sen. *Ben.* 4, 3, 2 *di uero tot munera, quae sine intermissione diebus ac noctibus fundunt, non darent*; Suet. *Nero* 31 *perpetuo diebus ac noctibus*.

quae ... ingurgitare: a similar telescoped construction is found in 3, 4 (55, 2 f.) *nihil amplius quam flere poteram*. E. Löfstedt (*Synt.* II, pp. 270 ff.) suggests that such constructions originate in an impersonal use of *solet* or *potest*. vGeisau (p. 76) lists these passages with "einige attraktionsartige Verbindungen ... die sich im Griechischen wiederfinden". His collection of material however does not consist of equivalent cases since he equates the instances mentioned with e.g. 6, 32 (154, 3) *quid aliud quam meum crastinum deflebam cadauer*, where we have ellipsis of a *verbum agendi*. Löfstedt's explanation, therefore, is to be preferred. See also LHSz p. 422 ff. Callebat (*S.C.*, p. 97) correctly defines *nil quicquam* as a "pléonasme de renforcement", here further reinforced by *rei*. The expression is found in the comic poets and later returns in Gellius and Apuleius.

merum: in ancient literature old women often are dipsomaniacs; cf. Ar. *Nu.* 555 and Dover *ad loc.*; Herod. 1, 85 ff.; *Anth. Pal.* 5, 273; 7, 329; 7, 353; 7, 455 ff.; 11, 409; Pl. *Cur.* 96; id. *Cist.* 120; Lucil. 765 f. (Krenkel); Ov. *Am.* 1, 8, 2; id. *Fast.* 2, 582; 3, 542; 3, 705; Hor. *Carm.* 4, 13, 4; Plin. *Nat.* 36, 32; Phaed. 3, 1; Petr. 79, 6 etc. See also A. W. Pickard-Cambridge, *Dithyramb tragedy and comedy*, Oxford ²1962, p. 164 and n. 4. In the *Met.* our *anus* is described as *delira et temulenta* (6, 25 (147, 3)); the old witch Meroe is not averse from a wee drop either, witness 1, 10 (9, 18), and at 9, 15 (214, 13) the miller's wife and her friend (also an *anus*) equally know how to deal with a bottle of wine. We know the type in sculpture through a copy from a Hellenistic original in the Munich Glyptothek.

saeuienti uentri: personification of the belly is a well-known figure in Roman literature; cf. e.g. Sen. *Ep.* 60, 4 *uentri oboedientes*; Hier. *Ep.* 58, 2 *plenus uenter facile de ieiuniis disputat*.

auiditer is found here for the first time in Latin. Later we find it in Arn. 5, 1 *sed cum liquoribus odoratis offendissent fragrantia pocula ... inuasisse auiditer*. Concerning adverbs ending in *-iter* see vdP. p. 119.

Gatscha (p. 151) points out that *ingurgitare* recalls Pl. *Cur.* 126 (about the *anus* Leaena): *hoc uide ut ingurgitat inpura in se merum auariter, faucibus plenis*.

79, 23 Tremens ad haec et stridenti uocula pauida sic anus: "Trembling, the terrified old woman answered in a squeaky little voice". For ellipsis of the *verbum dicendi* see vdP. p. 49.

66

Feldbrugge (p. 123) suggests a parody of epic (cf. Walsh p. 28). The hypothesis is supported by the fact that *stridere* is used mostly by poets, e.g. Tib. 1, 3, 72 *tunc niger in porta serpentum Cerberus ore/ stridet*; see LS *s.v.*

Tremens is ambiguous: trembling may be caused by fear or old age but also by excessive drink. Cf. Ov. *Met.* 10, 414 *Horret anus tremulasque manus annisque metuque/ tendit* and Sen. *Ep.* 24, 16 *epulae cruditatem adferunt, ebrietates neruorum torporem tremoremque.*

In classical Latin *uocula* occurs only sporadically: Cic. *Att.* 2, 23, 1; Prop. 1, 16, 27. For the increased use of diminutives see Bernhard pp. 135 ff. Here the use of a diminutive is entirely functional: fear almost chokes her. See also Médan p. 198.

"at uobis, fortissimi fidelissimique mei hospitatores iuue- _{79, 24-80,2}
nes, adfatim cuncta suaui sapore percocta pulmenta praesto sunt, panis numerosus, uinum probe calicibus exfricatis affluenter immissum et ex more calida tumultuario lauacro uestro praeparata": ""But, gentlemen, my heroic and gallant guests, there is plenty of everything ready for you — a delicious stew, lots of bread, plenty of wine ready poured into properly polished cups, and hot water ready as usual for your quick bath"." The robbers' invective and suspicion appear to have been mistaken: everything is arranged as it should be. Note the variation of syndetic and asyndetic links (Bernhard p. 84) as well as the alliteration of *p* and *f* which may illustrate the nervousness of the old woman. As often, *at* (a certain correction in φ) introduces an exclamation; see Callebat, *S.C.*, pp. 89 and 422; vdP. p. 171; Chr. Harrauer p. 82. In two-part expressions such as *fortissimi fidelissimique* alliteration is common; see Bernhard p. 220.

hospitatores: an awkward textual problem. The choice lies between a) *hospitatores* and b) *sospitatores*. F and φ read a) but a later hand has changed F to read b) (also the reading of ς). The editors are divided. Hildebrand, Eyssenhardt, Helm, Giarratano, Vitali, Terzaghi and Scazzoso opt for a), Oudendorp, Robertson, Brandt-Ehlers, Frassinetti and van Thiel for b) (vdVliet conjectures *hospites et sospitatores*). *Sospitator* occurs elsewhere in Apuleius in the sense of "rescuer", "saviour" (6, 28 (150, 16); 7, 10 (161, 21); 7, 14 (164, 15); 9, 3 (205, 1)). In Christian literature it is often an epithet of Christ, e.g. Arn. 1, 53 *(Christus) ab omnium principe deo sospitator est missus.* According to Fordyce on Catul. 34, 24 *sospitare* is "solemn liturgical language" (cf. also Pl. *Aul.* 546 *di...sospitent* and Liv. 1, 16, 3). On the other hand *hospitator* occurs nowhere else, *teste Thesauro.*

The reading *hospitatores* must be retained:
1. It is *lectio difficilior* (alteration of *sospitatores* into *hospitatores* is most improbable, unlike the reverse).
2. The *anus* is the robbers' *hospita* (cf. 79, 15 f.) and a *hospitium* is often a *deversorium militum* (cf. ThLL *s.v.* 3041, 10 ff.). Hence *hospitatores*

may be given a pregnant sense here: "you who are billeted with me" (OLD "lodger", "guest"). For the use of military terms by and about the robbers see appendix I. Words in *-tor* are discussed in Callebat, *S.C.*, pp. 35 ff., Brink on Hor. *Ars* 163, Goodyear on Tac. *Ann.* 1, 24, 2 and H. Quellet, *Les dérivés latins en -or*, Paris 1969.

iuuenes is used here adjectivally; see Bernhard p. 105 and LHSz p. 158. For *adfatim* see comm. on 75, 2.

After their exertions the robbers deserve their dinner; cf. the Horatian adage *tu pulmentaria quaere/sudando* (Hor. *S.* 2, 2, 20). The old woman has prepared *pulmenta* (a synonym of *pulmentaria*, cf. Kiessling-Heinze *ad loc.*). The word — which may be translated "stew" — belongs to the *sermo cotidianus*, see Callebat, *S.C.*, p. 42.

exfricatis: it is not clear from the editions what the mss. read. Helm has *exfricatis* (no misprint, cf. *app. crit.*), whereas Giarratano and Robertson have *ecfricatis*. Apart from this difficulty little that is sensible may be said about the spelling (cf. 1, 2 (2, 13) *exf-*; 1, 7 (6, 17) *eff-*; also Sen. *Ep.* 95, 36).

De Rooy's emendation *immistum* for *immissum* is unnecessary. *Immittere* may be used for liquids, cf. Col. 9, 14, 17 (on bees and honey) *optimum est per aditum uestibuli siphonibus dulcia liquamina immittere*, see also 3, 23 (70, 1) and vdP. *ad loc.*

tumultuario, "fast", "hurried", is another item of military terminology (see appendix I), cf. 1, 16 (14, 17).

80, 3-6 In fine sermonis huius statim sese deuestiunt nudatique et flammae largissimae uapore recreati calidaque perfusi et oleo peruncti mensas dapibus largiter instructas accumbunt: "When she finished speaking, they undressed at once and refreshed their naked bodies in the glow of a huge fire. They poured hot water over themselves, anointed themselves with oil and took their places at the tables which were generously laid with various dishes". See Bernhard p. 83 on the varied conjunctions.

sermonis huius: cf. 3, 14 (62, 21) and vdP. p. 110. As often in Apuleius the demonstrative pronoun is placed after the noun; see Bernhard p. 23.

The alternative for *largiter*, *large* does not occur in Apuleius; see Callebat, *S.C.*, p. 175.

mensas accumbunt: cf. 8, 8 (183, 16) and 10, 17 (249, 29). Gatscha (p. 149) cites Catul. 64, 304 *large multiplici constructae sunt dape mensae*.

CHAPTER VIII

A second group of robbers enters the cave. At the drinking-party a robber from the first group refers to the achievements of the second group in disparaging terms.

Commodum cubuerant et ecce quidam longe plures numero 80, 6-8 iuuenes adueniunt alii, quos incunctanter adaeque latrones arbitrarere: "They hardly had taken their places at table when, lo and behold, very many other men arrived, whom you would un-hesitatingly have sized up as robbers too". The longwindedness of this sentence is remarkable, in particular the adjectival clause *quos...arbi-trarere*: people other than robbers are hardly to be expected here. See for *commodum...et* vdP. p. 23, for *ecce* vdP. p. 87. Chr. Harrauer (p. 1) points out that *commodum* occurs 25 times in the *Met.*, 3 times in the *Fl.*, not at all in the *Apol.* Her conclusion that therefore *commodum* belongs to the *sermo cotidianus* is scarcely acceptable. See for the de-velopment of a temporal adverb paratactically connected by *et* LHSz pp. 481 f. and the passages quoted there.

quidam: *quidem* of F and φ has been corrected in ς; cf. e.g. 2, 24 (44, 16) *introductis quibusdam septem testibus* and de Jonge *ad loc.* See also Graur, pp. 378-382 and in particular p. 380. See for *plures numero* comm. on 79, 15.

incunctanter: "without hesitation"; the word occurs from Ulpian on-wards (*dig.* 40, 2, 20) and Apuleius. It is not entirely clear why Chr. Harrauer (p. 37) calls it a "Juristenterminus"; cf. 90, 9 *quidam procurrens e domo procerus et ualidus incunctanter lanceam mediis iniecit ursae prae-cordiis*; 9, 1 (203, 3); 9, 36 (230, 12) etc.

adaeque: the word belongs to the *sermo cotidianus*; it occurs in Plautus and then again in Apuleius and later authors; see Bernhard p. 134. ThLL remarks *s.v.*: "in enuntiatis affirmativis non legitur ante Apul. et Iubam gramm."

arbitrarere: for the impersonal use of the second person see LHSz p. 419; J. Wackernagel, *Vorlesungen über Syntax* I, Basel ²1926, pp. 109 f.

Nam et ipsi praedas aureorum argentariorum⟨que⟩ num- 80, 8-10 morum ac uasculorum uestisque sericae et intextae filis aureis inuehebant: "For they, too, were bringing in loot: gold and silver coins and vessels and robes of gold-brocaded silk". Perry (*Anc. Rom.*, p. 256 and *TAPhA* 54 (1923) pp. 218 f.) mistakenly sees a "self-contra-diction" or a "logical absurdity" in this sentence. The second group

obtained their booty in the house of Demochares: see 88, 14-16 *iubeo singulos commilitonum asportare, quantum quisque poterat auri uel argenti* and 91, 1-3 *confestim itaque constrictis sarcinis illis, quas nobis seruauerant fideles mortui*. The words *et ipsi* refer back to the booty of the first group: see 3, 28 (72, 29-73, 1) *totas opes uehunt raptimque constrictis sarcinis singuli partiuntur*. The similarity with *Onos* 21 is obvious:
εἶτα ὀλίγῳ ὕστερον ἧκον νεανίσκοι πολλοὶ κομίζοντες σκεύη πλεῖστα ὅσα χρυσᾶ καὶ ἀργυρᾶ καὶ ἱμάτια καὶ κόσμον γυναικεῖον καὶ ἀνδρεῖον πολύν.

The rhyme of repeated *-orum* produces no very attractive effect.

praedas aureorum argentariorumque nummorum ac uasculorum: ς and all modern editors add *-que* after *argentariorum*. Though sometimes conjunctions have been added mistakenly in our texts of the *Met.* (cf. Blomgren p. 4, n. 1), the reading of F and φ can hardly be defended here. The parallel *CIL* 6, 43 *officinatores monetae aurariae argentariae* is insufficiently dependable. See also Bernhard p. 56.

80, 10-12 **Hi[i] simili lauacro refoti inter toros sociorum sese reponunt, tunc sorte ducti ministerium faciunt**: "When they too had been refreshed by a bath, they lay down at table among their comrades; then those who had been drawn by lot served the meal". As is fitting the robbers bathe before their meal; see Balsdon, *Life*, pp. 26-32.

sorte ducti ministerium faciunt: the expression *sorte ducere* first occurs in Cicero (*Rep.* 1, 51). From then on it is the usual term for appointing by lot; on the development of the term see J. H. Schmalz, *ALL*, 9 (1896) p. 578. At 79, 12 also they had drawn lots, that time to assign guard duties. Similar appointments by lot occur in a military context, see Plb. 6, 35, 11: οἱ δὲ προκριθέντες ὑπὸ τῶν οὐραγῶν ἐκ τῆς πρώτης ἴλης τέτταρες, ἐπειδὰν διαλάχωσι τὰς φυλάκας. Christ's clothes are divided by lot among the Roman soldiers: St. Mark 15, 24 *Et crucifigentes eum diuiserunt uestimenta eius mittentes sortem super eis quis quid tolleret*; St. Luke 23, 34; St. John 19, 24.

See for *facere* as "Allerweltsverbum" LHSz p. 755. The expression *ministerium facere* is also found in Justin. 32, 3, 16 *(Daci) cogebantur ministeria ... uxoribus, quae ipsis ante fieri solebant, facere*. Petronius (22, 6) uses *ministerium* in the same sense, for serving at meals: *pueri detersis paulisper oculis redierant ad ministerium*.

80, 12-14 **Estur ac potatur incondite, pulmentis aceruatim, panibus aggeratim, poculis agminatim ingestis**: "There was unbridled eating and drinking, as they absorbed meat in heaps, bread in mounds, and cups in serried ranks". This sentence is remarkable for rhyme (*-tur, -tur*; 3× *-is*; 3× *-atim*), alliteration of *p* and assonance of *a*. Of the three members *pulmentis ... agminatim*, the nouns and the adverbs each have equal numbers of syllables. Feldbrugge p. 53 is right in underlining the comic character of the passage. The form *estur* occurs regularly

— but not solely — in the comic poets, e.g. Pl. *Mos.* 235 *dies noctesque estur, bibitur*; id., *Poen.* 835 *bibitur, estur quasi in popina*. See for the impersonal passive comm. on 74, 10.

  aceruatim: a similar use is found in 6, 10 (135, 9) and *Apol.* 35 (40, 20 f.). It is used metaphorically at 9, 11 (211, 20) *plagas ingerentes aceruatim*; cf. also Lucr. 6, 1263; Cic. *Clu.* 30; id., *Orat.* 85. See also for adverbs in *-tim* vdP. pp. 33 f. and the literature quoted there. According to ThLL *aggeratim* occurs here only. *Agminatim* is an Apuleian neologism: it is also used at 89, 24, but in a literal sense, which is the sense it has later in Ammianus Marcellinus (e.g. 18, 6, 23) and Solinus (25, 4).

Clamore ludunt, strepitu cantilant, conuiciis iocantur, ac iam cetera semiferis Lapithis ⟨ti⟩tuban⟨t⟩ibus Centaurisque similia: "There was shouting and joking, noise and singing, swearing and banter and for the rest it was just like the staggering of the half-wild Lapiths and Centaurs". Gaiety increases apace with the number of syllables of the three cola *clamore...iocantur* (5-6-7). This and previous sentences speed up the narrated as against the narrating time. At the end of a meal people often enjoyed *sermones, ut castitate integros, ita adpetibiles* (Macr. I, I, 4), but here *aut bibat, aut abeat* (Cic. *Tusc.* 5, 118) is rather more to the point; see also Balsdon, *Life*, pp. 45-53. In book I, too, in Aristomenes' story, Socrates starts his account during a meal, as does Thelyphron in bk 2. In bk 9 the story of the cuckolded husband starts in an inn, and Philesitherus' experiences are related after a breakfast and a solid drink.

  cantilant: the word occurs only in Apuleius; apart from our passage, it is found in *Fl.* 3(5, 4); 15(21, 3) and 17(32, 22).

  cetera semiferis Lapithis titubantibus Centaurisque similia: the revelry is such as to suggest a comparison with the famous meal of the Lapiths and Centaurs. This meal was proverbial in antiquity; see Cic. *Pis.* 10, 22 *quasi aliquod Lapitharum aut Centaurorum conuiuium*; Iul. Val. I, 13; Lucian. *Symp.* 45; *Nachträge zu Otto* p. 87 (Sonny). Visual art offers unnumbered instances, of which the western frieze of the temple of Zeus at Olympia is one of the most famous.

  The present passage contains a vexed textual problem: F has *tebcinibus centaurisque*. A great many proposals have been made to emend the enigmatic *tebcinibus* or *tebanibus*. Among these are Helm's *cenantibus* (Helm III), which is easily defensible from a palaeographical point of view, though the meaning is somewhat flat. Helm is followed by vThiel. Perhaps one might consider, in this context, *tuburcinantibus* (Smits) "fressen" rather than "essen", a word also used elsewhere by Apuleius (6, 25 (147, 10 f.) *prandioque raptim tuburcinato*) but this word is palaeographically less probable. Nicolaas Heinsius' *euantibus* has gained many supporters: Helm I, II, Giarratano, Terzaghi, Frassinetti and Vitali; Einar Löfstedt also favours this reading (*Hermes*, 41 (1906) p. 320) and offers a plausible explanation for the corruption: *euantibus* → *euantibus* →

teuanibus. (He omits acknowledging the conjecture as Heinsius'). *Euans*, however, is used only of those in the grip of Bacchus' ecstasy (Bacchants, Satyrs, priests etc.). Robertson's proposal to delete *tebcinibus* and to add after *Centaurisque* the word *semihominibus* (he refers us to Ov. *Met.* 12, 531[1]) appears too violent an intervention. The conjecture printed above was suggested by Smits (*Mnemosyne* 1974 p. 417); it has the advantages of palaeographical defensibility and suitability in the context (the staggering recalls 80, 13 f. *poculis agminatim ingestis*). An earlier case of *titubatio* was found at 2, 31 (51, 8) where Lucius returns under the influence *titubante uestigio* to Milo's house. We opt, then, though tentatively, for *titubantibus*[2].

80, 16-17   Tunc inter eos unus, qui robore ceteros antistabat: "Then one of them, who surpassed the others in strength…"

    antistabat: usually Apuleius construes this verb with a dative, e.g. 86, 2 f. *animi robore ceteris antistaret*; 8, 2 (177, 12 f.), but outside the Apuleian corpus there are parallels for the construction with the accusative, e.g. Mela 3, 54 *Scadinauia… ut fecunditate alias ita magnitudine antestat*; Iul. Val. 3, 3.

80, 17-21   "nos quidem", inquit, "Milonis Hypatini domum fortiter expugnauimus. Praeter tantam fortunae copiam, quam nostra uirtute nacti sumus, et incolumi numero castra nostra petiuimus et, si quid ad rem facit, octo pedibus auctiores remeauimus.":"…said, "*Our* group gallantly captured the house of Milo of Hypata. In addition to the enormous amount of loot we acquired by our prowess, not only did we get back to base without casualties, but, if it is to the point, we actually returned with eight extra feet"."

    The notions *tutum* and *honestum* have an important part in Roman literature; see A. D. Leeman, *Orationis Ratio. The Stylistic Theories and Practice of the Roman Orators, Historians and Philosophers*, 2 vols. Amsterdam 1963, pp. 23, 28, 246. Cf. Rhet. Her. 3, 3 *Utilitas in duas partes in ciuili consultatione diuiditur: tutam, honestam. Tuta est quae conficit instantis aut consequentis periculi uitationem qualibet ratione… Honesta res diuiditur in rectum et laudabile.* This is applicable — *mutatis mutandis* — to the robbers: the *honestum* is expressed in lines 17-19, the *tutum* by *incolumi numero*. The other party is reproached for the opposite: they have lost Lamachus (non-*tutum*) and *per balneas et aniles cellulas*

---

[1] *Sic*: line 536 is meant.
[2] We thank Mr. S. R. Duintjer Tebbens for his contribution to the discussions concerning this question. He is inclined to follow up a suggestion of Kronenberg's, (who tried *turbantibus*, before deciding to delete *tebanibus* (*Mnemosyne* 1928 pp. 31 f.) and to read *disturbantibus* (cf. 95, 15 f. *sic ad instar Attidis uel Protesilai dispectae disturbataeque nuptiae.* Another marriage!)

reptare cannot be called *honestum*. A similar analysis may be made at 5, 29 (126, 14 ff.). See vdP. pp. 63-64 for more rhetorical devices in the *Met*.

The robber's speech shows a careful rhetorical structure: note the fine rhetorical antitheses: *nos quidem* (17) vs *at uos* (21); *Milonis...expugnauimus* (17 f.) vs *qui...adpetistis* (21 f.); *praeter...sumus* (18 f.) vs *sarcinis...omnibus* (24) and *incolumi...remeauimus* (19 f.) vs *ipso... reduxistis* (22 f.).

Whether under the influence of drink or rhetoric or both, the robber transforms a simple case of breaking and entering into a regular military campaign: cf. 80, 18 *expugnauimus*; 80, 20 *castra nostra*; 81, 2 *inter inclitos reges ac duces proeliorum*. See also Appendix I. The speaker's own achievement is further underscored by the adjective *Hypatini* (18): *Hypata* is situated as far away as Thessaly (vs. *Boeotias urbes* 22).

inquit: Robertson, followed by Frassinetti and Scazzoso, wishes to insert *qui* after this word and to punctuate with a comma rather than a period after *expugnauimus*. He compares the construction at 80, 21. The insertion appears to be superfluous since the ms. reading produces a satisfactory sense and "variatio" is as common in Apuleius as parallelism.

praeter: for the sake of variation Apuleius here uses the preposition rather than *non solum tanta copia...sed etiam incolumi numero*. The frequency of this preposition in Apuleius is noteworthy; see F. H. Parriger, *A anschouwelijkheidsdrang als factor bij de betekenisontwikkeling der Latijnsche praepositie*, diss. Utrecht 1941, pp. 85 f.

incolumi numero: the combination does not occur very often; cf. Cic. *Ver.* 3, 125 *incolumis numerus manebat dominorum*; Vell. 2, 120, 2. Like *debilis* (23) the word *incolumis* is originally used of persons.

si quid ad rem facit: cf. *Apol.* 31 (36, 13) *piscis ad quam rem facit nisi ad epulas?* See Callebat, *S.C.*, p. 173; Waszink pp. 433 f.; OLD *s.v. facere* 30. The modesty the reader senses in the speaker is immediately seen to be false when the eight feet are mentioned. Feldbrugge p. 54: "Geestig haalt Lucius zichzelf er nog even bij; hijzelf en het paard — de andere ezel was omgekomen — zijn natuurlijk bedoeld!" The increasing number of syllables in the last four words of the sentence (2-3-4-5) is noteworthy.

"At uos, qui Boeotias urbes adpetistis, ipso duce uestro 80, 21-24 fortissimo Lamacho deminuti debilem numerum reduxistis, cuius salutem merito sarcinis istis, quas aduexistis, omnibus antetulerim": "But *your* group, which made for Boeotian towns, actually lost your heroic leader Lamachus, and have come back with your numbers reduced. *I* would have set his safety — and quite right, too — above all those packets that you have brought with you.""

deminuti: "robbed of": the same construction is used as in *capite deminuere*, which, in view of the relative rarity of the construction (see OLD *s.v.*), may be significant. In loosing Lamachus the second group has lost face.

cuius: the relative is rather far removed from the antecedent *Lamacho*, see Bernhard pp. 29 f.; de Jonge on 2, 4 (27, 11).

merito: the word sounds very self-satisfied; its sense appears to disagree with the use of the potential construction.

istis: though the booty is certainly worthwhile, Lamachus' death is much more important. Hence *istis* has, apart from its usual value, a disparaging function (not mentioned by Callebat, *S.C.*, p. 274), which is further emphasized by *sarcinis:* "(small) pieces of baggage".

81, 1-5 "Sed illum quidem utcumque nimia uirtus sua peremit, inter inclitos reges ac duces proeliorum tanti uiri memoria celebrabitur. Enim uos bonae frugi latrones inter furta parua atque seruilia timidule per balneas et aniles cellulas reptantes scrutariam facitis": ""But as far as he is concerned, in whatever way his too great courage has cost him his life, the memory of so great a man will be honoured among famous kings and marshalls. But you — excellent robbers — amble with small and servile pinchings along baths and old-age-homes doing a little business in scraps and rags"."

quidem (1) corresponds with *enim* (3) which here has the sense of *sed*; see O. Hey, *ALL*, 13 (1904) pp. 207 f.; id. *ALL* 14 (1905) pp. 270-275; Löfstedt, *Per. Aeth.*, p. 34; Helm, *Quaestiones Apuleianae, Philologus*, Suppl. Band 9 (1904) p. 573; Bonnet pp. 317 f. LHSz pp. 508 f. The same usage is found at 91, 12 (*latrones*) *conquiescunt. Enim nobis anus ... ordeum ... largita est.*

utcumque: in all probability a conjunction here as at 1, 20 (18, 23); therefore a comma should be printed after *peremit.*

Callebat's statement (*S.C.*, p. 257) that in *sua* we have to do with a "substitution d'un possessif à un démonstratif" is hardly correct. At all periods of latin *suus* may also refer to the object, whereas in later Latin the usage is widened even further; see Bernhard p. 113; LHSz p. 175. The meaning here is *proprius*; see Hoppe p. 103; Löfstedt, *Krit. Apol.*, pp. 95 f.

memoria celebrabitur: this expression is also found in Tac. *Hist.* 1, 78 (Nero); Suet. *Claud.* 11 (Germanicus); Cic. *Fin.* 2, 103; Sen. *Dial.* 6, 2, 5 (Marcellus); id., *Ep.* 99, 23. Lamachus is in illustrious company.

bonae frugi: of course ironic; see Callebat, *S.C.*, p. 468; cf. 1, 7 (7, 17 f.) *lacinias quas boni latrones contegendo mihi concesserant.*

timidule: according to the Thesaurus material placed at our disposal this is the only passage in which the word occurs. See Bernhard p. 137 for diminutives in Apuleius in general.

balneas: in the baths both of Athens and of Rome thefts, in particular of clothes, were a regular feature; cf. Catul. 33, 1 *O, furum optime balneariorum.* Kroll *ad loc.* cites Pl. *Rud.* 382 and Petr. 30, 8. In *dig.* 47, 17 we find the chapter heading *De furibus balneariis.* See also Marquardt I, 281, n. 2.

aniles cellulas: Bernhard (p. 111) cites *anilis* among the instances of

"Ausdehnung des Adjektiv-Gebrauchs", but the adjective *anilis* replaces the possessive genitive also at, e.g., Verg. *A*. 7, 416; Plin. *Ep*. 5, 16, 2.

scrutariam facitis: the speaker's scorn reaches its climax: "you do a little trade in scraps"; cf. Lucil. in Gel. 3, 14, 10 *Quidni? et scruta quidem ut uendat scrutarius laudat | praefractam strigilem, soleam inprobus dimidiatam*. The combination *facere* + trade occurs very early; cf. Pl. *Epid*. 581 *ego lenocinium facio?* Compare also expressions such as *medicinam facere = mederi*; Löfstedt, *Per. Aeth*., p. 165.

CHAPTER IX

A robber of the second group tries to defend himself against the accusations of the first spokesman. Start of the robber-stories.

81, 6-8 Suscipit unus ex illo posteriore numero: "tune solus ignoras longe faciliores ad expugnandum domus esse maiores?": "One among the last group spoke up and said: "Are you the only one who doesn't know that larger homes are much easier to conquer?""

The second robber in some irritation tries to refute the first: to begin with he expresses scorn that the first does not know that it is easier to break into larger houses. This is subsequently elaborated: a numerous staff does not care for their master's possessions, whereas a man without servants carefully guards his own property. The robber is ready to give factual proof.

suscipit: with the verb in this position asyndeton is found elswhere, in particular with verbs of speaking and seeing; cf. e.g. 5, 10 (110, 18) *suscipit alia*; see Bernhard pp. 11 f.; LHSz pp. 403 f.

tune: the pronoun is used in conversation in order to enhance the liveliness of an interchange; see Callebat, *S.C.*, p. 93; LHSz pp. 173 f.; Hofmann, *LU*, pp. 100 f.; cf. 1, 22 (20, 7) *an tu solus ignoras*.

81, 8-10 Quippe quod, licet numerosa familia latis deuersetur aedibus, tamen quisque magis suae saluti quam domini consulat opibus: "For though in a large house a great deal of staff is present, yet every individual cares more for his own safety than for the master's possessions".

numerosa: the adjective has developed from the meaning "rhythmic" in the classical period, to "numerous"; cf. e.g. Cic. *Orat.* 50, 168 *genus illud tertium explicetur quale sit, numerosae et aptae orationis?* See Ernout, *Les Adj.*, p. 45; Chr. Harrauer p. 182. Cf. 5, 8 (109, 4) *populosam familiam.*

deuersari: here the verb has lost its original meaning "to stay for the night", as also e.g. at 1, 21 (19, 14) *dic...quibus deuersetur aedibus;* 1, 21 (19, 17) *inibi iste Milo deuersatur.* Note the *variatio* of *domus* (7) and *aedes* (9).

81, 10-13 Frugi autem et solitarii homines fortunam paruam uel certe satis amplam dissimulanter obtectam protegunt acrius et sanguinis sui periculo muniunt. Res ipsa denique fidem sermoni meo dabit: "But simple folk living alone hide away

76

their small or even quite considerable substance acting as though they had nothing, and guard it fiercely and protect it even at risk of their life's blood. Actual facts indeed will prove my thesis".

paruam uel certe satis amplam: the robber corrects himself, possibly because of the Chryseros story that follows immediately. Chryseros was possessed of *copiosa pecunia* (17) and a *magna opulentia* (18 f.).

obtectam protegunt: a similar *annominatio* is found in 6, 20 (144, 1-7) *obseratis...reserat*, a passage not mentioned by Bernhard in his list of instances of this figure in the *Met*. (pp. 237 f.). See Bernhard pp. 323 f. for *annominatio* in the *Apol*. and p. 333 for the same figure in *De dogm. Plat.*

res ipsa denique fidem sermoni meo dabit: cf. Lucr. 5, 104 *dictis dabit ipsa fidem res*. Bailey *ad loc*. points out that *fidem facere* is more usual in this sense. *Dare fidem* is normally "to make a promise"; cf. Gel. 17, 10, 4 *Hoc uirum iudicii subtilissimi ingenue atque uere dixisse res indicium facit.*

For *denique* see vdP. pp. 42 f.

Vix enim Thebas ⟨h⟩eptapylos accessimus: quod est huic 81, 13-16
disciplinae primarium studium, sed[d]um sedulo fortunas
inquirebamus popularium: "We had barely arrived at Thebes of
the seven gates when — a primary requirement in this profession of
ours — we made an intensive investigation into the wealth of the citizens'
houses."

The text presents us with a nasty problem. After *studium* F and φ write *sed dū sedulo*, whereas they present the last word of the sentence as *populari*. Opinions differ: Salmasius deleted *sed dum* and was followed by Hildebrand, Eyssenhardt, Helm, Giarratano, Terzaghi, Brandt-Ehlers, Frassinetti, Vitali and Scazzoso (Hildebrand also adds *et* after *accessimus*). They correct the final word of the sentence to *popularis* (acc. plur.). VdVliet and Robertson also delete *sed dum* but print Pricaeus' *popularium*. Wiman, supported by Armini (1928), proposes the solution we have finally chosen. Further conjectures for *sed dum*: *scilicet* (Oudendorp), *sectim* (Gruter), and one might also think of *secreto* (Smits).

Of the several solutions to the textual problem, deleting *sed dum* is very plausible. Salmasius saw a dittography resulting from *studium*, Helm (Praef. *Fl.* p. LI) thought it had arisen under the influence of *sedulo*. Wiman's *sedum...popularium* is also very attractive. He compares 84, 2 *domus attiguae...fortunas arbitraturus*; his solution is supported by Armini who cites 78, 13 *sedes illa et habitatio* and 8, 23 (194, 28) where *sedes* is used in the same sense. Armini also points to Apuleius' use of *uariatio* (7 *domus*, 9 *aedibus*). Finally, a mistakenly duplicated letter occurs often enough. If *sedum* is read, Pricaeus' *popularium* becomes necessary. Robertson rejects the solution on the grounds that in the *Met*. *populares* is used six times in the sense of *ciues* and only once as an adjective. His argument is far from strong. Oudendorp's *scilicet* is also attractive, though its position is rather unusual.

Gruter's *sectim* deserves an honourable mention. *Secreto*, too, is not impossible: the word occurs elsewhere in Apuleius; a combination like *secreto sedulo* is found at 3, 16 (64, 5) *quos me sedulo furtimque colligentem tonsor inuenit*, and an asyndetic juxtaposition is found at 1, 18 (16, 8) *et ego curiose sedulo arbitrabar iugulum*. In the end Wiman's solution appears to be the most attractive, though *non liquet* might be even more appropriate.

As regards the sentence as a whole: the asyndetic, paratactic construction is not uncommon in the *Met.*; cf. e.g. 3, 26 (71, 24-26) and vdP. *ad loc.*; Callebat, *S.C.*, pp. 439 f. The phrase starting with *quod* should be taken as a parenthesis; parentheses are more often introduced by *quod* as at 7, 26 (174, 7 f.) *sed quod solum poteram, tacitus licet serae uindictae gratulabar*; see Callebat, *S.C.*, p. 463.

heptapylos: an epitheton ornans (Bernhard p. 145) which also occurs in Hyginus, *Fab.* 275, 4, and Schol. Stat. *Theb.* 3, 198 and 7, 252. It is found in Latin for the first time during the second century; the ending indicates that it was still felt to be Greek. In Greek literature it is, of course, well known from Hom. *Il.* 4, 406 and *Od.* 11, 263 onwards; cf. also Juv. 13, 26 f. *rari quippe boni; numera, uix sunt totidem quot/Thebarum portae*; see for the situation of Thebes in Boeotia vThiel I p. 103 and comm. on 83, 6; cf. 80, 22 *Boeotias urbes adpetistis* and 91, 3 *Plataeae terminos*.

81, 16-19 nec nos denique latuit Chryseros quidam nummularius copiosae pecuniae dominus qui metu officiorum ac munerum publicorum magnis artibus magnam dissimulabat opulentiam: "And as a result we discovered a certain Chryseros, a moneychanger who possessed a large fortune. For fear of calls upon him for expenditure in the public interest he concealed his great wealth with great skill".

Chryseros is another significant name; see comm. on 84, 15.

nummularius: cf. Mart. 12, 57, 7 f. *hinc otiosus sordidam quatit mensam / Neroniana nummularius massa*; Petr. 56 *quod...putamus secundum litteras difficillimum esse artificium? ego puto medicum et nummularium: ...nummularius, qui per argentum aes uidet*. Callebat, *S.C.*, p. 29 notes that *nummularius* has replaced *argentarius* which was in the classical period the more usual term.

munerum publicorum: Pomponius explains in *dig.* 50, 16, 239, 3 what it is the miser wishes to avoid: *munus publicum est officium priuati hominis, ex quo commodum ad singulos uniuersosque ciues remque eorum imperio magistratus extraordinarium peruenit*. See Vallette's note on our passage. Note the anaphora of *magnis...magnam*.

81, 19-21 Denique solus ac solitarius parua, se⟨d⟩ satis munita do-

78

muncula contentus, pannosus alioquin ac sordidus, aureos folles incubabat: "He lived alone and lonely, content with a small but burglar-proof little house, and despite his ragged and dirty clothes, he slept on bags of gold".

solitarius: the word may be synonymous with *solus*: see de Jonge p. 119 "solitarius est enim idem atque solus". He compares 3, 8 (58, 6) *hominem solitarium tres tam ualidos euitasse iuuenes*. Here, however, *solus* is employed in the objective sense of "sine ullo comite" and *solitarius* more subjectively "solitary", "living by himself"; cf. Cic. *Off.* 2, 39 *solitario homini atque in agro uitam agenti opinio iustitiae necessaria est*. Vallette therefore translates "Vivant seul et retiré" and Helm, beautifully preserving the *annominatio*, "Einsam und einzeln wohnend". LS, then, are not entirely right in noting a redundancy here.

alioquin: characteristically used with two adjectives linked by *ac*; see Bernhard p. 127 and vdP. p. 52. The word underscores the contrast with *contentus*.

aureos folles incubabat: Bernhard p. 218 speaks of a proverbial expression. See Otto, *Sprichw.*, pp. 173 f. and *Nachtr. zu Otto* p. 106 (Sonny) and p. 173 (Sutphen); cf. e.g. Quint. *Inst.* 10, 1, 2 *uelut clausis thesauris incubabit* and Abaelard, *sermo 33* (p. 588 Cousin), *(episcopi) non aliter se digne censent episcopari, nisi splendidius et accuratius uiuant, et obliti cibarium panem, quo antea uescebantur, corde in Aegyptum reuertentes de heremo, ollis carnium impudenter incumbant*. In this proverbial sense *incubare* is only here construed with the accusative.

Ergo placuit ad hunc primum ferremus aditum, ut contemp- 81, 21-24
ta pugna manus unicae nullo negotio cunctis opibus otiose potiremur: "So we decided to go for him first and get all his wealth easily and with no trouble — with only one opponent we expected no contest".

ferremus aditum: the expression is modelled on *ferre gradus, ferre uestigia*; cf. 8, 16 (190, 9) *nulli contra nos aditum tulerunt*; see Médan p. 246. On *ferremus* Bernhard p. 52 remarks: "Apulejus setzt in Anlehnung an die gesprochene Sprache in den weitaus meisten Fällen den blossen Konjunktiv". Callebat, *S.C.*, p. 359 expresses himself with greater care. He thinks it probable that in such paratactic constructions there may be influences from popular language, "facilités analogiques, expression non élaborée", and from literary language, "tendance archaïsante, influence des stylistes". He supports this with many instances.

potiremur: once again a military term; see Appendix I. The robbers will be disappointed in their expectations.

CHAPTER X

The robbers' very first undertaking is not precisely successful.

81, 24-25 Nec mora, cum noctis initio foribus eius praestolamur: "And straightaway, as soon as night fell we stood ready at his door..."

    nec mora cum: see on 77,7.

    noctis initio = nocte ineunte, prima nocte. ThLL offers no instances of *initio* as an abl. of time combined with the genitive of a word denoting a natural time unit such as *nox, dies, uer*; on the other hand we do read in Nep. *Cinn.* I, I *initio adulescentiae*.

    praestolamur: Fest. 223 M(= 250L) notes: *praestolari is dicitur, qui ante stando ibi, quo uenturum excipere uult, moratur*. This meaning does not fully fit the context (Helm: "...stehen wir... bereit"); the irony of the situation consists in the fact that on the contrary Chryseros is ready for the bandits; see vdP. p. 45.

81, 25-26 quas neque subleuare neque dimouere ac ne perfringere quidem nobis uidebatur: "however, we thought best not to lift it out of its socket or to wrench it open (with a crowbar), let alone to break it down (with an axe)". With this tricolon we may compare I, 10 (9, 21) *non claustra perfringi, non fores euelli, non denique parietes ipsi quiuerint perforari*.

    ne...quidem is used not only to denote what is less obvious than the item mentioned before ("not even"), but also something that is even more obvious ("let alone"; "not to mention"); cf. Cic. *Div.* 2, 8, 21 *sin autem id (sc. quod futurum est) potest flecti, nullum est fatum; ita ne diuinatio quidem, quoniam ea rerum futurarum est*; Hand, *Turs.*, IV pp. 60 f. In our passage the three elements are enumerated in order of increasing violence and noise and therefore increasing risk.

81, 26 ualuarum sonus: *ualuae* is the word for a folding door with two, three or four leaves, closing off a wide entrance, used especially in temples and other large buildings, see RE *s.v.* Where the *parua domuncula* of 81, 20, called a *gurgustiolum* below (82, 10), is represented as possessing such *ualuae*, we may speak of "*amplificatio (hyperbole)* of the situation", vdP. p. 197.

82, 1 cunctam uiciniam: *abstractum pro concreto*; cf. 3, 2 (53, 21) and 3, 27 (72, 20) *ministerium = minister*; see vdP. p. 37 and the literature mentioned there.

If the mention of *ualuae* raises some doubt whether Chryseros' *domuncula* is really so very *parua* (81, 20), the words *cunctam uiciniam* raise the question whether he is really *solus ac solitarius* (81, 19).

nostro exitio = ad nostram perniciem: the use of the final dative is a hyperurbanism acc. to Löfstedt, *Synt.* I² pp. 190 f.; cf. LHSz pp. 100 f.

suscitaret: see Bernhard pp. 18 f. concerning the position of the finite verb (last word but one); also O. Möbitz, *Glotta* 13 (1924) p. 124; here hiatus is avoided by the device.

Tunc itaque sublimis ille uexillarius noster Lamachus spec-   82, 1-3
ta[ta]tae uirtutis suae fiducia...: "It was, then, in these circumstances that our splendid leader Lamachus, confident in his tried and tested courage..." The inferential force of *itaque* is founded in *tunc*, which denotes not just a point in time as such, but the difficult situation, or rather the difficulty of the situation whih demands specific measures; thus also *tunc* at 82, 15. As usual in the *Met. itaque* has second position, see Bernard pp. 27 f.

sublimis: "splendid", "illustrious"; acc. to Médan p. 194 "sens poétique", cf. Hor. *Ars* 165 and Brink *ad loc. Sublimus* also occurs, see vdP. p. 34.

uexillarius: "gonfalonier", "standard-bearer", a military term used here only to denote a leader of bandits; see Médan p. 255.

Lamachus: another significant name and one which the robber has in common with the famous Athenian general who died in battle near Syracuse during the Sicilian expedition (Thuc. 6, 101, 6). On the irony of this name see Walsh p. 158. On significant names in general see comm. 84, 15 and 85, 15. Hesychius glosses the name as ἄμαχος, ἀκαταγώνιστος; it seems preferable to explain the name as λαόμαχος.

spectatae uirtutis: though the robber-narrator qualifies his late commander in this way the reader has no independent knowledge of the matter nor is he given any further information.

qua clauis immittendae foramen patebat, sensim inmissa   82, 3-5
manu claustrum euellere gestiebat: "put his hand through the wide keyhole, feeling his way around, with the intention of ripping the lock loose."

clauis immittendae foramen: F and φ have *claui* but according to Robertson the *s* has been erased in F; *clauis* is the reading in α. Helm reads with the older editors *claui* and is joined by Terzaghi and Vitali, but Robertson is right (as are Giarratano-Frassinetti, Scazzoso and Brandt-Ehlers) in adopting the reading of the recentiores. He refers to Sall. *Or. Phil.* 3 *exercitum opprimundae libertatis*; Tac. *Ann.* 12, 24 *sulcus designandi oppidi*; K.St. I p. 740; Löfstedt, *Synt.* I² pp. 169 ff.; see also LHSz p. 75. The "keyhole" is big enough to put a hand and arm through it; the bar (*claustrum*), however, is kept in place by bolts (cf.

1, 14 (13, 5)) which may only be removed by means of a large key (*clauis*), see Dar.-Sagl. IV, pp. 1245 f. *s.v. sera*; Marquardt I, pp. 232 ff.; H. Diels, *Antike Technik* ²1920, pp. 53 ff.; R. Fellmann, *Riegelbeschlagbleche, Ur-Schweiz-La Suisse primitive* 27 (1963), pp. 39 ff.; Marg. Molt pp. 82 f.; vdP. pp. 53 f. While unlocking by means of a key may be difficult enough (cf. 1, 14 (13, 21)), ripping out the entire mechanism (*claustrum euellere*) demands not just "eine räubermässige Kraft" (vThiel I, p. 102, n. 113), but is bound to be impossible in view of the cramped position of the arm in the keyhole.

claustrum: Médan (p. 207) remarks that usually one finds the plural forms of *claustrum* only; see however Gel. 14, 6, 3 *Euryclia Telemachum quo genere claustri incluserit.*

patebat: in the light of what follows an ominous word, see the note on *patibulatum* (82, 9).

sensim: to some extent the etymological sense is still felt in the present passage.

82, 5-6 Sed dudum scilicet omnium bipedum nequissimus Chryseros uigilans et singula rerum sentiens: "but Chryseros, most wicked of all bipeds, evidently long since ready and aware of everything…"

dudum: here doubtless used "cum notione longinquitatis", ThLL *s.v.* B 2 "i.q. *iamdiu, iampridem*", notwithstanding Médan (p. 224), who glosses with *modo, paulo ante*.

scilicet: "of course" not because Chryseros' readiness could have been expected, but because afterwards the sequence of events forces the band to draw the conclusion: "evidently".

omnium bipedum nequissimus: the same expression is found in Plin. *Ep.* I, 5, 14 where Modestus uses it to qualify a certain Regulus. Here the conclusion as to Chryseros' depravity is based on the fact that he is ready for the bandits and cruelly but definitely renders their professional activities impossible; cf. Men. *Mon.* 816 (Jaekel) φασὶν κακίστους οἱ πονη-ροὶ τοὺς καλούς.

bipedum: since Lucius, in the shape of a quadruped, is part of the scenery the use of this word in the robbers' story is highly humorous.

uigilans: here not so much "lying awake" (Helm: "war natürlich längst wach") but "prepared", "on the alert" (Scazzoso: "all'erta").

uigilans…sentiens…tolerans: "Partizipialkonglomerat", see Bernhard pp. 41 f., LHSz. p. 384; possibly it has the function here of slightly postponing the description of Chryseros' active intervention and thus increasing the tension in the reader.

singula rerum: cf. 75, 18 *nimio uelocitatis*. See also comm. on 88, 20.

82, 6-9 lenem gradum et obnixum silentium tolerans paulatim adrepit grandique clauo manum ducis nostri repente nisu

82

fortissimo ad ostii tabulam offigit: "... took care to walk quietly and preserve a steadfast silence. He crept graduallay closer and then suddenly and violently impaled our leader's hand on the door-panel by means of a huge nail".

lenem gradum: according to Médan p. 246 an "expression renouvelée" modelled on *lenis somnus*.

obnixum silentium tolerans: cf. Aus. *Ep.* 29, 28 *obnixum, Pauline, taces*; *obnixum* is joined to *silentium* through enallage; referring to Chryseros the adjective here has the full force ThLL attributes to it: "respicitur magis pertinacia animi"; the same state of mind is expressed by the participle *tolerans* i.e. *seruans*, acc. to Médan p. 240 equally an "expression renouvelée"; according to the material provided by the ThLL at Munich our passage is the only one in which the word is used in this sense.

grandi: not simply synonymous with *magno*, see vdP. on 3, 15 (63, 1) and the literature mentioned there; see also comm. on 76, 8.

offigit: according to Médan p. 179 "langue archaïque", cf. Pl. *Mos.* 359 f. *ego dabo ei talentum primus qui in crucem excucurrerit/sed ea lege ut offigantur bis pedes, bis bracchia.*

et exitiabili nexu patibulum relinquens gurgustioli sui 82, 9-10 tectum ascendit: "and leaving him fatally riveted, as a living bar to the door, he went up on the roof of his hovel".

exitiabili: according to Médan p. 199 "rare mais classique"; in Apuleius the word occurs eight times, all of those in the *Met.*; concerning the use of adjectives in *-bilis* in Apuleius see Gargantini p. 34.

patibulum: Scaliger's conjecture *patibulatum* was adopted by Ouden- 82, 10 dorp, who referred to Pl. *Mos.* 56 *ita te forabunt patibulatum per uias* and from vdVliet onwards modern editors adopt the conjecture. If as we prefer, the mss. reading is preserved, there are two possibilities: one may suppose with Hildebrand that *patibulum* refers to the *fores* to which Lamachus has been nailed — even though he is nailed by only one hand, not two; more humorous is the interpretation that regards Lamachus himself as the *patibulum* (for omitted *eum* see Bernhard pp. 159 f.), so that there is a play on the double meaning of *patibulum*, for the word means (1) a beam or board put on the shoulders of a person to be crucified, whose hands are fastened to the ends; on arrival at the place of execution the *patibulum* with the condemned man attached, is affixed to a vertical pole, cf. Pl. *Carbonaria* fr. 2 *patibulum ferat per urbem, deinde adfigatur cruci*; see Mommsen, *RStrR*, pp. 918 ff.; J. Schneider in: Kittel, *ThWbNT* s.v. σταυρός (with literature). But a *patibulum* is also (2) a wooden bar, Nonius p. 366, 15 M (= 582 L): *patibulum, sera qua ostia obcluduntur, quod hac remota ualuae pateant.* One may regard as black humour the suggestion that Lamachus now functions more or less as a bar that must be removed if one is to open the *ualuae*. For a contemporary accustomed from early years to find, often shaky, etymological connections and thus linking *patibulum* with *patere, patebat* in line 4 possibly acquires an ominous connotation — afterwards.

gurgustioli: the meaning of this word is rendered correctly by Marg. Molt (on 1, 23 (21, 11)) as "domus parua", "casa"; she is wrong, however, in stating "Tantum hic uocabulum hoc inuenitur", as appears from our passage.

tectum ascendit: vThiel's remark (I, p. 102) "dass er zu diesem Zweck aufs Dach steigt, ist ein realistischer Umstand (vgl. Lukian *v.h.* II 46) auf den Apuleius kaum geachtet hätte" badly undervalues Apuleius and can hardly be taken seriously. Chryseros is unable to leave his house through the door to fetch help and makes the best of the situation by climbing on to the roof — a realistic touch doubtless due to Apuleius' own invention.

One may note the cinematographic effect of the story sequence: *adrepit* (Chrys.)…*clauo* (Chrys.) …*manum ducis nostri* (Lam.) …*repente* (sudden reversal = the attacker attacked)…*nisu* (Chrys.)…*patibulum* (Lam.)…*ascendit* (Chrys.).

82, 11-14 atque inde contentissima uoce clamitans rogansque uicinos et unum quemque proprio nomine ciens et salutis communis admonens diffamat incendio repentino domum suam possideri: "and from there he yelled at the top of his voice calling on his neighbours each by his own name and trying to rouse them. He warned them that they were in danger too because his house was in the grip of a sudden blaze".

contentissima uoce: cf. Cic. *Lig.* 6 *quantum potero uoce contendam*; the superlative occurs here only.

clamitans rogansque uicinos: "Dem weiteren Begriff wird der engere angefügt" (Bernhard p. 168); the expressions are not merely getting narrower but also more precise: *clamitans* (absolute) *rogans uicinos* (more precise) *unum quemque proprio nomine ciens* (still more exact). Pricaeus' conjecture *corrogansque* ("fortasse recte", Robertson) has its attractions (*e.g.* the alliteration with *clamitans*), but it is not necessary.

diffamat: the verb has the primary meaning of spreading an evil rumour: Ov. *Met.* 4, 236 *uulgat adulterium diffamatumque parenti/indicat*; Tac. *Ann.* 14, 22 *se…praua diffamantibus subtraheret*. Apuleius is the first author known to use the word in a neutral or even good sense: 100, 9 *sorores, quarum…formonsitatem nulli diffamarant populi*. Médan (p. 156) speaks of "signification élargie".

incendio repentino domum suam possideri: Chryseros, the miser, is apparently interested not just in money but also in poetry. He is inspired by Hor. *Ep.* 1, 18, 84 *nam tua res agitur, paries cum proximus ardet*. It is true that the expression *mea* (*tua* etc.) *res agitur* is "quasi-proverbial", (see *Nachträge zu Otto* p. 206 (Sutphen)), but it is employed in the contexts of a fire only in Horace and here. The rhetoric to be observed in his words, however, should be attributed to the narrator. For the rest the neighbours

84

might not have reacted if instead of "Fire!" he had shouted "Robbers!".

Sic unus quisque proximi periculi confinio territus sup-
petiatum decurrunt anxii : "So they all, every one of them in a panic
because the danger was so close, came running out anxiously to help".

proximi periculi confinio: once again it becomes clear that Chryseros
does not live as *solitarius* as all that.

confinio: on the use of this word in singular and plural, see de Jonge
p. 77 on 2, 7 (39, 11); cf. 5, 21 (119, 5 f.) *tanti mali confinium sibi ...
metuentes*.

Though *territus* agrees with *unus quisque*, the predicate and the predi-
cative adjective belonging to it are plurals, cf. 10, 5 (240, 8) *quisque prae-
sentium ... insimulabant*; Cypr. *Ep.* 11, 1 *unus quisque sibi placentes et
omnibus displicentes*; see Callebat, *S.C.*, p. 336.

suppetiatum: the verb is not transmitted before Apuleius, except
possibly in Cic. *Att.* 14, 18, 2 where Montegnani wished to restore it *per
coniecturam*; see Médan p. 182, Marg. Molt on 1, 14 (13, 12).

CHAPTER XI

Chryseros' action has placed the robbers in a tight situation. But... aux grands maux les grands remèdes! The tone of the story causes the reader to identify and sympathise with the robbers' mentality to a remarkable degree.

82, 15-18 Tunc nos in ancipiti periculo constituti uel opprimendi nostri uel deserendi socii remedium e re nata ualidum eo uolente comminiscimus: "At that point, faced with the dilemma of either being caught or deserting a comrade, we devised — with his consent — a drastic solution which grew out of the circumstances".

nos: the addition of the first-person pronoun draws the attention away from Chryseros, who so far had been spotlighted, and places the robbers in the centre. The pronoun, then, is not used "sans raison spéciale" (Médan p. 215).

in ancipiti periculo: cf. 7, 19 (168, 16) *ancipiti malo laborabam*; in the other instances in the *Met. anceps* always refers to a double-edged weapon.

constituti: *constitutus* several times functions as a substitute for the present participle of *esse* 7, 8 (160, 8); 10, 29 (260, 16); 11, 21 (283, 9). Schrijnen-Mohrmann I, p. 10 regard this as a loan from legal language; see Callebat, *S.C.*, p 156.

opprimendi nostri: the gerundive construction is used in middle-passive sense and depends on *periculo*; P. A. Aalto, *Untersuchungen*, p. 106 quotes the passage as *uel opprimendi uel deserendi socii remedium e re nata ualidum*, thus allowing the genitive to depend on *remedium*; we do not agree.

e re nata: see comm. on 76, 23.

comminiscimus: thus F, followed by Helm, Robertson, Frassinetti Scazzoso and vThiel; Beroaldus proposed *comminiscimur*, a conjecture favoured by the fact that elsewhere in the *Met.* Apuleius always treats the verb as a deponent with only one exception, 10, 28 (259, 3) *prandio commento* (cf. *Apol.* 34 (40, 16); 58 (66, 9)), an exception which has little force in the present context since the perfect participle of deponents regularly has a passive sense (cf. LHSz p. 139; Ernout-Thomas p. 204). On the other hand a number of verbs, in "classical" Latin deponent, show active forms in Apuleius: Médan p. 12 mentions *adulare, altercare, laetare, percontare*. Callebat, *S.C.*, p. 156 is right in characterizing Beroaldus' proposal as "séduisante" but at the same time it seems best to follow Robertson's decision who notes "fortasse recte" but does not feel free to depart from the ms. reading.

Antesignani nostri partem, qua manus umerum subit, ictu
per articulum medium tem⟨p⟩erato prorsus abscidimus at-
que ibi brachio relicto, multis laciniis offulto uulnere, ne
stillae sanguinis uestigium proderent, ceterum Lamachum
raptim reportamus: "With a blow directed straight through the
joint, we completely severed that part of our leader where the lower arm
joins the upper. We left the arm there, and wrapping the wound in many
rags, lest drops of blood should leave a trail, we hurriedly made off with
the rest of Lamachus".

antisignani nostri partem: "Verdinglichung" of Lamachus' person; just
so *ceterum Lamachum*.

antisignani: once again (cf. 82, 2) a military term used to denote the
leader of the bandits; see Appendix I.

qua manus umerum subit: a precise circumlocution for the elbow, which
immediately afterwards is referred to as *articulum medium*. Lamachus has
put his lower arm through the hole; "aiming" (*ictu temperato* is a justifiable
correction in ς, cf. 56, 14) at the elbow, then, is quite easy. For the safety
measure cf. Hdt. 2, 121 β where, not just the arm but the head is cut off,
and not only with the consent (*eo uolente*) but on the very initiative of the
victim. Fraser on Paus. 5, 177 notes many variants of the tale which
appears to be found in many parts of the world.

raptim reportamus: if we remember how much the robbers like to use
military terminology, the use of *reportare*, a word in military contexts
often employed for bringing away the booty (cf. Cic. *Agr.* 2, 61 *praedam ac
manubias...reportare*) acquires a particularly ironic connotation. Note
the triple repetition of consonants (*r p t*) illustrating the speed of the
action; cf. 5, 23 (121, 7) *patulis ac petulantibus sauiis* (*p t l*); 7, 25 (173, 17)
solutum et solitarium (*s l t*).

Ac dum trepidi religionis urguemur graui tumultu et in-
stantis periculi metu terremur ad fugam...: "And anxious to
do our duty but deeply disturbed and panicked into flight by terror of
our imminent danger..."

trepidi religionis: F's reading is adopted by almost all modern editors;
Helm III² and Helm-Krenkel follow Oudendorp and Eyssenhardt who
read *regionis* with ς; so does vdVliet, who also adopts Pricaeus' *trepidae*;
Hildebrand is right in saying: "*Trepidi religionis* optime dicuntur latrones,
qui de sacramenti fide solliciti, deserere vulneratum Lamachum nolunt.
Eadem fere ratione apud Tacitum legitur: Ann. VI. 21. *trepidus admira-
tionis et metus*;" cf. Latte, *RRG*, p. 39: "Religiosität bedeutet eben für
den Römer nicht eine Gesinnung, die die ganze Persönlichkeit prägt,
sondern die ständige Bereitschaft, auf jedes Anzeichen einer Störung
des gewohnten Verhältnisses zu den Göttern mit einer begütigenden
Handlung zu antworten und einmal übernommenen Verpflichtungen
nachzukommen."

urguemur: it seems unnecessary to follow vThiel's hesitant suggestion to delete the word.

For the genitive with *trepidus* cf. Verg. *A.* 12, 589 *trepidae rerum*; see LHSz p. 81 and the literature mentioned there.

instantis periculi metu: the *anceps periculum* (lines 15, 16) has now become *instans*, cf. Plin. *Ep.* 6, 16, 12 *quamquam nondum periculo appropinquante, conspicuo tamen et, cum cresceret, proximo.*

terremur ad fugam: ThLL has no examples of *terrere ad*, but cf. Sen. *Ben.* 7, 31, 5 *neminem ad excitandas domos ruina deterruit.*

82, 24-25   nec uel sequi propere uel remanere tuto potest uir sublimis animi uirtutisque praecipuus: "while he, so elevated in mind and outstanding in courage, could neither follow us at speed nor stay behind in safety".

uir...praecipuus: if we take *sublimis* as nominative with *uir* (not genitive with *animi*) the arrangement is chiastic; parallelisms precede in *uel sequi propere uel remanere tuto* and follow in *multis adfatibus multisque precibus* and, with anaphora of the preposition, *per dexteram Martis, per fidem sacramenti.*

82, 26-28   multis nos adfatibus multisque precibus querens adhortatur per dexteram Martis, per fidem sacramenti, bonum commilitonem cruciatu simul et captiuitate liberaremus: "with many an appeal and many a prayer he tearfully adjures us by Mars' right hand and our solemn bond of friendship to rescue a good comrade simultaneously from torment and from captivity."

adfatibus: see vdP. p. 55; for the use of the plural of abstract nouns in *-us* see Bernhard pp. 101 ff.

per dexteram Martis: once again a wry sort of humour: the man who has just lost his (right) arm (though not precisely in a valiant fight) invokes the right arm of the god of war to exhort his fleeing comrades. See Tatum (1969) p. 503.

per fidem sacramenti: see vdP. p. 188 and Chr. Mohrmann, *Études* 1², pp. 237 ff., who emphasizes the almost always neglected sense of "lien", "union sacrée".

nos...adhortatur...liberaremus: an asyndetic construction in which Médan p. 17 notes that the rules of the sequence of tenses have been neglected; see however LHSz p. 551 and J. Lebreton, *Études sur la langue et la grammaire de Cicéron*, Paris 1901, p. 239.

cruciatu simul et captiuitate liberaremus: the word *cruciatu* may refer (1) to the terrible physical pain Lamachus is at present suffering or (2) to his prospective torture; the captivity is certainly prospective. In the case of (1) *liberare* means "to free from", in the case of (2) "to keep free from", *captiuitate liberare* in any case means "to keep (free) from being captured". It seems preferable, partly in view of the added *simul*, to

88

regard both nouns as referring to a prospective situation; this interpretation avoids a zeugmatic use of *liberare*. For the underlying thought cf. Sen. *Tro.* 329 *mortem misericors saepe pro uita dabit*.

Cur enim manui, quae rapere et iu⟨gu⟩lare sola posset, 82, 29-30
fortem latronem superuiuere?: "For why should a brave robber survive his hand, that could rob and throttle as no other?" The emotionally loaded rhetorical question (see LHSz p. 467) is rendered in *oratio obliqua* by the reporting robber. Thus the latter adds a humorous touch of relativity. The exclamation itself possibly parodies formulas used in the *declamationes* of the rhetorical schools, as well as Stoic tenets concerning suicide (cf. Sen. *Ep.* 77).
rapere et iugulare: We become aware of this characteristic now for the first time and from the man himself: it had not been said or implied before. The fact that Lamachus picks out these activities marks the robber's ethic.
sola: in this instance not "alone" but rather "as no other", cf. Ter. *Ph.* 854 *sine controuersia ab dis solus diligere*; *Fl.* 3 (3, 8 ff.) *Hyagnis fuit ...rudibus adhuc musicae saeculis solus ante alios catus canere.* See on this "steigerndes *solus*" Löfstedt, *Verm. Stud.*, pp. 183-185.
manui superuiuere: as if robber and hand each have an independent existence.

Sat se beatum, qui manu socia uolens occumberet: "He 82, 30-83,1
would count himself lucky to die voluntary at the hand of a comrade". Whereas according to Hor. *S.* 1, 1, 117 only rarely someone may be found *qui se uixisse beatum dicat*, our robber of all people in his dangerous situation thinks he may apply the statement to himself; cf. also Catul. 23, 26 f. *et sestertia quae soles precari/centum desine: nam sat es beatus*; see comm. on 6, 28 (150, 3-5).
occumberet: it is hard to decide whether the speaker in direct speech used a present or a future tense.

Cumque nulli nostrum spontale parricidium suadens per- 83, 1-4
suadere posset, manu reliqua sumptum gladium suum diu-
que deosculatum per medium pectus ictu fortissimo trans-
adigit: "When he failed, for all his urging, to persuade any of us to commit parricide on a willing victim, he drew his sword with his surviving hand, kissed it for a long time and thrust it with a powerful stroke through the middle of his breast".
spontale parricidium: the adjective *spontalis* according to the ThLL material at Munich occurs in only one other place: Apul. *Met.* 11, 30 (291, 2) *spontali sobrietate*; the adverb *spontaliter* is read in Sid. Apol. *Ep.* 8, 9, 2 *idque non modo non coactus uerum etiam spontaliter facio*; in our passage *spontale* does not mean "spontaneous", "voluntary",

i.e. "willed by the acting subject", but "desired by the object of the action".

spontale...persuadere: if not an oxymoron (see Médan p. 327, Bernhard pp. 238 f.), at least a paradox.

suadens persuadere: on word-play in general in Apuleius see Médan pp. 310 ff., Bernhard pp. 228 ff., Callebat, *S.C.*, pp. 470 ff. (under the latter's heading "Jeu verbal entre forme simple et composée" this passage may be added).

parricidium: the use of this word is in full accord with Paul. *Sent.* 5, 24, 1 *lege Pompeia de parricidiis tenetur, qui patrem, matrem, auum, auiam, fratrem, sororem, patruelem, matruelem...patronum, patronam... occiderit* and Fest. p. 247 L (= 221 M) *parricida non utique is, qui parentem occidisset dicebatur, sed qualemcumque hominem indemnatum.* Cic. *Tusc.* 5, 6 makes a neat transferred use of the word: *uituperare quisquam uitae parentem (i.e. philosophiam) et hoc parricidio se inquinare audet...?* See Koestermann on Tac. *Ann.* 15, 73, 3; Summers pp. 166-168.

diuque deosculatum: note the alliteration and assonance: in *deosculatum* *e* before *ō* approximates *i* (E. H. Sturtevant, *The Pronunciation of Greek and Latin*, Philadelphia²1940, p. 112) and *ō* in this word differs but little from *ū* in *diu* (Sturtevant, *ibid.* pp. 116 f.). Concerning *deosculatum* see de Jonge p. 53 on 2, 10 (33, 18) and vdP. p. 177 on 3, 24 (70, 5) where there is a similar situation with regard to the ointment-box; see further P. Flobert, *Les verbes déponents latins*, Paris 1975, pp. 364 (where Ennod. *Ep.* 6, 23 should read 5, 23) and 369.

gladium suum...per medium pectus...transadigit: cf. Verg. *A.* 12, 508 *crudum/transadigit costas et cratis pectoris ensem.* The addition *suum* ("his very own...") possibly accentuates the contrast with *nulli nostrum*.

83, 4-6 Tunc nos magnanimi ducis uigore uenerato corpus reliquum ues[ti]te lintea diligenter conuolutum mari celandum commisimus: "Then we paid hommage to the strength of our noble leader, carefully wrapped the remainder of his body in a linen cloth and entrusted him to the sea to conceal".

uenerato: perfect part. of deponent verb here also used in a passive sense (cf. *deosculatum*). The usual term for a funerary eulogy is *laudare*; Apuleius uses *uenerari* with regard to gods or at least in a religious context; the one exception — apart from this place — is 102, 1, where Psyche says to her parents: *quid lacrimis inefficacibus ora mihi ueneranda foedatis?* We may safely conclude that the word (like *trepidi religionis*) indicates the robbers' particular attachment to their *antesignanus* who is also their *socius*.

ueste: F has *uestitū*, in which *ū* has apparently been added by a later hand to replace *e*, φ has *uestite*; modern editors read *ueste* (Kronenberg *uesti*, but elsewhere mss. always have abl. *ueste*) following Lütjohann, who feels that *uestite* has resulted from contamination of *uesti* and *ueste*, citing a comparable case at 1, 11 (10, 21), where he argues *commodum* and *commodo* have been contaminated into *commododum*.

mari celandum commisimus: scholars proposed various solutions to the difficulty that (Boeotian) Thebes is situated at a considerable distance from the sea and that Lamachus therefore cannot be entrusted to the sea on the spot. Bétolaud notes p 430: "La scène se passe à Thèbes, où coulait le fleuve Ismène, dans lequel le corps de Lamachus fut jeté, le porta dans la mer, et qu'ainsi on a pu dire, par une sorte d'anticipation, qu'il avait été jeté dans la mer. Peut-être, d'ailleurs, Apulée n'y a-t-il pas regardé de si près".

According to Walsh p. 158, n. 2 we have to do with "a typical Apuleian loose end"; Perry, too, speaks of "self-contradiction or logical absurdity" (*Anc. Rom.*, p. 254); we may compare Pl. *Am.*, in which play the harbour (of Thebes!) has an important function in the action, and Pl. *Epid.* in which Thesprio travels from Thebes to Athens by sea and thus creates unnecessary difficulties for himself, see vdP. p. 74.

vThiel I, p. 103 is of the opinion that in the "Vorlage" Thebai Phthiotides which is near the sea was referred to, but that Apuleius transferred the action to Boeotian Thebes by his addition *heptapylos* (81, 14) — see however already 80, 22 — and that he "ohnehin das Itinerarium des Originals (änderte) weil ihm dessen geographische Genauigkeit nicht bewusst oder gleichgültig war". Against this interpretation one may raise the basic objection that thus the novel is seen merely as a mimesis of existing reality and that the novel's own world is ignored (see also note on 85, 5 *domesticis uenationibus*).

celandum: Helm-Krenkel translate "um sie zu bergen", Vitali: "lo affidammo alla custodia del mare"; *celandum*, however, does not so much express the notion that the body is given to the sea to *keep* or *hold* (for which *seruandum* is the appropriate word) but to *hide*; Brandt-Ehlers translate correctly: "ihre Spur zu verwischen". Apparently the robbers do not yet feel safe. Van Thiel's remark (I, p. 103), then, is not entirely right: "Danach (i.e. nach dem Selbstmord des Lamachus) aber besteht offenbar keine Gefahr mehr; die Räuber finden genügend Zeit, den Leichnam einzuhüllen, zum Meer zu tragen und darin zu versenken." At best one may say that the danger is no longer acute.

Et nunc iacet noster Lamachus elemento toto sepultus: 83, 6-7
"And now our friend Lamachus is at rest, with an entire element as his grave". Active as he was a short moment ago, the warrior has now found his peace. Like *sedere* (see note on 85, 11) *iacere* is often used with an implication of utter inactivity (OLD).

iacet noster Lamachus: the subject follows the predicate; cf. Verg. *A.* 2, 557 (here too the body has been mutilated)*iacet ingens litore truncus*.

elemento toto sepultus: Bernhard p. 215 incorrectly mentions this passage as an instance of hypallage of the adjective (it is not even necessary to remark in this respect that Lamachus lacks an arm).

Note the highly rhetorical use of language at the end of the chapter:

anaphora and homoeoteleuton	*multis...adfatibus multisque precibus*
anaphora	*per dexteram Martis, per fidem sacramenti*
interrogatio	*cur enim manui ... fortem latronem superuiuere*
annominatio	*suadens persuadere*

CHAPTER XII

The clever plans of the second robber are foiled by an old woman.

Et ille quidem dignum uirtutibus suis uitae terminum 83, 8-9
posuit: "And whereas he at least brought his life to an end worthy of his
qualities..."

dignum uirtutibus suis: the qualification sounds serious or ironic ac-
cording as one hears the voice of the robber-narrator or the author
Apuleius; the same applies to *sollertibus coeptis* below.

uitae terminum posuit; for the circumlocution see Bernhard p. 184,
Médan p. 240; the expression may (but does not always) indicate suicide,
cf. Cic. *Sen.* 23, 82 *si eisdem finibus gloriam meam, quibus uitam essem*
terminaturus.

Enim uero Alcimus sollertibus coeptis †eum† saeuum For- 83, 9-10
tunae nutum non potuit abducere: "Alcimus on the other hand
could not keep Fortune's adverse gaze from his clever enterprise".

enim uero: the contrast lies in the fact that Alcimus true enough
(*quidem*) is called as brave as Lamachus, but that he does not end his life
as gloriously; Alcimus' activities for that matter do not show up his
courage either. For the adversative sense of *enim uero* see Médan p. 232;
Furneaux on Tac. *Ann.* 2, 64.

eum saeuum: F has *eũ sęuũ*, φ offers *eu sęç̆ũ*, both the *u* above the *c*
and the dot underneath having been added by a different hand. The
younger manuscripts have *tamen saeuum*, the reading adopted by Helm;
the chief objection to *eum* is that the adjectival use of this pronoun is
extremely rare in Apul. (Callebat, *S.C.*, p. 266; Wolterstorff p. 200).
Different scholars have proposed different solutions; we only mention
some of them: Giarratano deletes *eum*, and is followed by Terzaghi and
Scazzoso; Armini (1932) p. 74 reads *eo saeuum*; his example is followed
by Robertson, Frassinetti, Vitali, *eo* meaning "thither", i.e. *ad dignum*
uirtutibus suis uitae terminum; Heraeus' conjecture *consecuum* is accepted
by Brandt-Ehlers, *consecuum* meaning "in accordance with"; this con-
jecture is palaeographically attractive, but according to ThLL the word
is not attested before the 5th cent. (Sid. *Ep.* 7, 14, 9 and Mamert. *St. An.*
138, 5); the adverb *conseque* has been restored *per coniecturam* by Lach-
mann at Lucr. 5, 679; Blümner, followed by Gaselee, reads *minus saeuum*,
Castiglioni (1931) proposed *saeuum scaeuae*. Each of these solutions has its
charms and its difficulties; we have not come to a decision.

adducere is the reading in F; Giarratano and Castiglioni (1931) read

93

with ς *abducere*; in view of 10, 24 (255, 17 ff.) *sed haec...feralem Fortunae nutum latere non potuerunt*, the reading *abducere* is to be preferred; for "*nutus*" = "eyes", "glands" see 6, 28 (150, 2).

83, 10-11 Qui cum dormientis anus perfracto tuguriolo conscendisset cubiculum superius...: "For having broken into the cottage of an old woman while she slept and having gone up to the upper bedroom..."

tuguriolo: according to Médan p. 135 a neologism that occurs also in Arn. 6, 3 and Hier. *Ep.* 112, 5.

83, 12-13 iamque protinus oblisis faucibus interstinguere eam debuisset: "and though he should have bumped her off at once by throttling her".

interstinguere: as appears from ThLL the word occurs rarely and in the senses of *exstinguere, restinguere, interimere*; in the latter, transferred, sense it is used here; cf. Lucr. 5, 761 (*aurae*) *quae faciunt ignis interstingui atque perire*.

debuisset: the robber-narrator knows exactly what his fallen comrade should have done.

83, 13-14 prius maluit rerum singula per latiorem fenestram forin-secus nobis scilicet rapienda dispergere: "he preferred first to throw her things out one by one through a fairly large window, for us to grab them of course".

scilicet, like *debuisset*, has something of the tone of an unregenerate schoolmaster; see also the note on 88, 18.

rerum singula: see comm. on 75, 18; 88, 18; Bernhard p. 107.

per latiorem fenestram: pour le besoin de la cause the *tuguriolum* improbably has a large window, on the upper story at that, cf. Scobie on 1, 16 (15, 1): "the window is high up from the floor and therefore probably small!"

forinsecus = *foras*: "out of the house"; see vdP. pp. 162 f.

83, 14-19 Cumque iam cuncta rerum nauiter emolitus nec toro qui-dem aniculae quiescentis parcere uellet eaque lectulo suo deuoluta uestem stragulam subductam scilicet iactare si-militer destinaret, genibus eius profusa sic nequissima illa deprecatur: "And when he had done a thorough job of heaving out all the stuff, he did not want to spare even the bed that the old woman was lying in, but meant to roll her out of her bed, drag the bed-clothes from under her — just imagine — and throw them out; but the rotten old hag threw herself at his feet and pleaded with him:"

94

nauiter, meaning "diligently", "actively", "zealously", is spoken with approval by the narrator-robber, though in Lucius' mouth it has an ironic tinge.

emolitus: as if throwing the old woman's things were a *moles*; once again irony.

nec...quidem: pleonastic use, equivalent to *ne...quidem* or *nec*; see Bernhard p. 123, Callebat, *S.C.*, p. 334.

toro: *torus* is mostly used in poetry, but is here employed ironically to signify the simple *lectulus* in the *tuguriolum* of the *anicula*.

aniculae quiescentis: after *dormientis anus* in lines 10 f., the repetition of the idea here ensures that both Alcimus' *uirtus* and his *sollertia* are shown in a dubious light; but from the robber's point of view the disastrous outcome is attributed to the old woman's *nequitia* (line 18).

lectulo suo: the addition here of *suo*, in itself superfluous (LHSz pp. 178 f.), is not merely a case of "umgangssprachliche Verwendung des Possessivpronomens" (Hofmann, *LU*, p. 137) but also a humorous touch ("her own bed"); also humorous is the use of *deuoluta* (instead of e.g. *deiecta*) as if the *anicula* has no will of her own and is a mere object that allows itself to be rolled away by a robber: the future will show him...

uestem stragulam: στρώματα; the combination of words is found eight times (in this or the reverse order) in Cicero's *Verrinae*; cf. Hor. *S.* 2, 3, 118. Isid. *Orig.* 19, 26, 1 remarks: *stragulum uestis est discolor quod manu artificis diuersa uarietate distinguitur*: *dictum autem quod et in stratu et in amictu aptus sit*. Blümner, *Privataltertümer* ³1911, p. 116 points out that a person lying in bed pulls *tapetia*, περιστρώματα over himself, while the *uestes stragulae* are spread underneath; this fits in with *subductam* in our passage.

subductam scilicet: "which, just imagine, he had dragged from under her"; Castiglioni (1931) p. 477 feels the use of *scilicet* in the context is inexplicable; various translators (Adlington-Gaselee, Vallette, Brandt-Ehlers) appear to ignore the word; Helm-Krenkel translate "natürlich"; *scilicet* is used here not just expressively and somewhat ironically, but it also maintains the narrator's perspective.

iactare: though *frequentativa-intensiva* in later Latin are often used in the meaning of the primitive verb (LHSz p. 297), *iactare* here has its full intensive sense and hence is very expressive; cf. *abiceret* (84, 1).

genibus eius profusa: In order to explain the well-known gesture, used from Homer onwards, Plin. *Nat.* 11, 250 remarks: *Hominis genibus quaedam et religio inest obseruatione gentium. Haec supplices attingunt, ad haec manus tendunt, haec ut aras adorant, fortassis quia inest iis uitalitas. Namque in ipsa genus utriusque commissura, dextra laeuaque, a priore parte gemina quaedam buccarum inanitas inest, qua perfossa ceu iugulo spiritus fluit*; see also ThLL VI 1878, 35 ff. and Onians, *Origins* pp. 180, 185. In Apul. also 9, 40 (233, 25) *simulansque sese ad commouendam miserationem genua eius uelle contingere*. The gesture has — at least in literature — a long life: Verg. *A.* 3, 607 f. *dixerat et genua amplexus geni-*

busque uolutans/haerebat. Choderlos de Laclos, *Les liaisons dangereuses*, lettre 90: "Je me suis avancé pour la secourir, mais elle prenant mes mains qu'elle baignait de pleurs, quelquefois même embrassant mes genoux: "Oui, ce sera vous, disait-elle, ce sera vous qui me sauverez".

nequissima illa: cf. 82, 5 *omnium bipedum nequissimus Chryseros.* According to Wolterstorff pp. 218 ff. this is one of the instances where Apuleius uses *ille* merely in order to substantize an adjective. *illa* itself, he feels, is used here as a weakly substantive notion joined by the adjective; the latter remark may be left to the author's responsibility. See vdP. p. 186 on pejoratively used *ille*.

83, 19-21 "Quid oro, fili, paupertinas pannosasque resculas miserrimae anus donas uicinis diuitibus, quorum haec fenestra domum prospicit?":"Why, my son, I beg you, are you giving these miserable ragged little possessions of a poor old body to the rich neighbours whose house this window overlooks?".

quid in the sense of *cur* appears to be borrowed from the *sermo cotidianus.* According to Callebat, *S.C.*, p. 92 it gives the question more animation and a more emotional character, it produces a pause before the actual question is asked. That aspect is strengthened here by the parenthetic insertion of *oro* (Bernhard p. 51) and the vocative *fili.*

fili: sometimes used more or less gently or even tenderly — or in order to mollify! — to a person younger than the speaker and not a blood relation; thus e.g. 9, 27 (223, 22) *Nihil triste de me tibi, fili, metuas* (the miller to the youthful lover of his wife).

paupertinas pannosasque: functional alliteration in an expression consisting of two similar parts (Bernhard p. 220): one hears the old woman's stutter.

paupertinas: "poor", "measly"; see Médan p. 175; Callebat, *S.C.*, p. 479; vdP. p. 100.

pannosas: "patched", "tattered", cf. Hor. *Ars* 15 *unus et alter/adsuitur pannus*; P.G. van Wees in a review of Callebat, *S.C.*, *Gnomon* 44 (1972), pp. 781 f. points out that the word is used of a thing (rather than a person) only here in the whole of Latin literature.

resculas: on *rescula/recula* (the reading in ς) see Leumann p. 216 and the literature on diminutives mentioned there; Callebat, *S.C.*, p. 509; van Wees p. 783.

quorum haec fenestra domum prospicit: a striking hyperbaton such as Apuleius likes to use (Möbitz p. 124). Bernhard feels that such an hyperbaton often produces an "anwiderndes, der...Situation...keineswegs angemessenes Pathos"; however the circumstances give the woman every reason for pathos; the fact that Apuleius expresses this so well in her choice of words is not surprising: Photis, too, who, at least in the Greek version, is unable to read and write, uses (3, 15 ff.) well chosen language (*lepidus sermo* 3, 19 (66, 4)), see vdP. pp. 119 f. For *prospicere* in the present sense cf. Hor. *Ep.* 1, 10, 23 *laudaturque domus longos quae prospicit agros.*

Quo sermone, callido deceptus astu et uera quae dicta sunt 83,21-84,3
credens Alcimus, uerens scilicet ne et ea quae prius miserat,
quaeque postea mis⟨s⟩urus foret, non sociis suis, sed in
alienos lares iam certus erroris abiceret, suspendit se fe-
nestra sagaciter perspecturus omnia, praesertim domus
attiguae quam dixerat illa, fortunas arbitraturus: "At
these words, misled by her clever ruse and thinking that what she said
was true, Alcimus of course was afraid, that the was throwing not only
all he had earlier thrown out but also what he still had to throw (con-
vinced of his error though he was) not to his comrades but into someone
else's yard; so he leaned out of the window to get a really good look at
everything, especially to make a guess at the wealth of the neighbours
the woman had mentioned". There is no need to place *astu* after *quae*
with Leo or to read with Blümner *ficta* for *dicta.* As appears from punctu-
ation and translation we prefer to combine *callido* with *astu,* cf. Sen.
Tro. 523 *nectit pectore astus callidos* ; Amm. 15, 5, 5 *astu callido consarcinata
materia.*

et ea, quae...quaeque: "not only what he..., but also what he";
for the combination *et...que* cf. Brut. Cas. *Fam.* 11, 13a, 5 *paratissimi et
ab exercitu reliquisque rebus* ; Plin. *Nat.* 15, 106 *communia et pomis omni-
busque sucis* ; see Bernhard p. 82.

miserat...missurus foret: for the use of subjunctive after preceding
indicative in equivalent phrases cf. 11, 9 (273, 16) *frequentabant...prae-
dicarent* ; see Médan p. 100; *foret* for *esset*: Médan p. 6.

non sociis suis, sed in alienos lares...abiceret: on the variation of con-
struction (here dative and prepositional phrase) see Médan p. 336; the
relation to *abiceret* here is not, however, entirely the same in the two cases:
sociis suis denotes an interested party, *in alienos lares* merely gives the
direction of the movement; see de Jonge on 2, 5 (29, 4 f.).

iam certus erroris: Alcimus is afraid that he, "though convinced already
of his error" is going to give the remainder, too, a wrong destination;
Blümner's transposition of these words after *abiceret* (resulting in a qualifi-
cation of *suspendit se fenestra*) has little to commend itself.

suspendit se fenestra: Alcimus just leans from the window; since, how-
ever, *se suspendere* is often (most often?) used in the sense of "hang one-
self" (e.g. Pl. *Rud.* 1415; id. *Trin.* 536; Cic. *de Orat.* 2, 278; Quint. *Inst.*
6, 3, 88) there may be, in view of the outcome, an ominous undertone
to the word.

sagaciter: basically used of an animal's sense of smell: Col. 7, 12, 7
(*Canes*) *si et aduenientem sagaciter odorantur* ; Plin. *Nat.* 10, 88 *uultures
sagacius odorantur.* The transition to metaphorical use is illustrated in
Cic. *de Orat.* 2, 186 *ut odorer, quam sagacissime possim, quid* (*iudices*)
sentiant.

On *sagire* and its derivates see Cic. *Div.* 1, 65 *sagire sentire acute est: ex quo sagae anus, quia multa scire uolunt; et sagaces dicti canes. Is igitur, qui ante sagit quam oblata res est, dicitur praesagire, id est futura ante sentire.*

attiguae quam: F reads *attigua* (*-ue?*) *ut* (*nt?*); according to Robertson the rewritten letters may hide *attigue quam*; the reading we have adopted is found in ç and is printed by modern editors.

arbitraturus: on *arbitrari* = *spectare* see vdP. p. 159.

84, 3-4 Quod eum strenue quidem, ⟨s⟩et satis inprouide conantem senile illud facinus...: "While he was trying to do this — energetically enough but rather heedlessly — that criminal old bag..."

set: F reads *et*. Colvius, followed by Oudendorp, proposed *sed*; Petschenig's *set* is palaeographically better, cf. Velius Longus (p. 70 Keil): '*sed*' *uero coniunctio, quamuis lex grammaticorum per t litteram dicat, quoniam d littera nulla coniunctio terminatur, nescio quo modo obrepsit auribus nostris et d litteram sonat cum dicimus*

> *progeniem sed enim Troiano a sanguine duci audierat.*

ubi quaerendum erat, contrane ac loquimur scribendum sit, an secundum scriptionem loquendum.

facinus: metonymy to indicate the person, cf. Cic. *Phil.* 11, 10 *Lucium fratrem* (*secum habet*): *quam facem, di immortales, quod facinus, quod scelus, quem gurgitem, quam uoraginem!*; Sal. *Cat.* 14, 1 *Catilina...omnium flagitiorum atque facinorum circum se tamquam stipatorum cateruas habebat.* See Médan p. 165, Callebat, *S.C.*, p. 85.

84, 4-7 quanquam inualido, repentino tamen et inopinato pulsu nutantem ac pendulum et in prospectu alioquin attonitum praeceps inegit: "gave him a shove, which, though feeble, was yet sudden and unexpected; as he was wobbling as he hung over the sill, and was moreover entirely engrossed in his examination, she sent him headlong". Note the multiple repetition of consonants, in particular *p* and *t*, as well as the melodious vowel variation.

repentino et inopinato: the second of the two coordinate adjectives gives the result of the first; similarly the second adjective in the combination *nutantem ac pendulum* serves to explain the first; see Bernhard p. 166.

alioquin: see comm. on 74, 18 and 76, 10.

in...attonitum: for the meaning "engrossed in" cf. 92, 10 *huic me operi attonitum clara lux oppressit.*

praeceps: here used as an adverb; see comm. on 78, 7 and Nipperdey on Tac. *Ann.* 4, 62.

inegit: according to ThLL *inigere* is used especially of animals, and by

98

extension also of a ship or a human (one instance of each); Alcimus, then, who wished to roll the old woman out of her bed as if she were an object, is himself now being pushed round by her as if he were an animal; see Médan p. 156.

Qui praeter altitudinem nimiam super quendam etiam uas- 84, 7-11
tissimum lapidem propter iacentem decidens perfracta dif-
fissaque crate costarum riuos sanguinis uomens imitus
narratisque nobis, quae gesta sunt, non diu cruciatus
uitam euasit:"As well as falling from a great height, he also landed
on a huge boulder lying nearby; his ribs cracked and burst open, and
he coughed up streams of blood from deep inside him, while he told us
what had happened. He was not long in agony before he escaped from
life".

quendam: see the note on 76, 6.

propter: FA show *praeter* (F rewritten), α has *prope*; Philomathes'
conjecture is accepted by modern editors.

diffissa: Hildebrand retains F's *diffusa*, and he is followed by Eyssen-
hardt, Helm, Giarratano-Frassinetti, Terzaghi, Scazzoso, vThiel; *diffissa*,
Beroaldus' conjecture is adopted by Oudendorp, vdVliet, Gaselee, Rob-
ertson (who cites 9, 40 (233, 24) *cerebrum diffindere*), Brandt-Ehlers,
Vitali.

The objection to *diffusa* is that in a literal sense it mostly refers to
liquids spreading from a central point. Hildebrand argued against *diffissa*
since the word is synonymous with preceding *perfracta*, but after Bern-
hard's discussion (esp. p. 168) of the "Synonymik koordinierter Begriffe"
which are characteristic of Apuleius (pp. 164-170) that objection can no
longer be used; we therefore adopt Beroaldus' conjecture,

crate costarum: note the functional alliteration; cf. Verg. *A.* 12, 508
transadigit costas et crates pectoris ensem; Ov. *Met.* 12, 370 (*hasta*) *laterum
cratem perrupit*.

riuos sanguinis uomens: cf. Verg. *A.* 11, 668 *sanguinis ille uomens
riuos cadit*; see Gatscha p 145.

uomens...narratisque: for the shift from participle in agreement with
the subject to ablative absolute see Bernhard pp. 42 f.

Quem prioris exemplo sepulturae traditum bonum secu- 84, 11-12
torem Lamacho dedimus: "We buried him as we had his predecessor,
and so gave Lamachus a worthy aide-de-camp".

sepulturae traditum: cf. Justin. 9, 4, 4 *bello consumptorum corpora
sepulturae reddidit* (referring to cremation); id. 12, 2, 15 *Corpus eius
Thurini publice redemptum sepulturae tradiderunt*.

Though the activities of the second robber do not precisely show
heroism, bodily strength or cleverness, the narrator attempts to suggest
that those were indeed Alcimus' qualities; *sollertia coepta* are ascribed to

him and when they prove unsuccessful this is felt to be due to Fortune's envy, but in fact they are prevented by an old woman who, when disturbed in her sleep, shows a great deal more *sollertia* than does her attacker; for forcible entry into a *tuguriolum* the word *perfringere* is surely too strong an expression; *conscendere cubiculum superius* equally suggests a less modest dwelling; the simple job of throwing out the poor possessions is glorified by the exaggerated phrase *nauiter emoliri*.

It is curious that the robbers apparently do not think of taking revenge on the old woman, but Heine's remark (p. 158) about Apuleius' *Met.* in general, applies here, too: after the climax in a story has been reached the characters lose their importance and drop from view.

CHAPTER XIII

The robbers give up and go to Plataeae, where they watch in wonder Demochares' rich and complicated preparations for a fair, at which bears are the main attraction.

Tunc orbitati⟨s⟩ duplici plaga petiti iamque Thebanis cona- _{84, 13-15}tibus abnuentes Plataeas proximam conscendimus ciuita-tem : "Then, assailed by the blows of a double loss and finally abandoning our Theban attempts, we went up the hill to Plataeae, the nearest town."
    tunc...petiti: cf. 102, 5 *Inuidiae nefariae plaga percussi*; for the passive use of *petere* with an abl. instr. see e.g. 10, 8 (243, 12) *falsis criminibus petito reo* (at 11, 20 (281, 28 f.) *spondeo* is probably to be taken with *libat* rather than *petitum*). The abl. instr. also at 100, 17, cf. L.S. *s.v.* II A; *petere* passively also e.g. Curt. 6, 1, 4 *(rex)...undique...petebatur*.
    Thebanis conatibus: Bernhard (p. 21) remarks that Apuleius prefers to put adjectives derived from proper names before their nouns.
    abnuere has the same construction at 6, 6 (132, 15) *At Venus terrenis remediis inquisitionis abnuens*; ThLL mistakenly also cites *Apol.* 76 (85, 8). Cf. *Paneg.* 7 (6), 9, 3 (p. 210, 18 f. Mynors) *sic quoque tibi rei publicae curis non erat abnuendum*. Médan p. 43, ThLL *s.v.* 113, 72 ff. regard *conatibus* as a dative, OLD *s.v.* 8 states that we have to do with an intransitive usage with ablative. Non liquet.
    Plataeas proximam conscendimus civitatem: Médan regards *conscendimus* as an "expression renouvelée" (p. 246). Cf. Eutr. 7, 13, 4 *conscendenti Capitolium*; it is synonymous with *ascendimus*: Plataeae is situated on the slopes of Mt. Cithaeron.
    civitatem: see vdP. p. 41.
    The period consists of three cola of equal length, the first two end with the verbal element, the third varies the pattern by inverting object and verb, thereby also producing a strong clausula (cretic + ditrochee).

Ibi famam celebrem super quo[n]dam Demochare munus _{84, 15-16}edituro gladiatorium deprehendimus: "There we caught up with the general topic of conversation, which concerned a man called Demochares, who was about to present gladiatorial games". For the paratactic character of the chapter see Bernhard p. 39. The same author (p. 256) also uses the passage to show that Apuleius employs a single style for all his characters. See also vdP. p. 119. Eicke, pp. 117 ff., disagrees.
    super quodam Demochare: on *super* instead of *de* see Callebat, *S.C.*,

pp. 237 f. Cf. 7, 1 (154, 16); 8, 21 (193, 12). Add *Soc.* 4 (11, 16), 10 (18, 12) etc.

Demochare: though in view of the numerous instances of this name collected in Pape and Forcellini it must have been a reasonably common one, there can be little doubt that Apuleius makes use of it as a significant name: "Peoplepleaser". Cf. Pricaeus: *"Democharis nomen, ut et aliorum multorum, ad negotium praesens accommodavit"*. Helm (Praef. *Fl.* pp. XXXII f.) seems to have been the first to notice (if we read his inverted commas aright) that Apuleius on several occasions explains his significant names. Cf. Junghanns p. 124, n. 9. Thus Demochares is, apart from his rank and riches, a *uir liberalitate praecipuus* who, more to the point, *publicas uoluptates instruebat* (84, 18; cf. 85, 9). Similarly BARBARUS 9, 17 (215, 11) is explained by his nickname Scorpio which he has been given *prae morum acritudine*: cf. the reference to the name 223, 22 f.; CANDIDUS gets its explanation 282, 10 in the words *equum...candidum*. In the case of CERDO it is clearly the whole story that explains the name, but in particular the words *negotiator...diem commodum peregrinationi cupiens*: 2, 13, (35, 22). See on this name I. van Wageningen, *Cerdo, sive de nominibus propriis Latinis appellativorum loco adhibitis, Mnemosyne* 40 (1912), pp. 147-172. DIOPHANES, in the same story, has an ironic name, see comm. on Babulus (85, 18). CHARITE, quite in character, *gratias summas ...meminisse non destitit* 7, 14 (164, 23 f.); CHRYSEROS 81, 17 ff. is a *nummularius copiosae pecuniae dominus* particularly characterized by the words *aureos folles incubabat*. HAEMUS, 7, 5 (158, 13) is *humano sanguine nutritus*; are we to understand that Tlepolemus uses the same story-telling technique that his creator uses? (See for a different explanation, Walsh p. 161, n. 1: "a jocose play on Mt. Haemus"). LAMACHUS 80, 22, probably understood as "he who fights for the people", is characterized by *duce fortissimo* and *sublimis uexillarius noster* (82, 2). Apuleius has Byrrhena characterize PAMPHILE fully and fluently 2, 5 (29, 5 ff.) *nam simul quemque conspexerit speciosae formae iuuenem, uenustate eius sumitur et ilico in eum et oculum et animum detorquet. Serit blanditias, inuadit spiritum, amoris profundi pedicis aeternis alligat.* PHILEBUS 8, 25 (197, 13) is named after his *puellae* i.e. his *chorus cinaedorum*. PHILESITHERUS' name is explained in the words *ardentem...uigilantiam* 9, 18 (216, 7). Though THELYPHRON calls himself a man of iron, 2, 23 (44, 2), Byrrhena is able to prevail upon him to tell the story of his loss of face (*perfecit, ut uellet* 42, 9). Haemus' father THERON is the hunter: 7, 5 (158, 12) *patre Therone aeque latrone inclito prognatus*; whether or not we keep the reading *atque* and give it epexegetic sense, Apuleius explains here also. For THIASUS a whole chapter, 10, 18 (250, 16-251, 10), serves as an explanation. The name THRASYLEON gets an immediate comment (86, 8 f.) in *ancipitis machinae subiuit aleam* and once again in *constanti uigore* (86, 17). In the case of THRASYLLUS the name serves as the climax of the preceding characterization: *luxuriae popinalis scortisque et diurnis potationibus exercitatus atque ob id factionibus latronum male sociatus nec non etiam manus infectus humano cruore, Thrasyllus nomine* 8, 1 (177, 7).

TLEPOLEMUS on the other hand seems to be left unexplained except in so far as he dares undertake a considerable campaign in order to regain his bride 7, 12 (163, 7). An explanation of the name, then, is found within the text itself in some 15 cases, enough to speak of a technique; and Apuleius confirms his technique at 8, 8 (182, 14): *Thrasyllus, praeceps alioquin et de ipso nomine temerarius*, see Heine p. 152, n. 3. This technique gives a notable, though not always immediately explicable, emphasis to the significant quality of the names. In the case of Demochares it adds to the unreal and ideal quality of this man as the intended victim of the robbers' subsequent attempt: one of the immediate results of a significant name is the reduction of the character involved to its essential function for the plot. Demochares pleases the people by his liberality, he pleases the robbers because of the wealth that allows him to be liberal, but beyond this we make his acquaintance no more than that of Babulus below. The same applies to the other significant names. If "each 'appellation' is a kind of vivifying, animizing, individuating" (Wellek and Warren p. 219), the type of appellation chosen by Apuleius in these cases is a highly economical one. Simple functionality, too, characterizes the names of (9, 2 (203, 25 ff.)) *Myrtilus mulio, Hefaestio cocus* and *Apollonius medicus*, Myrtilus being the charioteer of Oinomaus (Schol. Soph. *El.* 505), Hephaestus keeping the home fires burning (Roscher *s.v.* 2036 f., Wissowa p. 231) and Apollo serving in his medical capacity (Roscher *s.v.* 433). There is no doubt that the valet (*cubicularius*) mentioned together with the other three must have an equally significant name, hence the conjecture Hypnofilus (Castiglioni for *Hypatafium* F) which does not entirely convince, however. Clytius (1, 24), Myrmex (9, 17), and Philodespotus (2, 26) have names that fit their functions without further explanation, as does Meroe (1, 7). Helm explains this name κατ'ἀντίφρασιν, but there is no suggestion that the *caupona* Meroe adulterates her wine, whatever else she does. For names employed κατ'ἀντίφρασιν see below on Babulus. For the pun on *merum* cf. Suet. *Tib.* 42: *In castris tiro etiam tum propter nimiam uini auiditatem pro Tiberio 'Biberius', pro Claudio 'Caldius', pro Nerone 'Mero' uocabatur*, and in particular, Aus. *epigr.* 20 (p. 327 Peiper):

> *Qui primus, Meroe, nomen tibi condidit, ille*
>   *Thesidae nomen condidit Hippolyto.*
> *Nam diuinare est, nomen componere, quod sit*
>   *Fortunae et morum uel necis indicium.*
> *Protesilae, tibi nomen sic fata dederunt,*
>   *Victima quod Troiae prima futurus eras.*
> *Idmona quod uatem, medicum quod Iapyga dicunt:*
>   *Discendas artes nomina praeueniunt.*
> *Et tu sic Meroe: non quod sis atra colore,*
>   *Ut quae Niliaca nascitur in Meroe:*
> *Infusum sed quod uinum non diluis undis,*
>   *Potare inmixtum sueta merumque merum.*

In view of Meroe's magic, Scobie (*Comm.* I, p. 95) suggests a connection with Meroe, an island in the Nile with a famous temple of Isis.

edituro: see Médan p. 81 for the use of the future participle in the sense of an adjectival clause; it occurs with poets from Verg. *A.* 8, 627 onwards. In prose, mostly historical and philosophical e.g. Sal. *Iug.* 106, 3; Cic. *Tusc.* 4, 14. See LHSz p. 390.

84, 16-18   et genere primarius et opibus plurimus et liberalitate prae-cipuus: "a man of the first rank by birth, extremely wealthy and out-standing in liberality". F has *pluribus* which was defended by Oudendorp (Sed alibi quoque *plura*, sine comparationis respectu dicuntur de quam multis); *plurimus* however is a very old correction (F in mg) as well as the *lectio difficilior*, in view of the symmetry generally accepted. Note the syndetic tricolon marked by alliteration and wordorder; Bernhard pp. 22, 70 f. Pricaeus notes that *primarius* is translated ἀρχικός in an Onomasticon Vetus: lacking in CGL.

84, 18   digno fortunae suae splendore: "with the splendour befitting his fortune"; *dignus* w. gen. in the *Met.* ony here. Pricaeus wished to change but was opposed by Oudendorp with a wealth of parallels. Cf. Balb. in Cic. *Att.* 8, 15 a 1; vGeisau, p. 244, LHSz p. 79.

84, 18   publicas uoluptates instruebat: "used to provide popular entertainment". Plutarch has little respect for these methods to obtain popular acclaim, cf. *Praec. ger. reip.* 5, 820D; 29, 821F; Friedländer, *SG*, II[8] p. 431 and notes 3-4. For the respective frequency of gladiatorial displays, as described here, in Italy and Greece see Friedländer *ibid.* pp. 427 ff. It may be, of course, that *instruebat* has the force of "happened to be organizing", but Friedländer *ibid.* p. 429 quotes an interesting example of an Italian official who gave eight such displays, CIL XI 6357 = Dessau 5057 (...*ob eximias liberalitates et abundantissimas in exemplum largitiones et quod ex indulgentia Aug. octies spectaculum gladiator. ediderit, amplius ludos Florales*...).

84, 19-21   Quis tantus ingenii, qui⟨s⟩ facundiae, qui singulas species apparatus multiiugi uerbis idoneis posset explicare?: "Who so talented, who so eloquent as to be able to unfold in apt words the individual aspects of the multiform preparations?" The "Unfähig-keitsbeteuerung" forms part of the *captatio benevolentiae*. See Curtius, *Eur. Lit.*, pp. 93, 168, 412. Heine p. 189 speaks of the "Unsagbarkeitsto-pos" and collects several instances in the *Met.*: 3, 9 (59, 5) *nec possum nouae illius imaginis rationem idoneis uerbis expedire*; 96, 19-22; 11, 3 (268, 3 ff.); 11, 25 (287, 5 ff.). See also Chr. Harrauer on 11, 25. Cf.

Heine pp. 188 f. and 189, n. 1. A. Obermayer criticizes Curtius' use of *topos* to describe opening formulas, see M. L. Baeumer ed., *Toposforschung*, Darmstadt 1973, p 256.

tantus ingenii: this use of the *gen. relationis* only here (Médan p. 36), cf. LHSz p. 79 who compare e.g. Vell. 1, 12, 3 *eminentissimus ingenii*. See vGeisau p. 247.

apparatus multiiugi: Médan p. 36 (cf. p. 176) assigns the word *multiiugus* to the *sermo cotidianus*; it does not, however, occur in Callebat, *S.C.* Apuleius uses the word several times, not only in the *Met.* (e.g. 6, 2 (139, 5)) but elsewhere as well, and we may conclude that for him at least it had lost the flavour of familiar speech. Scholars agree in taking *apparatus* as "preparation" with the exception of Butler who translates "show".

It is obvious that the subsequent description must be one that shows   84, 21 ff. *ingenium* and *facundia* as well as *uerba idonea*. Unhappily scholars disagree on the interpretation of the passage. It is clear that there are three types of human participants in the show, gladiators, hunters and criminals; it is equally clear that animals — for the time being of undetermined species — play their voracious part; but how the material apparatus mentioned is related to the various events is not at all obvious.

Gladiatores isti famosae manus, uenatores illi probatae   84, 21-22 pernicitatis, alibi noxii perdita securitate...: "Here gladiators of famed strength, there hunters of proven speed, there convicts with the abandon of despair". As often, the third member shows *variatio* (several instances among the tricola collected by Bernhard pp. 67 ff.), a variation which is functional since it is this last group whose activity is described in the rest of the sentence.

gladiatores ... famosae manus: cf. 10, 18 (250, 26) *famosos gladiatores*; Firm. *math.* 7, 26, 2 (under a particular constellation *famosi gladiatores nascentur*; cf. 8, 7, 5). *Famosus* here in the sense of "well-known","famous", rather than "ill-famed"; cf. *diffamare* at 82, 13. Porph. *ad* Hor. *Ep.* 2, 1, 81 has *famosissimi comoedorum*. Pricaeus quotes Donatus *ad* Ter. *Hec.* 797: *nam et meretrix et gladiator nobilis dici solet*, a statement fully supported by the evidence collected in ThLL *s.v. gladiator*, see e.g. Porph. *ad* Hor. *Ep.* 1, 1, 4 *Veianius nobilis gladiator post multas palmas consecratis Herculi Fundano armis suis in agellum se contulit*.

famosae manus: gen. qual., like *probatae pernicitatis* in the next line (here strong hands, there swift feet), see ThLL *s.v. manus* 354, 52. Curiously enough parallels of this sense of *manus* ('strength') with an adjective are lacking; in the majority of cases it occurs in the ablative. Possibly *manus* should be taken in the sense of "troop" and the genitive explained as a gen. epexeg.

uenatores ... probatae pernicitatis: *uenator* for the first time in the specialised sense of θηριομάχος, the man who fights wild animals in the arena; cf. *uenatio* below 84, 25. See also Tert. *mart.* 5, 1 *Alii inter uenatorum taureas scapulis patientissimis inambulauerunt*, Veget. *mil.* 2, 24, *dig.* 48, 19, 8, 11 (Ulp.), Cass. *Variar.* 5, 42, 1. *Pernicitas* in the *Met.* only here and 8, 16 (189, 21), cf. *Fl.* 21 (42, 7) *equum ... uiuacis pernicitatis.*

isti...illi...alibi: the adverbial use of *isti* occurs, with certainty, in Plautus (e.g. *Mil.* 255, and elsewhere at least in the A tradition), Turpil. *com.* 105, Pompon. *Atell.* 33 R. (*istic* Frassinetti), afterwards not until our passage (ThLL *s.v.* 514, 34 ff.). *illi* occurs more often (legitur inde a Plauto... fere 5oies per totam Latinitatem, editur fere 20[ies], ThLL *s.v.* 367, 84 ff.). Floridus' adoption *istic...illic* (ς) was therefore rightly rejected by Oudendorp.

noxii perdita securitate: the two main explanations of *perdita securitate* are those of Oudendorp and Hildebrand, of which the first is lively and insecure, the second safe and dull; Oudendorp: "Cave *perdita securitate* intelligas amissa, sed *uesana*; qualis perditorum et desperatorum hominum esse potest." Hildebrand: *"Perdita securitas* puta esse *uitae securitas amissa*, de cuius salute nulla spes esse potest." Both meanings of *perditus* occur in the *Met.* e.g. 6, 19 (142, 22: "lost"); 9, 23 (220, 21: "abandoned"). Translators distill a few more shades of meaning: "in heilloser Gemütsruhe" (Helm), "con cinica indifferenza" (Carlesi) clearly follow Oudendorp; "without hope of reprieve" (Adlington-Gaselee) "voués désormais à un sort sans espoir" (Vallette) obviously side with Hildebrand. Brandt-Ehlers' "vogelfreie Verbrecher" probably derives from the first, Butler's "criminals guilty past all reprieve" from the second explanation, though both depart a little from the straight and narrow path of strict interpretation. We prefer Oudendorp's choice. Note the too easily forgotten irony of this description occurring in a robber's report concerning his own professional activities.

84, 22-25 — suis epulis bestiarum saginas — instruentes confixilis machinae sublic⟨i⟩as turres tabularum nexibus, ad instar circumforaneae domus: "...busy fixing towers — provision to fatten the beasts with meals of themselves! — of beams joined with boards forming a complicated machine in the image of a movable house". The text is most uncertain; among the manuscripts F reads *bestiaru saginas instruentes c̃fixilis machinae sublicae turres stabularum nexibus ad instar* ...; φ corrects through expunction to *tabularum*. Full information concerning the relevant proposals has been collected in *Apul. Gron. III*, where also the arguments in favour of Westendorp Boerma's conjecture printed above are given.

suis epulis bestiarum saginas: to be construed as an apposition with *turres*, cf. Bernhard p. 24. It is clear that the victims are regarded with a fascinated horror enhanced by their unconcern. The topos is not new. Pricaeus quotes Artemid. Dald. *Onirocr.* 2, 54 (p. 183, 22 Pack): Θηριομαχεῖν πένητι ἀγαθόν· πολλοὺς γὰρ ἕξει τρέφειν. καὶ γὰρ ὁ θηριομαχῶν ἀπὸ τῶν ἰδίων σαρκῶν τὰ θηρία τρέφει. Among Christian authors the situation provides a topos in the problem of resurrection, e.g. Tert. *Res.* 32, 1; Athenagoras *Res.* 4 and Oehler's parallels *ad loc.*; Greg. Nyss. *De hom. opif.* 26, 1; Methodius *Res.* 1, 20, 4-5.

sagina is used here in its basic meaning (the fattening of animals), but Apuleius seems to be playing also with the specific usage of *gladiatoria sagina*, the mash fed to gladiators: Prop. 4, 8, 25; Sen. *Ep.* 15, 2; Tac. *Hist.* 2, 88.

confixilis: only here; see Bernhard p. 139, Médan p. 118.

machinae: the structure of a house is also called *machina* by Venantius Fortunatus 1, 19, 9: *machina celsa casae triplici suspenditur arcu.* Cf. Z. Pavlovskis, *Man in an Artificial Landscape. The Marvels of Civiliza-tion in Imperial Roman literature*, Leiden 1973, p. 53.

sublicias: according to Médan p. 139 the ms. reading *sublicae* represents an accessory form for *sublicius*; the Thesaurus material at Munich pro-vides no parallel.

turres: certainly not part of the palace of Demochares (Bernhard p. 206) but part of the temporary structures built for the event.

floridae picturae: the *pegmata* described by Josephus *B.J.* 7, 5, 5 are adorned with tapestries, Martial 8, 33, 3 mentions gilding, Claudian. 17 (*Paneg. d. Manl. Theod. Cons.*) 328 f. (p. 139 K.) speaks of *pictae trabes.* Here we may imagine that the *tabulae* just mentioned as well as the enclosures (*receptacula*) of the *uenationes* show pictures. *Floridus* may refer both to (representations of) flowers, and to bright colours; cf. respectively 10, 29 (260, 9) and 2, 12 (35, 9) (*gloria*) or 7, 8 (159, 26) *ueste muliebri florida.*

uenationes were held in the morning for preference and exhibited *uenatores*, trained in schools like the gladiators. The word *uenatio* in the sense of a fight between man and beast in the forum (cf. Vitr. 5, 1, 1), the circus or the amphitheatre (Cass. Dio 66, 25 calls the Colosseum a θέατρον κυνηγετικόν) occurs as early as Cic. *De off.* 2, 55. See also *Met.* 10, 35 (265, 24). *Venationes* frequently form the subject of wall-paintings, mosaics and other forms of art. See e.g. *Enciclopedia dell' arte antica s.v.*, Dar.-Sagl., V fig. 7372, L. Foucher, *Venationes à Hadrumète, OMRL*, 45 (1964), pp. 87 ff.

Qui praeterea numerus, quae facies ferarum: "Furthermore, 84, 26-85,1 what a number of beasts there were, how many species!" *Facies* in the sense of "species" e.g. Manilius 5, 190 *ferarum/diuersas facies*; cf. *ibid.* 4, 739; Col. 10, 189 *Quot facies (lactucarum).* In this sense the word refers to the entire habitus, rather than to head or face, see ThLL *s.v.* 48, 83 ff. There is no need to quote parallels for the fact that several species were present at once; Pricaeus mentions perhaps the most famous one: Androclus and the Lion in Gell. 5, 14, 7: *Multae ibi saeuientes ferae e.q.s.*

Nam praecipuo studio forensis etiam aduexerat generosa 85, 1-2 illa damnatorum capitum funera: "For he had taken particular care to import exotic animals too — fine coffins, those, for condemned criminals". Until Eyssenhardt editors usually printed *forensi* with some of the *recentiores*. Pricaeus and Oudendorp placed commas before *forensi* and after *etiam* and took the former in the sense of "exotic".

Kronenberg (*Mnemosyne* 1928, pp. 29-54) supports his ingenious conjecture *foris* (>*foresis*, cf. 1, 11 (10, 21) *commo[do]dum*, 83, 5 *ves[ti]te* and Helm, Praef. *Fl.*, p. LIII for similar examples) by referring to *Apol.* 15 (18, 12) *sine ullo foris amminiculo*. He convinced Robertson and Brandt-Ehlers. The majority of scholars, however, now adopt N. Heinsius' *forinsecus* (thus, among others, Helm, Giarratano-Frassinetti, Scazzoso).

The basis for these conjectures disappears if *forensis* (F) can be made to yield sense. It was defended by Armini (1932), who takes it with an understood *feras*. It may be objected that this presents us with a rather harsh type of apposition (*forensis* ...: *funera*), but it is certainly no less acceptable than the apposition proposed above (84, 22-23); *illa* indeed often indicates the emphatic repetition of an item just mentioned, cf. Callebat, *S.C.*, p. 279. Epexegetic apposition is discussed by e.g. Löfstedt, *Per. Aeth.*, p. 326; Svennung, *Pall.*, pp. 197 ff. LHSz pp. 428 ff.

generosa: cf. 1, 4 (4, 12) *serpentem generosum*. The word is used elsewhere, too, of wild animals: e.g. Sen. *De ira* 2, 16, 1 *Animalia...generosissima habentur quibus multum inest irae*. Cf. Plin. *Nat.* 8, 48; Juv. 14, 81.

funera: for the history of this topos see Russell on Ps-Long. *De subl.* 3, 2. Apuleius uses it also at *Met.* 5, 18 (117, 6) *saeuissimae bestiae sepeliri uisceribus*.

85, 2-3   Sed prae⟨ter⟩ ceteram speciosi muneris sup[p]ellectilem: "but in addition to the rest of the material for this spectacular show...". *Praeter* is an ancient and reasonable correction for $\bar{p}$ (F). Oudendorp (comm.) follows Sciopp. and Salm. in reading (with the "Pithoeanus") *prae cetera speciosi (c.q. tam speciosi) muneris supellectile. (ceterā, suppelectilē* F). The attempt has not met with the approval of later editors. *suppellectilem* is also the mss. spelling at 9, 31 (226, 21) and (e.g.) Amm. 22, 8, 42. Walde-Hofmann[3] *s.v.* reject *-pp-*, Ernout-Meillet (who doubt the etymology *super-l.*) admit *-pp-* as a variant spelling.

The Thesaurus material at Munich does not present any clear evidence that *suppellectilis* was an acceptable form in antiquity. In hexameter poetry the word *supellex* appears to occur only at the end of a line.

85, 3-4   totis utcumque patrimonii uiribus: "with absolutely all the resources of his patrimony". Yet Demochares still has some *aurei* to bestow upon the bearers of Nicanor's letter (86, 28), cf 88, 13 *argentum copiosum*.

utcumque: Médan (p. 157) speaks of a "signification élargie" and translates "absolument"; cf. Callebat, *S.C.*, p. 322 (synonymous with *utique*).

immanis ursae comparabat numerum copiosum: "he was 85, 4-5
collecting a large number of enormous she-bear", a strange combina-
tion; the expression recalls e.g. Cic. *Phil.* 2, 66 *maximum uini numerus
fuit*. The collective genitive occurs also 87, 14 f. *hoc genus bestiae*; Sall.
Jug. 6, 1 has a collective sing. in *leonem atque alias feras primus...
ferire*; see K.St. II,1, p. 68; Löfstedt, *Synt.* I², p. 18; LHSz pp. 13 f.;
Callebat, *S.C.*, p. 247.

The pleonastic combination *numerus copiosus* is hard to parallel, but
see Vulg. I *Macc.* 1, 18 *copiosa nauium multitudine*.

The reason for the use of the feminine *ursae* here and 88, 20 is that the
she-bear is bigger than the male (cf. ἡ ἄρκτος?); also e.g. Ov. *Met.* 12, 319
fusus in Ossaeae uillosis pellibus ursae. A stronger parallel is Verg. *A* 5,
37 *horridus...pelle Libystidis ursae* (see also *A.* 8, 368). Médan p. 196.

85 5-8

Nam praeter domesticis uenationibus captas, praeter largis
emptionibus partas amicorum etiam donationibus uariis
certatim oblata⟨s⟩ tutela sumptuosa sollicite nutrieba[n]t:
"Besides those caught in his own hunts, besides those obtained by a
lavish purchase, he was also feeding, conscientiously and with costly care,
those offered him by competing friends as gifts for various occasions".
Since to take *oblata* (F) with *tutela sumptuosa* would cause us to assume
the omission of a verb of similar meaning after *certatim*, it is simpler to
accept the traditional correction *oblatas*. The error *nutriebant* is hard to
explain except as a simple mechanical one. Robertson's (crit. app.)
oblatae...nutriebantur presents no improvement. It is probably better to
retain *Demochares* as the subject throughout. A period noteworthy for
its carefully repeated word-order winds up the description of the scene
in general; the particular aspect that enables the robbers to go to work
follows in the next chapter.

domesticis uenationibus: it is hardly likely that bears were actually
found in the neighbourhood of Plataeae in Apuleius' time, but it is more
important to note that they do in the landscape of the novel.

partas: Pricaeus compares Donatus on Ter. *Ph.* 46: *proprie dicitur par-
tum de eo quod labore quaesitum est.*

oblatas: see Callebat, *S.C.*, p. 452, on the ellipsis of *ursas*. *largis emp-
tionibus*: Symm. *Ep.* 5, 62 speaks of *ursorum negotiatores* (Friedländer,
S.G., II⁸ p. 548).

sollicite: Pricaeus quotes Sen. *VB.* 14, 3 *Ut feras cum labore periculoque
uenamur et captarum quoque illarum sollicita possessio est.* But since
Seneca adds *saepe enim laniant dominos*, the parallel is not exact: *sollicite*
in our passage must, in view of both *tutela sumptuosa* and the context of
disease (ch. 14), refer to the quality of the care, rather than to the danger.

CHAPTER XIV

A disaster strikes, creating just the right opportunity for the robbers.

Et si ... ursus homuncionem comest,
quanto magis homuncio debet ursum
comesse.   Petronius 66

85, 8-10 Nec ille tam clarus tamque splendidus publicae uoluptatis apparatus Inuidiae noxios effugit oculos: "But such notable and splendid preparation for the public's entertainment did not escape Envy's baleful eyes". As so often in Apuleius, the high point in the description of a situation or activity is immediately followed by a let-down. Cf. e.g. the comment on 75, 18-20; 76,14; 77,22. Such reversals are often introduced by a more or less general phrase, see Junghanns p. 58, n. 87. Often Fortuna is responsible, on occasion other divinities or abstractions as is the case here. Cf. also Heine p. 170 and n. 1.

nec: adversative, cf. e.g. 90, 7 *nec tamen.*

publicae uoluptatis: technical term as above 84, 18; cf. e.g. Script. Hist. Aug. Treb. Poll. *Gall.* 9, 4 *alios dies uoluptatibus publicis deputabat*; Fl. Vopisc., *Aurel.* 34, 6 *sequentibus diebus datae sunt populo uoluptates ludorum scaenicorum (e.q.s.)*; cf. Cassiod. *Var.* 6, 13, 9 *et cum lascivae uoluptates recipiant tribunum, haec non meretur habere primarium?* (LS incorrectly add Tac. *Hist.* 3, 83 where *uoluptas* refers to lascivious activities.)

apparatus: see on 84, 20.

Inuidiae noxios...oculos: INVIDIA is frequently personified from Pl. *Per.* 556 onwards; see e.g. Sen. *Pol.* 9, 4 *edax et inimica semper alienis processibus Inuidia*; ThLL *s.v.* 205, 71 appears not to distinguish between instances of the personification of *Inuidia* and instances where it is a collective emotion, but treats separately those passages in which *Inuidia* is obviously conceived as a goddess; the most detailed description occurs in Ov. *Met.* 2, 760 ff., see Böhmer's extensive note *ad loc.*, in which our passage, however, is lacking. See also Helm-Krenkel p. 405. *Inuidia* here is comparable to Greek φθόνος unlike Hyg. praef. 17 (Rose) where she is to be identified with Ζῆλος. On the notion see G. J. D. Aalders, *De oud-Griekse voorstelling van de afgunst der godheid, Med. Kon. Ned. Ak. Lett.* NR 38, 2 (1975).

Similar personifications of other attributes occur in the *Met.*: CONSUETUDO 6, 8 (134, 1) apparently occurs only here; FIDES 3, 26 (71, 21), 10, 24 (255, 27) cf. vdP. p. 189, and e.g. Pease on Cic. *N.D.* 2, 61, Nisbet-Hubbard on Hor. *Carm.* 1, 24, 7, Wissowa, pp. 54 etc., Latte, *RRG*, pp. 237, 273; IUSTITIA 2, 22 (43, 16) de Jonge p. 91; 3, 7 (57, 7) vdP. p. 66, e.g. Hor. *Carm.* 1, 24, 6; METUS 10, 31 (262, 16) cf. Verg. *A.* 6, 276 and Norden *ad loc.* (with a reference to R. Engelhard, *De personificationibus, quae in poesi atque arte Romanorum inveniuntur*, Göttingen 1881, p. 26); MISERICORDIA 11, 15 (277, 7) cf. Servius on Verg. *A*. 3, 607 (*misericordia* treated as a *numen*), see Chr. Harrauer p. 94; PROVIDENTIA 6,15 (139, 10) see Pease on Cic. *N.D.* 2, 73; QUIES 11, 15 (277, 7), Liv. 4, 41, 8 has a *fanum Quietis* but Ogilvie *ad loc.* shares Latte's doubts concerning the passage; see also August., *C. D.* 4, 16; RIVALITAS 10, 14 (255, 20), the only possible parallel Publ. Syr. R 7; SOBRIETAS 5, 30 (127, 13), see Fernhout *ad loc.*, also Merkelbach p. 28; see further Prud. *Psych.* 244 etc., Dracont. *Rom.* 6, 65; SOLLICITUDO 6, 9 (134, 16); Grimal *ad loc.* speaks of a pessimistic conception of love, but gives no parallels for the personification; TERROR 10, 31 (262, 16), see above *Metus*, cf. Ov. *Met.* 4, 484 f.; TRISTITIES 6, 9 (134, 17), no parallels; VERITAS 8, 7 (181, 17), cf. Hor. *Carm.* 1, 24, 7 and Nisbet-Hubbard *ad loc.*; VOLUPTAS 6, 24 (147, 1), see Pease on Cic. *N.D.* 2, 61.

Further personifications of abstracts in Strilciw p. 107. See in general Wissowa pp. 327 ff.; Latte, *RRG*, pp. 233 ff.; Fernhout p. 12 is concerned with these personifications as arguments in favour of an allegorical interpretation of *Amor and Psyche*; cf. Walsh p. 212; Mantero p. 9, n. 1. It is interesting to note that no Greek counterparts of these personifications occur in the *Onos*, nor does the latter work contain any comparable ones.

noxios...oculos: of course Invidia has harmful eyes: Ov. *Met.* 2, 780 *sed uidet ingratos intabescitque uidendo/ successus hominum*; Cic. *Tusc.* 3, 20 gives the same information in prosaic fashion: *nomen inuidiae, quod uerbum ductum est a nimis intuendo fortunam alterius.* Cf. Verg. *Ecl.* 3, 103; *A.* 11, 337; Hor. *Ep.* 1, 14, 37. It is against her that people seek protection by means of a *bulla*, e.g. Macr. 1, 6, 9: *nam sicut praetexta magistratuum, ita bulla gestamen erat triumphantium, quam in triumpho prae se gerebant inclusis intra eam remediis quae crederent aduersus inuidiam ualentissima.* See also Friedrich on Catul. 5, 11. Lesky p. 564, n. 1 feels that the word *noxios* reflects a Greek βάσκανος and uses this passage as an argument in favour of a Greek "Vorlage".

effugit oculos: on the word-order see Bernhard p. 18.

Nam diutina captiuitate fatigatae simul et aestiua flagran- 85, 10-13
tia maceratae, pigra etiam sessione languidae, repentina correptae pestilentia paene ad nullum rediuere numerum: "Exhausted by their long captivity and at the same time weakened by the summer heat, and furthermore grown sluggish through their long inactivity, the bears were seized by a sudden epidemic and their number reduced almost to zero". The two striking features of this period are the relatively even lengths of its cola and the absence of a subject noun such as *ursae* or (as vdVliet wished to print) *bestiae*; *repentina...pestilentia* varies the word-order.

diutina captiuitate fatigatae: notwithstanding the excellent care just mentioned! We hear of the long captivity when it is needed for the story, as we hear of Lucius' *gladiolus* when he uses it 3, 5 (56, 2 ff.) and of the gardener's wife when she thwarts the ass's purpose by raising the alarm (76, 14). For the narrative technique, see S. Vestdijk, *Muiterij tegen het etmaal*, I,³1966, pp. 176 ff., who speaks of it under the heading "economy". Plin. *Ep.* 6, 34, 3 tells of delays that occurred in the transport of animals intended for the show.

simul et aestiua flagrantia maceratae: *măceratae* in the *Met.* only here, literally "steeped in moisture"; *măcer*, "thin", of course formally has no part in this word since *măcerare* does not occur, but it is just possible that the transferred sense may have undergone some influence from *măcer*. Cf. the word-play in Pl. *Capt.* 133 ff. (*măceror/*, *măcesco...măcritudine*) and, though subtler, in *Epid.* 320 ff. See Walde-Hofmann³ *s.v.* The same applies to the use of the word in Symm. *Ep.* 2, 76, 2 (Mon. Germ. Hist. Auct. Ant. VI 1 p. 65): *interea nos ursis saepe promissis et diu speratis sub ipso articulo muneris indigemus. uix enim paucos catulos maceratos inedia et labore suscepimus.*

pigra etiam sessione languidae: Pricaeus compares Sen. *Ep.* 122, 4 *ita sine ulla exercitatione iacentibus tumor pigrum corpus inuadit.* Though Seneca is speaking of birds that are being fattened in a cage, the notion of disease is close by. *Sessio* in this sense also in Cic. *Att.* 14, 14, 2 (Tyrrell and Purser note that *sedere* is often the equivalent of *"otiosum esse"* in the letters; see also on c. 11 (83, 7)). Cf. Médan p. 162.

repentina correptae pestilentia: *corripere* is a common term for disease striking man or beast; often used with an almost pleonastic *repente*, cf. 10, 28 (259, 15); Verg. *G.* 3, 472.

paene ad nullum rediuere numerum: it is hard to parallel the combination *nullus numerus* in this sense (different in Cic. *Phil.* 3, 16 *homo nullo numero* "a man of no account"); cf. Suet. *Vesp.* 19 *...redigerentque ad breuissimum numerum.* The word-order is treated by Bernhard p. 18;

rediuere: cf. 3, 23 (69, 19) *praeteriui*; Neue-Wagener III³, p. 432; Médan p. 6.

85, 13-14   Passim per plateas plurimas cerneres iacere semiuiuorum corporum ferina naufragia: "All about in most of the squares one could see animal wrecks of half-dead bodies". Cf. Verg. *A.* 2, 364 ff. *plurima perque uias sternuntur inertia passim/ corpora perque domos et religiosa deorum/ limina.* There is no need to change *plurimas* to *plurima* with Colvius: once again we have to do with a quotation with *variatio*. According to vThiel I p. 105 we have here one of the illogicalities ("Ungereimtheiten") that betray the hand of Apuleius in this passage, which is, he feels, entirely without humour. One might counter by saying that to put a rhetorical exaggeration like this into the robber's mouth is undoubtedly humorous — a humour underscored by the explosive alliteration of *passim p.pl.pl.*

semiuiuorum: cf. 9, 25 (222, 2); also *semimortuus*: 1, 14 (13, 8); 6, 26 (148, 22). Of the two words *semiuiuus* occurs more frequently in classical

Latin; however, the suspicion that the Romans' perspective differed from ours (cf. 88, 1 *semitectos*: "half open") is untenable in view of the absence of other pairs such as *semianimis/seminecis*. See also vdP. p. 37 *pericula salutis = pericula uitae*.

ferina naufragia: *naufragium* is also used in metaphorical sense in 6, 5 (131, 25) *fortunae naufragio*. The present use is close to Soph. *El.* 729 f. πᾶν δ'ἐπίμπλατο/ναυαγίων Κρισαῖον ἱππικῶν πέδον. Cf. *ibid.* 1444; Jebb compares [Dem.] *or.* 61, 29. See also D. v. Nes, *Die maritime Bildersprache des Aischylos*, Diss. Utrecht, Groningen 1963, pp. 152 f. In Latin literature both *naufragus* and *naufragium* are often used metaphorically, e.g. Cic. *Cat.* 1, 30 *undique conlectos naufragos* (Catiline's men), cf. *ibid.* 2, 24. *Phil.* 13, 3 *addite illa naufragia Caesaris amicorum*... Ov. *Tr.* 1, 5, 36 *et date naufragio litora tuta meo*; *Pont.* 1, 2, 60; 2, 9, 9. See also Neuen- schwander p. 47, Strilciw p. 107, Bernhard p. 193. We have been unable to inspect the Greifswald dissertation of J. Kahlmeyer, *Seesturm und Schiffbruch als Bild im antiken Schrifttum*, 1934.

Tunc uulgus ignobile, quos inculta pauperies sine delectu ciborum tenuato uentri cogit sordentia supplementa et dapes gratuitas conquirere, passim iacentes epulas accur- runt: "In these circumstances the common people, whom sordid poverty, with no choice of diet, forces to search for extra food, however unpleasant, and any free meals for their emaciated bellies, fell upon these feasts, that were lying everywhere". The two short cola of the main clause enclose a very long adjectival clause which, though it presents a necessary aspect of the situation, does so at unnecessary length. *Tunc* ("in those circum- stances") here introduces the general activity, in the next sentence the particular plan.

uulgus ignobile: unlike the rather abstract *uulgus indoctum* of 76, 2, these are very concrete people. In both cases the word *uulgus* is given a plural construction. For the pleonastic *ignobile* see Bernhard p. 175.

inculta pauperies: "sordid poverty", cf. Hor. *Ep.* 2, 2, 199 *p. immunda*; *incultus* in the *Met.* only here.

sine delectu ciborum: *delictu* F; *delectu* F²; φ *delictu*; cf. 8, 17 (190, 18) *sine ullo dilectu*. Robertson prints *dilectu*. ThLL despairs *s.v. delectus*: "commiscetur in usu cum *dilectus* (...) neque codices neque editiones certam distinguendi facultatem suppeditant". OLD prefers *dilectus*; but, in view of the fact that the problem is insoluble, there seems to be in- sufficient reason why we should not follow F's corrector.

More interesting is the question whether the expression should be taken with *inculta pauperies* (thus Robertson) or with *tenuato uentri* (thus Helm). We incline to the first since a choice of foodstuffs would represent a form of *cultus*, whereas not so much the absence of choice but of foodstuffs as such would be responsible for a *uenter tenuatus*.

epulas accurrunt: cf. 3, 21 (67, 20) *me accurrit*, vdP. p. 156.

Tunc e re nata suptile consilium ego et iste Babulus tale comminiscimur: "Then I and Babulus there devised a subtle scheme to deal with the situation that had arisen".

e re nata: cf. 76, 23 *e re nata capto consilio* and comm. *ad loc.*

Babulus: *babulus* F φ; *bubalus* Colvius, *bardulus* Beroaldus, *baburus* Sopingius, *balbulus* (or *balbillus*) Oudendorp, *baculus* Eyssenhardt, *Eubulus* Bursian, Robertson[1], *Zabulus* vdVliet, *Diabulus* Rohde. External support for the ms. reading is weak, cf. Ter. *Ad.* 915 where Dziatzko-Kauer retain *babulo* (see Kauer's defense of that reading in *WS* 24 (1902), pp. 537-541). Pape-Benseler mention Βαβύλος but have no Βαβούλος.

Whether or not *babulus* ("the babbler") is intended as a name is hard to say, but the descriptive quality is obvious: the man does not say a word. Among the conjectures Colvius' *bubalus* merits an honourable mention (a *bubalus* ("bison") is hardly likely to hit upon a neat, subtle plan), and indeed both Βούβαλος and *Bubalus* occur as names of freedman (ThLL *s.v.* 2220; for the spelling *babulus* instead of an intended *bubalus* cf. *Mittellateinisches Wörterbuch s.v.*); see also Fr. Bechtel, *Die historischen Personennamen des Griechischen bis zur Kaiserzeit*, Halle 1917 (Hildesheim 1964) p. 581. Most scholars agree that a significant name κατ'ἀντίφρασιν is required. Such names also occur elsewhere in the *Met.*: *Alcimus* (83, 9), however strong he may be, is thrown out of the window by an old woman — the chapter also plays with an "all brawn, no brain" contrast.

The name also occurs historically, see Pape-Benseler *s.v.*, Bechtel p. 37. There are instances of all of the following names in Pape-Benseler *s.vv.* ARETE 9, 17 (215, 16), wife of Barbarus, is hardly as virtuous (or prayed for) as her name suggests. See Bechtel p. 612. ARISTOMENES is the great hero but in 1, 13 (12, 3-5) we find him in a cold sweat, trembling uncontrollably under the bed. See Bechtel p. 71. DIOPHANES 2, 14 (36, 10 ff.) tells the story of his unfortunate journey, not realizing that as a fortune teller he should have foreseen it. His name, though probably meaning "he who is famous through Zeus", seems to hint at an explanation "through whom Zeus manifests himself" (cf. Tatum, *Aspects*, p. 76) by the very contrast with the characterization *mente uiduus necdum suus*. See Bechtel p. 439; vdP. p. 27 with reference to modern literature. PANTHIA 1, 12 (11, 11) is the All-Divine one, or κατ ἀντίφρασιν the demonic one; see Bechtel p. 525. The ironic intent of the name seems to be reinforced by the epithet *bona* 1, 13 (12, 6). SOCRATES 1, 6 (5, 18 etc.), who occurs in the same story, is sketched (particularly in 6, 5-13) as the very opposite of the philosopher: *diuinae prudentiae senex* 10, 33 (264, 14) as Tatum (*Aspects* pp. 76, 146) rightly remarks; see Bechtel p. 414.

Unam, quae ceteris sarcina corporis ⟨p⟩raeualebat, quasi cibo parandam portamus ad nostrum receptaculum: "One bear, which exceeded the others in body-weight, we carried off to our hide-out as if to prepare her as food".

[1] See also Rode - Burck p. 226.

unam: cf. 3, 5 (55, 21) *unus denique*, below 86, 2 *unus e numero nostro*, 3, 10 (59, 16) *una[m] de ceteris*; see Callebat, *S.C.*, p. 289, vdP. p. 84 and the literature mentioned there.

sarcina: it is not necessary to read *sagina* with ς and Oudendorp, though *sarcina* in the sense of weight (non-figurative) is late and rare. Médan p. 153 compares 88, 18 and 92, 14, but in those passages the aspect of the heavy load of stolen goods carried approaches the use very closely to the original meaning of a (military) pack, load. Here that aspect is lost, though the aspect of weight carried is not: *portamus*. Cf. Apul. *Pl.* I, 18 (103, 9) *ualitudo obteritur...pabuli sarcina immodice inuecti*; Cassian. *Coll.* I, 14, 8 *deposita hac...sarcina corporali*.

⟨*p*⟩*raeualebat*: a certain correction, but it is the only instance of the verb in the *Met.* Though there are many passages in which *praeualere* is construed with an abl. and quite a few in which a dative is employed (e.g. August. *C.D.* 16, 39 *nam quod ei praeualuit Iacob...*), the Thesaurus material at Munich does not provide instances of the two constructions used in combination.

quasi cibo parandam: one of the several humorous touches in the episode: the robbers presently show themselves sufficiently hungry to give the lie to this boastful *quasi*.

ad nostrum receptaculum: this hiding place is mentioned only here; at 87, 29 a different one is sought. *Receptaculum* in the sense of a place of shelter, a retreat, is commonly used in military or semi-military contexts; e.g. Cic. *Pis.* 11 *templum... receptaculum ueterum Catilinae militum*; Plin. *Nat.* 10, 100 *Perdices spina et frutice sic muniunt receptaculum, ut contra feram abunde uallentur*.

eiusque probe nudatum carnibus corium seruatis sollerter 85, 21-25
totis unguibus, ipso etiam bestiae capite adusque confi-
nium ceruicis solido relicto tergus omne rasura studiosa
tenuamus et minuto cinere perspersum soli siccandum
tradimus: "and her pelt was properly laid bare of flesh, while all the claws were expertly preserved, and the brute's head, right down to the line of the neck, was left whole; we thinned down the whole skin with careful scraping, and sprinkling it with fine ash we laid it out in the sun to dry". vdVliet wished to change the object *nudatum corium* to *nudato corio;* the conjecture, however unnecessary, serves to remind us of a slight anacoluthon: Apuleius substitutes *tergus omne* for the object. Bernhard p. 94 does not mention this case. See also comm. on 77, 6, and vdP. p. 140.

nudatum: cf. Verg. *A.* I, 211 *tergora diripiunt costis et uiscera nudant*. Here however the process described is so different that if there is a reminiscence it is a humorous one. The process is one of curing rather than tanning, see R. J. Forbes, *Studies in Ancient Technology* V, Leiden 1957, p. 3.

ipso...relicto: it is to be noted that the two items most essential for the success of the plan are placed centrally and expressed in two clauses that are both preceded and followed by pairs of clauses, all three pairs consisting of clauses of roughly equal length. The plan itself is not mentioned until the very end of the chapter, showing that the chapter numbers were added by a competent scholar.

rasura studiosa tenuamus: for the sort of instruments Roman tanners used for this process see Forbes, fig. 14 showing scrapers found at Vindonissa near Basle. *Rasura*, "scraping", in the *Met.* only here.

minuto cinere perspersum: it is not clear whether plain ashes from a fireplace or some other powder (cf. *cinis lixiuus* Plin. *Nat.* 15, 67 or *aluminis cinis* Plin. *Nat.* 28, 244) is meant. See also *Met.* 9, 12 (212, 10) *farinulenta cinere sordide candidati*. As often we are not told the provenance of the materials or instruments used. See also comm. on 88, 10 *gladio*.

soli siccandum tradimus: for this age-old curing process see Forbes p. 3.

85, 25-86,1 Ac dum caelestis uaporis flammis examurgatur, nos interdum pulpis eius ualenter saginantes sic instanti militiae disponimus sacramentum: "And while it is drying in the flames of heat from the sky we meanwhile stuffed ourselves with its meat and so allotted duties for the coming sortie...": *examurgat*; F, *examurgatur* ς; the very slight correction is doubtless correct. The verb occurs only here. Cf. *amurca, amurga,* ἀμόργη watery part 'which runs out when olives are pressed' (LSJ). For the style see comm. on 75, 9; 77, 7.

nos interdum pulpis eius...saginantes: apparently the robbers suffer from the same *inculta pauperies* (85, 15) and its attendant hunger as the *uulgus ignobile*; this is hardly surprising after the failures of Lamachus and Alcimus. It is to be noted that the robbers now eat the very animals that had been acquired to eat them or at least their colleagues. Eating the animals killed in the arena both occurred and was regarded with revulsion. Scintilla sickens at the sight of a piece of bear's meat (Petr. *Sat.* 66), cf. Friedländer and Marmorale *ad loc.* (who omit our passage) and Ciaffi, p. 122; Tert. *Apol.* 9, 11 notes: *Ipsorum ursorum aluei appetuntur cruditantes adhuc de uisceribus humanis*, see also Mayor *ad loc.* Cf. Min. Fel. 30, 6: *Non dissimiles et qui de harena feras deuorant inlitas et infectas cruore uel membris hominis et uiscere saginatas.*

pulpis: cf. Is. *Orig.* 11, 1, 81 *Pulpa est caro sine pinguedine*; Cato *Agr.* 83; Mart. 3,77,6.

interdum, as usual in the sense of *interim*, see vdP. p. 28.

sic instanti militiae disponimus sacramentum: the military terminology used throughout the robbers' tales is discussed in Appendix I. It is clear that the robbers see their occupation as a *militia*; here, however, the word *militia* is used for the particular sortie; cf. e.g. [Quint.] *Decl.* 339 (p. 340, 13) *...qui, etiamsi utiles consiliis futuri essent, indigni tamen propter dedecus proximae militiae erant.* (At 2, 18 (39, 20) the word is used for the love affair with Fotis, at 11, 15 (277, 27) for the service of Isis.)

disponimus sacramentum: for *disponere = aliquid administrare, iubere*, cf. ThLL *s.v.* 1425, 56.

Médan p. 255 translates "sous la garantie du serment", but for *sacramentum* we should take "mutual obligation" as the basic meaning, such mutual obligation being the very content of military duty. Helm's "Verabredung" is rather weak. See comm. on 82,27 and the literature quoted there. The same sense seems to be most fitting also at 90, 15 *ne ululatu quidem fidem sacramenti prodidit*: "not even by howling did he betray the duty entrusted to him".

ut unus e numero nostro, non qui corporis adeo, sed animi 86, 1-3
robore ceteris antistaret: "that one of our number, who excelled the rest in strength not so much of body as of mind". The antithesis is discussed by Bernhard p. 60. The entire phrase echoes and elaborates on 80, 16 f. *unus, qui robore ceteros antistabat*. The construction of the verb with the dative is the uusal one, the accusative occurs in the *Met.* only at the place just cited. See Callebat, *S.C.*, p. 183.

ut unus e numero nostro: cf. above on 85, 19. The characterization of Thrasyleon (concerning the name see above comm. on 84, 15 and below on 86, 8) as a *uir fortis* starts here (for vigour of mind contrasted with vigour of body see e.g. Sen. *Ep.* 66, 1 *posse ingenium fortissimum ac beatissimum sub qualibet cute latere*), and continues 86, 10 *uultu sereno*; 86, 15 *fortissimum socium nostrum*; 86, 17 *constanti uigore*; 89, 15 f. *non tamen sui nostrique uel pristinae uirtutis oblitus*; 90, 12 ff. *egregium decus nostrae factionis...immortalitate digno illo spiritu...generoso uigore ...uitam fato reddidit* (a climax!). See also Tatum, *Aspects*, pp. 134 f.

atque is in primis uoluntarius, pelle illa contectus ursae 86, 3-6
subiret effigiem domumque Democharis inlatus per opportuna noctis silentia nobis ianuae faciles praestaret aditus: "and above all was a volunteer, should cover himself with that skin to assume the appearance of a bear and be led into Demochares' house. At the right moment at the dead of night he would give us easy access through the door".

atque is: takes up *unus* and thereby gives *non qui... antistaret* a parenthetical quality.

atque is in primis uoluntarius: a necessary precondition for the required *animi robur*. Note also that by volunteering Thrasyleon becomes as responsible for his own death as Lamachus was for his.

pelle illa contectus ursae subiret effigiem: both elements of the plan mentioned here are described with greater intensity in the next chapter: *contectus* becomes *sese recondit* (86, 10), *subiret effigiem* becomes *prorsus bestiam factum* (86, 16). *Effigies* here clearly "disguise", cf. 2, 1 (24, 26) *in aliam effigiem*. Apparently there are no parallels for the combination *subire effigiem*, and it is hard to say whether an element of stealth is implied.

domumque Democharis inlatus: the subject matter of chapters 16 and 17. *domum inferre* also Col. 12, 1, 5, cf. ThLL *s.v.* 1374, 60, 1378, 56 (our passage). Cf. *Met.* 2, 2 (25, 11 f.) *repente me nescius forum cupidinis intuli*.

per opportuna noctis silentia: intensified in 88, 7-8 *examussim capto noctis latrocinali momento*. See Bernhard p. 103 for the plural *opportuna silentia*.

nobis ianuae faciles praestaret aditus: the word-order emphasizes *ianuae*: the access provided is to be the easiest imaginable.

CHAPTER XV

Brave Lion becomes a bear of fortitude.

Nec paucos fortissimi collegii sollers species ad munus 86, 6-7
obe[di]undum adrexerat: "This clever disguise stirred not a few
of our gallant band to undertake the task".

nec paucos: the reader had been informed that there were numerous
members of the company at 80, 6 *longe plures numero iuuenes*.

fortissimi collegii: it seems that the robber stresses the fortitude of the
band to defend his men against the words *debilem numerum* uttered by
his colleague (80, 23), even though they were intended in a different
sense. The choice of the word *collegium* is remarkable in so far as it
appears to depart from the largely military aspect of the terminology
used so far.

sollers species: the expression is rather bold: *species* is used in much the
same sense as e.g. Sen. *Ben.* 4, 34, 1 *fallaces...sunt rerum species quibus
credidimus*, but *sollers* emphasizes the implication that this "semblance"
is of the robbers' own creation. Heinsius' *sollertiae spes* ("the hope of
showing their mettle"), though an excellent phrase and palaeographically
reasonable, is unnecessary.

ad munus obeundum: F's *obediendum* was corrected very early (ς).
A defense is not likely to succeed, though several Christian texts construe
oboedire with a direct object: Ambr. *Hex.* 5, 10, 29 p. 163, 14 *piscis
sollemniter oboedit* (*obaudit* Schenkl) *mandata caelestia*; cf. Greg. Tur.
Franc. 2, 23 *ut...non oboediatur* (*obaudiatur* Krusch-Levison) *sacerdos dei*;
for more examples in the *Vetus Latina* see ThLL s.v. 135, 62 ff. The
combination *munus obire* occurs also Liv. 3, 6, 9. The military aspect is
treated in Appendix I.

adrexerat: see vdP. p. 79.

Quorum prae ceteris Thrasyleon factionis optione delectus...: 86, 8
"Of them it was Thrasyleon, picked in preference to the rest by the band's
choice". In Lamachus the robbers had lost their leader, a fact Apuleius
emphasizes at 80, 22; 82, 2; 83, 5, now they resort to democratic practices
in deciding between the volunteers.

prae ceteris: Callebat, *S.C.*, p. 209 notes that this archaic expression
underwent a revival during the 2nd cent. A.D.

Thrasyleon: the humorous twist of this significant name has been
noted at the chapter heading above. Since Apuleius could have named
the man Thrasymenes, Thrasycles or even Arctinus, this feature is
doubtless intended. See also Introd. p. 4.

factionis optione: cf. e.g. 2, 18 (39, 22) *uesana factio*; 3, 8 (58, 10) and vdP. p. 75 *ad loc. Factio* is usually employed *in malam partem* and thus it refers at 3, 28 (72, 23) to the band of robbers. That the present narrator uses it here of his own band in another touch of Apuleian humour. At 90, 13 Thrasyleon will have become the *egregium decus nostrae factionis*.

optio: in the *Met.* the word occurs here only. When feminine it usually refers to the possibility of choice between two or more items (e.g. Liv. 8, 33, 16), but in certain contexts, particularly legal ones, it may also refer to a choice already made e.g. Quint. *Inst.* 7, 8, 4 (dealing with the question whether a certain choice may be revoked). Cf. also Sen. *Con.* 1, 5 *passim*. It may then also mean "wish" as at Petr. 86, 1; Quint. *Inst.* 5, 10, 97. Passing from the activity of choosing to the item chosen the word achieves a wide currency in the sense of a military official; cf. Fest. p. 184 M (= 201 L) *optio est optatio, sed in re militari optio appellatur is, quem decurio aut centurio optat sibi rerum privatarum ministrum, quo facilius obeat publica offica*. See also Ernout-Meillet *s.v.*, O. Keller, *Optio, RPH* 1897, pp. 7 f.

86, 9   *ancipitis machinae subiuit aleam*: "who undertook the risk of this dangerous stratagem". There is no case for F's *subibit* which was corrected very early. ThLL *s.v.* 25, 31 gives the meaning of *anceps* as "fallax" and indeed the disguise is destined both to deceive the victim and to betray its wearer.

subiuit aleam: cf. Sen. *Ep.* 117, 20 *temere me geram, subibo* (*subito* mss.) *huius uoti aleam*; also Col. 3, 21, 6. The development of the word *alea* may be illustrated by Suet. *Cl.* 33 *aleam studiosissime lusit*; *Jul.* 32 *iacta alea est*; Hor. *Carm.* 2, 1, 6 *periculosae plenum opus aleae*.

The pause after *aleam* is not very strong.

86, 9-10   Iamque habili corio et mollitie tractabili uultu sereno sese recondit: "Straightaway he cheerfully covered himself in the skin which fitted well and was easy to pull because of its softness". It is the last they see of Thrasyleon.

habili corio et mollitie tractabili: Bernhard p. 175 is, of course, right in listing the phrases as an instance of the many redundancies which characterize Apuleius' style, yet *habili* may well imply the easy fit (cf. Verg. *A.* 9, 365 f. *tum galeam Messapi habilem cristisque decoram / induit*) and *mollitie tractabili* the aspect of pliability. Bernhard p. 31 points out the chiastic arrangement; note also the numbers of syllables (3-3-4-4), which appear to have been arranged in a kind of counterpoint with the chiasmus.

uultu sereno: the immediate association of *serenus* is an unclouded sky. It is used for Socrates in Cic. *Tusc.* 3, 31. Cf. Lucr. 3, 293 *pectore tranquillo fit qui uoltuque sereno;* see for many more instances Nisbet and Hubbard on Hor. *Carm.* 1, 37, 26 and, in particular, Pease on Verg. *A.* 4, 477.

recondit: the verb may be used for putting up a sword in its sheath and it is not quite clear whether in our passage the aspect of hiding or that of enveloping prevails.

86, 10-13 Tunc tenui sarcimine summas oras eius adaequamus et iuncturae rimam, licet gracilem, setae circumfluentis densitate saepimus: "Then with a fine suture we matched the outer edges and the line of the seam, narrow though it was, we covered with the dense hair flowing around it".

sarcimen occurs here only. Whether Apuleius intends the word in the sense of the activity (thus Médan p. 110: "couture") or the concrete sense of "thread" (thus e.g. Butler), or in the resultative sense of "seam" (thus e.g. Helm, Vallette) is not clear. J. Perrot, *Les dérivés latins en -men et -mentum*, Paris 1961, p. 123 does not address himself to the question, but translates "couture"; he feels that in view of the notion the word belongs to the "langue populaire".

sarcimine adaequare is probably little more than a circumlocution for "sew together", though by *adaequare* Apuleius may refer to the precise fitting together of the *orae*. ThLL *s.v.* 562, 1 mistakenly lists our passage under II "intransitive". On *orae* see Festus 183 M (= 196 L) *orae extremae partes terrarum, id est maritimae dicuntur, unde et uestimentorum extremae partes, quae quidem et primae dici possunt*. Médan p. 265 lists the word as poetic.

iuncturae rimam refers to the slit still remaining after the activity described in *sarcimine...adaequamus*. The narrator hastens to add *licet gracilem* (see Médan p. 236, vdP. p. 80) in order to preserve the impression of extreme care thus far created and continued in the words *setae... saepimus*.

circumfluentis: if we take it literally with ThLL *s.v.* 1145, 9 the word indicates that *seta* here refers to rather long hair which, though not the more common meaning, is perfectly possible: the sword of Damocles is suspended *saeta equina* (Cic. *Tusc.* 5, 62), cf. *Met.* 6, 28 (150, 12f.) *caudaeque setas incuria lauacri congestas...perpolibo*. In spelling *seta* rather than *saeta* F is inconsistent with itself (cf. 3, 24 (70, 11) *sęta*) and, in giving *seta* at all, apparently among the minority of manuscripts. Cf. Forcellini *s.v.*, Ernout-Meillet *s.v.*

86, 13 saepimus, ad ipsum: though it is not a matter of great moment whether we print a period or a comma after *saepimus*, a comma seems to express rather better the flow of activity which consists of five elements: sewing the seam, combing the hair over it, fitting the head, cutting airholes and (finally) the climactic entry into the cage. The editors are divided.

86, 13-14 ad ipsum confinium gulae, qua ceruix bestiae fuerat execta, Thrasyleonis caput subire cogimus: "we forced Thrasyleon's head right up to the top end of the gullet, where the beast's neck had been cut open".

confinium gulae: "the throat-line" (i.e. the borderline between head and throat); cf. above 85, 23 *adusque confinium ceruicis*.

qua ceruix bestiae fuerat execta: see vdP. p. 54 on form and function of the pluperfect. The picture is not entirely clear.

Thrasyleonis caput subire cogimus: the word *cogimus* indicates a very tight fit, cf. Vallette: "en forçant un peu".

86, 14-15   paruisque respiratui circa nares et oculos datis foramini-
bus: "after supplying him with little breathing-holes round his nostrils and eyes". Leo added ⟨*et obtutui*⟩ after *respiratui* and the addition was adopted by Robertson and Frassinetti. The syllepsis is indeed striking, but it is doubtful whether it is beyond Apuleius, cf. e.g. 11, 23 (285, 9 ff.) *dicerem, si dicere liceret, cognosceres si liberet audire. Sed parem noxam contraherent et aures et linguae illae temerariae curiositatis.* VdVliet and Leo judged that where *curiositas* refers to *aures* a parallel *loquacitas* ought to refer to *linguae*. See on this type of problem J. Willis, *Latin textual criticism*, Urbana 1972, pp. 115 f.[1]

respiratui: in Apuleius only here; *respiratus* is a rare word which was restored at Cic. *N.D.* 2, 136 by Lambinus. Pease, however, follows F. Skutsch in retaining the ms. reading *respiritu*. See Neue-Wagener I³, p. 795. It occurs also at Hippocr. *progn.* 5 (p. 125 Kühlewein, in *Hermes* 20 (1890)): *grandis autem respiratus et post multum tempus desipientiam ostendit.*

86, 15-18   fortissimum socium nostrum prorsus bestiam factum in-
mittimus caueae modico prae[de]stinatae pretio, quam constanti uigore festinus inrepsit ipse: "We led our heroic comrade, completely transformed into an animal, to a cage we had bought quite cheap, and with stout heart he crept straight into it of his own accord".

fortissimum socium nostrum: see above on 86, 2. The phrase gains weight in view of *fortissimi collegii* (86, 6) above, and it becomes functional in view of the contrast provided by the next phrase.

prorsus bestiam factum: the metamorphosis of Thrasyleon is, though in the previous chapter there was but question of a disguise, almost total.

---

[1] A related, though not identical, problem occurs at 11, 5 (269, 25 f.) ...*et qui nascentis dei Solis inchoantibus inlustrantur radiis Aethiopes* where Robertson adds after *inchoantibus* ⟨*et occidentis inclinantibus*⟩. It is quite true that elsewhere the Aethiopians are said to live both in the east and in the west, but did Apuleius say so? And if Apuleius did not, could the reader be expected to supply the west from memory? The answer to both questions seems to be: "probably not".

See Tatum, *Aspects*, p. 135 who points out that in chapter 21 we read of the death of a bear (90, 10: *lanceam mediis iniecit ursae praecordiis*). However, that entire chapter carefully distinguishes between the point of view of Thrasyleon himself and that of his attackers and other by-standers, who see a bear. Even the butcher at the end (90, 22 ff.) starts on a bear, but finishes up with a *magnificus latro*. At any rate we need to remind ourselves that Lucius is relating a mock-metamorphosis of which he himself heard the account when an ass...

inmittimus caueae modico praestinatae pretio: the cage is mentioned here for the first time. This time (cf. comm. on 85, 24) we are indeed informed as to its provenance, and on inspection it turns out to be one of the funnier notions of the episode.

modico pretio: the supply no doubt having outstripped the demand; a modest investment in the service of Mercury.

praestinatae: LS list *praedestinatae* in our passage as used in the meaning "provided beforehand"; in the case of *destinare* there are several examples of the meaning "to purchase", e.g. Pl. *Mos.* 643, Cic. *Att.* 13, 33, 2. There is no reason to suppose that *praedestinare* could not have been employed in the same sense; but the ThLL material at Munich provides no evidence that it ever was so used. There are two possible solutions, then: to suppose with Beroaldus that a scribe unfamiliar with *praestinare* added (perhaps automatically) -*de*-, or to assume an original *destinare* that was not recognized in this sense and glossed with *prae*. The first seems to be the simpler solution. For *praestinare*, a Plautine term used some 10 times in the *Met.*, see Desertine p. 20[1], Callebat, *S.C.*, pp. 484 f.; see also Marg. Molt p. 52.

O. S. Powers, *Studies in the commercial vocabulary of Early Latin*, Diss. Chicago 1944, pp. 22-26 discusses both *destinare* and *praestinare* and suggests that notwithstanding Festus 223 M (= 249 L) *prae*- gives no connotation of previousness.

constanti uigore: see above on 86, 2.

festinus: cf. e.g. 1, 5 (5, 8); 2, 6 (29, 19); 2, 13 (36, 9); Verg. *A.* 9, 488 f. *ueste tegens tibi quam noctes festina diesque/ urgebam*. See Marg. Molt p. 51, who refers to the *sermo cotidianus*; Callebat, *S.C.*, pp. 411 f. agrees with Löfstedt, *Synt.* II, pp. 368 f., that the usage is poetic rather than colloquial. Its frequency increases in Christian authors.

quam...inrepsit: for the direct obj. see 3, 24 (70, 4) *inrepit cubiculum* and vdP. *ad loc.* The verb indicates that Thrasyleon has to go on all fours, both because of his disguise as a bear and presumably because of the size of the cage's door. See also 88, 8 *prorepit cauea*.

ipse: is placed at the end, doubtless both in order to produce an acceptable clausula and to emphasize once more the fact that Thrasyleon has volunteered for the task, as well as the fact that he is no real bear, who presumably would be reluctant to enter the cage.

---

[1] The author defends *praedestinare* on p. 66.

Ad hunc modum prioribus inchoatis sic ad reliqua fallaciae pergimus: "The preliminaries having been begun in this manner we then moved on to the rest of the deception".

ad hunc modum: cf. e.g. 3, 21 (67, 19) and Callebat, *S.C.*, p. 214.

prioribus inchoatis: the *priora* refer to all the preparations for the production of an acceptable bear. With *inchoatis* there is a notable redundancy. Bernhard p. 181 discerns a further redundancy in the use of *sic*, which in his opinion refers to the preceding participle. There is no reason, however, why we should not take it to refer to the next stages with Helm ("folgendermassen"); cf. 2, 25 (45, 21).

reliqua fallaciae: see comm. on 88, 18 ff. *cuncta rerum*.

It is not clear why vThiel I p. 13, n. 33 lists the present chapter among passages of ecphrasis that cannot be visualized.

CHAPTER XVI

Demochares is presented with a very special bear.

86, 19-21 Sciscitati nomen cuiusdam Nicanoris, qui genere Thracio proditus ius amicitiae summum cum illo Demochare colebat, litteras adfingimus: "We found out the name of one Nicanor who was the scion of a Thracian family and on very friendly terms with this Demochares, and we made up a letter from him to go with the bear". At the risk of seeming to be in a rut, it is attractive to interpret *Nicanor* as yet another significant name: Valpy notes "A victoria deductum nomen" (and continues with a somewhat low assessment of the Dauphin's Greek: "Graecis enim νίκη victoria est, et νικᾶν vincere"). The name "he who conquers men/a man" (see H. Frisk, *Griechisches etymologisches Wörterbuch*, Heidelberg 1954-1972, *s.v.* ἀνήρ) may in that case have a double function; it forms a beautiful contrast with Demochares, but in addition it points ahead to the sad outcome of the venture (90, 18).

The *genus Thracium* is no "blind motif"; Hildebrand is quite right in remarking "Thraciam A. commemoravit, quia silvestris et montosa ursis ceterisque feris frequentia lustra praebebat, quod consideraverant latrones, ita ut eo magis callidum consilium apertum fiat".

For *proditus* Scioppius proposed *productus*; he was wrong: cf. 1, 23 (21, 9) *generosa stirpe proditum*; Soc. 24 (35, 6) *inclute, parua prodite patria*, a quotation from Accius (cf. Warmington II 522). Apart from Apuleius this in any case rather infrequent sense of *proditus* occurs mainly (?) in poetry.

ius amicitiae colere: according to Médan an "expression nouvelle" (p. 240); *amicitiam colere* occurs frequently from Pl. *Cist.* 26 onwards.

adfingimus is a generally accepted emendation in ς for *adfigimus* which occurs in F and φ and is printed by Eyssenhardt only. LS and OLD translate *adfingere* in this passage as "to forge", but though the prefix *ad-* has in some cases lost its meaning — cf. 1, 17 (16, 1 f.) *adficto ex tempore absurdo ioco* — this is not the case here and the interpretation of ThLL is to be preferred: "fictis nova addere falsa". Cf. 8, 6 (180, 21 ff.) *frontem adseuerat et dolorem simulat et cadauer... circumplexus omnia quidem lugentium officia sollerter adfinxit*, where once again OLD does not give the prefix its value and translates "to simulate", "counterfeit".

86, 22-23 ut uenationis suae primitias bonus amicus uideretur ornando muneri[s]dedicasse: "to make it seem that his good friend had earmarked the first-fruit of his hunting as an adornment of the gladiatorial games".

For the extended use of *primitiae* cf. 10, 29 (260, 15 f.) *ac dum ludicris scaenicorum choreis primitiae spectaculi dedicantur.*

muneri is once again a certain correction of ς for *muneris* of F and φ. The same error occurs in *CIL* IX 2197, see P. Aalto, *Untersuchungen*, p. 65, n. 2.

Unfortunately for the robbers the *munus* will take on an entirely unexpected shape.

86, 23-25 Iamque prouecta uespera abusi praesidio tenebrarum Thrasyleonis caueam Demochari cum litteris illis adulterinis offerimus: "Late in the evening, we took advantage of the cover of darkness to present Thrasyleon's cage to Demochares together with the forged letter".

Apuleius employs forms of *uespera* only, not of *uesper*; see Neue-Wagener I³ pp. 855 f. for a general survey.

abutor is here used in the sense of "make a full use of", "profit from"; cf. Lucr. 5, 1033 *sentit enim uim quisque suam quod possit abuti*, also the Greek ἀποχρῆσθαι.

adulterinus in the sense of *falsus* is not uncommon; it occurs from Pl. *Bac.* 266 onwards and is used specifically of counterfeit coins, seals and keys.

86, 25-27 qui miratus bestiae magnitudinem suique contubernalis opportuna liberalitate laetatus: "amazed at the animal's size and overjoyed at his old buddy's opportune generosity".

In most cases the rather frequent *contubernalis* (see Callebat, *S.C.*, p. 46) means no more than "friend"; possibly there is a link with the martial name of Nicanor and *commilito* (in the original sense) is the appropriate association.

86, 27-87,1 iubet nobis protinus gaudii sui gerulis decem aureos, ut ipse habebat †, e suis loculis adnumerari: "he ordered that we, the bringers of such joy, should forthwith be paid ten gold pieces from the cash-box he always had with him (?)".

gaudii gerulus is a suggestive and unique expression. ThLL *s.v.* is wrong in treating it on a par with 6,20 (144,5), where Psyche calls herself *diuinae formonsitatis gerula* and with *Apol.* 77 (86, 16) where a *uerborum gerulus* is mentioned. For *gerulus* see vdP. p. 199.

ut ipse habebat presents editors with almost insuperable difficulties. Among the many proposed interpretations or alterations of the text none is really satisfactory.

1. Hildebrand wished to delete *ut ipse habebat* with some recc. Eyssenhardt agreed. Hildebrand offered as an alternative the conjecture: *ut*

ipse gaudebat. There are older conjectures on the part of Heinsius: *ut is se habebat* and Colvius: *ut ipse aiebat* (Lütjohann and vdVliet agree, Robertson comments "fortasse recte").

2. The order is changed by vdVliet and Robertson in the wake of Lütjohann p. 464: *iubet nobis protinus gaudii sui ut ipse habebat* (Rob.; vdVl. of course reads *aiebat*) *gerulis decem aureos e suis loculis adnumerari*.

3. Most editors maintain *ut ipse habebat*, but their interpretations are far from being the same. Helm thought that the Greek ὥσπερ εἶχεν was being imitated[1] and at first interpreted that expression as "qua erat liberalitate" (cf. Butler: "being a generous fellow"), later as 'sine mora' (cf. Helm-Krenkel: "wie er da ging und stand"). The latter interpretation — the one preferred by Oudendorp — was adopted by Frassinetti. However, the function of *ipse* remains unclear, as does the need for this equivalent of *protinus*.

It goes without saying that Robertson's interpretation fits the change of order mentioned above: he agrees with Kronenberg in interpreting *habebat* as *persuasum habebat*, and is (of course) followed by Grimal, and also by Vitali (who does not adopt the textual change!).

The most obvious translation is: "as he had himself". If we link this with *decem aureos*, as do e.g. Gaselee ("as he had great store in his coffers"), Brandt-Ehlers ("er persönlich hatte es ja") and Scazzoso ("che aveva a disposizione"), Colvius' ironic question: "si non habuisset, jussissetne numerari?" is to the point (unless we suppose that *ipse* is used emphatically and Demochares' wealth is underscored by a reference to his private coinage). Colvius' objection is void if *ut ipse habebat* is taken with the subsequent *e suis loculis*. In that case, moreover, the use of the imperfect is accounted for: Demochares is sketched as "the man with the cash-box", forever ready to be the benefactor. The curious word-order, however, argues against this interpretation.

For *loculi*, see Mayor on Juv. *Sat.* 1, 89.

ut nouitas consueuit ad repentinas uisiones animos homi- 87, 1-2
num pellere : "as novelty commonly attracts people to sudden manifestations". The expression is not without its irony; cf. Riefstahl p. 65: "kleine und grosze Schwächen der Menschen werden mit Überlegenheit festgestellt". It is unnecessary to replace the tradition's *pellere* by *pellicere* (Beroaldus, Robertson) or *impellere* (Pricaeus), though *pellere* here does have the meaning of the latter; for the frequent use of *simplex pro composito* in "Late Latin" see Löfstedt, *Spätlat. Stud.*, pp. 50 ff.; id., *Verm. Stud.*, pp. 117 ff.

For *repentina uisio* cf. 2, 13 (36, 4) *attonitus* [*et*] *repentinae uisionis stupore*.

---

[1] Thus also Lesky pp. 563 f., who uses this grecism also as an argument in favour of his hypothesis that the Thrasyleon episode is taken from the Greek original.

87, 2-3 multi numero mirabundi bestiam confluebant: "a large crowd gathered to see the animal"; acc. to ThLL this is the only occasion on which *mirabundus* is construed with an object; for adj. in *-bundus* with obj. see vdP. p. 26.

87, 3-4 quorum satis callenter curiosos aspectus Thrasyleon noster impetu minaci frequenter inhibebat: "but our friend Thrasyleon rather cleverly kept their curious stares constantly at a distance by threatening sallies". More people suffer from *curiositas* than Lucius alone and Thrasyleon has donned his bear's skin (in more senses than one) in order to fight just that.

callenter, a synonym of *callide*, is an Apuleian neologism that does not occur elsewhere in Latin (Médan pp. 124, 140).

In refuting Scriverius' conjecture *frequente* (Scriv. objects to the fact that *callenter* and *frequenter* qualify *inhibebat* asyndetically) Oudendorp remarks that *frequenter* might be taken also with *minaci* (ἀπὸ κοινοῦ).

The hyperbaton *quorum...aspectus* is remarkable, but in view of the frequency of this figure in the *Metamorphoses* (see Bernhard pp. 25 ff.) it is probably too farfetched to suggest that we have here a case of illustrative wordorder.

87, 5-6 consonaque ciuium uoce satis felix ac beatus Demochares ille saepe celebratus: "and he, so often praised by the unanimous voice of his fellow-citizens as "that most happy and prosperous Demochares..."

The same functional alliteration occurs at 3,2 (53, 12) *cuncti consona uoce flagitant*; there the function is, of course, a different one since function is determined by the context.

Médan p. 363 regards *felix* and *beatus* as synonyms; in many cases there is indeed no difference in meaning, cf. 2, 7 (31, 4 f.) *felix et...beatus cui permiseris illuc digitum intingere*; 5, 17 (116, 12 f.); 11, 22 (284, 7), but here *beatus* seems to lend greater precision to *felix* and denotes material happiness. See e.g. Fordyce on Cat. 61, 149.

87, 6-7 quod post tantam cladem ferarum nouo prouentu quoquo modo Fortunae resisteret: "since after so great a disaster to his animals he somehow thwarted hostile Fortune with a fresh supply".

Vallette points out (p. 21, n. 3) that *clades* in this case is not an exaggeration and compares Symmachus' indignation (*Ep.* 2, 46) in a similar case.

prouentus is used here in its original meaning of "yield", "harvest"; at 2, 12 (35, 7) and 96, 11 it is synonymous with *euentus*; in addition Apuleius elsewhere uses the word in the *Met.* in the (usual) pregnant sense of "success", "favourable result", cf. 10, 26 (257, 26 f.) *priusquam...*

digesta potione medicinae prouentus (φ: *euentus*) *appareat*; this sense possibly plays a secondary role in our passage.

Helm-Krenkel are right in treating *Fortuna* as a personification; for the sense "angry Fortune" see Junghans p. 163, n. 76; at 85, 9 her part was played by *Inuidia*.

87, 7-9

iubet noualibus suis confestim bestia iret, iubet summa cum diligentia reportari: "[he] ordered that the animal go forthwith to his park, and that it should be transported very carefully". The most important mss. (F φ A) intend (though F and φ do not produce altogether clearly) *bestiam iret, iubet*. This reading is, of course, senseless, but UES show *bestiam ire, iubet...reportari*, which is entirely possible.

Lütjohann regarded *iret, iubet* as a dittography resulting from ⟨*resist*⟩-*eret, iubet* of 87, 7 and wished to delete the words. He is followed by Helm (see Praef. *Fl*. p. LI), Gaselee, Robertson, Brandt-Ehlers, Frassinetti, Vitali and vThiel. Oudendorp, too, was inclined to delete: *iubet...reportari* might have crept into the text as an explanation of *iubet...ire*. The second phrase is a further explanation or sharper definition of the first according to Armini also (1928, p. 293), but for him this was good reason to retain the text (of UES), as Hildebrand and Eyssenhardt had done before him (vdVliet changed into *bestiam inmitterent, iubet ... deportari*, see below), and in which he was followed by Giarratano, Terzaghi and Scazzoso. The reading we, too, prefer keeps very close to the manuscript tradition, with no more emendation than *bestia* for *bestiam* (for added *m* see Helm Praef. *Fl*. p. XLVII).

There is an excellent parallel for repeated *iubet* with varied construction: 1,23 (21, 2 f.) *et cum dicto iubet uxorem decedere utque in eius locum adsidam iubet* (the chiasmus is illustrative). In comparison with the passage just quoted there are three syntactic-stylistic differences (apart from the chiasmus): *parataxis* instead of an *ut* construction, an imperfect subj. instead of a present subj., as well as asyndeton. These phenomena are typically Apuleian; see Callebat, *S.C.*, pp. 358-360. In both cases the repetition of *iubet* echoes the agitation of the person who issues the order.

noualibus is dative (thus also v. Geisau p. 96 and *Index Apul. s.v.*) rather than local abl. (Médan p. 56) taking the place of an acc. of direction; see vdP. p. 191. The meaning of the word can hardly be the usual one of "fallow land". According to Oudendorp *noualia* or *nouales* (the *Index Apul.* is in no doubt concerning the gender here: it is neuter!) are *praedia rustica*. Hildebrand rightly objects to this interpretation, but his argument is not felicitous: "Si in praedia rustica ille (sc. Thrasyleon) religatus esset, quid inde commodi redundare potuit ad latrones?" In fact, the robber-narrator takes great pains (ch. 17) to prevent the bear from being sent away! It would be a more forceful argument to point out that in the subsequent objection there is no reference to a strenuous expedition as one might expect if *noualia* denoted land outside the city, but that the only objection is to *committere*. In any case it seems probable that the *noualia* are to be thought more or less in the immediate neighbourhood of the *domus Democharis* and have the function of a *uiuarium*, a παράδεισος; thus Hildebrand, who compares Aus. *Mos.* 332, (also Forcellini *s.v. novale* and Vallette p. 22 n. 1).

Two possible interpretations present themselves for *reportari*: it may mean "to be brought back" (in that case the repetition of *iubet* is also functional since two activities are referred to), but it is perhaps simpler to regard the word as a synonym of *deportari*, which was mistakenly adopted in the text by vdVliet (and after him Helm I/II, Gaselee, Giarratano and Scazzoso). See Wiman p. 36, Armini 1932, pp. 75 f., Löfstedt, *Per. Aeth.* p. 274 concerning *reportare=deportare*. It is also possible that *re-* here is void of meaning, see Waszink p. 490, Svennung, *Pall.* pp. 602 f.

CHAPTER XVII

The two robbers offer their services as attendants to the bear, but their help is not appreciated.

"Caueas"..."domine, fraglantia solis et itineris spatio fatigatam coetui multarum et, ut audio, non recte ualentium committere ferarum.": "Do be careful, sir, about bringing this animal, worn out as it is by the heat of the sun and its long journey, into contact with a lot of animals which, from all I hear, are not by any means well".

caueas...committere: the present subjunctive instead of imperative is colloquial style. See Médan p. 21; Callebat, *S.C.*, p. 100; LHSz p. 335. From Cic. *Att.* 3, 17, 18 onwards *cauere* is construed with the infinitive, see Médan p. 77; Callebat, *S.C.*, p. 311. LHSz pp. 346 ff. show the extension of the use of the infinitive after similar verbs.

fraglantia solis: see comm. on 74, 9. For the orthography of *fraglantia* see Appendix II.

fatigatam: as at 85, 5 ff. *ursam* or *bestiam* has been left out. See Callebat, *S.C.*, p. 452. The arguments are well chosen, cf. 85, 10 f. *diutina captiuitate fatigatae simul et aestiua flagrantia maceratae*. As regards the *fraglantia solis* the statement is not even untrue: cf. 85, 25 f. *ac dum caelestis uaporis flammis examurgatur*, but the *iter* of the bear (that was) was of the kind *unde negant redire quemquam*.

coetui: here in the concrete meaning of company rather than the abstract "social intercourse"; the latter retains something of the original verbal action (cf. 74, 18).

multarum...ferarum. this, of course, contradicts 85, 12 f. *paene ad nullum rediuere numerum*. Theoretically there are three possible explanations:

1. Apuleius commits an error in his logic, as he does elsewhere, see vdP. p. 74.

2. A more probable explanation would be that not only bears but other animals as well are housed in the *noualia*; no information is given concerning their state of health, however, and therefore it seems better

3. to assume that the robber pretends not to be fully informed. This corresponds with the not displeasing understatement *non recte ualentium* and the addition *ut audio*, an irony which is obvious for the listener/reader, who knows that *ut uidi* would be the truth.

committere: Hildebrand objects to the interpretation that the word has its usual meaning of *tradere* and opts for that of *coniungere* ("monet latro ne D. ursam recte valentem cum morbidis coniungat neve ita eius stragem efficiat"). ThLL, however, correctly interprets the word as meaning *conferre, admouere*.

87, 12-14 Quin potius domus tuae patulum ac perflabilem locum, immo et lacu aliquo conterminum refrigerantemque prospicis?: "Why don't you rather look round your own house for a spot that is open and airy — better still, next to a pond, where it is cool?" In both pairs of adjectives belonging to *locum* the second adjective explains the first; see Bernhard p. 166. The alliteration of respectively *p* and *r* may be functional. Note the increasing number of syllables as well as the variation in the use of copulative (*et*, however, belongs to *immo*; for the combination see Callebat, *S.C.*, p. 328).

As at 3, 17 (65, 1) Oudendorp prefers *perflatilem*. He is wrong, see vdP. p. 131.

lacu aliquo: ablative according to Médan p. 37; *Index Apul. s.v. lacus* (as appears from the order in which the references occur); ThLL and OLD *s.v. conterminus*, but the latter with the addition *si vera lectio*. The usual dative, however, is much more probable (thus ThLL *s.v. lacus*); *aliquoi*, proposed by Oudendorp to effect a dative and accepted by Robertson and Brandt-Ehlers, is unnecessary. Parallels for dative *lacu* are found in Stat. *Silv.* 1, 1, 83 and *ibid.* 1, 5, 53; for dative *aliquo* see vdP. p. 38.

lacus is more likely to refer to a pond belonging to the house than to a lake as Helm-Krenkel translate.

87, 14-16 An ignoras hoc genus bestiae lucos consitos et specus roridos et fontes amoenos semper incubare?: "Or don't you know that this species of animal always lives in dense woods, moist caves and by pleasant springs?"

The syndetic tricolon *lucos...amoenos* shows homoeoteleuton in the adjectives but varying endings in the nouns; there is some symmetry in the number of syllables and a notable (also functional?) sigmatism. The elements named are in increasing order applicable to, and hence arguments in favour of, the *locus domus Democharis*. For the collective *bestia* see Médan p. 211 and the commentary on 85, 4.

consitus finds an interpretation elsewhere in the *Met.*: cf. 5, 1 (103, 10 f.) *lucum proceris et uastis arboribus consitum*; 8, 18 (191, 19) *nemus quoddam proceris arboribus consitum*; 10, 30 (261, 5) *mons...consitus uirectis et uiuis arboribus*. Weyman p. 349 compares Jul. Val. 3, 24 *locum arboribus consitum*. Combination with *lucus* occurs also in Lact. *Phoen.* 9 and Ennod. *Opusc.* 4, 42.

roridus, synonymous with *roscidus* which occurs elsewhere in Apuleius (see Marg. Molt p. 31), is very rare: according to the lexica it occurs, apart from our passage, only in Prop. 2, 30 b, 26 *rorida antra* and *ibid.* 4, 4, 48 *rorida terga iugi*. After *roridos* A adds *frigidos*, ς *et colles frigidos* (also in Oudendorp's text). The A reading however disturbs the symmetry, the reading in ς produces a syndetic tetracolon that is less persuasive and also less usual than the tricolon. See Bernhard pp. 74 ff.

incubare: in the sense of "to live", "stay in/near" it occurs from Pl. *Cas.* 110 onwards. The construction with the accusative is a novelty and

is subsequently found only at *Met.* 7, 7 (159, 9 f.) *tabernulam quandam...*
incubabant; Avien. *Orb. terr.* 529; Petr. Chrys. *serm.* 17.

Talibus monitis Demochares perterritus numerumque perditorum secum recensens non difficulter adsensus, ut ex arbitrio nostro caueam locaremus, facile permisit: "Much alarmed by these warnings Demochares mentally reviewed his numerous losses, and reaching the same conclusion without hesitation he readily permitted us to put the cage wherever we liked".

The participles piled up here (*perterritus* and *adsensus* are connected by -*que*, *recensens* has a causal function vis à vis *adsensus*; all three are participles of compound verbs with varied prefixes, but *per-* is picked up in *perditorum* and *permisit*) cause a certain tension; one is waiting for Demochares' reaction, but his consent is given *non difficulter*, even *facile*. Oudendorp, then, is wrong in wishing to delete the final words with Elmenhorst and Scriverius ('mera enim est glossa praecedentium').

perditorum: abstract (vdVliet adds *animalium* after *secum*). Giarratano-Frassinetti, Robertson, Brandt-Ehlers, Scazzoso and vThiel read *perditarum* with ς without acknowledgement in their respective crit. app. For the *mutatio generis* compare 5, 17 (116, 20) *trucis bestiae* referred to in 116, 22 by *eum*. See Fernhout *ad loc.*; v. Wageningen on Min. Fel. 17, 2; LHSz p. 432.

"Sed et nos", inquam, "ipsi parati sumus hic ibidem pro cauea ista excubare noctes, ut aestus et uexationis incommodo bestiae fatigatae et cibum tempestiuum et potum solitum accuratius offeramus": ""Furthermore", I went on, "we are ourselves prepared to keep watch at night, right here in front of this cage, so that we can be more precise in giving the beast his food on schedule and his usual drink, worn out as he is by the trials caused by heat and discomfort"".

Once again the fatigue of the bear/Thrasyleon is mentioned; the same arguments, different words. Thrasyleon's own situation, by now, certainly involves both *aestus* and *uexatio*. For the expressive combination *hic ibidem* see Callebat, *S.C.*, p. 530; LHSz p. 125.

excubare: just as bears are wont to *incubare*, robbers' routine involves *excubare* — here an indoor activity! — cf. 79, 11 f. *quo speculatores e numero latronum...noctibus excubabant*.

cibum tempestiuum et potum solitum: it is useful to remember that *tempestiuus* in combination with *epulae* and the like usually means "ahead of" rather than "on schedule" (see Koestermann on Tac. *Ann.* 11, 37, 2) and that the *potus* is likely to be somewhat *insolitus* for Thrasyleon.

accuratius: probably a true comparative, viz. *quam uos*: Demochares' reaction is a little peevish: *nihil indigemus labore isto uestro*.

"Nihil indigemus labore isto uestro", respondit ille, "iam paene tota familia per diutinam consuetudinem nutriendis ursis exercitata est". "He answered, "We don't at all need you to do this job; pretty well all my staff have had plenty of practice in feeding bears"".

consuetudinem: both "custom", "practice" and "social intercourse", "contact". For the latter sense in the *Met.* see Fernhout on 5, 9 (110, 10 f.) *procedente consuetudine et adfectione roborata.* The combination *diutina consuetudo* also occurs in Sen. *Ep.* 112, 1.

Note how the robber (or Lucius, or Apuleius) is proceeding "dialectically": the first request of the robber-narrator, packaged most skilfully, does not fail to impress Demochares. He consents and the robbers appear to have gained their point. A second, apparently very reasonable, request follows. But the robber, in his enthusiasm, has overstepped the mark. He slips on *accuratius*: Demochares has no need of *labor iste uester*, he has his own men for those duties! The mission, then, has succeeded only partially. A slight disappointment is hard to suppress and the departure is rather abrupt (see note on 87, 27 ff.).

CHAPTER XVIII

The attack on Demochares' house: Thrasyleon shows a lion's courage.

Post haec ualefacto discessimus et portam ciuitatis egressi 87, 27-29
monumentum quoddam conspicamur procul a uia remoto et
abdito loco positum: "After this we took our leave and departed.
Having gone out through the city gate we noticed a grave-monument
in a remote and secluded spot, well away from the road".

ualefacere is a somewhat unusual synonym for *ualedicere*; it occurs e.g.
in August. *Ep.* 65, 2 and Hier. *Ep.* 120, 11. If written as one word it may
be regarded as an abl. abs. without a noun, see Waszink p. 223, LHSz p.
141 f. In all likelihood *uale* was originally the subject, which later lost
its independent entity, as in *uale dicto*, e.g. Ov. *Tr.* 1, 3, 57.

Alternating perf. and pres. is not uncommon in the *Met.*; see Bernhard
p. 153, Callebat, *S.C.*, pp. 428 f. Bernhard regards it as 'eine zu gesuchte
Interpretation' to look for a rationale in such cases, but the present
conspicamur (itself an expressive word, see vdP. p. 129) in this case
reflects another element of tension after the slight disappointment
Demochares has caused. Cf. Lindsay's translation: "So there was nothing
for it but to say goodbye".

Bernhard p. 167 regards *remotus* and *abditus* as synonyms, but the
latter is a result of the former.

Ibi capulos carie et uetustate semitectos, quis inhabitabant 87, 29-88,3
puluerei et iam cinerosi mortui, passim ad futurae praedae
receptacula reseramus: "The coffin there, now only half closed
because of decay and age, which the dead inhabited who had long since
turned to dust and ashes, we opened everywhere, as storage for our
future booty".

capulos: in the more usual sense of "handle", "hilt" it occurs in *Met.*
1, 13 (12, 13) *capulo tenus*; the meaning "coffin" also in 8, 13 (187, 12):
Charite capulum (φ; generally accepted against F's *caput*) *Tlepolemi
propter assistens*; 10, 12 (245, 16) *coperculo capuli remoto*. Nonius p. 7 L.
takes the word as a neuter and explains: *capulum dicitur quicquid aliam
rem intra se capit. nam sarcophagum, id est sepulchrum, capulum dici
ueteres uolunt, quod corpora capiat.*

The overtones of the word are hard to assess, witness the qualifications
in Bernhard p. 134 (vulgar), Médan p. 171 (archaic), Ernout on Lucr.
2, 1174 (belonging to comic language). Callebat may be right in classi-
fying the word among professional terminology of the *sermo cotidianus*
(*S.C.*, p. 44).

semitectos: "half covered", or rather "half open"; see comm. on 85, 14
semiuiuorum; the conjectures *semiconfectos* (vdVliet), *semiretectos* (Plas-
berg), *semirutos* (Damsté, Thomas) are therefore unnecessary. Since at
Sen. *VB* 25, 2 the word is a conjecture, no longer accepted, by Lipsius,
it may count as an Apuleian neologism, which was picked up by Arn.
6, 25 and Amm. 19, 11, 13. See Médan pp. 132 f. concerning the favourite
prefix *semi-*.

For *quis = quibus* see vdP. p. 159.

inhabitabant: used transitively at 78, 19 (if the addition *quam* is correct),
see comm. *ad loc.* Seeing that the inhabitants are *cinerosi mortui* the verb
is used somewhat ironically.

cinerosi: one of Apuleius' neologisms (Bernhard p. 139; Médan p. 119).
It is a rare word and in this sense ("turned to ashes") strictly Apuleian,
see L. Gargantini p. 38; at 7, 27 (175, 3) *cinerosam canitiem* signifies
"covered with ashes". See Ernout, *Les Adj.*, pp. 57 and 81.

ad … receptacula reseramus: note the vowel parallelism; a *receptaculum*
occurred above at 85, 20 f. vThiel I p. 105, n. 119 disapproves: "Die
Beschreibung der vermoderten Leichen ist im Geschmack des Apuleius".
Apuleius' penchant for macabre scenes is revealed also in Photis' de-
scription of Pamphile's departure (3, 17), the description of the dead
bodies on the road at 8, 17, the slave's body eaten by ants at 8, 22.
Heine pp. 149 f. gives further examples of a similar *deformitas* in the *Met.*

The lack of piety with regard to the dead and their graves shown here
is entirely consonant with the given typology of the robbers. However,
it is not the hand of Hades but of Haemus that will fall upon the dese-
crators. As far as the graves themselves are concerned, Vallette p. 23,
n.l. has remarked that in the *Met.* only interment is mentioned and cre-
mation does not occur. The fact finds its explanation on the one hand in
the impossibility of the latter in several cases (e.g. Socrates in 1, 19;
Lucius' guard in 7, 26); on the other hand it fits in with historic reality,
since cremation at this time (i.e. the time in which the novel is set) is
becoming less and less usual. See Marquardt p. 377.

88, 3-5   **et ex disciplina sectae seruato noctis inlunio tempore, quo
somnus obuius impetu primo corda mortalium ualidius
inuadit ac premit**: "and, according to the teaching of our school,
we waited for the moonless time of night, when unsought sleep first
attacks human hearts and holds them in a stronger grip". As the theoret-
ical background of the robbers' profession is mentioned once again the
narrator rises to epic heights! Cf. 81, 14 ff. *quod est huic disciplinae
primarium studium: sedulo fortunas inquirebamus popularium.* Both
disciplina and *secta* are terms from the philosophic realm: the combination
of the two places the metaphor beyond doubt (in the translations it is
usually disregarded; cf. Adlington-Gaselee: "according to the custom of
our band"). The metaphor's function is a double one: on the one hand
it is in conformity with the lofty heights of the subsequent language with

136

its epic colouring; on the other hand it emphasizes the very discrepancy between the lofty language and the trivial reality described. The word *secta* is also used by the robbers in 92, 23 and 6, 31 (153, 3), but in a slightly different sense (something like "profession"). See furthermore Fernhout on 5, 15 (115, 10).

seruato=obseruato; we are told by Servius on Verg. *A*. 6, 198 that this is a technical term that occurs mainly in epic poetry. Cf. Verg. *A*. 6, 338 f. *dum sidera seruat/ exciderat puppi* (*Palinurus sc.*); *ibid*. 5, 25 *seruata... astra*; Luc. *Phars*. 1, 601 *doctus uolucres augur seruare sinistras*. See Norden, *Komm.*, p. 231. Weyman p. 363 regards Amm. 17, 2, 3 *obseruata nocte inluni* as a reminiscence.

inlunio: cf. 9, 33 (227, 20) *inluniae caliginis*; the adj. occurs in Apuleius only. (Oudendorp reads *illunae* "ut nox suum habeat epitheton" and resists *illunis* (Salmasius) since Apuleius in the case of pairs prefers the adjectives in *-us*, but there is justified criticism in Hildebrand: "haec ipsa terminatio in Mss. constanter reservata admonere eum debebat, ut cautior esset.")

somnus obuius: personification (Bernhard p. 190), and indeed not an uncommon one (Feldbrugge p. 116). Cf. 92, 10 f. *me...clara lux* (!) *oppressit*; for the meaning "unsought" cf. Quint. 12, 2, 2 *uirtutem...obuiam et inlaboratam* (*et* was deleted both by Radermacher and Winterbottom).

mortalium: not necessarily poetic, but the word does fit in the elevated style of the present passage; see Ogilvie on Liv. 1, 9, 8.

impetu primo: the first sleep is deepest (hence *ualidius*). Apuleius obviously alludes to Verg. *A*. 2, 268 f. *tempus erat quo prima quies mortalibus aegris/incipit et dono diuum gratissima serpit*; cf. *ibid*. 1, 470 f. *primo quae prodita somno/Tydides multa uastabat caede*; ibid. 5, 857 *uix primos inopina quies laxauerat artus*.

cohortem nostram gladiis armatam...uelut expilationis uadimonium sistimus: "we stationed our cohort, armed with swords... as a kind of guarantee of looting". 88, 5-7

cohortem: see Appendix I; the swords return in the description of the counterattack on the part of the staff (89, 9).

uelut...uadimonium: correctly paraphrased by Valpy as "veluti satisfacturi sponsioni factae de direptione ejus." For the use of the juridical term *uadimonium* in the *Met.* see Bernhard p. 194; vdP. p. 97; Summers pp. 149 f. Here we have a witty play on the technical term *uadimonium sistere* ("appear before the court").

Nec setius Thrasyleon examus⟨s⟩im capto noctis latrocinali momento prorepit cauea statimque custodes, qui propter sopiti quiescebant, omnes ad unum, mox etiam ianitorem ipsum gladio conficit: "Thrasyleon (was) no less (active): he seized precisely the robbers' moment in the night, crept out of his cage and at 88, 7-10 once with a sword killed to a man all the guards who were lying asleep neerby and then also the actual porter".

nec setius Thrasyleon: after a glance at the exertions of the robbers we come to a description of Thrasyleon's deeds, of which, however, only the results are visible to the robbers; the activities themselves therefore can be known only through reconstruction. Therefore we are not told how Thrasyleon managed to obtain a sword, nor how, in his bear suit, he could have wielded it.

examussim: literally "perpendicular"; most often, as here, used in the derivative sense "precise", "careful". After Plautus the word does not occur until Apuleius. See 2, 30 (50, 8) *adplicant examussim*; 10, 2 (237, 21); 11, 27 (288, 26 f.). Desertine p. 17, Callebat, *S.C.*, p. 476; de Jonge and Chr. Harrauer *ad loc.* agree that Apuleius has borrowed from Plautus.

capto noctis latrocinali momento: the expression *momentum capere* is new, but analogous to the well known *tempus* (or *occasionem*) *capere*. Bernhard, Médan and de Jonge on 2, 14 (36, 18) fail to mention the fact that *latrocinalis* is an Apuleian neologism, used later by e.g. Amm.; cf. Amm. 27, 2, 3 *latrocinalia castra*; *ibid.* 31, 5, 7 *latrocinales globi*. The expression as a whole produces a comic effect; see Feldbrugge p. 105.

propter: adverb. See comm. on 77, 13; *prope* (a few mss.) and *probe* (Pricaeus) were effectively rejected by Oudendorp.

omnes ad unum: less frequent than *ad unum omnes* which was preferred by Oudendorp; see however Hand, *Turs.* I, p. 104. Perry (1923, p. 219) curiously speaks in this context of *"several* servants on guard" (our italics).

gladio: vThiel I p. 105 thinks it exceedingly strange that Thrasyleon suddenly has a sword at his disposal, but one may easily suppose that it came from one of the *custodes*; cf. Graves: "killing all the houseguards… with one of their own swords." The irony of being killed by one's own sword also occurs at 7, 13 (164, 11), where the robbers themselves are the victims!

88, 10-13 clauique subtracta fores ianuae repandit nobisque prompte conuolantibus et domus alueo receptis demonstrat horreum, ubi uespera sagaciter argentum copiosum recondi uiderat: "and, abstracting his key, he threw open the double doors. As we rushed straight in and were well into the interior of the house, he showed us the strong-room where he had closely watched a quantity of silver being stored the night before".

subtracta: the prefix has the force of "from under" (the janitor lies on top of his key).

repandit: also occurs at 9, 20 (218, 8) *Myrmex…repandit fores et recipit…dominum*. The Thesaurus material at Munich provides no instances of *repandere* outside Apuleius.

alueo: only here used for the interior of a house; nearest is the meaning "beehive" cf. Tib. 2, 1, 49 *rure leuis uerno flores apis ingerit alueo*. Possibly Apuleius plays with this sense: the robbers fly (like bees) to and fro (*conuolare; gladiis armati*), in the *alueus* a bear is sniffing (*sagaciter*) around, smelling out some ... silver!

horreum = gazophylacium; see vdP. p. 198.

uespera: abl. of time (= *uesperi*); see Callebat, *S.C.*, p. 193.

sagaciter: really "with a sharp nose" (particularly of hounds. See also comm. on 84, 1.), therefore typical of a bear, but here applied to *uidere* (synaesthesia, cf. Wellek-Warren, *Theory of Lit.* (Per. ed.), pp. 83 and 283 (bibliography)). The place of the adverb is interesting, all the more since the expected *sagaciter uiderat* would also have produced a good — if not a better — clausula: a dicretic as against the present spondee+cretic.

confertae manus uiolentia: "with joint forces". *Confertae* is a 88, 14
correction in ς for *confarte* about which there can be no doubt; *conferta manus* is a military term; cf. Caes. *Gal.* 1, 24, 5 *acies confertissima*; Sal. *Cat.* 60, 6 *in confertissimos hostes*; Curt. 3, 2, 13 *conferta robora*. Compare also *Met.* 5, 14 (114, 13) *conferto uestigio*; the reading *conferta uox* 5, 3 (105, 14) is disputed, the interpretation dubious; see Fernhout and Grimal *ad loc.*

iubeo singulos commilitonum asportare quantum quisque 88, 14-18
poterat auri uel argenti, et in illis aedibus fidelissimorum
mortuorum occultare propere rursumque concito gradu
recurrenti⟨s⟩ sarcinas iterare: "I ordered each of my comrades
to bring as much gold or silver as each could carry, and hide it quickly
in the homes of our most loyal dead accomplices, and then run back at
the double again to get another load".

aedibus: Brant's conjecture *sedibus* was rejected as early as Oudendorp and Hildebrand; they point out that both *aedes* and *domus* are often used for a grave (cf. 88, 1 *inhabitabant*); Apuleius, however, is the first to use *aedes* in this sense. Cf. *CIL* 3, 8289 *has pro meritis aedes carissimo coniugi memoriam posuit*; ibid. 14, 480 for the singular: *hanc aedem posuit* etc.

fidelissimorum: at 91, 2 the dead are also called *fideles*; cf. the robbers' outburst at 91, 4 ff.: *reputabamus merito nullam fidem in uita nostra repperiri, quod ad manis iam et mortuos odio perfidiae nostrae demigrarit*.

rursum...recurrentis: redundant use of *rursum*: see Marg.Molt p. 24; vdP. p. 98. *recurrentis* is Hildebrand's emendation for *recurrenti* (F): "*s* littera a sequenti vocabulo *sarcinas* absorpta". φ has *recurrentes* (altered to *recurrenti*), which is the reading followed by Oudendorp, Eyssenhardt, vdVliet, Gaselee and Vitali; this reading is also to be found in ThLL *s.v. itero*.

concito gradu: cf. 5, 31 (128, 22 f.) *concito gradu*; 2, 6 (29, 19); 4, 2 (75, 16) etc. Weyman p. 366 regards Amm. 24, 6, 12 *concito gradu* as imitative.

sarcinas iterare: the idiomatic use of *iterare* also occurs e.g. in Ov.

Met. 4, 749, where he says of the nymphs: *semina...iterant iactata per undas*; Stat. *Ach.* 1, 909 *inmitis quotiens iterabitur ensis* (see Dilke *ad loc.*).

88, 18-20 quod enim ex usu foret omnium, me solum resistentem pro domus limine cuncta rerum exploraturum sollicite, dum redirent: "but because it would be in the interest of all, I would stay alone by the threshold of the house and keep a close eye on everything, until they returned".

quod...omnium: the robber-narrator is a born teacher; cf. 81, 14 f. *quod est huic disciplinae primarium studium*; the number of explicatives (*nam, enim*) is also very large.

me...exploraturum: the transition to reported speech is the easier since (slightly zeugmatic) *iubeo* serves as a *verbum dicendi*. On reported speech in the *Met.* see Bernhard p. 52 f.

resistentem=*restantem*; the example nearest to this in sense is 2, 4 (27, 17) *pedes imi resistunt*. See de Jonge *ad loc.*

cuncta rerum: also at 83, 15. In the fourth book we find furthermore the following partitive genitives of this type: 75, 18 *nimio uelocitatis*; 76, 13 *procliue montis;* 82, 6 *singula rerum*; 83, 13 *rerum singula*; 86, 19 *reliqua fallaciae*; 97, 5 *profundum pelagi*; 97, 11 *terrae plusculum*; 98, 12 *uenerationis incertum*; 99, 14 f. *profundum maris*; 103, 3 f. *per deuexa rupis*. See vGeisau pp. 261 ff.; Médan pp. 265 f.; Bernhard pp. 206 f. Austin on Verg. *A* 2, 332 has an excellent note on the origin of this gen. part.; some additions in his comm. on *A*. 1, 422.

Both Lesky p. 563 and vThiel I p. 105, n. 119d note that the motif of the robber who stays behind occurs elsewhere in the *Met.* (3, 28; 7, 1), but their conclusions concerning Apuleius' dependence on the Greek original in this passage are utterly different. See introduction.

88, 21-22 siqui de familia forte uigilassent: "should any of the household chance to have awoken". For the partitive use of *de* Callebat, *S.C.*, p. 201 compares Dessau 6824 *si quis de propinquis*; *ibid.* 2354 *si qui de collegiis...si quis de tironibus*. See also Waszink pp. 311 f.

The notion "wake up" is certainly apt here in view of the context at 88, 28 ff. *quidam seruulum...inquietus proserpit* etc., but Stewech's conjecture *euigilassent*, though accepted by all editors, is unnecessary; cf. Svennung, *Oros.*, p. 151: "Warum nehmen die Wörterbücher für dieses Verbum nur die Bedeutung "wachen" (Ggstz. *dormire*) auf, da es doch, soviel ich sehen kann — wie *evigilare* — auch mit 'aufwachen', 'erwachen' ('aufstehen') übersetzt werden kann?" As evidence Svennung quotes: Pl. *Mil.* 215 *uigila, ne somno stude*; *ibid.* 218 *uigila inquam, expergiscere inquam* and a few further instances from Plautus; Verg. *A.* 4, 573 *praecipites uigilate uiri* (showing the same alliteration as our passage); Suet. *Vesp.* 21 *maturius semper ac de nocte uigilabat; dein perlectis epistulis...amicos admittebat*, where Graevius and others wrote

140

euigilabat against the mss.; id. *Claud.* 33, 2 *somni breuissimi erat, nam ante mediam noctem plerumque uigilabat, ut tamen interdiu nonnumquam…obdormisceret* (here, too, editors read *euigilabat*). These and other instances mentioned by Svennung find many parallels from the Thesaurus material at Munich, e.g. Suet. *Aug. 78 si uel officii uel sacri causa maturius uigilandum esset*; Cels. 4, 32 (185, 23 M.) *ex quocumque morbo inualescit, si tarde confirmatur, uigilare prima luce debet*; Col. 11, 1, 14 *igitur primus omnium uigilet* (sc. *uilicus*). See G. Nyström, *Variatio sermonis hos Columella*, Diss. Göteborg 1926, p. 32; LHSz p. 302.

Quis enim, quamuis fortis et intrepidus, immani forma 88, 22-26
tantae bestiae noctu praesertim uisitata non se ad fugam
statim concitaret, non obdito cellae pessulo pauens et
trepidus sese cohiberet: "For who, however stout-hearted and
fearless, on seeing the enormous shape of that huge beast, especially at
night, would not at once take the flight, and in fear and trembling bolt
the door of his room and lock himself in?"

A sonorous and rhetorical period built on the antithesis *fortis et intrepidus* versus *pauens et trepidus*, with the aim to convince the audience that the subsequent incident could not reasonably have been foreseen.

immani forma tantae bestiae: the generally accepted emendation by a later hand *tantae* (for original *tanta*) provides parallelism of cases, chiasmus in number of syllables.

noctu praesertim: not a superfluous addition, for Demochares had said that the staff was *nutriendis ursis exercitata* (87, 25 f.).

uisitata: no iterative value, cf. 89, 1 f. *uisa…bestia*. See Médan p. 183; Callebat, *S.C.*, pp. 141 f.

se ad fugam…concitaret: the expression *se in fugam concitare* occurs in Liv. 22, 17, 6 where a similar situation — Hannibal's trick with the cattle — is described also in rhetorical terms. See Weissenborn-Müller *ad loc.*

obdito: in the sense *ianuae (foribus) opponere* the verb *obdere* occurs before Apuleius only in the comic poets; for the meaning *nectere* see vdP. p. 137.

cella: often used for a slave's room; see e.g. Marquardt p. 248.

CHAPTER XIX

Once again the robbers' plans are foiled by a chance occurrence: a slave wakes up and the domestic staff attack the bear.

88, 26-27 His omnibus salubri consilio recte dispositis occurrit scaeuus euentus: "When with sound planning we had all this properly arranged, we were met by an unlucky chance". For the narrative technique ("at the very moment that things go well...") see comm. on 85, 8-10; *scaeuus euentus* might well be printed with a capital: the divine element is underscored by 89, 1 *diuinitus*. See comm. on 75, 15-18. Bernhard p. 19 notes the emphatic placement (final verb would have produced much the same clausula).

   salubri consilio: cf. 3, 29 (74, 1 f.) *consilium me subit longe salubrius*; 10, 7 (241, 23) *placuit salubre consilium*. The combination which occurs from Cicero (e.g. *Att.* 8, 12, 5) onwards is quite common; see ThLL *s.v. consilium* 451, 6 f. and 455, 22-27.

   scaeuus ("nasty") occurs in a similar sense in Sallust, *Orat. Lep.* 5 p. 148, 19 Kurfess: *quae cuncta scaeuos iste Romulus quasi ab externis rapta tenet*; (Ernout translates: "cette caricature de Romulus"). Médan p. 199 gives an incomplete account of the frequency of the word; cf. e.g. Gel. 12, 13, 4; Script. Hist. Aug. Ael. Spart. *Pesc. Nig.* 7, 1; Servius on Verg. *A.* 3, 351 has a curious remark in which two senses of the word are employed: *Scaeua porta dicta est non a pugnis ante se factis scaeuis, id est malis — nam et ante sic dicta est — nec ab itinere ingressis scaeuo, id est sinistro — quod ingressi non recto eunt itinere, sed sinistro — sed a cadauere Laomedontis, hoc est scenomate, quod in eius fuerat superliminio.*

   Note the contrast *recte...scaeuus*. See also comm. on 75, 19, Vallette p. 7, n. 2, Fernhout on 5, 9 (109, 23).

88, 27-28 Namque dum reduces socios nostros suspensus opperior...: "For while I was waiting on tenterhooks for our comrades to be back..." Note the prevalence of *s* (continued in the next clause).

   Namque...reduces socios: a Vergilian echo (*A.* 1, 390 *namque tibi reduces socios classemque relatam/nuntio*) which may be added to Gatscha's list.

   Namque occurs both in first and in second place in Apuleius; see Bernhard p. 28 and vdP. p. 42 (with further literature).

   reduces socios nostros: they had at 88, 19 been despatched to hide as much gold and silver as they could carry. The narrator is naturally in suspense, since, in this Apuleian world, the sort of untoward happening

142

as is described subsequently is of course part and parcel of his experience; *nostros* includes the bear/Thrasyleon; cf. Perry 1923, p. 219, who mistakes the tamosphere when saying that "Thrasyleon and the speaker are quietly waiting for their comrades to return."

quidam seruulum st⟨r⟩epitu[s] scilicet diuinitus inquietus 88, 28-89,1 proserpit leniter: "one of the slave-boys, disturbed inevitably by the noise by divine agency crept silently forth".

The text is by no means certain: except for *stepit*; F reads as printed; *seruulus* ς. There are three main problems:

I. *seruulum* or *seruulus*; 2. *strepitus* or *strepitu*; 3. *scilicet* or *scilicet uel* (or some other disjunctive).

I. *Seruulum* is changed to *seruulus* in ς. Giarratano follows the conjecture comparing 9, 35 (229, 10). Robertson and Scazzoso follow suit. Helm hesitates ("fortasse recte") and notes 9, 37 (231, 22) *quidam de seruulis*, cf. Novák, *Čezké Museum Filologické* 10 (1904), p. 1.

There are several instances of gen. in *-um* in the *Met.*: *aureum* 7, 4 (156, 24); *denarium* 1, 24 (23, 2); 2, 13 (35, 24 f.); 8, 25 (197, 12); *inferum* 11, 5 (269, 16); 11, 11 (274, 19 f.); 11, 21 (283, 6); *liberum* 5, 28 (125, 19); 9, 8 (208, 14); *nummum* 2, 23 (43, 30); 6, 23 (145, 22); *pastophorum* 11, 17 (279, 18); 11, 30 (291, 16); *superum* 4, 32 (100, 15); 11, 11 (274, 19); for *seruuulum* ours seems to be the only instance. See Neue-Wagener I³ pp. 166 ff., *seruuulum* p. 180. At *Soc.* 7 (14, 20) the mss. are divided between *hariolorum* and *-lum*.

2. *Strepitus* is generally corrected to read *strepitu*. A causal genitive, however, might be defended; cf. 2, 15 (37, 7) *mihi uero fatigationis hesternae etiam nunc saucio*; above 78, 3 *postumae spei fatigati* (and comm. *ad loc.*); vGeisau pp. 243 and 250; LHSz p. 75. (There are no further instances of *inquietus* with genitive: much to Hildebrand's disgust Oudendorp attempted to use Gel. 9, 13, 8 *ut quiescerent pugnae*, modern editors of Gellius, however, print ...*ut quiescerent. Pugnae facta pausa est.*) The case for *strepitus*, however, is weak since *-s* is easily explained either as an instance of anticipation (*diuinitus, inquietus*) or of dittography (perhaps produced auditively) of the s- by the subsequent *scilicet* (?). *scilicet* (?).

3. *Scilicet*. The problem lies in the combination of *strepitu(s)* and *diuinitus*. A number of scholars reason that if the *seruulus* wakes up because of a noise, this cannot also be termed *diuinitus*. They add (a) a disjunctive element or (b) remove either *diuinitus* or *strepitu(s)*. Some scholars on the other hand (c) defend the ms. reading by pointing out that the two need not be mutually exclusive.

(a) Among the first group are Vossius (*scilicet an*), vdVliet (*scilicet audito uel*), Giarratano (*scilicet audito uel*), Helm (*scilicet uel*). We may add the possibility that *scilicet* hides a single disjunctive *siue*; cf. *As.* 17, 1 (51, 18) *spiritu uero agitantur siue gubernantur omnes in mundo species.* W. M. Lindsay, *Notae Latinae*, Cambridge 1936, pp. 279 and 291 f. remarks on a possible confusion of abbreviations for *scilicet* and *siue*; see also Doris Bains, *A Supplement to Notae Latinae*, Hildesheim 1963, p. 43 (*s.* = *siue* sometimes in glossaries; more commonly *s.* = *scilicet*).

(b) Of the others Stewech and Heinsius read *diutino*, Oudendorp *diutini* for *diuinitus*; Wover deletes *strepitu scilicet* as a gloss.

(c) The ms. reading is rightly defended by Armini 1928, p. 294 with the paraphrase "quidam seruus strepitu dis scilicet ita gubernantibus inquietus factus proserpit." Van der Paardt prefers to take *scilicet* more closely with *inquietus* (an ironic "what else could we have expected") and compares Liv. 1, 4, 4 *forte quadam diuinitus*.

89, 1-4 uisaque bestia, quae libere discurrens totis aedibus commeabat, premens obnixum silentium uestigium suum replicat et utcumque cunctis in domo uisa pronuntiat: "and on seeing the beast, which was running loose all over the house, he kept absolutely quiet, and turned in his tracks and somehow informed everyone what he had seen in the house".

bestia: from the *seruulus'* point of view, but of the pathos of 88, 23 ff. nothing remains!

discurrens…commeabat: a general impression of movement without direction.

premens obnixum silentium: cf. 82, 7 *obnixum silentium tolerans*. Chryseros creeps up preserving a careful silence in order to catch Lamachus; our *seruulus* on the other hand silently returns in order to raise the alarm. One may suspect a conscious reference; the passages are each other's opposites. The enallage of *obnixus* results in a passive and resultative use (expressing constancy, obstinacy); there is a redundancy with *premens*, but an expressive one: we almost see the slave clap his hand to his mouth and hold tightly inside whatever wants to get out. A similar sense of physical effort at 90, 16 *obnixo mugitu*. Cf. also Verg. *A*, 4, 332 *obnixus curam sub corde premebat*, (cf. Pease *ad loc.*) and Aus. *Ep.* 29, 28 *obnixum, Pauline, taces* (where *obnixum* is used adverbially). See also Médan p. 262 who quotes Sil. 12, 646 as a parallel for *premens… silentium*, where we read: *sic adeo orantes pressere silentia*.

uestigium suum replicat: the slave does not walk backwards like Cacus' cows, but folds over, or turns around the direction of his track. *Vestigium* collective as at 82, 21. Médan p. 240 remarks on the novelty, p. 245 on the picturesque aspect of the expression.

utcumque: "somehow or other", cf. above on 85, 3. See Callebat, *S.C.*, p. 322 with examples and literature; Médan p. 157. The narrator's point of view is given. The frequency of *u* throughout the period is remarkable and may be functional in announcing the threatening disaster.

89, 4-5 Nec mora, cum numerosae familiae frequentia domus tota completur: "In no time the whole house was full to crowding with the

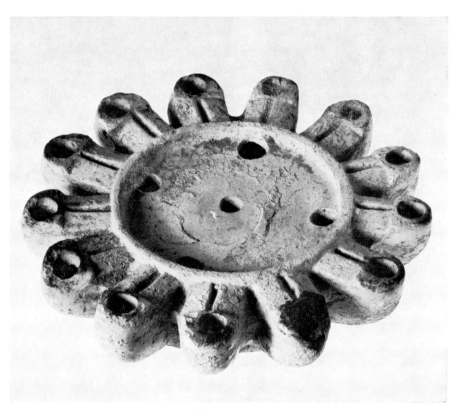

See p. 145-6.

numerous staff". Once again we are not informed as to where these people come from: the point is that they are suddenly there. The effect is underscored by assonance and alliteration (*u*, *f*), but in particular by the word-order; enclosed within the phrase *nec mora cum ...completur* we find

numerosae (a) *familiae* (b) *frequentia* (c) *domus* (b) *tota* (a)

and we note that the numeric strength of the staff (*frequentia*) is at once the central notion and centrally placed between chiastically arranged nouns and adjectives. Médan p. 269 remarks that *nec mora cum numerosae* shows a dactylic sequence, but it is doubtful whether this is due to the epic colouring of the passage.

Taedis, lucernis, cereis, sebaciis et ceteris nocturni luminis 89, 6-7 **instrumentis clarescunt tenebrae:** "Torches, lamps, tapers, candles and all the other instruments of nocturnal light dispelled the shadows". In general it may be said that the four specific kinds of lighting mentioned are quite comprehensive in so far as they comprise both the three main methods (torch, lamp, candle) and include expensive (*cereus*) as well as cheap (*sebacius*) forms. Yet Apuleius adds *et ceteris nocturni luminis instrumentis*, no doubt for the rhetorical value of the extra words, which strengthen the effect of *clarescunt tenebrae*. This is not to say that there are no forms of lighting to be found other than those mentioned, see below.

Note the homoeoteleuton *taedis, lucernis, cereis, sebaciis et ceteris... instrumentis*.

Taeda refers to all easily combustible woodsplinters and is a loanword from Greek (δαίδα) through Etruscan. In the sense of "torch" the word is most commonly used in religious, funereal and nuptial contexts (cf. e.g. 95, 4 f.). Several types of torche are mentioned, see J. Mau, *RE* VI, 1945 ff., and in particular R. J. Forbes, *Studies in Ancient Technology* VI, Leiden 1958, p. 128, who speaks of "torches...manufactured from sticks of resinous wood bound with rushes, papyrus or vine tendrils and treated with resin, pitch or wax". See also *ibid.* p. 130 for torch-holders. There appears to be no appreciable difference between *fax* and this sense of *taeda*.

lucerna, to be associated with *lūcere*, but with short root; according to Walde-Hofmann the formation is not entirely clear. On the history of lamps in the ancient world see A. Hug, *RE* XIII, 2, 1566-1613 *s.v. lucerna*; Forbes pp. 147-163.

Mention may be made of the existence of lampstands that could hold multiple *lucernae*; cf. P.Nol. 19, 404 ff. Hanging lamps have also been found. Martial's lamp with many wicks

Inlustrem cum tota meis conuiuia flammis

totque geram myxos, una lucerna uocor.

(14, 41) has been vindicated by several finds. Forbes' illustration p. 155, which shows one with thirteen wicks, found at Holdeurn near Nijmegen, is reproduced at the end of our volume.

cereus: Mau, *RE* VI, 1951 maintains "der öfter genannte cereus ist deutlich Fackel, nicht Kerze". He appears to have our place in mind as well. See however Forbes pp. 136 ff. who describes candles made in ancient Rome by a dipping process. *Cereus* is obviously a candle (or taper[1]) made of beeswax. Forbes' contention (p. 137) that *cerei* were for the rich, *sebacii* for the poor, however probable in itself, is not supported by Martial 14, 40 (which he quotes) or even 42: the first epigram deals with a *cicindela* (firefly, small lantern) as a servant of a *lucerna*, in the second a *lucerna* has disappeared and is replaced by a *cereus*:

> *Hic tibi nocturnos praestabit cereus ignis,*
> *subducta est puero namque lucerna tuo.*

See however Festus 54 M (= 47 L) *candelis pauperes, locupletes cereis utebantur*. See further Collart on Pl. *Cur.* 9.

sebacius: the form in *-ius* has been printed with the mss. since Hildebrand, and where *CIL* VI 3038 has *sebacia* (probably neuter plural) one is surprised to find *sebaceus* in Walde-Hofmann[3] *s.v. sebum*; *sebum* is hard animal grease, cf. Forbes p. 132.

Columella 2, 21, 3 tells us that *candelas sebare* is an activity allowed on religious holidays and it seems likely that we have to do with candle-dipping; Amm. 18, 6, 15 tells the story of a lamp (*lampas*, some kind of lantern) tied to a pack-animal which is sent off in one direction in order to deceive the Persians who are to think *praelucere sebalem facem duci* ("that a tallow torch was carried before the general"); Rolfe rightly translates "torch" here, rather than candle, though he admits the latter meaning in a footnote.

et ceteris...instrumentis: other types of lighting are hard to find; other variations are, in particular, the *lanterna*, whether *cornea* (with horn windows) Mart. 14, 61 (entitled *Lanterna cornea*)

> *Dux lanterna uiae clusis feror aurea flammis*
> *et tuta est gremio parua lucerna meo.*

or *uesica*, ibid. 62

> *Cornea si non sum, numquid sum fuscior? aut me*
> *uesicam, contra qui uenit, esse putat?*

and the *cicindela* mentioned above. Cicero (*Att.* 4, 3, 5) mentions a *linea lanterna*, probably even cheaper than Martial's two types.

Note the antithetic juxtaposition in *clarescunt tenebrae*. For antithesis in general see Bernhard pp. 59 ff. See also vdP. p. 141 and the literature mentioned there.

89, 7-9 **Nec inermis quisquam de tanta copia processit, sed singuli fustibus, lanceis, destrictis denique gladiis armati muniunt aditus:** "Not one of the entire number came forth unarmed, but individually armed with clubs, lances or even drawn swords they manned

---

[1] A taper consists of a fat wick with a little wax or tallow, a candle of a thin wick with a great deal of wax or tallow. See also Plin. *Nat.* 16, 178 and M. v. Assendelft, Comm. on Prud. *Cath.* 5, 15 and 20 (in preparation).

the entrances". The correction *aditus* (F has *aditis*) is doubtless correct.

de tanta copia: after *quisquam* the genitive is usual; Callebat, *S.C.*, p. 191 notes that the exceptional *de* here is used with an "expression plus large"; cf. 10, 12 (245, 14) *ac ne de ipso quidem populo quisquam*.

fustibus, lanceis, destrictis denique gladiis: Bernhard p. 68 speaks of an obvious crescendo. It is achieved by means of *denique*, which appears to be stronger here than a simple *et* (see vdP's enumeration of possible meanings of *denique* pp. 42 f.), as well as by the addition of *destrictis*, and some alliteration and homoeoteleuton.

Note the competent behaviour of the robbers' opponents.

Nec secus canes etiam uenaticos auritos illos et horricomes
ad comprimendam bestiam cohortantur: "No less do they sick on the hunting dogs — long-eared and shaggy they are — to overcome the animal".

nec secus: at first sight the comparative element is not entirely clear, in particular if one starts out from the usual sense *"non aliter"*. However, *non secus* may well mean *non minus*, cf. Ernout-Meillet *s.v.* p. 1074, and the items compared may well be the verbal actions *muniunt... cohortantur*. Vallette's "en même temps" appears to be due to the derivation of *secus* from *sequor*; see LHSz p. 248. For the sense "moreover" (e.g. Butler, Schwartz, Scazzoso) it is hard to find proper parallels. (Though F has *sedus*, changed to *setius* by a later hand, there can be little doubt that *secus* (φ) is correct.)

uenaticos: Médan p. 177 assigns the word to the "langue archaïque", but apart from Enn. *Ann.* 340 V; Pl. *Capt.* 85, *Mil.* 268 and Varro *R.* 2, 9, 2; 3, 3, 3, it also occurs in Cic. *Ver.* 4, 31; Nep. *Pel.* 2, 5; Hor. *Ep.* 1, 2, 65; Sen. *Ben..* 2, 34, 1-2; Col. 7, 12, 3. See also *Met.* 8, 31 (202, 2); 9, 2 (203, 22) as well as our next chapter (89, 22). See also Justin 23, 1, 9; Symm. *Ep.* 4, 18, 2 (Seeck), Porphyrio on Hor. *Ep.* 1, 18, 49. *De diff. scriptoribus* (ed. Beck, 1883) notes (p. 88, 6) *uenatorium ferramentum dicimus, uenaticum canem*.

auritos illos: on hearing this the ass grins — or should we say that Apuleius makes Lucius grin reminiscently as he is passing the story on? For long-eared dogs, cf. Verg. *G.* 1, 308 *auritosque sequi lepores* and Servius *ad loc.* Médan maintains (p. 159) that the word means no more than "qui a des oreilles", but expensive, long-eared hunting dogs certainly existed. In fact there appear to have been two schools of thought among ancient breeders: the ears should be short and thin according to Xen. *Cyn.* 4, 1 (though the text is not entirely certain), Poll. 5, 57, Oppian *Cyn.* 1, 404 f. (and Mair *ad loc.*); large and soft, however, according to Arr. *Cyn.* 5, 7; Var. 2, 9, 4 also has *auriculis magnis ac flaccis*. (Grat. *Cyn.* 1, 269 merely has the ears pointing forward). O. Keller, *Die antike Tierwelt*, Leipzig 1909, I p. 123: "Langhaarige Jagdhunde waren in vorrömischer Zeit nicht Mode, ebensowenig solche mit Hängeohren." He gives an exhaustive survey of dogs on pp. 91-151.

horricomes: Oppian 1, 422 λάσιος. Grattius' favourite dog has a *discreta...
collo/caesaries neu pexa nimis neu frigoris illa /impatiens*. Arr. *Cyn.* 6, 1
allows both long- and short-haired dogs, provided the coat is thick and
soft. Oudendorp notes that most compounds with *coma* have *-comus* (thus
e.g. *anguicomus* Ov. *Met.* 4, 699, *auricomus* Verg. *A.* 6, 141, *flammicomus*
Prud. *Psych.* 775 etc.); for *horricomis* cf. 7, 11 (162, 14) and *inanimis* e.g.
1, 3 (3, 12) and Marg. Molt *ad loc*. See comm. on 89, 12 *retrogradis*.

The chapter develops the *scaeuus euentus* very neatly from a small
thing to an immense noise: a slave wakes up, warns others, the house is
full, the lamps are lit (we do *not* ask how the bear could have been seen
before, see 88, 3 *inlunio tempore!*), the people appear to be fully armed,
take (with a great show of discipline) their stations at the entrances and
are supported *for the hunt* by the appropriate dogs. If it is the narrator's
intention to show that Thrasyleon never had a chance, he succeeds very
well.

CHAPTER XX

The narrator reports Thrasyleon's struggle against the dogs and his own intervention.

Tunc ego sensim gliscente adhuc illo tumultu retrogradi 89, 11-14 fuga domo facesso, sed plane Thrasyleonem mire canibus repugnantem, latens pone ianuam ipse, prospicio: "Then, while the uproar still increased, I gradually made my escape from the house, walking backwards, but I had a clear view of Thrasyleon's astonishing stand against the dogs, concealed as I was behind the door".

tunc ego...domo facesso: there may be a slight inconsistency in the position of the narrator; he was placed *pro domus limine* at 88, 19, now he appears to have been inside, and he certainly gives us a clear picture of what has happened there. One may think of *domo* in the sense of "from the atrium to the outer door", but see below 89, 19 *domo prolapsus est* and 89, 23 *domo...processerant*, where respectively Thrasyleon and the hunting dogs come from the house into the public street. It may be, then, that the narrator-robber is here tabelled as a prevaricator by his novelist-creator. Borth speaks of an "unreliable narrator" (see Ph. Stevich, ed., *The Theory of the Novel*, New York 1967, pp. 100-102).

sensim: the robber more or less feels his way out of the house (the adverb is to be taken with *facesso* rather than with *gliscente*). The hyperbaton is made possible by the intervening *gliscente...tumultu*, which constitutes a colon, cf. E. Fraenkel, *Kl. Beiträge* I, pp. 123 f. If this interpretation is correct, the attention is directed at the narrator (*ego*) in a very circumspect manner: *sensim* shows that he does not panic, *gliscente... tumultu* that the need for his retreat is urgent, *retrogradi fuga* that his is a strategic retreat, not a rout. Moreover, the narrator hastens to add that he cleverly (*latens pone ianuam ipse*) continues on the scene as an observer.

adhuc emphasizes *gliscente*, thus giving it equal weight with the finite verb, acc. to Bernhard p. 127.

facesso: cf. 3, 10 (59, 14 f.) *cuncti theatro facessunt*, 6, 11 (136, 10), 8, 30 (201, 6), 9, 22 (219, 21 f.), 10, 30 (261, 19). We need not assume that this archaic verb has retained any of its legal flavour here as at 3, 5 (55, 25) (vdP. pp 55 f.), but it certainly enhances the poetic quality, see Helm-Krenkel p. 34. *Retrogradis* (instead of *retrogradus*) cf. *Vet. Lat.*, II *Macc.* 14, 44 rec. P (de Bruyne) *illisque retrogradibus factis*. See also Médan p. 139, and our note on 89, 9 f.

plane...prospicio: the hyperbaton once again is made possible by the fact that the two intervening phrases are distinct cola, see Fraenkel *ibid.*

mire canibus repugnantem: the narrator does not mention any success-

149

ful blows on the part of his admired colleague, who, in the nature of things, does not bite. See also the note on 90, 18.

Note that the sentence as a whole has an *ababa* structure in which *a* represents the narrator, *b* the tumult.

What follows might well serve as a motion picture scenario: the amplification of the basic theme is expressed almost entirely in visual terms; no noise is mentioned (see however the notes on 89, 17 and 89, 21).

89, 14-17 Quamquam enim uitae metas ultimas obiret, non tamen sui nostrique uel pristinae uirtutis oblitus iam fa⟨u⟩cibus ipsis hiantis Cerberi reluctabat: "For though he was approaching life's finishing post, yet forgetting neither himself nor us nor his old courage, he went on fighting against the very jaws of gaping Cerberus".

quamquam...obiret: for the subjunctive see vdP. p. 31.

uitae metas ultimas: *meta* occurs 10, 35 (266, 7) in the sense of the end of the day. The present expression has a poetic flavour, cf. Verg. *A.* 10, 472 *metasque dati peruenit* (sc. *Turnus*) *ad aeui.* See also Varro *Men.* 544; Ov. *Trist.* 1, 9, 1. The image first occurs in Simonides 85, 13: βιότου ποτὶ τέρμα; Gatscha p. 148; cf. Aesch. *Fr.* 708 M (362 N) εἰ μὴ τέρμα συντρέχοι βίου, Soph. *OT* 1530 etc.

sui nostrique uel pristinae uirtutis: one may hesitate between two interpretations: *a* the narrator refers to two elements, the relationship expressed in *sui nostrique* and the *constans uigor* of 86, 13 or (preferably) *b*, there are three elements *sui* (the bear Thrasyleon did not forget himself, i.e. his fame), *nostri* (he did not forget us, i.e. he did not betray us) and *pristinae uirtutis* (subsuming the two previous elements under the appropriate moral heading); vdP. p. 62 points out that *uel* here has the sense of *et.* Gatscha p. 154 cites Sal. *Cat.* 58, 12 *memores pristinae uirtutis.*

fa⟨u⟩cibus: the correction (an inevitable one) was made in ç; cf. 6, 19 (142, 24) *tonantibus oblatrans faucibus mortuos.* For Cerberus swallowing all things, see 1, 15 (14, 13 f.). Some translators, e.g. Vallette, Brandt-Ehlers, Helm-Krenkel, treat *faucibus* as a kind of local ablative, but others, e.g. Adlington, Butler, Vitali, prefer the (equally possible) dative dependent on *reluctabat.* Cf. e.g. Curt. 6, 2, 6 *Inter quas unam rex conspexit maestiorem quam ceteras et producentibus eam uerecunde reluctantem*; also 8, 2, 11; Plin. *Nat.* 10, 15 *continuae nauigationi etesiae reluctantur*; and, finally Jul. Val. 2, 32 *uiuendi clausulae reluctantem* (sc. *Darium*).

Thus the many dogs become the one Cerberus (see also Clouard n. 60). Bernhard is certainly wrong in treating *faucibus ipsis hiantis Cerberi* as a mere euphemism for death (p. 213); it is on the contrary an imaginative expression enhancing the horror of this particular death, a device which in turn emphasizes the *uirtus* immediately preceding.

For *fauces* as the "jaws" of a dangerous animal cf. e.g. Prop. 3, 5, 43 f. *num tribus infernum custodit faucibus antrum/Cerberus* where *fauces* are the instrument of defence (whether through bark or bite is not stated)

150

rather than of swallowing. Barking is the more usual connotation, cf. 6, 19 (142, 24) quoted above, Sil. 13, 845 *illatrat ieiunis faucibus Orthrus*, Fronto p. 228, 27 N (217, 18 vdH) *trinas latrandi fauces*. Here there may be an oblique reference to the noise, though in the context a reference to biting jaws would be preferable. See also 92, 2 (with *exercere!*). For active *reluctare* see LHSz p. 292 and Callebat, *S.C.*, p. 294 (possibly an expressive and archaic flavour). Strilciw p. 110 lists the phrase under the heading periphrasis.

Scaenam denique, quam sponte sumpserat, cum anima re- 89, 17-19
tinens nunc fugiens, nunc resistens uariis corporis sui schemis ac motibus tandem domo prolapsus est: "In a word, while life remained, he sustained the rôle that he had voluntarily adopted and, now retreating, now stopping, with various gestures and movements of his body, at last he slipped out of the house".

scaenam: Callebat, *S.C.*, pp. 65 f. explains: "mise en scène". The figurative sense, however, sometimes refers to the act performed or rôle played by an individual (as here and at 8, 8 (183, 6-7) *scaenam pessimi Thrasylli perspiciens*), sometimes to the enactment of a specific scene (e.g. 8, 8 (183, 20-21)) *omnemque scaenam sceleris inluminauit*. See also comm. on 94, 20. Concerning Apuleius' use of theatrical imagery see Heine p. 207.

denique: it is hard to decide whether the word presents a final stage, sums up, gives an instance or a conclusion or merely notes a transition. Cf. vdP. pp. 42 f., Callebat, *S.C.*, p. 325. It seems best to take it as combining the instance and the summary: in the fact that Thrasyleon continues his rôle we see a conclusive instance of his courageous struggle.

quam sponte sumpserat: cf. 86, 3 *uoluntarius*.

cum anima retinens: *cum* "as long as": ThLL s.v. 1362, 25, cf. e.g. Amm. 26, 1, 14 *uictura cum saeculis Roma*; *anima* here in the sense of the principle of life. (There is no need to change *anima* to *animo* (H. Blümner, *Mélanges Nicole*, Genève 1905, p. 30): if we take *animo* in the sense of "courage", "enthusiasm" it repeats part of the previous sentence, if in the sense of "consciousness" it hardly improves on the ms. reading.) H. W. Prescott, *Marginalia on Apul. Met.*, *CPh* 6 (1911) p. 348 explains that the robber prolongs his life by continuing to play his rôle; Heine p. 200, n.l. is probably right in rejecting the inverted emphasis and preferring the simpler explanation that the robber plays his rôle as long as there is life in him.

nunc fugiens, nunc resistens: the picture is one of swift motion. The contrasting combination occurs several times, e.g. Liv. 4, 59, 6; Amm. 17, 13, 10.

uariis corporis sui schemis ac motibus: the narrator continues to describe the act that unfolds before his eyes in terms of theatrical spectacle. Cf. Non. 56 M (= 79 L) *Petauristae a ueteribus dicebantur qui saltibus uel schemis leuioribus mouerentur*; cf. *ibid.* 61 M (= 85 L) *Sanniones dicuntur a sannis qui sunt in dictis fatui et in motibus et in schemis*. The word *schema* was also applied to dance movements: Naev. *Lyc.* 31 (33 f. Warm.) *per-gite/thyrsigerae Bacchae* [*modo*], *Bacchico cum schemate*. The obscene show of the *spintriae* at Suet. *Tib.* 43 is performed in front of pictures, *ne cui in opera edenda exemplar imperatae schemae deesset.* The examples quoted indicate that "archaic" (Médan p. 172) is incorrect as a qualification of the word *schema*. First declension forms are quite common. Cf. Neue-Wagener I³, p. 502, Desertine p. 73. Leumann-Hofmann p. 261 provide examples of loan words treated similarly. See J. André, *Emprunts et suffixes nominaux en latin*, Paris 1971, p. 6 on *schema, schemae* and p. 19 on *schēma, schēmata* (cf. M. Leumann, *Kleine Schriften*, Zürich etc. 1959, p. 173).

89, 20-21   Nec tamen, quamuis publica potitus libertate, salutem fuga quaerere potuit: "And yet, though he had escaped into the open street, he still could not seek safety in flight".

publica...libertate: possibly elliptical for *libertate uiarum publicarum.* Acc. to Médan p. 194 *publicus* in the sense of "common to all" is poetic; see however Cic. *Ac.* 1, 25 *uerba...publica*, and Sen. *Ep.* 122, 9 *dies publicus. Libertas* is a relative notion, both philosophically speaking and in the *Met.* In our passage it means no more than the bear's escape to the street, at 9, 2 (204, 13 f.) it signifies the ass's escape from his pursuers, though he is now locked up in the master bedroom. Liberty is meaningful only if combined with *salus*, cf. 6, 28 (150, 6) where Charite addresses the ass as *praesidium meae libertatis meaeque salutis*; in our passage, however, *salutem* is placed in an ominously contrasting juxtaposition with *publica...libertate.*

The function of this sentence is not so much to announce the approaching end — that had been done by 89, 14 f. *quamquam ... obiret* — but to show how close Thrasyleon came to an escape. For the narrative function of *nec tamen* cf. the note on 90, 7. Note the alliteration *publica potitus ... potuit.*

89, 21-24   Quippe cuncti canes de proximo angiportu satis feri satis-que copiosi uenaticis illis, qui commodum domo similiter insequentes processerant, se ommisce[u]nt agminatim: "For all the dogs from the next street, pretty ferocious specimens and pretty numerous, joined in a pack the hunting dogs which had just streamed out of the house in pursuit". To judge by the length of the describing phrases (both 24 syllables, admittedly not a reliable criterion of information) the two packs of dogs are of similar numerical strength. Their mixing together makes a beautiful cinematographic scene. Doubtless the dogs are of different kinds (cf. above on 89, 10); one imagines the mongrels from the city-alleys now joining the pure-bred hunting pack. At night dogs must have been quite a menace, cf. Cato *Agr.* 124: *canes interdiu clausos esse oportet, ut noctu acriores et uigilantiores sint.*

152

The prevalence of *c* and *q* in this sentence may be intended to illustrate the noise.

de proximo angiportu: scholars dealing with Roman comedy now appear to agree that *angiportum* (or *angiportus*) cannot refer to a small alley between the houses represented on the stage. See e.g. G. E. Duckworth, *The Nature of Roman Comedy* (1952) pp. 87 ff., W. Beare, *The Roman Stage* (³1964) pp. 256-263. Yet it seems that "alley" must be the basic meaning: see J. André, *Les noms latins du chemin et de la rue*, REL 28 (1950) pp. 104-134 (on *angiportum* pp. 124-129). He points out[1] that Apuleius contrasts *angiportum* with *platea* (see 85, 13) both in Plataeae and in Hypata (*angiportus* 1, 21 (19, 17)): Milo's house is situated in an alley, see also Marg. Molt and Scobie *ad loc.*; 3, 2 (53, 1) as against the *platea* at 2, 27 (47, 5) and 2, 32 (51, 10)). For a discussion of the problem concerning the declension of the word see André *ibid.* 125 ff. Médan p. 172 thinks that the word belongs to the "langue familière", Callebat, *S.C.*, p. 481 thinks it is of comic origin.

The — at first sight excessive — precision of the phrase materially enhances the visual effect of the scene.

satis feri satisque copiosi: both terms serve to increase the element of danger. Heine points out that Apuleius likes to populate his scenes with dangerous beings, such as wild dogs (p. 149 and n. 1).

uenaticis illis: see above 89, 10. At the end of chapter 19 the hunting dogs are urged on, here both groups appear to act of their own accord: *similiter insequentes*.

domo processerant: here clearly out of the building into the street.

se ommiscent: *se ommisceunt* F; *sese ommisc͡ent* φ (*u* by a second hand); ς has *se ommiscent*; *commiscent* occurs in the margin in φ. Helm points out that a similar pair with *ob-* and *com-* occurs in *Apol.* 40, 1 (*commutescere*) and *Apol.* 113, 22 (*ommutescere*). For third conjugation forms of *miscere* see ThLL *s.v.*; Neue-Wagener III³ p. 269; Svennung, *Pall.*, p. 104 (literature in n. 3); Leumann-Hofmann p. 89. These forms, from which the Romance forms derive, are relatively late. Cf. W. Meyer-Lübke, *Einf. in das Studium d. rom. Sprachwiss.*,³1920 p. 193; *Rom. Etym. Wörterbuch* 5604; H. Lausberg, *Romanische Sprachw.* III, Berlin 1962, p. 175. It is more likely therefore that the *u* in F is due to a scribal tendency than to the scribe's original; cf. Médan p. 143.

The word is a hapax legomenon except for *Visio Pauli* 13 p. 16, 6 J. (Cf. Weyman, *ALL* IX p. 138).

For the neologism *agminatim* see comm. on 80, 14.

Miserum funestumque spectamen aspexi, Thrasyleonem 89, 24-90,3 nostrum cateruis canum saeuientium cinctum atque obsessum multisque numero morsibus laniatum: "I saw a piti-

---

[1] Arguing partly against P. W. Harsh, *Angiportum, platea and uicus*, CPh 32 (1937) pp. 44-58, who maintains that both *angiporta* and *platea* are general words for (normal) streets in Apuleius.

able and deathlike sight: our friend Thrasyleon encircled and besieged by packs of ravening dogs and torn by their numerous bites". Bernhard p. 47 remarks on the loose structure of the sentence: an extended apposition almost overwhelms the main clause. Far from indicating lack of polish, however, the sentence's structure is effective in the narrative. So too are the homoeoteleuton (*miserum funestumque ... nostrum ... canum saeuientium cinctum atque obsessum ... laniatum*), wordplay in *spectamen aspexi* (Bernhard pp. 228 f.), alliteration in *cateruis canum ... cinctum*. On the military terms *cinctum atque obsessum* see Appendix I.

multisque numero: see comm. on. 79, 15. Here the word *numero* serves in part to enhance the somewhat funereal sound effect.

morsibus: awkward questions might be asked as to the effect of these bites on Thrasyleon's costume; vThiel asks similar questions of the entire episode, pp. 105 f.

90, 3-6 **Denique tanti doloris impatiens populi circumfluentis turbelis immisceor et in quo solo poteram celatum auxilium bono ferre commilitoni, sic indaginis principes dehortabar:** "At last, unable to bear such misery, I mingled in the (small?) groups of people milling about and, using the only available means to give disguised help to my good comrade, I tried to discourage the ring-leaders of the chase as follows":

tanti doloris impatiens: the narrator tries to show himself in the best possible light with his audience: here we note his good intentions, presently (*in quo solo poteram ...*) he speaks of the limitations of his position.

populi circumfluentis turbelis: doubtless woken by the disturbance they add to it. The picture is not entirely clear as to who these people are: the narrator is more interested in the aspect of confusion.

Festus 355 M (= 485 L) notes: *Turbelas apud Plautum* (*Pseud.* 110) *turbas significat*; this is where the trouble starts, since in the line mentioned ms. A indeed has *turbula* but otherwise *turbella* is read as at *Bac.* 1057; cf. Leumann-Hofmann p. 217 (sub C). See also G. K. Strodach, *Latin diminutives in -ello/a- and -illo/a-*, Philadelphia 1933, p. 95. It may be, then, that *turbela* is in effect an Apuleian neologism. Apart from the *Met.* passages mentioned below it also occurs *Soc.* 12 (20, 8), at least in the Aug. version (*turbulae* mss.). See also e.g. Vet. Lat. II *Macc.* 15, 29 (cod. P); Amm. 14, 10, 2; August. *CD* 8, 17; 9, 3; 10, 27. LS translate "little crowd", a sense not mentioned by Forcellini. Cf. 3, 29 (73, 15) *inter ipsas turbelas Graecorum*. VdP. *ad loc.* treats the suffix *-ela* as vulgar, Callebat, *Latomus* 31 (1972) p. 1105 thinks that this is uncertain as is the diminutive sense.

On the latter question see I. S. T. Hanssen, *Latin Diminutives*, Bergen 1952, p. 130 (who compares *fugela - fugella*) and B. Zucchelli, *Studi sulle formazioni latine in -lo- non-diminutive*, Univ. degli Studi di Parma, 1970, p. 34. In our passage a diminutive would be no more functional than at 7,

1 (154, 14 f.) *immixtus ego turbelis popularium. Turbula* (e.g. 10, 35 (266, 5)) appears to be used in much the same sense.

immisceor: the reflexive is noted by Médan p. 13.

circumfluentis: the picture of the bear surrounded by dogs is now expanded with a further circle.

et in quo solo poteram: see Callebat, *C.S.*, p. 225 on the relational/instrumental use of *in*: "sous le rapport de"; cf. comm. on 94, 23 *triennio maior in aetate*. There is no need to delete *in* with vdVliet or to try *exin* with Robertson.

celatum auxilium: Lipsius' *celatim* need not be adopted, despite Apuleius' penchant for adverbs in *-im*: apparently the help, rather than its proffering, is disguised.

indaginis principes: the ring-leaders. The word *indago* maintains the fiction of the "bear". The careful differentiation between points of view is apparent in the juxta-position with *commilitoni*. In the subsequent speech *bestia* is, of course, required by the plot, but the comment that follows is directed at the audience in the robbers' hideout and therefore speaks of *infelicissimo ... iuueni*.

dehortabar: *de conatu*; on the tenses (*inmisceor ... dehortabar*) see Callebat, *S.C.*, p. 427. Médan p. 178 regards the word *dehortari* as archaic, but see Nep. *Att.* 21, 6; Sen. *Ep.* 76, 29.

"O grande", inquam, "et extremum flagitium, magnam et uere pretiosam perdimus bestiam": ""This is a serious business, a disastrous error", I said, "We are destroying an important, really valuable animal"." 90, 6-7

grande: see comm. on 82, 8.

extremum "nefarious": see vdP. pp. 55 f. See also comm. on 79, 17 for a similar intensifying function in invective.

magnam: see 86, 26 *miratus bestiae magnitudinem*; as for the value cf. Demochares' pleasure *sui contubernalis opportuna liberalitate* (*ibid.*).

perdimus: it is hard to choose between "destroy" or "lose".

The subsequent *artes* (90, 8) may indicate that the present speech is intended by the narrator as only an example of all the things he "really" said. The *artes* may be spelled out as being (a) an attempt to arouse fear for Demochares' displeasure, and second thoughts concerning the destruction or loss of valuable property, but also (b) the narrator's attempt to pose as one of the attacking group (*perdimus*).

CHAPTER XXI

The narrator's intervention being of no avail Thrasyleon dies, though no faster than most heroes in Italian opera, but no one dares to touch the bear until a butcher brings forth the robber's body.

The narrator reflects on life and presents the booty to his audience.

90, 7-8 Nec tamen nostri sermonis artes infelicissimo profuerunt iuueni: "But my wily words were of no avail to that most unfortunate of men".

nostri: on its placement see Bernhard p. 24, on its employment for mei LHSz p. 20, but let us not forget Babulus.

For the artes see above on 90, 5-6. The infelicity is largely explained by the scaeuus euentus of 88, 27 which caused Thrasyleon's lack of success. Though infelix is not a very frequent word in the Met., it is remarkable that in eleven of the thirteen instances it refers to the situation of someone or something that has sustained or is about to sustain the loss of life or some equally important attribute. The two exceptions are 93, 13 f. infelicis rapinae praeda, referring to Charite, and 101, 25 infelicem senectam, referring to Psyche's parents. It may be argued that in those cases the same implication of a loss is present, though the adjective is transferred to an abstract. The superlative occurs twice (apart from our passage): 5, 23 (121, 18) Amor has been burnt and has left the embraces infelicissimae coniugis; at 9, 38 (232, 20), in the bloodiest passage of the entire novel, a father commits suicide ad instar infelicissimi sui filii.

90, 8-12 quippe quidam procurrens e domo procerus et ualidus incunctanter lanceam mediis iniecit ursae praecordiis nec secus alius et ecce plurimi, iam timore discusso, certatim gladios etiam de proximo congerunt: "For a tall, strong fellow ran out of the house and without a moment's hesitation aimed his lance at the bear's heart; another did the same and then, lo and behold, lots of people, having shaken off their fear, vied with each other to come right up to him and belabour him with their swords".

F's initial slip in writing gladiis, then correcting to gladios need not concern us; the slip c̄gerit for c̄gerūt, easily corrected in ς, does not appear to hide any error at a deeper level.

quippe quidam procurrens...procerus: the alliteration in two pairs seems to underscore the sudden turn of events.

procurrens e domo: a swift motion and a precise direction whose sud-

156

denness is a worthy continuation of the *scaeuus euentus* (88, 27). For the expression see also 5, 7 (108, 14); Liv. 4, 4, 30.

procerus et ualidus: Thrasyleon's valour of course requires a worthy and visible opponent in addition to his bad luck; the hyperbaton *quidam ...procerus* serves to tie this notion to the suddenness noted above.

incunctanter: for the word see on 80, 7 (Apuleian neologism). ThLL *s.v.* interprets the lack of hesitation as "neglegitur periculum mortis", but it is at least as significant for the mentality of the robber-narrator who wishes to justify himself.

mediis iniecit ursae praecordiis: though it cannot be said that the expression contains specifically poetic words, the hyperbaton (with resulting emphasis on *ursae*: the proper point of view is maintained here as well) appears to produce a certain poetic flavour.

The subsequent commata describe the overall motion very vividly: first one, then another, then many, then closing in.

nec secus alius: see above on 89, 9; in our passage *nec secus* may well have the usual sense of *non aliter*.

et ecce plurimi: Heine p. 174 is right in reminding us of the common use of *ecce* in comedy to introduce a new arrival, wrong in saying that here it refers to ("verweist auf") Thrasyleon's battle against overwhelming odds: *ecce* rather invites us to visualise the sudden numerical increase once the danger is past: *iam timore discusso*. The latter expression occurs here only, though there are several examples of the verb used with other words for fear: 7, 1 (154, 12) *discussa sollicitudine*; V. Max. 1, 7, 8 *metu ... discusso*; Plin. *Nat.* 28, 84; Sen. *Oed.* 793; V. Fl. 4, 700 *discussa ... formidine Auerni*. The use of the word *discutere* in the *Met.* is confined to dispelling sleep, fatigue, drunkenness or fear (cf. ThLL *s.v.* 1374, 31 ff.) with the exception of 2, 1 (24, 17) *nocte discussa*.

de proximo: the adverbial expression occurs also 2, 4 (27, 13), 11, 6 (270, 15) and 11, 23 (285, 17); cf. de Jonge p. 27, Bernhard p. 107 on prepositions with neut. sing; Svennung, *Pal.* 275 f. Cf. Tert. *Apol.* 27 and Mayor *ad loc.*; further parallels for this use of *de* ThLL *s.v.* 79, 48-84; Waszink p. 242 (*de longinquo*); LHSz p. 266.

gladios ... congerunt: though *congerere* in a context of arms usually refers to missiles, Phaedr. 3, 2, 3 has *alii fustes congerunt* (farmers are cudgelling a panther in a pit). Cf. Stat. *Theb.* 5, 160 f. (bare hands).

Enimuero Thrasyleon egregium decus nostrae factionis 90, 12-18
tandem immortalitate digno illo spiritu expugnato magis
quam patientia neque clamore ac ne ululatu quidem fidem
sacramenti prodidit, sed iam morsibus laceratus ferroque
laniatus obnixo mugitu et ferino fremitu praesentem casu⟨m⟩
generoso uigore tolerans gloriam sibi reseruauit, uitam fato
reddidit: "But Thrasyleon, that dazzling jewel of our band, when at last not his endurance but his actual ability to survive — worthy though it was of immortality — was wrested from him, not by a cry nor even by a

shriek did he betray his oath, but mangled and cut about as he was he nobly endured his inevitable fate with sustained roar and animal cries, and so kept glory for himself while he surrendered his life to fate":

The second hand that added the *virgula* to *casu* in F belonged to a reasonable corrector.

This period containing the description of Thrasyleon's death and his *elogium funebre* is carefully built from a point of view of colometry. Not only are the two halves almost equal in length (64 × 59 syllables) but each half consists of a symmetrical group:

enimuero	-	factionis	20	)	(	sed	-	laniatus	16
tandem	-	patientia	24	} × {	obnixo	-	tolerans	27
neque	-	prodidit	20	)	(	gloriam	-	reddidit	16

The last element of the second symmetrical group, however, is split into two parallel elements, a parallelism that is the more effective because of the frame within which it is placed.

enimuero strongly marks the start of the description of the other half of the picture. Cf. above comm. on 83, 9.

egregium decus: see above on 86, 17. The use of an abstract in conveying praise or blame is treated by Bernhard p. 98. Cf. Cic. *Phil.* 11, 14 *lumen et decus illius exercitus paene praeterii* (ironic; cf. Ilona Opelt, *Schimpf-wörter* p. 139). Cf. also *dedecus* (above, comm. on 79, 17).

nostrae factionis: see comm. on 86, 8 (and 92, 15 f.).

tandem ... spiritu expugnato: the word *spiritus* in the *Met.* ranges from plain "breath" (e.g. 1, 4 (4, 1), 9, 24 (221, 6)), to "divine spirit" (e.g. 8, 27 (199, 6), 11, 28 (290, 3)): *spiritu fauentis Euentus*). Between those extremes a variety of possibilities is represented: thus Zephyr's breeze that carries Psyche is a *spiritus* (4, 35 (103, 3) = 5, 16 (115, 117)) as is the river-breeze at 6, 12 (137, 13). A little more ghostly seems the *spiritus* that wafts the dishes to Psyche at 5, 3 (105, 9). On the other hand there is also a series of passages in which *spiritus* denotes the principle of life — in some cases still closely related to "breath", e.g. 10, 26 (258, 7), and visibly at 7, 1 (154, 9) *ex anhelitu recepto spiritu*, cf. 11, 6 (270, 28); in other cases that link seems forgotten, e.g. 8, 14 (188, 6) *inedia statuit elidere sua sententia damnatum spiritum*. Sometimes that principle appears to be able to exist by itself: e.g. 6, 17 (141, 15) *nam si spiritus corpore tuo semel fuerit seiugatus* ..., 2, 28 (48, 6) and it may be the object of one's own or others' actions, thus e.g. 2, 15 (29, 8) *inuadere spiritum*, 3, 23 (69, 10) *uincire spiritum*, 4, 34 (101, 26) *fatigare spiritum*, 5, 6 (107, 28) *diligere spiritum*. In our passage we have *expugnare spiritum* which also occurs at 9, 29 (225, 1). In both cases the plain translation "life" appears to fit the context best, but only if we immediately associate the possibility of a continued (separate) existence.

expugnato: agreement, as usual, with the nearest noun.

immortalitate digno: see below on 91, 1 *sed a gloria non peribit*.

magis quam patientia: endurance is the aspect that enables Thrasyleon to continue in his role even in the face of death. The narrator elaborates on the notion in the next phrases. For *expugnare patientiam* see 7, 19 (168, 25).

neque clamore ac ne ululatu quidem: Apuleius employs the negative + *ac ne ... quidem* construction some 24 times in the *Met.* and usually *ne ... quidem* represents the reinforced negative: "not even", enclosing the weaker term. Our passage may be explained in this way if we accept Vallette's suggestion that *clamor* refers to articulate speech, *ululatus* to inarticulate utterance. It is however hard to prove that this is the intention and Helm quotes one parallel where the second term is not the weaker one: in that case the reinforced negative must mean "and altogether not...", "let alone": 4, 28 (96, 20 f.): *tam praeclara pulchritudo nec exprimi ac ne sufficienter quidam laudari sermonis humani penuria poterat.* Cf. also 6, 26 (148, 6) where the two items *salus* and *nex* appear to be more or less on a par. See also comm. on 81, 25. See in general on *ne ... quidem* H. David-H. L. W. Nelson, *Gai Institutionum Commentarii IV* I, Leiden 1954, pp. 88 ff.

fidem sacramenti: see comm. on 82, 27 and 86, 1. Vallette *ad loc.* compares the gladiators' oath, citing Seneca, *Ep.* 37, 1 f.; Summers on 82, 27 (p. 166) and our passage (p. 169) emphasizes the military connotation. See also below on *uitam fato reddidit*, the philosophical attitude.

morsibus ... laniatus: see above on 90, 2; as to the structure of the sentence we have here the first of three noteworthy parallel pairs in this second half of the period. Bernhard p. 89 notes that the second, *obnixo mugitu et ferino fremitu* consists of 2 × 6 syllables; we may add that the first shows similarly equal lengths. See also above on 90, 2.

obnixo mugitu: see above on 89, 3 for the sense of *obnixus*; *mugitus* is most commonly used of the lowing of cattle, rarely of the noises made by other animals. Rufin. *patr.* 1, 2 col. 302B (Migne 21) uses it of a lion. The transfer of *mugire* to human noises is not uncommon: at 8, 8 (183, 6) *mugitus* is used of Charite: *ferinos mugitus iterans*, and at 9, 21 (218, 19) the word appears to have lost the aspect of noise altogether, while retaining that of pain or grief: (Barbarus) *tacitos secum mugitus iterans.*

fremitus occurs only here in Apuleius; the combination *mugitus ... fremitus* also Sil. 16, 264 ff. ... *taurus ... mugitu ...| impleuit tecta et fremitu suspiria rauco | congeminans ...* Cf. Rufin. *patr.* 1, 2 quoted above.

praesentem casum generoso uigore tolerans: *praesens* here emphatic: "immediate"; *generosus*, "noble" with abstract also 2, 2 (26, 3) *generosa probitas*; *Fl.* 17 (33, 19) *generosa modestia*. Cic. *Tusc.* 2, 16 still treats *generosa* with *uirtus* as a metaphor (cf. Dougan *ad loc.*).

At this point, just before the robber-narrator reaches the climax of his eulogy, it may be noted that though he has told us that Thrasyleon fights (89, 13 and 16), no actual battle activity on his part is described; on the contrary, we hear that he leaves the house (*domo prolapsus est* 89, 19), that he cannot reach safety (89, 20), that he is bitten (90, 2), hit with a spear (90, 10) and swords (90, 12) and that he roars (90, 17). His one claim to fame is the fact that he does not betray his oath (90,

15) and that he is able to take what comes (90, 17 f.): on the resemblance of the latter aspect to the stoic see below, but all in all we appear to have a carefully elaborated piece of irony; cf. the description of Lamachus.

A certain parallelism may be noted between the vowel sounds of 90, 2 *multisque numero morsibus* and 90, 17 *mugitu et ferino fremitu*. The robber-narrator doubtless intends nothing but praise for a well-sustained role, his reporter Lucius, or their novelist-creator, may well intend an ironic reference to Thrasyleon's complaint...

The narrator winds up his *elogium* with an epitaph (on *CE* 431 — 1st c. A.D. — the dead person agrees that this is appropriate: *uerba meo cineri saltem gratissima dona*). The antithesis has parallels on many a stone, e.g. *CE* 56 *mors animam eripuit, non ueitae ornatum apstulit*; *CE* 922 *Ars nobi]s et uera fides duo cum bona constent [cedet] liuor iners, fama perennis erit*. These inscriptions date respectively to 1st c. B.C. and 1st. c. A.D.; A. Ferrua, *Antiche iscrizioni inedite di Roma* III, *Epigraphica* 32 (1971) pp. 90-126 mentions p. 107 a probably Christian inscription: *mentis pro meritis animam rebocabit ad astra [Simpliciae tantum membra tenet tumulus.* Cf. e.g. *CE* 618, 1254, 1366, 1392; R. Lattimore, *Themes in Greek and Latin Epitaphs*, Urbana ²1962, p. 242. But our narrator, not content with his present success, produces a second epitaph below 90, 24-91, 1, repeating himself as far as the antithesis is concerned. It is not so easy to find prose parallels on the stones: Cagnat has suggested that stone cutters had sample collections from which clients chose suitable poetic utterances; cf. Lattimore pp. 18 ff.; an extensive bibliography concerning Latin funeral inscriptions is to be found in H. Geist-G. Pfohl, *Römische Grabinschriften*, München 1969, pp. 243-248.

gloriam sibi reseruauit: *gloria* is not a common notion in the *Met*. It occurs 9 times only, sometimes in the sense of the fame or the good reputation of the family: 1, 2 (2, 7); 7, 8 (160, 6); 9, 35 (229, 17); sometimes in the sense of fame acquired personally: 2, 12 (35, 9), 10, 8 (250, 25); 11, 27 (289, 9). Once it refers to Psyche's child (as something she may be proud of: 5, 12 (112, 18)). In our chapter it refers both times to Thrasyleon's reputation with his comrades, but the first time it is treated as a simple abstract quality, the second time (91, 1: *a gloria non peribit*) it is noticeably more concrete.

When *gloria* first appears in a funeral inscription, it seems to be something that ends with death: *CE* 8: *mors perfecit ut essent omnia tua breuia, honos fama uirtusque, gloria atque ingenium*; in *CE* 610 it may survive, but still is very much part of the living person; cf. e.g. *gloria uitae CE* 1186, 8. *CE* 1142 speaks of a *gloria mortis* (referring to the prospect of husband and wife to be joined in death). *CE* 1251 (3rd c. A.D.), however, appears to spell out what is meant in our passage: *Manibus infernis si uita est gloria uitae,/uiuit et hic nobis ut Cato uel Cicero*: a personal glory not much distinct from fame. On the development of the notion see e.g. U. Knoche, *Der römische Ruhmesgedanke* (1934) now in H. Oppermann (ed.), *Römische Wertbegriffe*, Darmstadt 1974, pp. 420-445. Cf. A. D.

Leeman, *Gloria*, Diss. Leiden, Rotterdam 1949, p. 123, n. 1; see also H. Drexler in *Helikon*, 2 (1962) pp. 3-36.

sibi reseruauit: rather "preserved for himself" than "reserved for himself". The first sense also at 1, 15 (14, 16), 6, 19 (143, 6), 7, 20 (169, 9), 7, 24 (172, 4), 10, 24 (242, 20), the second at 3, 11 (60, 20), 7, 22 (171, 2), but it is not in all cases easy to distinguish between the two. *Sibi gloriam reseruare* is hard to parallel, but at *Paneg.* 12, 23, 4 we read *tibi gloriam... seruabat*; cf. Cypr. *Ep.* 14, 3, 1 *conponere mentes eorum ad seruandam gloriam suam*.

uitam fato reddidit: for the exact formula cf. *CE* 1901 (= *CIL* XI 7376): *uita(m) fato reddidi*; cf. *CIL* 3335 *animam fatis reddidit*. *Reddere* is quite common in similar formulas (e.g. *debita fatis CIL* III 423; *debitum naturae* VIII 16374, 16410; *obitum naturae* VIII 10892; cf. *CE* 1532 *uitam reddidi*; 1559 *anima caelo reddita est*; 1612 *reddito natu(rae spiritu...)* = *CIL* VIII 724; and *CIL* XIII 2016 *si fati condicionem reddidero*.

The exact meaning of *fatum, Fatum*, or even *Fatus* (e.g. in the formula *uoluit hoc Fatus meus, CE* 1537, 1538 (1540) etc.) is hard to catch: it seems to be a general notion of inescapability to which people, but understandably the relevant dead person in particular, are subject.

Tanto tamen terrore tantaque formidine coetum illum 90, 19-20
turbauerat...: "But he managed to instill such terror and dread into the gathering..." A remarkable alliteration (cf. Médan p. 306, Bernhard p. 222) introduces the discovery, much later, that it had not been a bear after all: the consistent distinction of the points of view of those who did and those who did not know of the deception now reaches its climax, a climax so captivating that we barely realize that our robber-narrator in the nature of things hardly stayed *usque diluculum*, let alone *in multum diem* to see what was going to happen to the corpse. The fact that *turbauerat* retains the subject of *reddidit* further serves to keep the now dead hero as the centre of the attention.

ut usque diluculum, immo et in multum diem, nemo quis- 90, 20-22
quam fuerit ausus quamuis iacentem bestiam uel digito
contingere: "that right up to daybreak, no, actually until full daylight, not one person dared so much as lay a finger on the animal even though it lay still".

usque diluculum: *usque* as a preposition denoting the time limit is rare in classical Latin (cf. LHSz p. 254 who quote Cic. *Att.* 3, 10, 1 *usque a.d. VIII Kal. Jun.* (cf. *Att.* 2, 15, 3) where Baiter read *usque ad ⟨a.d.⟩* thus clarifying the problem), occurs increasingly often in later Latin (e.g. Cels. 7, 7, 15 *usque mortis diem*); in Apuleius it is confined to our passage, see Callebat, *S.C.*, p. 222.

diluculum: Suet. fr. p. 160, 15 (Re) *diluculum quasi iam incipiens parua diei lux*; today the lexica prefer to explain: "dilucere + -ulum" (OLD *s.v.*); cf. ThLL *s.v.*, Ernout-Meillet *s.v. lux*.

in multum diem: cf. 3, 20 (67, 17) *in altum diem*; in Livy the expression is *in multum diei* (e.g. 9, 44, 11) or *ad multum diei* (e.g. 10, 32, 6, cf. Curt. 8, 14, 28).

nemo quisquam: see Médan p. 324, LHSz pp. 205, 802, Callebat, *S.C.*, p. 98, cf. comm. on 79, 21 *nil quicquam*; both expressions belong to the *sermo cotidianus*. Here the sense is obviously emphatic (Callebat).

fuerit ausus: for the conjugation ("verschobenes Perfectum") see Médan p. 6; LHSz p. 322; below comm. on 92, 1.

quamuis iacentem bestiam: Helm prints a comma after *iacentem* following Oudendorp. They are joined by e.g. Giarratano-Frassinetti, Scazzoso, vThiel. But Hildebrand, followed by Eyssenhardt, vdVliet, Gaselee, Robertson, Brandt-Ehlers, dispenses with a comma. A very similar situation occurs at Prop. 1, 15, 13 where (e.g.) Butler-Barber, Paganelli and Camps do, Enk and Schuster do not print comma's around *quamuis...uisura*. Probably *quamuis* lifts out the participle sufficiently to produce a lightly separate *colon* or *comma*. Cf. E. Fraenkel, *Kl. Beitr.* I, p. 91. But in view of differing fashions in punctuation one cannot be sure that the printed or omitted comma conveys a decision on the degree of integration of the phrase into the surrounding area. Cf. 5, 31 (128, 21) *quamuis absenti*; Médan pp. 236 f.

90, 22-24   nisi tandem pigre ac timide quidam lanius paulo fidentior utero bestiae resecto ursae magnificum despoliauit latronem: "until finally, reluctantly and fearfully, a butcher with a little more courage than the rest opened up the animal's belly and stripped the heroic robber of his bear".

nisi: Löfstedt, *Verm. Stud.* p. 33, discussing adversative *nisi* (pp. 29 ff.), remarks that psychologically the thought *"nemo ausus est nisi lanius"* dominates; see also Médan p. 233 and Callebat, *S.C.*, pp. 352 f.

pigre: Médan p. 207 "à contre-coeur".

quidam: see comm. on 76, 6.

lanius: not the man who had thrown the spear or one of the other attackers of 90, 10 ff. but a wholly appropriate professional.

paulo fidentior: cf. 5, 2 (104, 14); *fidentior*: cf. 1, 3 (3, 14) and Marg. Molt *ad loc.*; Callebat, *S.C.*, p. 131.

utero...latronem: the text has been doubted. F has *magnificum* but *ū* in rasura and written by a later hand, probably over an original *o*. The latter may be explained as due to perseveration; the corrector was doubtless right. Editors have differed, however, on the question whether to retain *bestiae* or *ursae* or both. Brantz deleted (saying "iugulo"!) *bestiae* as a gloss, Philomathes *ursae* followed by Eyssenhardt. Equally drastic are the solutions of Lütjohann (*ursae magnifico ⟨corio⟩*, which preserves F.'s original *o*) and of Plasberg (*ursae magnificum ⟨mimum⟩*). Most editors however retain both *bestiae* and *ursae*. Some regard *ursae* as genitive, others interpret it as dative. The genitive is defended by Hildebrand ("per graecismum"), vdVliet (app. crit.), Médan p. 102, Robertson (cf. K. St. I p. 474, who compare στερεῖν + gen. and such parallels as Hor. *Sat.* 2, 3, 27 *miror morbi purgatum te illius.* Whether or not that genitive is a grecism is a disputed question; cf. Löfstedt, *Synt.* II, p. 416 concerning gen. with *regnare*). Petschenig, *W.S.* 4 (1882), p. 147 and vGeisau p. 251 regard *ursae* as dative. The former compares 3, 1 (52, 7 f.) *me securae quieti reuulsum* and 11, 4 (269, 6) *laeuae...cymbium dependebat,* the latter Tert. *Val.* 32, 5 *despolior sexui meo*; see Hoppe p. 29; within the context however (*ubi, etsi despolior, sexui meo deputor*) the dative seems to be due rather more to *deputor.* Thus the one proper parallel for the dative with *despolio* disappears, and as a result Pricaeus' conjecture *ursa* becomes rather more attractive. A definitive solution, however, is impossible to reach.

The difficulty of the passage should not blind us to the Apuleian humour which manages to have the narrator praise Thrasyleon's performance while at the same time playing with the notion that the robber is beaten at his own game; moreover, as Walsh has it, the story serves as a "timely warning to men who wear the guise of animals!" (p. 158)

Sic etiam Thrasyleon nobis periuit, sed a gloria non peribit: 90, 24-91,1 "So it was that we lost Thrasyleon, too, but he will never be lost to glory".

F has *non periuit,* Stewech proposed *non peribit.* Arguments in favour of the ms. reading are, apart from the fact that it is there,

1. some instances of epanalepsis in which the second term acquires a different qualification from the first: 4, 32 (100, 8 f.) *mirantur...mirantur omnes*; cf. 7, 24 (172, 7 f.) *moriturus...moriturus integer* (Bernhard p. 234). It is to be noted, however, that in both cases the first term is given a *quidem.*

2. the strength of the verb: "sed quum summa insit in voc. *periuit* totius enuntiationis vis et efficacia, nemo dubitabit, quin recte hic habeat" (Hildebrand). Immo dubitamus.

In favour of the future (apart from the frequency of the *u/b* interchange (cf. Helm Praef. *Fl.* p. XLVI))

1. Stewech quoted 81, 3 *celebrabitur* (and we may add that there are further parallels between the stories of Lamachus and Thrasyleon). Add

2. the very banality of the future tense (Vallette *ad loc.,* Walsh pp. 59, 158: "sententious rhetoric", also Ogilvie-Richmond on Tac. *Agr.* 46, 4);

3. the irony of the fact that this is the last thing said about Thrasyleon.

It is hard to decide, but on the whole the balance is slightly in favour of *peribit.*

a gloria: *a* refers to the point of view taken; cf. 7, 18 (168, 1); Callebat, *S.C.*, p. 198, OLD *s.v.* 25 a.

Thrasyleon, like Lamachus, is given a core characteristic borrowed from the well-known picture of the Stoic. In Lamachus' case it is his willingness to die since he cannot maintain his essential character; cf.

e.g. A. Bonhoeffer, *Die Ethik des Stoikers Epiktet*, Stuttgart 1894, p. 30 and note 41. (82, 30 *sat se beatum qui manu socia uolens occumberet* seems to stamp him as a προκόπτων rather than a *sapiens*, cf. e.g. Sen. *De prov.* 2, 10); in Thrasyleon's case it is the *patientia* which enables him to maintain the role assigned to him (Bonhoeffer, *ibid.*).

91, 1-4 Confestim itaque constrictis sarcinis illis, quas nobis seruauerant fideles mortui Plataeae terminos concito gradu deserentes istud apud nostros animos identidem reputabamus...: "So we quickly tied up the bundles that our faithful dead had kept for us, and leaving the city limits of Plataeae at the double we kept meditating on this fact, that...".

confestim...constrictis: note the repetition of the first syllable and, with *itaque sarcinis illis*, the assonance of *i*. The phrase *constrictis sarcinis* shows that the original meaning of *sarcina* is no longer felt. The expression occurs also at 3, 28 (73, 1).

fideles mortui: see comm. on 88, 16, where the contrast with *nullam fidem in uita nostra* (91, 4 f.) is noted. *fideles*: the dead may be trusted to do nothing but *seruare*; *fides*: "trustworthiness" is discussed by E. Fraenkel, *Kl. Beitr.* I, p. 16.

Plataeae terminos: the singular Πλάταια also e.g. at Hom. *Il.* 2, 504, Herodotus 8, 50 (cf. Stein on 1, 82 Μαλέαι), Thuc. 2, 4, 8. See *RE* 20, 2 (2255). The lexica give no Latin instances: Apuleius doctus at work! For *termini = fines* in the sense of domain cf. Cic. *Dei.* 36; Liv. 38, 40, 2; Just. 44, 1, 1; Tert. *Marc.* 4, 26. See also E. Mikkola, *Die Abstraktion im Lateinischen* I, Helsinki 1964, pp. 40 (138, 141). Tac. *Ann.* 12, 13, 5 has *terminos urbis propagare* where the original sense of boundary stones is still very close.

concito gradu: see comm. on 88, 17 and 75, 16 (*cursu concito*).

apud nostros animos: see comm. on 75, 12 *apud mea praecordia*.

deserentes...reputabamus: not the physical but the mental activity is central.

91, 4-6 merito nullam fidem in uita nostra repperiri, quod ad manis iam et mortuos odio perfidiae nostrae demigrarit: "it is our own fault that loyalty is not to be found in this life, since through hatred of our treachery she has emigrated to the shades of the dead".

merito: "with reason"; thus the provoker of the tale (80, 24) had felt that *merito* he preferred Lamachus to all the treasure the present group is lugging to the cave. In the *Met.* adverbial *merito* always precedes the verb it qualifies.

nullam fidem: the personification is deferred to the causal clause.

quod...demigrarit: see Médan p. 17, Callebat, *S.C.*, p. 362 on the sequence of tenses ("résultat durable d'une action"). For personified Fides cf. 3, 26 (71, 21) and vdP. p. 189. Fides leaving this world is a common enough topos, e.g. Ov. *Met.* 1, 129 and Bömer *ad loc*; in particular the description in Sil. 2, 484 (cf. M. v. Albrecht, *Silius Italicus*, Amsterdam 1964, pp. 55 f.), where the Goddess had moved to heaven. Here she has moved to the dead, in Petronius *Sat.* 124 (lines 249 ff.) she has followed Pax to the realm of Dis (cf. Stubbe *ad loc.*, the passage is omitted by Ciaffi).

ad manis…et mortuos: see Bernhard p. 220 on the alliteration.

manis: see 6, 30 (151, 27) and Helm-Krenkel *ad loc.* who translate "Die Guten". Here that translation is particularly apt from the robbers' point of view. See also comm. on 92, 5.

perfidiae nostrae: the parallels quoted above show that *nostrae* refers to the human race; the fact that a robber reflects on human *perfidia* is, of course, as Helm-Krenkel point out, highly humorous.

Sic onere uecturae simul et asperae uiae toti fatigati tribus 91, 6-8
comitum desideratis istas quas uidetis praedas adueximus:
"And so the lot of us, worn out by the weight of our baggage and the rough road, and three men short, have brought in the stuff you see there".

asperae uiae: F has *aspere uiae*; Scaliger proposed *asperitate*, Armini *asperie*. Neither Scaliger's irreproachable Latin, nor Armini's enrichment of the language by a new but not impossible word are needed. Hildebrand explained *asperae uiae* by linking it with *onere*; it appears equally possible and possibly preferable to let it depend on *fatigati*; see the parallels quoted (e.g. *fessi rerum*, Verg. *A.* 1, 178) on 78, 3. If this interpretation is right, we have another case of mixed construction: cf. Bernhard pp. 150 f. See 3, 2 (52, 23) *magistratibus…et turbae miscellaneae cuncta completa*, and vdP. p. 30 who quotes also 8, 1 (177, 7 f.) *luxuriae popinalis scortisque et diurnis potationibus exercitatus*.

toti fatigati: on the confusion of *omnes* and *toti* see Callebat *S.C.*, p. 287. Even so one may hesitate between Helm's "ganz ermüdet" and Vallette's "épuisés tous". The latter produces a notable contrast with *tribus comitum desideratis*.

desideratis most probably was the original raeding in F; when it disappeared, *desertis*, a marginal reading in φ, gave rise to the unnecessary conjecture *defectis* which Hildebrand proposed as a refinement of Oudendorp's *defecti s(cilicet)*. Helm cites e.g. Caesar *B.G.* 7, 51, 4 *eo die milites sunt paulo minus septingenti desiderati*.

istas quas uidetis praedas adueximus: see Callebat, *S.C.*, p. 274 on emphatic *istas*. The phrase refers back to 80, 24 *sarcinis istis quas aduexistis* and thus forms a verbal frame around the reported activities of the second group of robbers. See Bernhard pp. 262 ff. on the stereotyped element in the introductions and endings of insets. In the mouth of the present robber-narrator *istas* sounds rather as an ironic quotation of the *istis* as used by the earlier speaker (one might use the term "antiphrastic depreciation").

CHAPTER XXII

The robbers go to sleep; Lucius is given dinner by the old woman, but prefers to feed on bread. The robbers hardly take time to rest and depart during that very night to return on sunrise.

91, 9-10 Post istum sermonis terminum poculis aureis memoriae defunctorum commilitonum uino mero libant: "That was the end of the conversation; from golden cups they poured libations of un-mixed wine, in memory of their dead comrades".

post istum sermonis terminum: cf. 5, 24 (122, 12) *et cum termino sermonis*; 3, 14 (62, 21) *cum isto fine sermonis*; literature in vdP. p. 110. *Istum* is not used in a deictic sense here, but refers to the previous chapters. See Callebat, *S.C.*, p. 273; Jahn-Kroll on Cic. *Brut.* 258.

poculis aureis: from a materialistic point of view the robbers are not too badly placed. Possibly the vessels have just been captured; cf. 80, 8-9 *aureorum...uasculorum*; 88, 14 ff. *iubeo singulos commilitonum asportare, quantum quisque poterat auri uel argenti*.

memoriae defunctorum...libant: a much more gruesome funeral sacrifice is mentioned at 8, 12 (186, 23 ff.) *at ego sepulchro mei Tlepolemi tuo luminum cruore libabo et sanctis manibus eius istis oculis parentabo*. See further vdP. p. 137; Latte p. 378.

uino mero: from Pl. *Am.* 430 onwards a frequent combination. The purity of the wine is mentioned emphatically, not only to mark the robbers' "affluent society" but in particular to show that religious precepts are being observed. Cf. Hor. *Carm.* 1, 19, 14 f. *uerbenas, pueri, ponite turaque / bimi cum patera meri*. Nisbet and Hubbard *ad loc.* refer to Fest. 474, 31 ff. L (= 348, 19 ff. M.) *spurcum uinum est quod sacris adhiberi non licet, ut ait Labeo Antistius Lib. X commentari iuris pontificii, cui aqua admixta est defrutumue, aut igne tactum est mustumue, antequam deferuescat.*

91, 10-12 dehinc canticis quibusdam Marti deo blanditi paululum conquiescunt: "then buttered up Mars with some hymns, and went to sleep for a while".

canticis quibusdam: if the translation "some" for *quibusdam* is right we have another case of *quidam* in the sense of *aliqui* (quite frequent in the *Met.*). Of course the sense "certain" is also eminently possible here. The meal had had a singing start as well: cf. 80, 14 *strepitu cantilant*.

Marti deo blanditi: not Mercury but Mars is the god of the(se) robbers (see also Appendix I). Cf. 7, 10 (162, 3 f.) *quin igitur ... supplicatum*

Marti Comiti pergimus?; *ibid.* (162, 10 f.) *copiosum instruunt ignem aramque cespite uirenti Marti deo faciunt*; 7, 11 (162, 14 f.) *hircum annosum et horricomem Marti Secutori Comitique uictimant.* Haemus/ Tlepolemus, when entering, indeed greets the robbers with *hauete...fortissimo deo Marti clientes* 7, 5 (158, 3-4).

The use of *blandiri* is remarkable, for the verb is used rarely with respect to the gods (cf. *Met.* 5, 31 (128, 20 f.)), but there the goddesses Ceres and Juno flatter the god Amor/Cupido *metu sagittarum*; Plin. *Pan.* 2, where there is question of the deified emperor; Mart. 1, 102 *Qui pinxit Venerem tuam, Lycori,/blanditus, puto, pictor est Mineruae*). Within the framework of the given typology of the robbers, however, the verb is entirely in its place: even towards their *patronus* the robbers are — in Lucius' eyes! — wholly without conscience and entirely calculating.

paululum conquiescunt: anticipating 92, 3 ff.

Enim nobis anus illa recens ordeum adfatim et sine ulla 91, 12-13
mensura largita est: "To us the old woman ladled out lots of fresh barley, without stint".

enim: a later hand in F wrote *et*, but Robertson judges there is sufficient space for an earlier *enim*, the reading of φ. Oudendorp agrees with Gruterus to read *at enim*, Eyssenhardt reads *at*, vdVliet with Lütjohann *enimuero*, but *enim* by itself may have adversative force. See comm. on 81, 3; Svennung, *Pall.*, p. 494, note 7; Callebat, *S.C.*, p. 329 (who does not mention this passage).

ordeum: F spells without *h* also at 1, 24 (22, 4); 3, 26 (71, 26); 7, 14 (164, 16); *Apol.* 93 (103, 20). In the six remaining cases (all of them in the *Met.*) the spelling with *h* is preferred.

adfatim et sine ulla mensura: both express the same notion, *adfatim* (see comm. on 75, 2) gives the point of view of the eater, *sine ulla mensura* that of the "serving staff", here therefore the *anus*. The variation of construction, then, may be called functional; see Bernhard p. 151.

ut equus quidem meus tanta copia et quidem solus potitus 91, 13-15
sali⟨ar⟩es scilicet cenas se ⟨esse⟩ crederet: "so that my horse, at least, when he got such generous rations and all for himself, too, thought that he must be at the Salians' feast".

equus quidem meus: Oudendorp notes: "non inscite conjecit vir doctus *quondam*; scil. quum adhuc eram Lucius". Oudendorp (quite rightly) regards the conjecture as superfluous, as appears from the references he provides, but its mention, as often with this type of conjecture, has some heuristic value. Here we may interpret the passage as a statement of the I-narrator (not the experiencing I), or, alternatively, as a statement of the experiencing I, who, for the very reason that he is given unpalatable food, becomes conscious of his humanity (his often-mentioned *sensus humanus*), as also at 74, 17. See Heine pp. 301 f. This first *quidem* is, of course, contrasted with the subsequent *uero*; note the repetition of *quidem* (in different senses).

saliares scilicet cenas se esse crederet: F and φ have *salies se cenasse...crederet*, with a space four letters wide between *cenasse* and *crederet*, but in F both the separation of *se* and *cenasse*, and the addition of the verb's final syllable (*se*) is the result of later interference. The correction *saliares* occurs in ç and is now generally accepted.

Most editors follow Helm: *saliares se cenas ⟨cenare⟩ crederet*. The present infinitive seems preferable to the perfect infinitive proposed by Lütjohann: *saliares cenas se cenasse* and vdVliet: *saliares se cenasse cenas* (adopted by Gaselee and Terzaghi; the latter wrongly claims the conjecture as his own, Frassinetti adopts that attribution without criticism).

Armini's conjecture (1928 p. 294) *saliares esse cenas crederet* goes in the right direction but has in common with the other solutions that it neglects the proper narrator's perspective. If we read *sc.* for *se* (cf. 77, 25) this defect is removed; if we, moreover, retain (the second) *se* as a probably necessary subject accusative, the reading *sali⟨ar⟩es scilicet cenas se ⟨esse⟩ crederet* is the inevitable result.

saliares ... cenas: Oudendorp and Hildebrand read *Salias* (sc. *cenas* or *epulas*) since they also retain the inf. *c(o)enasse*; no parallels are to be found but their argumentation impressed Forcellini, Lewis-Short and Georges, all of whom cite our passage *s.v. Salii*. Helm, in his crit. app., refers to 7, 10 (162, 9) *epulas saliares* where F (originally) reads *epulas alias res* and 9, 22 (219, 22) *cenas saliares*. There is, then, sufficient reason to accept the emendation in ç.

The *cenae saliares* are proverbial. Cf. Hor. *Carm.* 1, 37, 2 ff. *nunc Saliaribus | ornare puluinar deorum | tempus erat dapibus*. Ps. Acro notes *ad loc.*: *Saliares cenae, quas Salii faciebant, dicuntur amplissimi apparatus fuisse, unde et in prouerbio erat Saliares cenas dicere opipares et copiosas.* Cf. Fest. 438 f. L (= 326 M.) *Salios a saliendo et saltando dictos esse quamuis dubitari non debeat, tamen Polemon ait Arcada quendam fuisse nomine Salium, quem Aeneas a Mantinea in Italiam deduxit, qui iuuenes Italicos* ἐνόπλιον *saltationem docuerit ... Salios, quibus per omnis dies, ubicumque manent, quia amplae ponuntur cenae, siquae aliae magnae† dum† (sunt, Aug.), Saliares appellantur*; Cic. *Att.* 5, 9, 1 *epulati essemus Saliarem in modum.* See further Otto, *Sprichw.*, p. 306. Priests' colleges like that of the Salii (serving Mars!) were exclusive clubs not exactly despising culinary pleasures. On the Salii see Wissowa pp. 555 ff.; Latte pp. 114 ff.; R. M. Ogilvie, *The Romans and their Gods*, pp. 79 ff.

esse: for this present infinitive (= *edere*) see Sommer p. 541.

91, 15-92,1 Ego uero numquam alias hordeo cibatus, cum minutatim et diutina coquitatione iurulentum semper esserim, rimatus angulum, quo panes reliquiae totius multitud⟨in⟩is congestae fuerant: "As for me, I had never before eaten raw barley, as I had always eaten it fine-milled and soft from long cooking, so searching the corner where the remaining loaves of bread from the whole store were stacked".

ego uero...esserim is a much discussed section of text. Appendix III gives a survey of the readings of manuscripts and editors.

minutatim: the adverb occurs fairly regularly from Pompon. *Atell.* 166 onwards, e.g. in *Apol.* 61 (70, 7); the participle *minutatum* is rare and late, but nevertheless is preferred to the reading of F by a number of editors. See vdP. p. 34 concerning adverbs in *-tim* in the *Met.*

diutina coquitatione iurulentum: *coquitatione* (here only, see Bernhard p. 99; Médan p. 109, is the generally accepted correction of Salmasius for F's *cogitatione*. ThLL *s.v. iurulentus* quotes the passage as *diutius coquitatione iurulentum*, but that must be due to a misprint.

iurulentum: occurs also in 2, 7 (30, 16), an equally disputed passage, where the word is deleted by Helm III² (but not by e.g. Robertson, Helm-Krenkel, Frassinetti) and in *Apol.* 39 (46, 4), where F has the spelling *iusulentus*, defended by Kübler, *ALL* 8 (1893), p. 137, note 1 (see however Helm, Praef. *Fl.*, pp. XLV f.). See Médan p. 203; Callebat, *S.C.*, p. 44; Ernout, *Les adj.*, pp. 93, 100.

esserim: this perf. subj. occurs here only. The usual form is *ederim*: cf. Pl. *Capt.* 473; id. *Cas.* 126; id. *Poen.* 535. Possibly the latter form is to be preferred in our passage as well.

rimatus angulum: yet at 4, 7 (79, 14) the ass (and his horse) had been tied to the entrance of the cave. See Stockin pp. 10 f. on the contradiction involved.

quo: according to Médan p. 55 *quo* here represents *ubi*, but the usual construction is *congerere in* + acc. and therefore *quo* must be used here in its "original" sense of "whither"; cf. Verg. *Ecl.* 3, 69 *locum, aeriae quo congessere palumbes*.

panes: Oudendorp, Hildebrand and Eyssenhardt read *panis* with φ, doubtless partly because of the feminine *congestae fuerant*. The agreement here, however, is with the apposition *reliquiae*: see Petschenig, *WS* 4 (1882), p. 142; LHSz. p. 429.

totius multitudinis: F has *multitudis*, the correction occurs in φ. All translators assume that *multitudo latronum* is meant, but the relevance of *totius* is less than clear in that case; *multitudo pan(i)um* is at least as attractive an interpretation.

congestae fuerant: once again "verschobenes Plusquamperfectum", see vdP. p. 54; Enk on Prop. 1, 3, 17. The present passage is not in Médan's list (p. 6).

fauces diutina fame saucias et araneantes ualenter exerceo: 92, 2 "I vigorously plied my jaws, sore and cobwebby as they were from my long fast".

saucias: 'Sauciae sunt fauces *fame*, quae illa sunt laesae. Sicut saucia dicitur omnis res sive animata sive inanima, quae quocunque modo aliquid pristini vigoris vel salutis amisit, quasi vulnere quodam adfecta', thus Oudendorp, who compares for the sense *famelicus* Sil. 15, 786, where a *belua male saucia* is pursuing a fish. Cf. Pl. *Cur.* 318 *lippiunt fauces fame.*

araneantes: the participle occurs only here in Latin. The expression is proverbial; cf. Cat. 13, 7 *tui Catulli plenus sacculus est aranearum.* See Otto, *SdR.*, p. 34. Our passage in *Nachträge zu Otto*, p. 52 (Weyman).

92, 3-5 **Et ecce nocte promota latrones expergiti castra commouent instructique uarie, partim gladiis armati, in Lemures reformati concito se gradu proripiunt**: "And late in the night, lo and behold, the robbers were woken up, struck camp and in various rig, most of them armed with swords, they set out at the double, transformed into ghosts".

et ecce: see vdP. p. 93; Heine p. 174, n. 1.

nocte promota: this new expression (Médan p. 240) also occurs at 7, 7 (159, 8) and 9, 20 (217, 20).

expergiti: this participle occurs also at 2, 14 (36, 23); 2, 26 (46, 8); *Apol.* 43 (50, 17). According to ThLL the participle belongs to *expergiscor* as an alternative form for *experrectus* which also occurs three times in the *Met.* The *Index Apul.* and OLD assign it to the relatively rare *expergere*. The ancient grammarians also distinguished between *experrectus* and *expergitus*; see Butler-Owen on *Apol.* 43 (50, 17). The passive sense is easily defended here: we just have to assume that the *anus* adds the function of rouser to those of cook and cleaning lady.

castra commouent: see Appendix I.

partim...reformati: all editors, starting with vdVliet, read a double *partim* with Elmenhorst: *partim gladiis armati, partim in Lemures reformati* (the addition first occurs in the margin in φ). If we accept the addition, the dicolon must be a further elaboration of *instructi uarie*; cf. Vallette, p. 27, n. 3: "Sans doute afin d'épouvanter "l'habitant" au cours d'une expédition nocturne". That aspect however is not mentioned at all when the attack is described (95, 8 ff.): probably *in Lemures reformati* represents the impression the robbers create as they leave for their nocturnal adventure, and does not refer to a special outfit.

In itself a second *partim* (postulated on the strength of *armatī* in F; the stroke has almost disappeared and may have been removed) is not necessary. At 7, 13 (164, 9) and 9, 9 (209, 5) single *partim* is found, though followed by respectively *alios* and *alibi*. Rossbach indeed wished to insert *alii* after *armati*, but possibly *partim* here has the sense "largely", as at Pl. *Pers.* 434 (see Forcellini and LS *s.v.*; cf. also Bailey on Lucr. 1, 483 and the discussion in Gel. 10, 13). In that case only *partim gladiis armati* further explains *instructi uarie*, while *in Lemures reformati* refers to the entire company: a much more logical notion.

Lemures: Apuleius tries (*Soc.* 15 (23, 19-24, 10)) to distinguish between Lemures, Lares and Laruae: *est et secundo significatu species daemonum animus humanus emeritis stipendiis uitae corpori suo abiurans. Hunc uetere Latina lingua reperio Lemurem dictitatum. Ex hisce ergo Lemuribus qui posterorum suorum curam sortitus placato et quieto numine domum possidet,* *Lar dicitur familiaris; qui uero ob aduersa uitae merita nullis sedibus incerta* *uagatione ceu quodam exilio punitur, inane terriculamentum bonis homi-* *nibus, ceterum malis noxium, id genus plerique Laruas perhibent. Cum uero* *incertum est, quae cuique eorum sortitium euenerit, utrum Lar sit an Larua,* *nomine Manem deum nuncupant.* Cf. Schol. Pers. 5, 185: *Lemures dicuntur* *dii manes, quos Graeci* δαίμονας *uocant, uelut umbras quasdam diuinitatem* *habentes. Lemuria autem dicuntur dies, quando Manes placantur.* See Beaujeu and Del Re on *Soc.* 15; Frazer on Ov. *Fast.* 5, 419 ff.; Latte p. 99, n. 1; R. M. Ogilvie, *The Romans and their Gods in the Age of Augustus,* London 1969, pp. 85 f.; *RE* XII 1931, 25 ff. For the ghostly element in the *Met.* see Heine p. 150, n. 7 and p. 316.

in...reformati: many instances of the use of *in* to indicate a transfor-mation are given by Médan p. 70 and Callebat, *S.C.*, p. 229. The various meanings of *reformare* are discussed by Callebat, *S.C.*, p. 153.

concito...gradu: see comm. on 88, 17.

Nec me tamen instanter ac fortiter manducantem uel 92, 5-7 somnus imminens impedire potuit: "But as for me, not even overwhelming sleepiness could stop me from continuously and valiantly chewing".

nec...uel: "not...even"; see Médan p. 235.

manducantem: "chewing"; an expressive usage, as Callebat, *S.C.*, p. 409 plausibly argues, rather than a borrowing from the *sermo cotidianus*.

Et quamquam prius, cum essem Lucius, unico uel secundo 92, 7-10 pane contentus mensa decederem, tunc uentri tam profundo seruiens iam ferme tertium qualum rumigabam: "And though, in former times, when I was Lucius, I used to leave the table satisfied after one or maybe two rolls, on this occasion, enslaved as I was to an unplumbable belly, I was almost on my third basket-full".

uentri tam profundo seruiens: see comm. on 79, 21. Cf. 7, 27 (175, 5 ff.) *et nunc iste securus incumbens praesepio uoracitati suae deseruit et insatiabi-lem profundumque uentrem semper esitando distendit.* See also Curtius 10, 2, 26.

iam ferme tertium qualum rumigabam: Bernhard p. 117 thinks that "three" is used here to indicate a relatively large number, but it is obvious that *tertium* is climactic after *unico uel secundo*, especially as it now qualifies not *panem* but *qualum*!

rumigare occurs here for the first time and is synonymous with *ruminare*; later it is found e.g. in Garg. Mart. *rur. boum* 12 and Arn. 5, 23.

Huic me operi attonitum clara lux oppressit: "Intent on this 92, 10-11 task I was surprised by the bright light of day". For the personification see comm. on 88, 3-5. Colvius' conjecture *attentum* is superfluous: cf. 10, 35 (265, 24 f.) *tota familia partim ministerio uenationis occupata, partim uoluptario spectaculo adtonita*; see also comm. on 84, 6.

CHAPTER XXIII

A highly placed and very lovely visitor.

Tandem itaque asinali uerecundia ductus, aegerrime tamen 92, 11-13
digrediens riuulo proximo sitim lenio: "So at long last my
assly sense of propriety led me to abandon my meal — though very
reluctantly — and I slaked my thirst in a nearby stream".

itaque: Oudendorp reads (with A) *denique*; in the *Met. tandem denique*
is indeed a regular redundancy (see vdP. p. 166), but the reading is not
compelling: *itaque* presents the consequence of *clara lux oppressit*. For
the position (usual in the *Met.*), see Bernhard p. 27; Scobie, *Comm.* I,
pp. 90 f., 103.

asinali: this adjective does not occur elsewhere (Bernhard p. 139;
Médan p. 115); it is synonymous with *asinarius* and *asininus*. The combi-
nation with *uerecundia* is unexpected — thus Callebat, *S.C.*, p. 470.
The form of the adjective may be explained as a humorous analogy of
uirginalis.

uerecundia: Lucius has retained this characteristic as a quadruped!
See Scobie, *Comm.* I, p. 124.

ductus...digrediens: for the juxtaposition of the two participles see
Bernhard p. 41.

sitim lenio: a welcome change for the *fauces sauciae* after three baskets
full of bread!

Nec mora cum latrones ultra anxii atque solliciti remeant: 92, 13-14
"It wasn't long before the robbers came back, even more tense and
excited".

There is no question of fear on the part of the robbers (cf. Helm-
Krenkel "ängstlich"): it is not clear whom they should fear — possible
pursuers? The robbers are on the contrary excited by their big catch.
Cf. 3, 21 (67, 20) *percita...ac satis trepida* and vdP. *ad loc.* (p. 156).

ultra anxii: thus the tradition in F and φ. Oudendorp and Gaselee read
ultro with ς (this is not impossible: at 2, 15 (37, 2) *ultro* has been transmit-
ted as *ultra* as well); Wasse proposed *retro*, Petschenig *uultu*; there are
additions by vdVliet: *ultra ⟨solitum⟩*; Helm crit. app. *ultra ⟨morem⟩*;
the largest following was gained by Haupt: *ultra ⟨modum⟩*, a reading
adopted by Helm, Robertson, Vitali and vThiel.

None of these show any particular likelihood from a palaeographical
point of view. Three solutions present themselves:

1. Proposal by B. L. Hijmans Jr.: read ⟨*non*⟩ *ultra anxii*. The addition

is a minor one and *non ultra* ("no longer") has parallels e.g. in Sil. 14, 103; 15, 808; Hier. *Ep.* 22, 6, 2. Moreover, in the remainder of the tale there is no question of *anxietas*. We have, then, a contrast between the hasty departure and the self-assured return of the robbers.

2. We retain the text and interpret *ultra* with Th. Stangl (*BPhW* 28 (1908), pp. 1486 f.) as a synonym of *satis*; it may be the positive of *ultime*; cf. 1, 7 (7, 9) *ultime adfectus*. See Marg. Molt *ad loc.* and Callebat, *S.C.*, p. 539. The Thesaurus material at Munich does not provide any parallel for this sense.

3. There *is* a parallel for *ultra* + positive in the sense of a comparative: Persius 3, 15: *o miser inque dies ultra miser hucine rerum/uenimus?* Here *ultra miser* must have the sense of *miserior* (thus also van Wageningen *ad loc.*). *Ultra anxii* "even more nervous" would have to be seen, like the ⟨*non*⟩ *ultra anxii* proposed under 1), in the light of the hasty departure described earlier.

The robbers' return at this moment — just after sunrise — has curious consequences with respect to the girl's marriage discussed in the subsequent chapters: the marriage must have taken place in the middle of the night! (E. H. Haight consistently speaks of the "weddingnight"; see her *Essays on Ancient Fiction* (New York 1936, repr. 1966), p. 163). We cannot but conclude that there is an element of untidiness in the composition (not seen by Perry or vThiel) and occasioned when Apuleius altered his "Vorlage", as may be seen when we compare *Onos* 22 τρισὶ δὲ ὕστερον ἡμέραις μεσούσης σχεδὸν τῆς νυκτὸς ἀναστρέφουσιν οἱ λησταί (where there is no inconsistency).

The fact that Apuleius gives a shortened version — obviously in order to give the story more speed — did not escape Junghanns, but curiously he thinks that the abbreviation left no traces (p. 143, n. 44). The only scholar who had difficulty with the passage appears to be Kerényi, who remarks that the girl's falling asleep (93, 21) better fits a nocturnal hour (K. Kerényi, *Die griechisch-orientalische Romanliteratur*, Darmstadt ²1962, p. 159, n. 27).

92, 14-20 **nullam quidem prorsus sarcinam uel omnino, licet uilem, laciniam ferentes, sed tantum gladiis, totis manibus, immo factionis suae cunctis uiribus unicam uirginem fil[i]o liberalem et, ut matronatus eius indicabat, summatem re[li]gionis, puellam mehercules et asino tali concupiscendam, maerentem et crines cum ueste sua lacerantem aduehebant**: "bringing no load at all, not so much as a rag, however valueless, but for all their swords, for all their considerable number of hands, let's face it, for all the combined forces of their troop, the only thing they were bringing with them was one single young lady, beautiful in looks and, as her ladylike apparel suggested, one of the local nobility, a girl, I promise you, to give ideas even to an ass like me. She was sobbing and tearing her hair and her clothes".

174

The sentence contains an anacoluthon, the only one Bernhard (p. 94) found in the whole of the *Met.* It is a simple enough case: "Der Ueber-gang vom Partizipium zum verb. finit. ist durch die Länge des Satzes hier begründet". Callebat, *S.C.*, pp. 363 f., gives no further instances either; see however comm. on 95, 21 ff.

sarcinam: Médan p. 153 mistakenly compares 85, 19; see comm. *ad loc.*

licet uilem: cf. 86, 12 *licet gracilem* and comm. *ad loc.*

ferentes: Bernhard pp. 43-45 collects the cases of "Nachstellung der Partizipia".

gladiis, totis manibus, immo factionis suae cunctis uiribus: a clear case of climax, as Hildebrand *ad loc.* and Bernhard p. 68 have noted. The climax is underlined by *immo* (Bernhard p. 127) and *cunctis* (more loaded than *totis*, see Callebat, *S.C.*, p. 288). The "Gesetz der wachsenden Glieder" which is working here renders the supplement by Löfstedt (and Bulhart): *gladiis totis* (thus also Helm, Gaselee, Robertson, Brandt-Ehlers, Frassi-netti, Vitali and vThiel) improbable, however attractive it is palaeo-graphically. In this respect Castiglioni's addition *tot gladiis* is rather better, but even this conjecture may be superfluous, as is Kronenberg's *sed tantis gladiis* (though it produces a beautiful double parallelism).

factionis: on the unfavourable connotation see vdP. p. 75.

unicam uirginem: Oudendorp thought that a *cinctam* had disappeared here. Robertson supplies *munitam* before *unicam uirginem* (thus also Brandt-Ehlers). Hildebrand however has pointed out that the climax is particularly well marked by *unicam uirginem*.

filo liberalem: F has *filio*; the same mistake is made by ms. P. at Pl. *Merc.* 755 *satis scitum filum mulieris*, the first instance of the sense "outward appearance" (the usual sense being "thread", "seam"). For further instances see Enk *ad loc.*; *liberalis* here may mean "beautiful", rather than "highly-placed", for as Hildebrand remarks her *nobilitas* is dealt with in the next phrase. Cf. Pl. *Epid.* 43 *forma lepida et liberali captiuam adulescentulam*; see Duckworth *ad loc*; Desertine p. 116. Weyman p. 345 notes imitation of Apuleius in Jul. Val. 1, 7.

matronatus: one of Apuleius' neologisms (not mentioned by Bernhard or Médan) and in this sense occurring here only. In view of the develop-ment of *matrona* in the direction of a synonym for *femina nobilis* there is no paradox.

summatem regionis: just as at 82, 22 f. there is confusion here between *religionis* and *regionis*, but here *regionis* is, of course, the right reading.

summas also occurs at 11, 1 (266, 15); 11, 10 (274, 8); 11, 22 (284, 1), in all of which cases it is used of Isis — a beautiful argument in favour of the identification of Charite and Isis, but one that escaped Merkelbach (*Roman*, pp. 75 ff.). The word was probably borrowed from Plautus who uses it at *Pseud.* 227, *Cist.* 25 and *St.* 492 (Hildebrand; Médan p. 177; not in Desertine).

mehercules occurs four times in the *Met.*; see Bernhard p. 129; Callebat, *S.C.*, p. 177. Heine p. 176 remarks that the situations in which *hercules* (and the like) are used have in common "dass sie den Erzähler zu einer

Unterbrechung der ruhigen Sprachbewegung veranlassen und sich in dem überraschten, wenn nicht gar erschreckten Ausruf 'hercules' erneut sein geringer Abstand zum und sein Ergriffensein vom Erzählten dokumentiert."

tali: mistakenly deleted by vdVliet after the ed. Basil. (1533) and Bursian, *SABW* 1881, p. 128 ("eine Randbemerkung eines alten Lesers"). Damsté (*Mnemosyne* 1928, p. 13) compares 5, 23 (121, 11) *tale corpus*; 7, 21 (170, 4) *amator talis*. A similar reaction on the part of Lucius, sexually easily excited, whether biped or quadruped, is absent from the *Onos* (Feldbrugge p. 55).

maerentem et crines cum ueste sua lacerantem: according to Médan pp. 267 f. one of the complete hexameters in the *Met.*; apparently he does not take into account the elision of the final syllable. More correct is his remark on p. 273: "l'accumulation de syllabes longues correspond à l'expression d'un sentiment de terreur ou de tristesse".

92, 20-22 Eam simul intra speluncam uerbisque quae dolebat minora facientes sic adloquuntur: "As soon as she was in the cave, in an attempt verbally to lessen here sorrows they spoke to her as follows".

According to many editors this text cannot be retained. Insertion of *ducunt* after *speluncam* is the most generally accepted cure; it was proposed by Haupt and adopted by Helm, Robertson, Vitali and vThiel. Bernhard p. 159 agrees. Other proposals are Lütjohann's ⟨*intrauerunt, deponunt*⟩, Walter's ⟨*condunt*⟩, Brakman's ⟨*claudunt*⟩, Scazzoso's ⟨*trahunt*⟩ (in his app., not in his text).

Others think *intra* corrupt. Oudendorp thought of *intrarant*, necessitating the deletion of *-que*; Bursian proposed *intrantes*, adopted by vdVliet and Gaselee; Petschenig wished to read *intrat* in which case too *-que* must be deleted.

Frassinetti, finally, proposes an intervention at *simul*: he reads *eam sistunt intra speluncam* and compares 100, 21 *montis in excelsi scopulo, rex, siste puellam* and the passage in *Onos* 22 which corresponds with ours: καὶ καταθέμενοι αὐτὴν ἔνδον...θαρρεῖν ἐκέλευον.

There appears to be no need however to change the transmitted text; and indeed Hildebrand, Eyssenhardt, Giarratano, Terzaghi, Brandt-Ehlers and Scazzoso leave it untouched. If one follows Kronenberg's reasoning (*Mnemosyne* 1928, p. 34) we have to do with a contamination of *simulatque intra speluncam sunt, eam adloquuntur* and *simul intra speluncam sunt et eam adloquuntur*. Hildebrand's paraphrase "eam latrones, quum intra speluncam essent et verbis minuerent causas ob quas illa dolebat" points in the same direction. The solution proposed by Wiman (pp. 36-38) and Chodaczek, *Eos* 34 (1932/3), p. 166 is more subtle. They treat both *eam* and *quae dolebat* as the object of *facientes* though their terminology differs. Chodaczek speaks of zeugma, Wiman of an ἀπὸ κοινοῦ construction, both are right. The construction ἀπὸ κοινοῦ is by no means rare in the *Met.*, see vdP. p. 51. For *eam...intra speluncam*...

facientes cf. 5, 2 (104, 14) *intra limen sese facit*. See Fernhout *ad loc.*; Löfstedt, *Per. Aeth.*, pp. 167 f.; Svennung, *Pall.*, pp. 563-565; Callebat, *S.C.*, p. 173.

Tu quidem salutis et pudicitiae secura breuem patientiam 92, 22-24
nostro compendio tribue, quos ad istam sectam pauper-
tatis necessitas adegit: "You've got nothing to worry about, your
life and honour are safe, just be a little indulgent while we take our
winnings, because you know, it was the neediness imposed by poverty
that brought us to this profession".

tu quidem: according to Callebat, *S.C.*, p. 93 this is an example of the
use of the personal pronoun in a lively dialogue, but it is, of course, an
instance of contrastive use as well, *tu quidem* being contrasted with *pa-
rentes autem tui*.

salutis et pudicitiae secura: *secura* with genitive is a poetic usage; see
vGeisau p. 246; Médan p. 36; Fernhout p. 111; LHSz p. 78. See also
comm. on 93, 16. After *secura* there is an obvious pause; the sentence,
then, has three commata of respectively 15, 16, 17 syllables (with a
ditrochee at the end).

patientiam...tribue: for *tribuere* with obj. used as a periphrasis for a
verb see vdP. p. 50.

nostro compendio..., quos: in view of *nostro* there is no need for an
antecedent for *quos*; see Bernhard p. 160; Callebat, *S.C.*, p. 113.

sectam: see comm. on 88, 3.

paupertatis necessitas: for such well-to-do people as the robbers appeared
to be, a beautiful argument!

Parentes autem tui de tanto suarum diuitiarum cumulo, 92, 24-93, 3
quamquam satis cupidi, tamen sine mora parabunt scilicet
idoneam sui sanguinis redemptionem: "As for your parents,
even if they are a bit mean, with their huge heaps of money they won't
hesitate for a moment to produce a really suitable ransom for their own
flesh and blood".

quamquam...cupidi: notwithstanding their attempt to put the girl
at ease, the robbers must sneer at her parents! For *quamquam* with adj.
see Médan p. 237. The sense of "avaricious" for *cupidus* also occurs e.g.
in Suet. *Vesp.* 16.

scilicet: Colvius proposes *ilicet*, without justification, however; the fact
that *sine mora* precedes may not in itself be a strong argument against
ilicet, but *scilicet* fits very well here as a reference to *breuem patientiam...
tribue.*

sanguinis: like the Greek αἷμα, often used in the sense of offspring; cf.
Ov. *Met.* 5, 514 f. *pro...meo ueni supplex.../sanguine proque tuo*; Verg.
A. 6, 835 *proice tela manu, sanguis meus.*

redemptionem: neither attempts nor methods to obtain the ransom from the parents are mentioned anywhere. Van Thiel I, p. 107, n. 121 (cf. *ibid.* p. 191, n. 73) thinks that the ransom will not have been mentioned in the "Vorlage": "Der Verfasser machte keine Worte über Dinge, die sich von selbst verstanden". More probability may be assigned, however, to Junghanns' theory (p. 143, n. 44) that the robbers of the "Vorlage" never thought of a ransom: "das Natürliche ist Verkauf als Sklavin oder Verschleppung (gewöhnlich in ein Bordell, wie die Romanliteratur zeigt, z.B. Xen. Eph. I 13-14; III 11, 12; V 5; Chariton I 12; Hist. Apoll. r. T. c. 33). — Apul. dagegen, dem es nur auf Ausgestaltung der Szene mit dem untröstlichen Mädchen ankommt, legt wenig Wert darauf, ob die Worte sachlich zur Lage der Räuber passen."

CHAPTER XXIV

The girl remains desperate.

His et his similibus blateratis necquicquam dolor sedatur 93, 4-5
puellae: "By this and similar blathering the girl's misery by no means
calmed".

The second *his* could have been omitted, cf. 10, 15 (247, 26) *his et
similibus altercati*; the addition of the word in our passage possibly
illustrates the blathering; the robbers' wishes seem, from their point of
view, reasonable (*idoneam redemptionem*) and acceptable to the girl's
parents; on the other hand the robbers do not appear to try to establish
contact with those parents in order to negotiate a ransom; but for the
girl their words are *blateratio* (she continues to weep) and the ass — com-
passionately co-experiencing the situation — takes her point of view:
the narrating and experiencing Lucius are not strictly separate here.

Apul. employs the verb *blaterare* three times in the *Met.* (apart from
our passage also 9, 10 (210, 8) and 10, 9 (243, 23)) and three times else-
where (*Apol.* 3 (4, 4), 34 (39, 27) and *Fl.* 9 (10, 24)). Fest. 34 M (= 30 L)
explains: *blaterare est stulte et praecupide loqui, quod a graeco* βλάξ (i.e.
"stolid") *originem ducit, sed et camelos, cum uoces edunt, blaterare dicimus*;
Non. 44 M (= 63 L) remarks: *blatis et blateras, confingis aut incondite et
inaniter loqueris ut a balatu*. According to Médan (p. 180) the word belongs
to the "langue familiaire"; see Callebat, *S.C.*, p. 513.

necquicquam: F has *necqquã qq* is a correction by a second hand, which
also adds *cu* over the correction. Among conjectures we mention those
by Haupt (*nequaquam*) and vdVliet (*nequiquam nequaquam*); all modern
editors read *necquicquam*.

Quidni? quae inter genua sua deposito capite sine modo 93, 5-6
flebat: "No, indeed: she put her head between her knees and wept with-
out ceasing".

quidni?: "of course not"; the original interrogative sense "why not"
faded very early (see LHSz p. 458); whereas we expect an answer to *cur*,
we do not to *quidni*; it emphatically confirms a previous positive state-
ment, cf. 6, 17 (141, 5-7) *Tunc Psyche uel maxime sensit ultimas fortunas
suas et uelamento reiecto ad promptum exitium sese compelli manifeste
comperit. Quidni?* It also emphasizes the negative contained in the pre-
ceding sentence, as is the case here; cf. Wilkins on Cic. *de Orat.* 2, 273,
K.St. II 2, p. 495. Often further explanation is supplied in a relative
clause. The formal interrogative *quidni?* causes a certain expectation

with respect to this clause. Callebat, *S.C.*, pp. 424 f., thinks that Apuleius uses the word both as an imitation of comic authors and as a borrowing from oratorical writing.

Usually the relative clause following *quidni* explains what precedes that word, cf. Catul. 79, 1 *Lesbius est pulcher: quidni? quem Lesbia malit/ quam te cum tota gente, Catulle, tua*; Cic. Quinct. 69 *"erat"*, *inquit, "illarum partium". quidni? qui apud te esset eductus*; strictly speaking this is not the case here (for that matter, no subjunctive is used) but the intention is clear: "her grief was far too strong for that, as was obvious from the fact that she continued weeping bitterly".

J. B. Bauer quotes Egyptian parallels for the posture described here, *Hermes* 87 (1959), pp. 383 f.; he considers Hor. S. 2, 8, 58 f. *Rufus posito capite, ut si / filius immaturus obisset, flere* 'eine rein äussere Parallele'; see however Gatscha p. 150.

93, 6-8 At illi intro uocatae anui praecipiunt, adsidens eam blando, quantum posset, solaretur alloquio, seque ad sectae sueta conferunt: "So they called the old woman inside and told her to sit down by the girl and comfort her as best she could with soothing chat, while they turned to the usual occupations of their profession".

Though the old woman left the cave at the beginning of the night, when the robbers went to sleep, in order to feed horse and ass, one had better not ask whether she stayed outside all night. If one asks with Helm-Krenkel (p. 25) how the ass standing outside can be aware of what is happening inside, the answer is found in 6, 25 (147, 4) *astans ego non procul.*

anui praecipiunt...solaretur: on the ellipsis of *ut* and the deviation from the rules of the sequence of tenses see the note on 76, 17.

adsidens eam: for the accusative cf. 1, 22 (20, 18 f.) *assidebat pedes uxor*; see Marg. Molt *ad loc.*; it is possible that *eam* should be linked with both *adsidens* and *solaretur*.

blando...solaretur alloquio: Var. *L.* 6, 57 remarks *adlocutum mulieres ire aiunt, cum eunt ad aliquam locutum consolandi causa*. One receives the impression that *alloqui* is used in particular for comforting among women (as is the case here). But Servius, when commenting on Verg. *A.* 10, 860 (*Mezentius*) *alloquitur maerentem* (*Rhaebum equum*), uses a more general expression: *est enim adloqui consolari*. In combination, though at some distance from one another, the words *alloquia* and *consolantes* are also found at Liv. 9, 6, 8. *Adloqui* is used in the more general sense of "to address" at 92, 22, where the robbers address the girl. Gatscha p. 149 draws attention to Catul. 38, 5 *solatus es allocutione* and mentions another six passages where there may be Catullan influence in Apuleius.

sectae sueta: that *latrocinia* are meant is to be expected, but becomes explicit only at 6, 25 (147, 6 ff.); see vThiel I, p. 107, n. 122.

On *sectae* see comm. on 88, 3-5.

sueta as a noun is not found before Apuleius (this is confirmed by the

180

ThLL material at Munich kindly placed at our disposal); Liv. 28, 24, 6 *rapto suetis uiuere* has the masculine form.

Nec tamen puella quiuit ullis aniculae sermonibus ab in- ceptis fletibus auocari, sed altius eiulans sese et assiduis singultibus ilia quatiens mihi etiam lacrimas excussit: "But the girl could not be distracted from her crying by any words from the old woman; on the contrary she bewailed her case even more and continued sobbing until her belly shook[1] and thus she forced tears even from me".

The girl's inconsolable condition will presently (ch. 26) occasion her to give a fuller report of her calamity and present the *anus* with an opportunity to distract her attention with the story of Amor and Psyche.

quiuit: see Neue-Wagener III³, p. 440.

eiulans: Apul. is the first author in whom *eiulare* is found in a transitive sense, cf. 3, 1 (52, 19 f.) *fortunas meas heiulabam* (see vdP. p. 28); 3, 8 (57, 23) *se lugubriter eiulantes*; also in Amm. 27, 12, 7 and 28, 1, 37.

altius: F has *alius*, which a second hand apparently tried to change into *altius*, the reading also in α. φ has *autius*, but a later hand has added a *c* above the line in between *a* and *u*. One might consider taking *altius* in the sense of *imo de pectore, profundiore gemitu* with Oudendorp; in three of the four places he quotes in defence of his interpretation *altius* is combined with a verb meaning "to sigh" (*ingemiscere, (ad)suspirare*); only 4, 29 (98, 6 f.) has a different verb: *inpatiens indignationis capite quassanti fremens altius sic secum disserit*. Possibly Oudendorp's proposal was suggested by the subsequent *ilia quatiens*.

assiduis singultibus ilia quatiens: Celsus clarifies (4, 1, 13) *ilia inter coxas et pubem imo uentre posita sunt*; according to the medical profession violent sobbing may result in a contraction of the *musculus rectus abdominis* or even a rupture (cf. the Dutch expression "hij bescheurde zich van het lachen").

ilia is mistakenly rendered (an pudoris causa?) "breast" (Helm, Schwartz and even Graves), "bosom" (Adlington-Gaselee), "sides" (Butler, Vallette), "body" (Brandt-Ehlers) or left untranslated (Rode-Burck, Scazzoso, Clouard, Grimal). Possibly Apuleius found his inspiration in Verg. *A*. 9, 415 *longis singultibus ilia pulsat*; see Gatscha p. 145.

mihi etiam lacrimas excussit: cf. Ter. *Hau.* 167 *lacrumas excussit mihi miseretque me eius*. An ass shedding tears of pity shows undoubted human traits, cf. 6, 32 (154, 3) *meum crastinum deflebam cadauer*, said by Lucius/the ass. This is, for the time being, the last occasion on which the ass puts himself forward; it is only after the tale of Amor and Psyche, in the passage just quoted, that he comes to the fore once again.

---

[1] Our English adviser assures us that 'until her belly shook' "is a phrase of (...) horrendous ugliness" and she implores us to paraphrase. We apologize for not agreeing to her request, pleading the fact that the dire atmosphere of the *Met.* does not allow us to soften any individual expressions.

Ac sic: "An ego", inquit, "misera, tali domo, tanta familia, tam cari⟨s⟩ uernulis, tam sanctis parentibus desolata et infelicis rapinae praeda et mancipium effecta inque isto saxeo carcere seruiliter clausa et omnibus deliciis, quis innata atque innutrita sum, priuata sub incerta salutis et carnificinae lani[g]ena inter tot ac tales latrones et horrendum gladiatorum populum uel fletum desinere uel omnino uiuere potero?": "And then she spoke: "Poor wretch that I am, bereft of a wonderful home, a large household, devoted servants and my sainted parents, the prey and property of ill-chanced robbery, locked up like a slave in this rocky prison and deprived of all the comforts to which I am born and bred, how can I, faced with uncertainty as to my fate and with the threat of hideous torture, and in the power of all these dreadful robbers and terrible ruffians, how can I stop crying — how can I even survive?"

ac sic: translators go different ways in order to render *sic*: 1. they leave the word out entirely (Schwartz; Helm-Krenkel's "Ach ich Aermste, *so* rief sie" is hardly meant as a translation of *sic*); 2. they take it in a temporal sense (Carlesi: "a un certo momento"); 3. they take it to refer to manner (Vallette: "et elle parlait ainsi", with reference to what is to follow). We prefer to give *sic* a regressive link ("And it was in this situation that she exclaimed...") cf. Cic. *Q.fr.* 1, 1, 5, 16 *atque etiam e Graecis ipsis diligenter cauendae sunt quaedam familiaritates si qui sunt uetere Graecia digni; sic uero fallaces sunt permulti et leues*; cf. Becker p. 16 "ab initio enuntiationis positum *sic* valet idem quod *tum*, ut vis insit nostri *in solcher Lage, unter solchen Umständen*"; our passage is not mentioned, but there are references to 3, 3 (53, 22), 3, 21 (68, 13), 4, 32 (100, 14). Add 1, 23 (21, 7) *et sic 'ego te' inquit,*... Rather less comparable is 2, 25 (45, 21) *denique sic ad illam: 'quin abis', inquam*... where *sic* points ahead. See vdP. p. 38 with the literature mentioned there.

Note the clever and carefully varied structure of the long period:

tali domo
tanta familia
tam caris uernulis } DESOLATA
tam sanctis parentibus

et infelicis rapinae praeda et / mancipium } EFFECTA

inque isto saxeo carcere seruiliter CLAUSA
et omnibus deliciis, quis innata atque innutrita sum, PRIVATA

sub { incerta salutis / et carnificinae laniena }

inter { tot ac tales latrones / et horrendum gladiato- / rum populum }

{ uel fletum desinere / uel omnino uiuere } potero?

182

tali domo, tanta familia, tam caris uernulis, tam sanctis parentibus desolata: the rhetorical effect is enhanced by alliteration, assonance, pathetic anaphora, tetracolon and climax; Bernhard p. 78; moreover we have an instance of the law of waxing members at work.

sanctis parentibus...infelicis rapinae...saxeo carcere: each of the three adjectives is not merely *epitheton ornans* but is used rather for rhetorical and evocative effect; for the use and meaning of *infelix* see comm. on 90,8.

Note in lines 13-16 the variation in the use of conjunctions: (*desolata*) et {(*praeda*) et (*mancipium*)} (*effecta*)... *que* (*clausa*) et (*priuata*); see Bernhard pp. 82 f.

seruiliter: the word is used both in active ("as a slave does") and passive sense ("as a slave is treated"): a) Cic. *Tusc.* 2, 55 *ne quid...seruiliter muliebriterue faciamus*; Tert. *Nat.* 2, 6 *conceditisne diuinitatem non modo non seruiliter currere*, b) Petr. 117 *post peractum sacramentum seruiliter ficti dominum consalutamus*; Flor. *Epit.* 1, 17 *quibus in terga quoque seruiliter saeuientibus*. In our passage the sense is obviously passive.

innata atque innutrita: according to Bernhard p. 223 a "beabsichtigte assonantische Verbindung".

sub incerta salutis et carnificinae laniena: F has *incerta*; Beroaldus' conjecture *incerto* is adopted by most editors. Hildebrand retains *incerta* in the opinion "virginem ideo potissimum esse perturbatam et afflictam, quod incerta est, num ita privetur misere an reservetur a latronibus"; he thinks that *sub incerta salutis et carnificinae laniena* is put instead of *sub incertae salutis et carnificinae laniena*, and therefore notes a case of enallage here.

Ph. Dust. *CJ* 63 (1967/68) pp. 266 f. also retains the ms. reading, but interprets (*ego*) *sub incerta...laniena* and translates "(I) under a torment, uncertain of safety and torture"; he takes *incerta* as nominative. In view of the position of the word this seems unacceptable. *Incerta* may be retained if it is given causative sense, cf. Liv. 31, 12, 6 *incertus infans natus, masculus an femina esset*; admittedly as OLD *s.v.* 8 g remarks, *incertus* in this sense is always followed by a dependent question, but it may be assumed that Apuleius allowed himself greater freedom in the way he used the word. If, finally, one assigns a dominant function to *incerta* vis à vis the noun *laniena*, the phrase may be translated "in the excruciating uncertainty of safety or torture". Concerning the genitive with *incerta* see LHSz p. 78; Ph. Dust notes a similar construction at 92, 22 *tu quidem salutis et pudicitiae secura*.

carnificinae: *carnificina* is the activity of the *carnifex*: "torture". The word is found as early as Plautus (*Capt.* 132, *Cist.* 203) and used by Apuleius on two other occasions: *Met.* 7, 27 (174, 25) and 8, 28 (200, 2).

laniena: F has *lanigena*, but according to most modern editors the g is deleted by a second hand (Giarratano, however: sed al. m. indux. g).

A *laniena* is properly a butcher's shop (*ubi caro uenit*, Var. *L.* 8, 55) but in Apuleius always has the sense of *laniatus*, "torture", see de Jonge on 2, 30 (50, 6), vdP. p. 42, Callebat, *S.C.*, pp. 74 f. Robertson places the words *et carnificinae laniena* after *inque isto saxeo carcere*; this is attractive to the extent that the ablative would then not depend on *sub* (used in a zeugma!) but on *in* that is more easily understandable in the context; palaeographically, however, the transposition is difficult to explain.

gladiatorum: a *gladiator* is not only someone who acts as a "sword fighter" (thus 84, 21), but in general also a "bandit" (thus 95, 9); Cicero, too, combines the word in this meaning repeatedly with *latro*: *Cat.* 2, 7 *quis gladiator, quis latro*; *Phil.* 14, 14 *in aliquem gladiatorem aut latronem*; *Phil.* 13, 16 *furiosus gladiator cum taeterrimorum latronum manu*.

93, 20-22 **Lamentata sic et animi dolore et faucium tendore et corporis lassitudine iam fatigata marcentes oculos demisit ad soporem**: "Such was her lamentation; worn out with mental distress, physical exhaustion, and her throat swollen with crying, she let her drooping eyes close in sleep".

lamentata sic: thus the mss., as well as most editors. Kirchhoff, however, has pointed out (*JKlPh Suppl.* 28 (1903), pp. 38 f.) that in Apuleius' *Met. sic* always has first, the participle second place (it may even be pointed out that in Apuleius *sic* always precedes the word it qualifies). Therefore he proposed to read *sic lamentata*; Giarratano and Frassinetti adopted the transposition. We do not feel, however, that it is necessary to depart from the tradition.

tendore: F has *tundore*, according to Helm *t* in ras., Robertson *tu* in ras. nimis angusta; *tēdore* is found in φ (but the Nasalstrich seems to have been added by a second hand); both *tundor* and *tendor* are ἅπαξ εἰρημένα; the problem is discussed at length by H. Quellet, *Les dérivés latins en -or*, Paris 1969, pp. 50 f. He mentions four arguments in favour of *tendore*:

1. Soon (94, 3) the word *tundere* occurs; it is possible that its proximity gave rise to the "correction".

2. A comparable passage in Cass. Fel. 34 reads *faucium tensione et grauedine*.

3. The meaning of *tendore* fits the situation better than that of *tundore*.

4. There is nothing unusual about the formation of *tendore*.

If one examines the force of these arguments the conclusion must be that 1. has some but not much force; concerning 2. Quellet himself admits that Cass. Fel. is a very late author (5th century). As regards 3., Q. gives *tundor* a transitive — reflexive meaning: "se frapper la gorge", which does not fit the situation very well, but the word may just as well have an intransitive sense: "the beating of the pulse in the throat". As to 4., the formation of *tundor* is no less usual than that of *tendor*. Notwithstanding these objections we have decided in favour of *tendore*, partly because of the strength of the combination of arguments, however weak their individual force; thus also Clouard, Robertson-Vallette and Frassinetti; see Boscherini, *St.It.* 31 (1959), pp. 116 f.; Ernout, *Philologica* 2, p. 46.

CHAPTER XXV

The girl wakes up immediately and is altogether desperate: she wants to commit suicide. Angry words from the old woman.

At commodum coniuerat nec diu, cum repente lymphatico 93, 22-94,3 ritu somno recussa longeque uehementius adflictare sese et pectus etiam palmis infestis tundere et faciem illam luculentam uerberare incipit: "She had only just closed her eyes, but it was no time at all before suddenly, like one possessed, she started awake and began to attack herself far more vehemently, and even to beat her breast with cruel hands and strike her lovely face".

The sentence offers a number of textual problems:

1. *At* is not the reading in F, which has *an*, but Helm's conjecture, now generally accepted; probably rightly, for F also has *an* for *at* (though corrected in the same hand) at 7, 27 (175, 11). See Helm, Praef., *Fl.* p. XLII. Van der Vliet deleted *an*, a measure to some extent approved by Robertson.

2. According to Lütjohann, after *recussa* there is a lacuna, which Helm decided to print. A number of proposals have been made to fill the lacuna, of which the following are worth mentioning: Lütjohann himself proposed ⟨*est*⟩ (adopted by Gaselee), Kronenberg ⟨*longe*⟩ (which produces an instance of *geminatio*; adopted by Robertson, Brandt-Ehlers and vThiel). The difficulty may also be avoided by deleting *que* with Kroll (Frassinetti uses the wrong type of brackets in his crit. app.).

No lacuna (and therefore no addition) is accepted by Giarratano-Frassinetti, Terzaghi, Vitali or Scazzoso. They quote Petschenig's defence *WS* 4 (1882), p. 147, who remarks that the copula is lacking elsewhere, e.g. at 4, 32 (100, 8-11) *duae maiores sorores ... procis regibus desponsae iam beatas nuptias adeptae*, sc. *sunt* (Scioppius in fact adds *sunt* before *adeptae*). A more convincing parallel, however, is to be found at 3, 2 (52, 21 ff.) *nec mora cum ... cuncta completa* (sc. *sunt*) *statimque lictores duo ... trahere me ... occipiunt*.

3. *Luculentam*, too, has been doubted: Hildebrand and Eyssenhardt have *luculenter*, Petschenig proposed *truculenter* (in his commentary on 5, 22 (120, 22) *corpus ... luculentum* Hildebrand, however, quotes our place as *faciem illam luculentam*!). But *luculentus* for bodily beauty is not unusual; cf. Pl. *Mil.* 958 *luculenta ac* (or *atque*) *festiua femina*; Ter. *Hau.* 523 *forma luculenta* (said of a *meretrix*); Apul. *Met.* 10, 30 (261, 11) *luculentus puer nudus*.

lymphatico ritu: "as one possessed"; cf. 8, 25 (197, 7 f.) *uelut lymphaticus exilire*; 8, 27 (198, 20) *lymphaticum tripudium*. Vallette p. 29, n. 5 points out that *lymphat(ic)us* is an adaptation of the Greek νυμφόληπτος, "possessed by the nymphs", i.e. out of one's mind. Concerning the (etymological) connection between *lympha* and *nympha* see Kiessling-Heinze on Hor. *Sat.* 1, 5, 97 and Ernout-Meillet *s.v.* Nymphs possessed of the gift of clairvoyance are discussed in E. Rohde, *Psyche II*, Tübingen [5/6]1910, p. 68, n. 2. The girl (Charite) in fact speaks prophetically: after her husband has died (though not in the manner of her dream in 4, 27), she commits suicide: 8, 14 (187, 21/22) *ferro sub papillam dexteram transadacto corruit*.

adflictare sese: it is impossible to say whether the verb is used here in its literal sense "prae luctu pectus palmis afflictare, tundere", or in the derived sense "maerere, lugere" (ThLL). A clear example of the figurative sense is to be found in Petr. 111, 3 *sic afflictantem se ac mortem inedia persequentem* (since *afflictantem se* picks up a previous *flere*); most translators take the word here in its literal sense, but Rode and Graves (e.g.) take it figuratively.

et pectus etiam palmis infestis tundere: functional alliteration of *p* and *t*; Gatscha p. 145 detects imitation of Verg. *A.* 1, 481 *tristes et tunsae pectora palmis*.

94, 3-5 et aniculae, quanquam instantissime causas noui et instaurati maeroris requirenti, sic adsuspirans altius infit: "and, though the old woman most earnestly enquired the reasons for her renewed lamentations, she fetched a deep sigh and spoke as follows".

Petschenig and Castiglioni proposed *quam* for *quanquam*; the correction was adopted by Giarratano and Scazzoso, mistakenly however, for "quamuis facilis sit error ... huic loco bene conuenit *quanquam* nam causas noui maeroris non statim profert puella" (Robertson).

adsuspirans: apart from 96, 5 the word occurs nowhere else in Latin; Bernhard p. 121 detects Greek influence in the double prefix; see LHSz p. 284.

infit: according to Bernhard p. 133 the word is a vulgarism, but he is mistaken. It is noteworthy that *infit* (which occurs in the present only, see LHSz p. 307) occurs in but few prose writers, most often in Apuleius, who uses it thirteen times. From Enn. *Ann.* 394 V. onwards it is a typically poetic word with an archaic sound. Before Apuleius it occurs in prose only in Livy (three times); see Ogilvie on Liv. 1, 23, 7. The poetic aspect appears to be strengthened by the heroic clausula.

94, 5-7 Em nunc certe, nunc maxime funditus perii, nunc spei salutiferae renuntiaui: "Oh yes, now for sure, now I am absolutely done for, now I have abandoned all hope of survival".

The girl utters her despair in a beautiful anaphoric tricolon with increasing numbers of syllables.

The inerjection *em* has been transmitted here only in the *Met*. According to G. Luck, *Ueber einige Interjektionen der lateinischen Umgangssprache*, Heidelberg 1964, *em* should be accepted in the text in two more passages: the first one is 8, 5 (179, 24), where F has *et cape uenabulum et ego sumo lanceam* and editors correct with Haupt to read *en cape* (Helm in his *app. crit.* had already suggested *em cape*). The other passage is 9, 23 (220, 21 f.), where all editors, without exception, read *hem qualis... matrona*. Luck p. 66 asks furthermore "ob bei Apuleius durchweg *em* oder durchweg *en* zu schreiben ist, oder ob unter besondern Umständen bald die eine, bald die andere Schreibung nötig ist". In his opinion *em* and *en* are but two different phonetic spellings of one sound (p. 49) and thus he rejects the current etymology of *em* as the imperative *eme* with apocope (see e.g. Hofmann, *L.U.*, p. 35).

In the cases of both *em* and *perii* Callebat (*S.C.*, pp. 498; 518) postulates comic influence. Cf. 2, 10 (33, 16 f.) *pereo ... immo iam dudum perii, nisi tu propitiaris* (in erotic context; see de Jonge *ad loc.*).

Laqueus aut gladius aut certe praecipitium procul dubio 94, 7-8
capessendum est: "Without doubt, I shall have to resort to the noose or to the sword, or at least the high-jump".

Apart from the continued tripartition the use of *aut* is remarkable since, once again, this is the only place in the *Met*. where it has been transmitted. By conjecture it has been restored at 2, 9 (32, 9) by Groslot (generally accepted) but Bernhard p. 84, n. 34 there proposes *atque* on good grounds (F has *at*, ς *ac*, Becker *et*). In the *Met. aut* has been pushed aside entirely by *uel* which occurs 190 times, a tendency which is definitely not found in the other works: in the *Florida* the proportion is 44 : 22, in the *Apology* 72 : 54, both times indeed in favour of *uel* (see Callebat, *S.C.*, p. 330). These numbers hardly offer material for Callebat's theory that the preference for *uel* in the *Met*. argues a "recherche littéraire concertée et artificielle". In the *Met. uel* is often used in a sense usually regarded as characteristic for *aut*, i.e. opposition between two alternatives (see however A. H. Weston, *On the use of aut*, CJ 29(1933/34), pp. 45-47). Why, then, is *aut* used here? Possibly we have to do with a reminiscence from Luc. *Phars*. 9, 106 f. *numquam ueniemus ad ensis | aut laqueos aut praecipites per inania iactus* (a parallel quoted by Hildebrand). For *aut/uel* see also Becker p. 13; Bernhard p. 126; LHSz p. 501.

The three methods of suicide are a choice from the *uiae multae, breues, faciles* that Seneca mentions in *Ep*. 12, 10, without specifying them, however; such a specification is found in *De Ira* 3, 15, 4: *uides illum praecipitem locum? illac ad libertatem descenditur, uides illud mare, illud flumen, illum puteum? libertas illic in imo sedet. uides illam arborem breuem, retorridam, infelicem? pendet inde libertas. uides iugulum tuum, guttur tuum, cor tuum? effugia seruitutis sunt. nimis tibi operosos exitus monstro et multum animi ac roboris exigentes? quaeris quod sit ad libertatem iter? quaelibet in corpore tuo uena!* See also A. L. Motto, *Seneca Sourcebook*, Amsterdam 1970, *s.v.* suicide. For contemporary possibilities one may compare *Opdracht*, a poem of the Dutch poet J. Bernlef, with the English motto "the more you think of dying / the better you will live" (from *Kokkels*, Amsterdam 1960):

met een scheermesje kan het	[it can be done with a shaving-blade
soms wel 2 keer per dag	even twice a day sometimes
met een broodzaag kan het	it can be done with a bread-knife
je twaalfuurtje bereiden	cutting sandwiches for lunch
met een gasslang kan het	it can be done with a gaspipe
rode kool in een half uur gaar	red cabbage is done in half an hour
in een badkuip kan het	it can be done in the bath
één keer per week en flink met zeep	once a week and use your soap
met een touw kan het	it can be done with rope
als je broekriem soms stuk is	if you've bust your belt]

The motif of suicide occurs repeatedly in the *Met.*, murder even more often; see Heine p. 150; vThiel I pp. 154 f. The girl (Charite) we may presume in 8, 14 uses a *gladius* (187, 21-22) *ferro ... transadacto*; the old woman prefers to use the *laquens*, but the robbers add the *praecipitium*: 6, 30 (152, 14 ff.) *quam ... cum suo sibi funiculo deuinctam dedere praecipitem.*

94, 9-11 **Ad haec anus iratior dicere eam saeuiore iam uultu iubebat, quid, malum, fleret, uel quid repente postliminio pressae quietis lamentationes licentiosas refricaret**: "At this the old woman got rather cross and frowning heavily told the girl to explain what the hell she was crying for, and why, after a short but deep rest, she had renewed her unbridled lamentation".

saeuiore: Elmenhorst and vdVliet preferred to read *seueriore*, but Oudendorp's explanation is certainly correct: "Vel sic tamen saevum praeferre poterat vultum, saevissima ei minans, *faxo viva exurare*"; Eyssenhardt's *uulto* is no doubt a printer's error (though metaplastic forms are not lacking in the *Met.*, see Médan pp. 3 f.).

malum: there are three possible explanations. Adlington translates "the cause of her sorrow" and therefore regards *malum* as a gen. plur. Gaselee adds in a note (p. 180, n. 2): "It is quite possibly right to put commas before and after *malum* and to translate: "why was she weeping, the plaguey thing". He, then, regards *malum* as an invective; so does Desertine p. 105; cf. Pl. *Am.* 403; *id. Aul.* 429; see LHSz p. 746. The interpretation of *malum* as an interjection, shared by Oudendorp, Hildebrand, Callebat, *S.C.*, p. 88, and almost all translators, appears to be the right one. *Bonum*, too, can serve as an interjection: 10, 16 (248, 22) *sciscitatus denique quid bonum rideret familia*. It is clear that in these two cases we have to do with ellipsis. But what was the original expression? Hofmann, *L.U.*, p. 32, discusses the question as follows: "Bréal Rev. Phil. 36, 29 dachte an Kürzung aus der Formel *abi (in) malam rem*, doch ist wahrscheinlicher die ebenfalls Plautinische Vollformel *malum (magnum) habebis* (z.B. Amph. 721, dann noch Cic. und Sen. Contr.) als Grundlage der Fluchellipse anzusehen, daneben ev. *malum dabitur*[1], das man an der Liviusstelle 4, 49, 11 *malum ... militibus meis ... nisi quieverint* ergänzen kann". A different explanation is found in Butler and Owen, commentary on *Apol.* 8 (9, 12 f.) *nam quae, malum, ratio est...*: "The word is not a direct vocative, but, having been originally an ellipse for *quod malum est*, is used in relation to the sentence, much as our own expletives, "the deuce", etc."

The most acceptable solution is that given by Thoresby Jones on Pl. *Men.* 390: "probably it stands for *malum tibi sit*", which is also Quinn's interpretation on Catul. 29, 21 *quid hunc malum fouetis* (where, with Kroll, he takes *malum* as an interjection).

The use of *malum*, here, in reported speech is striking. ThLL provides only one further instance: Heges. 5, 31.

postliminio pressae quietis: Médan p. 157 rightly says that *postliminio* here practically functions as a preposition "after", "au sortir de" (but p. 254 he translates "de nouveau"!). Cf. 2, 28 (48, 7) *postliminio mortis* "after death", the same expression at 10, 12 (245, 17). On 3, 25 (71,2) *postliminio redibis* Vallette remarks (p. 81, n. 1) that at 1, 25 (23, 3); 94, 10; 5, 7 (108, 23); 9, 21 (219, 11) *postliminio* means *rursus*; apparently he takes *postliminio* with *refricaret* (as does vdP. p. 184); this may also appear from his translation: "pourquoi, quand tu dormais si bien, tu t'abandonnes de nouveau, par un brusque retour, à des lamentations désordonnées?" It is by no means clear, however, how *pressae quietis* is to be fitted into the construction.

An excellent discussion of *postliminio* in the *Met.* is found in Norden, *Privatrecht*, pp. 84 f. See also Bernhard p. 194; Marg. Molt p. 109; de Jonge p. 108; Summers p. 155.

From Vallette's translation as quoted above it appears that he follows Pricaeus, as do most other translators, and takes *pressae* as *prementis* just as the compound *compressus* has an active sense in V. Fl. 1, 491. According to Oudendorp and Hildebrand *pressa* here means "adstricta, compressa et sic brevis", which fits the context very well (cf. *nec diu, cum*), but it is difficult to produce parallels for this meaning: as a stylistic term *pressus* is "concentrated", "pithy", "lucid" rather than "brief" (Quint. *Inst.* 8, 3, 13; 10, 1, 102), and elsewhere in the *Met.* where Apuleius uses *pressus*, 5, 5 (106, 16 f.) *pressiore cautela* and 5, 10 (111, 19) *cogitationibus pressioribus*, the meaning is "(more) concentrated".

The meaning "deep sleep" for *pressa quies* is supported by the existence of the expression *artus somnus*, which achieves the same sense by means

---

[1] cf. Ogilvie *ad loc*: "*fiet* or the like must be understood".

of the same metaphor; cf. Cic. *Rep.* 6, 10, 10 *me artior quam solebat somnus complexus est*; Cic. *Inv.* 2, 14 *artius ... dormire*; Suet. *Aug.* 16 *arto somno deuinctus*. Moreover Non. 237 M (= 354 L) notes with *altum* (cf. Verg. *A.* 10, 63 f. *quid me alta silentia cogis/rumpere*) the synonyms *pressum* and *obscurum*.

lamentationes licentiosas refricaret*: the polysyllables suggest the duration of the weeping bout (see W. Empson, *Seven types of ambiguity*, Pelican, p. 29).

refricaret* is the reading in φ and α and the original reading in F, changed by a later hand to the more common *replicaret*, which was preferred by Oudendorp, Eyssenhardt, Helm I-II, Vitali. *Refricare* is used by Cicero in the sense of "tear open wounds" (e.g. *Att.* 5, 15, 2). It is more artificial, but fits the rhetorical context (in which the words of an *anus iratior* are represented in reported speech!)

94, 11-13 "Nimirum", inquit, "tanto compendio tuae redemptionis defraudare iuuenes meos destinas?" "I know what you're up to", she said, "you're planning to do my boys out of their huge profit from your ransom". The old woman has the interest of "her boys" at heart; see comm. on 79, 14.

nimirum* emphasizes her indignation; cf. 5, 28 (126, 7 ff.) *Tunc indignata Venus exclamauit ...:* "... *nimirum illud incrementum lenam me putauit ...*"; 11, 29 (290, 11 f.) *nimirum perperam uel minus plene consuluerunt in me sacerdos uterque*. For the etymology see LHSz p. 421.

defraudare* is usually construed with a double accusative, but the construction with acc. and abl. of separation is neither rare nor original (Médan p. 33) witness ThLL. *s.v.* Cf. 9, 28 (224, 12 f.) *defraudatis amatoribus aetatis tuae flore*.

94, 13-15 Quod si pergis ulterius, iam faxo lacrimis istis, quas parui pendere latrones consuerunt, insuper habitis uiua exurare: "If you go on like this, I shall ignore your tears, which robbers think nothing of, and see to it that you are burned alive". The old woman's threat to have the girl "burnt alive" is of course inconsistent with the preceding reaction, but she is, after all, *iratior*.

For *faxo* + subj. see Fernhout pp. 174 f.; Callebat, *S.C.*, p. 504; LHSz p. 530. *Insuper habere* as a synonym for *contemnere* is not uncommon in later Latin; see Callebat, *S.C.*, p. 239. In the *Met.* it has been transmitted here only; Oudendorp also reads it, with Colvius, at 1, 12 (11, 13 f.) for F's *subterhabere*.

CHAPTER XXVI

The girl tells her story; a disrupted wedding.

Tali puella sermone deterrita manuque eius exosculata: 94, 16-18
"parce", inquit, "mi parens, et durissimo casui meo pieta-
tis humanae memor subsiste paululum: "These words frightened
the girl, she kissed the old woman's hand and said: "Spare me, mother,
and for pity's sake give me a little help in my dreadful situation"."

manu is the reading in φ; F originally also offered the abl., but a later
hand added a stroke above the *u*. Helm wished to read *manus* and was
followed by Robertson, Brandt-Ehlers, Vitali and vThiel (it is to be
noted that the various readings as reported in ThLL are entirely er-
roneous). Helm refers to 2, 28 (48, 10) *huius diu manus deosculatus*, but
also mentions a parallel for the singular: 11, 6 (270, 16) *manum sacerdotis
osculabundus*. Cf. also Tac. *Hist.* 1, 45, 1 *exosculari Othonis manum*.
The reading *manuque eius exosculata* (preferred by the other editors as
well as ThLL *s.v.*) is remarkable to the extent that it presupposes a) a
passive use of *exosculari* and b) juxtaposition of agreeing participle and
abl. abs. Both of these may easily be defended: *exosculari* is used as a
passive also at 11, 17 (280, 3 f.) *exosculatis uestigiis deae* and after Apu-
leius by Amm. 22, 7, 3 and Greg. T. *Hist.* 5, 2. See also Médan p. 10,
Callebat, *S.C.*, p. 515. For the variation in constructions cf. Amm.
26, 8, 1 *in societatem ... adscitus et suscepta cura palatii*. See Bernhard
pp. 42 f.; Blomgren p. 61; LHSz p. 385.

mi parens; *mi* for *mea*, as at 96, 6 *mi erilis*; 5, 16 (115, 23) *mi soror*.
More instances in Fernhout *ad loc.*; Callebat, *S.C.*, p. 124; many in-
stances outside Apuleius in Neue-Wagener II³ p. 368. LHSz p. 426 and
Hofmann, *L.U.*, p. 139 compare Bavarian "na, mei Liaber", said to a
woman, and 'mon petit', equally said to a member of the female sex
(they refer to L. Spitzer, *Stilstudien II*, München 1928, p. 517). Lucius
calls a *caupona* at 1, 21 (19, 14) *parens optima*; Milo is addressed as *parens
meus* at 3, 7 (57, 11).

subsiste: cf. 2, 27 (47, 14 f.) *per pietatem publicam perempto ciui sub-
sistite*; 3, 23 (69, 25); 5, 19 (118, 3); 6, 2 (130, 14); 11, 2 (267, 20). It is
listed as a case of "Umdeutung" by Löfstedt, *Verm. Stud.*, p. 102. See
also vdP. p. 175.

Nec enim, ut reor, aeuo longiore maturatae tibi in ista 94, 18-21
sancta canitie miseratio prorsus exaruit. Specta denique
scaenam meae calamitatis: "For I cannot believe that, seasoned
as you are by many long years, so white-haired and venerable, all sense

of pity has dried up in you. So please lend an ear to the tale of my un-
doing". Oudendorp, Robertson, Brandt-Ehlers and Frassinetti prefer
maturae with α and the first hand in F and φ; *maturatae* is offered by the
second hand in F, since this must be what is meant by *ma͞tate*; additions
in φ suggest *mutatae*. It is hard to choose in this case. An argument
against *maturae* lies in the fact that where the word is linked with *aeuum*
not the abl. of cause but rather the gen. of relation is employed, e.g. Verg.
A. 5, 73 *aeui maturus Acestes*. Oudendorp and Robertson mention Suet.
Cal. 44, 1 *plerisque centurionum maturis iam*. The passage is not relevant
since *maturis ad missionem* is meant. It seems best, therefore, to choose
with Helm (and most editors) *maturatae*, which in addition is the *lectio
difficilior*.

ista makes the dialogue livelier, as is very well illustrated by Callebat,
S.C., p. 270.

miseratio ... exaruit: the imagery is typically Ciceronian as ThLL
teaches us *s.v. exarescere* meaning *euanescere, interire*; cf. Cic. *Brut.* 82
(*orationes*); *Tusc.* 3, 75 (*opinio*); *Fam.* 9, 18, 3 (*facultas orationis*).

denique: used in the sense of *ergo, igitur*. See M. Helbers-Molt, *Mne-
mosyne* S. III, 11 (1943), p. 131; Callebat, *S.C.*, p. 325.

scaenam: used here in the sense of "dramatic story", but the meaning
"show" also plays a role, as appears from *specta*. See comm. on 89, 17;
Heine p. 207.

94, 21-23 Speciosus adolescens inter suos principalis, quem filium
publicum omnis sibi ciuitas cooptauit, meus alioquin con-
sobrinus, tantulo triennio maior in aetate: "There is a hand-
some young man, leader among his peers, whom the whole populace
voted their favourite son; actually, he is my cousin and only three years
my senior".

principalis (a correct emendation in ς; F has *principales*) is regarded
as a noun by Callebat, *S.C.*, p. 163, apparently without necessity.

Oudendorp was the first to point out (and Hildebrand and Vallette
repeat) that *filius publicus* is not just an honorific as is *castrorum filius*
(acc. to Suet. *Cal.* 22, 1 the soldiers' name for Caligula), but also an
official title. Cf. W. Liebenam, *Städteverwaltung im römischen Kaiserreiche*,
Leipzig 1900, p. 131: "Recht häufig sind im Osten Ehrungen, als υἱός,
θυγάτηρ, μήτηρ πόλεως ... (sie sind) Ehrenbürger, Ehrenmitglieder, weil
die betreffenden gleichsam Sohnespflicht gegen die Städte oder Genossen-
schaften erfüllt haben und deshalb von der Gemeinde als Angehörige
angesehen werden".

consobrinus: Charite and Haemus/Tlepolemus are probably children
of two sisters. In early periods Rome allowed no marriage between rel-
atives of up to and including the sixth degree, but gradually the rule was
relaxed. The first known instance of a marriage between first cousins is
recorded by Liv. 42, 34, 3, where Sp. Ligustinus says: *cum primum in
aetatem ueni, pater mihi uxorem fratris sui filiam dedit* (in the year 171

B.C.; Summers p. 172 n. 1 misprints 117 B.C.). During the Republic and the pre-christian Empire such a marriage remained legal; thus Cicero says concerning his client Cluentius' sister: *quae breui tempore post patris mortem nupsit A. Aurelio Melino, consobrino suo* (Cic. *Clu.* 5, 11). The Emperor Marcus Aurelius and his wife Faustina also were full cousins. According to St. Augustine, *C.D.* 15, 16, such a marriage was in fact exceptional. See A. Rossbach, *Untersuchungen über die römische Ehe*, Stuttgart 1853, pp. 431 f.; Marquardt p. 31; Norden, *Privatrecht*, p. 108; P. E. Corbett, *The Roman Law of Marriage*, Oxford 1930, pp. 47-51; Balsdon, *Roman Women*, p. 175; Summers, pp. 171 f.

triennio maior in aetate: the use of *in* is remarkable. Helm refers to 2, 2 (25, 16) *senex iam grauis in annis*; cf. 2, 11 (34, 1) *uini cadum in aetate pretiosi*. See Ruiz de Elvira, pp. 99-110, for more cases of instrumental use of *in*. Here it is rather the abl. of limitation that has been replaced. Thus also Callebat, *S.C.*, p. 225 who compares Arn. 1, 36 *in uini melior...potu*; Cypr. *Ep.* 55, 24 offers a further parallel: *episcopi in aetate antiqui, in fide integri*, which Schrijnen-Mohrmann I, p. 123 also take as an ablative of limitation or respect. It is precisely the little difference in age that renders Tlepolemus so attractive to Charite. Age-difference in itself at first had no importance from a legal point of view; cf. Norden, *Privatrecht*, p. 106: "War die Voraussetzung der Pubertät erfüllt, so fragte man nicht weiter nach dem Alter der Nupturienten und liess auch die Tatsache eines etwa zwischen beiden bestehenden grossen Alterunterschiedes völlig unberücksichtigt". Under Augustus and Tiberius this was changed. Men above sixty and women above fifty years of age were forbidden to marry. Hence the violent attacks on the marriage between Apuleius and Pudentilla, whose age (incorrectly in fact) was given as sixty: *Apol.* 67 (75, 25 f.) *sexagesimo anno aetatis ad lubidinem nubsisse*. Concerning the question of her real age see Butler & Owen, pp. XIX f.

qui mecum primis ab annis nutritus et adultus indiuiduo 94, 23-25
contubernio domusculae, immo uero cubiculi torique: "he was brought up with me from his earliest years and grew up inseparable from me in the same house, even in the same room, the same bed".

According to J. H. Schmalz, *BPhW* 25 (1905), p. 366 *primis ab annis* imitates Verg. *A.* 2, 87 *pauper in arma pater primis huc misit ab annis*; cf. *ibid.* 8, 517 *primis et te miretur ab annis*. That there is such a reminiscence is by no means certain.

adultus: one of the conditions of a *iustum matrimonium* was the partners' adulthood. According to Ulp. *Reg.* 5, 2 the man had to be *pubes*, the woman *(uiri)potens*. Justinian fixed the ages with greater precision (*Inst.* 1, 10 pr.): men had to be 14, women 12 years of age. See Rossbach, *Unters.* pp. 403-420; Marquardt p. 127; Norden, *Privatrecht*, p. 105; Corbett p. 51; Summers p. 172.

indiuiduo contubernio: Roman law meant by *contubernium* the cohabitation of male and female slaves, of master and female slave, of a free

woman and a slave (Paul. *Sent.* 2, 19, 6). "From its meaning of 'tent'
the word also indicates the place where such cohabitation took place,
and Apuleius seems to take this latter sense of the word here and apply
it to free persons who are living together out of wedlock" (Summers pp.
172 f.). See also Norden, *Privatrecht* pp. 116 f. Even without approving
of his conclusions in this respect, however, one has to agree with Merkel-
bach, when he remarks, *Roman* p. 75, n. 6, that the present *indiuiduum
contubernium* conflicts with the situation as presented at 8, 2 (177, 10 ff.).
Most probably Charite is indulging in some wishful thinking here.

    domusculae: this diminutive occurs here only. Oudendorp thinks it
strange that an important citizen should live in a *domusculum*, but
Hildebrand is right in reminding us of Charite's *iucunditas recordationis*.
See Hofmann, *L.U.*, p. 195; LHSz p. 773. Robertson toys with the notion
of adding *coaluerat* after *torique* (with a reference to 2, 3 (26, 14)) but
apart from the fact that the disappearance of this verb would not be
easy to explain, the piling up of participles is functional in characterizing
Charite's emotional state.

94, 25-26   sanctae caritatis adfectione mutuo mihi pigneratus: "he
was pledged to me — and I to him — by the emotion of true love".

    Robertson, Brandt-Ehlers, Frassinetti and vThiel adopt Pricaeus'
mutua, whereby *adfectione* is given an attribute and a chiastic order
results. Cf. 2, 10 (33, 18 f.) *nam ego tibi mutua uoluntate mancipata sum.*
The use of *mutuo* is quite apt here, however; see Callebat, *S.C.*, p. 259
concerning the meanings of this adverb in Apuleius. For the figurative
use of the legal term *pignerare* one may consult Norden, *Privatrecht*, p.
180 n. 2; vdP. pp. 96 f.; Summers p. 101. Mutual affection, i.e. *consensus*
on the part of the candidates for marriage, had not always been a require-
ment, "but as free marriage, i.e. marriage without *manus*, became the
predominant marital institution, consent was necessary, whereas mere
cohabitation was regarded as concubinage. As Ulpian succinctly states:
nuptias non concubitus, sed consensus facit" (Summers p. 173 quoting
dig. 50, 17, 30). See also Balsdon, *Roman Women*, p. 182.

94, 26-95,2 uotisque nuptialibus pacto iugali pridem destinatus, con-
sensu parentum tabulis etiam maritus nuncupatus: "and by
nuptial vows he had been long since destined for the marriage-bond, and
with our parents' consent he was already called my husband in an
official document".

    According to Norden, *Privatrecht*, p. 92, *pactum iugale* here refers to an
unwritten betrothal for which the technical term is *condicio*. Apparently
he takes *pacto iugali* as an ablative. A remarkable, but not impossible,
asyndeton results. Summers, pp. 174 f., has a different explanation.
He argues against Norden's interpretation that Apuleius should have
used *despondere* rather than *destinare* as at 4, 32 (100, 10), cf. however

e.g. *dig.* 23, 2, 36 *nisi a patre desponsa destinataue* (ThLL *s.v.*, however, has no instances of *destinare* in the sense of *despondere* referring to male persons). His own explanation is as follows: "The phrase *uotis nuptialibus pacto iugale* (sic!) refers to religious vows and the *pactum dotale*. The latter was a formless agreement which set the conditions upon which the dowry was given to the prospective husband by the father of the bride. These conditions customarily dealt with the disposition of the *dos* in event the marriage was terminated by any means or did not in fact occur". Actually Summers replaces one difficulty by another, for why does Apuleius write *pacto iugali* if he means *pacto dotali*? (For *pacta dotalia* see Corbett, *Rom. Law*, pp. 198-200). Moreover the difficulty of the asyndeton remains. It seems best, therefore, to regard *pacto iugali* as a dative (against Index Apul. *s.v. pactum*) and to treat, with Hildebrand, *pacto iugali destinatus* as synonymous with *desponsus*. Concerning vdVliet's addition ⟨*erat*⟩ after *pridem*, see comm. on 94, 25.

consensu parentum: cf. Summers p. 174: "The agreement of the parties to the marriage... did not result in a legal marriage for those *in potestate*. Under such circumstances consent of the *pater familias* was required under the rules of classical Roman law for both *filius familias* and *filia familias*. The only exception to this rule was that the consent of the grandfather of a male who intended to marry also was required if the male's father was himself in the *potestas* of the grandfather. The phrase *consensu parentum ... maritus nuncupatus* in our passage consequently reflects a typical legal situation where the husband to be is *in potestate*". See also Rossbach, *Unters.*, pp. 395-399; Corbett, *Rom. Law*, pp. 57 f.

tabulis: this official document was called in full *tabulae nuptiales* (*nuptiarum*) or *dotales* (*dotis*); yet other names may be found in Marquardt p. 48, n. 2. In this contract a number of financial matters are arranged (e.g. the size of the dowry) and in our case apparently it contained the consent of the groom's father. The contract however does not constitute the marriage itself. See Norden, *Privatrecht*, pp. 93 f.; Balsdon, *Roman Women*, pp. 183 f.; Summers p. 175. For the employment of the juridical term *nuncupatus* see Summers pp. 108 f.

ad nuptias officio frequenti cognatorum et adfinium sti- 95, 2-4
patus templis et aedibus publicis uictimas immolabat: "in preparation for our marriage, attended by a large crowd of relatives and in-laws doing their duty, he was making sacrifice in the temples and shrines of the town".

officio: the social duty to assist at weddings. See Rossbach, *Unters.*, p. 293, n. 920; Balsdon, *Roman Women*, p. 183. Here used for the group on whom such duty fell (hence *abstractum pro concreto*). Such a group at first consisted of friends and relatives, later, as here, of relatives only.

immolabat: according to Oudendorp and Hildebrand the sacrifice indicates *confarreatio*, but Norden, *Privatrecht*, p. 113 and Summers p. 176, n. 1, easily refute that opinion by pointing out that such a marriage required the presence of the *pontifex maximus* and *flamen Dialis* and hence could not be contracted in the provinces. (On *confarreatio* and other forms of marriage see Corbett, pp. 68-90).

Marquardt p. 52, n. 4 thinks that we have to do here with "ein nach griech. Sitte vor der Hochzeit von dem Bräutigam dargebrachtes Opfer".

95, 4-5 domus tota lauris obsita, taedis lucida constrepebat hyme-
naeum : "strewn with laurel-branches and bright with torches, the whole house rang to the bridal-song".

Apuleius is the only one who construes the verb *constrepere* (a neologism) with an inner object; cf. II, 10 (273, 23) *argutum tinnitum constrepentes*. On the decorations cf. Juv. 6, 78 f. *longa per angustos figamus pulpita uicos,/ ornentur postes et grandi ianua lauro*. See K. Baus, *Der Kranz in Antike and Christentum*, Bonn 1940 (Nachdruck 1965), p. 96; Fried-länder on Juv. 6, 51.

hymenaeum: the true *hymenaeus* was sung at the end of the day as appears from Catul. 61 and 62 (moreover the groom is absent at the moment described); these, then, are "hymnes de circonstance" (Vallette p. 31, n. 3). Burck's interpretation (Anm. p. 227) that the word *hymenaeus* here means the wedding-day and the start of the festivities can hardly, in view of *constrepebat*, be right. Cf. Claud. 9, 21 (ed. Gesner) *frondoso strepuit felix Hymenaeus Olympo*. For *taedis* see comm. on 89, 6.

Note the asyndeton (see Bernhard p. 56), the parallelism, the effective use of the various sounds.

95, 5-8 tunc me gremio suo mater infelix tolerans mundo nuptiali
decenter ornabat mellitisque sauiis crebriter ingestis iam
spem futuram liberorum uotis anxiis propagabat: "at that moment my poor mother held me on her lap and was dressing me in proper bridal clothes; as she showered me with tender kisses she was already supporting her hope of children to come with anxious prayers"...

spem futuram is the correction in φ (F has *spe futura* which can scarcely be right; Oudendorp and Hildebrand tried respectively *spe foeturam* and *spes foetura*, ingenious but hardly convincing solutions). The entire expression *spem ... propagabat* is exceedingly affected; see Médan p. 343.

gremio: cf. Fest. p. 364, 26 ff. L (= 289 M) *rapi simulatur uirgo ex gremio matris aut, si ea non est, ex proxima necessitudine, cum ad uirum trahitur, quod uidelicet ea res feliciter Romulo cessit*; Catul. 61, 3 *qui rapis teneram ad uirum | uirginem, o Hymenaee*; ibid. 61, 58 ff. Festus' explanation of the custom — the Sabine Rape (thus, though with some reservations, Balsdon, *Roman Women*, p. 184) — can hardly be right: on the contrary it is much more likely that the famous story is an aetiological myth. See Rossbach, *Unters.*, p. 330; Marquardt p. 53 (in particular note 3); P. Fedeli, *Il Carme* 61 *di Catullo*, Friburg 1972, pp. 47 f.

infelix: not at that moment but retrospectively.

tolerans: in this literal sense not very common. See de Jonge p. 26; vdP. p. 70.

ornabat: concerning bridal garments see Rossbach, *Unters.*, pp. 275-286; L. M. Wilson, *The clothing of the ancient Romans*, Baltimore 1938, pp. 138-145; Balsdon, *Roman Women*, p. 183.

crebriter: see comm. on 76, 12.

sauiis ... ingestis: cf. 5, 23 (121, 7 f.) *patulis ac petulantibus sauiis ... ingestis; osculum ingerere* occurs in Suet. *Gram.* 23, 3.

spem futuram liberorum: enallage, in order to avoid *spem futurorum liberorum*; see Bernhard p. 215.

uotis anxiis: cf. Balsdon, *Roman Women*, p. 195: "Death took a heavy toll of women and children in childbirth".

cum inruptionis subitae gladiatorum impetus ad belli fa- 95, 8-11
ciem saeuiens, nudis et infestis mucronibus coruscans: non caedi, non rapinae manus adferunt: "when a sudden inrush of swordsmen attacked, raging in the semblance of war and flashing their deadly blades; but not to murder or rapine did they set their hands".

Helm's punctuation after *coruscans* has been adopted, but not his conjecture *fit* after *gladiatorum*, which was accepted by Robertson, Brandt-Ehlers, Vitali, vThiel and Scazzoso. Bernhard p. 158 supposes an ellipse of *esse* (though such an ellipse is not very common in the subordinate clause) and regards Helm's supplement as superfluous (p. 158, n. 2). An ellipse of *fieri* is more likely however: a good parallel instance occurs at 1, 10 (9, 11) *quae cum subinde ac multi nocerentur* (unless Armini's explanation of this passage is the more correct one; see Marg. Molt *ad loc.*; Callebat, *S.C.*, p. 117). This very passage is Löfstedt's point of departure in his discussion of the ellipse of *fieri*, *Verm. Stud.*, pp. 89-92. He compares among other instances Tac. *Ann.* 4, 20 *unde dubitare cogor, fato et sorte nascendi, ut cetera, ita principum inclinatio in hos, offensio in illos*, on which Dräger notes "sc. *fiat*" and Nipperdey "ergänze den allgemeinen Verbalbegriff 'entstehen', 'bestimmt werden'". See also S. Wahlén, *Studia critica in declamationes minores quae sub nomine Quintiliani feruntur*, Diss. Uppsala 1930, p. 55, n. 1. The ἀπροσδόκητον, too, argues in favour of an ellipse.

If one is unwilling to adopt Helm's punctuation, one must, with Oudendorp, have recourse to a *constructio ad sententiam* (*gladiatorum impetus ... adferunt*), a fairly harsh instance. See Callebat, *S.C.*, pp. 336 f.; further literature in vdP. p. 36.

cum: for this use of *cum* in the sense of *cum repente* (le *cum* de rupture, cf. J. P. Chausserie-Laprée, *L'expression narrative chez les latins*, Paris 1969, p. 584, n. 2: "Tableau détaillé, émouvant et gracieux de la scène où se produisit l'enlèvement de la future épousée par des brigands. Ces quatres imparfaits successifs sc. *immolabat, constrepebat, ornabat, propagabat* font peser, au sein de chaque évocation, la menace et l'attente d'un *cum de rupture*". The author makes a very interesting comparison with Voltaire's Jeannot et Colin (Pléiade, p. 145).

inruptionis ... gladiatorum impetus: see Bernhard pp. 173 f. on the more or less redundant combination. For *gladiatorum* see comm. on 93, 18.

ad belli faciem: on this use of *ad* ("modal"), see Médan pp. 61 f.; Callebat, *S.C.*, pp. 213 f.; vdP. p. 144.

infestis: Scioppius' conjecture (instead of F's *infertis*) is now generally accepted (and therefore preferred to Beroaldus' *insertis* adopted by Oudendorp and to other ingenious emendations). Hildebrand tried to defend the tradition ("nihil nisi gladios viderat"), but the form *infertus* (*infercio*) is very doubtful; it is true it is also transmitted at *Aetna* 66, but it is rejected by Goodyear *ad loc*. In view of 8, 2 (177, 21 f.) *die, quo praedonum infestis mucronibus puella fuerat astu uirtutibusque sponsi sui liberata* it seems best to read *infestis* here as well.

coruscans: a poetic verb; see Bernhard p. 212; Médan p. 191; Fernhout p. 21.

95, 11-12 "sed denso conglobatoque cuneo cubiculum nostrum inuadunt protinus: "but in densely closed marching order they burst into our room forthwith".

conglobato ... cuneo: in view of the original meaning of *globus* and *cuneus* a somewhat curious military term. Cf. 8, 15 (189, 11) *cuneatim*. Notice the alliteration of *c* (strengthened by the subsequent *cubiculum*).

95, 12-15 Nec ullo de familiaribus nostris repugnante ac ne tantillum quidem resistente miseram, exanimem saeuo pauore, trepido de medio matris gremio rapuere: "And while not one of our household fought back or offered even *that* much resistance, they tore me from my mother's fearful arms, poor wretch that I was and fainting with wild terror".

This real abduction proves a very different matter from the fictitious abduction which forms part of the marriage ceremony.

tantillum is regarded by Callebat as borrowed from comic language (*S.C.*, p. 520). On the deictic function of the adverb see vdP. p. 61.

miseram, exanimem saeuo pauore, trepido de medio ... gremio: F originally had *misera*, changed by a later hand to *miseram*. Robertson reads *misera ⟨formidine⟩ exanimem, saeuo pauore trepidam, de medio ... gremio*, for which he compares 9, 20 (218, 2 f.) *misera trepidatione ... deductus*; to Oudendorp's *trepidam* (though adopted by vdVliet, Gaselee, Brandt-Ehlers, Frassinetti, Vitali and vThiel) Hildebrand long ago quite rightly objected: "quominus enim *saevo pavore trepidam* coniungantur, obstat sententiarum connexio, quum quae iam *exanimis* est puella, deinde *trepida pavore* dici nequeat. *Exanimare* enim vero ut *enecare* de omnibus commotionibus Romani dicunt, quibus animus ita perturbatur, ut de sede sua quasi deiiciatur". The same goes for Helm's suggestion ⟨et⟩ *trepidam* (approved by Lehnert) which however requires *saeuo pauore* to be taken with *exanimem*. Wower's proposal *trepidae* (with *matris*) is a better one since it provides *matris* with a reinforcing adjective, but the objections to *trepido* as transmitted are hardly valid, since *medium … gremium* will have been taken as a unity. The supplement ⟨me⟩ (Blümner; vdVliet) is unnecessary; for the absence of the pronoun, see Bernhard pp. 159 ff.; Callebat, *S.C.*, pp. 112 f.

Sic ad instar Attidis uel Protesilai dispectae disturbatae-   95, 15-16
que nuptiae: "Thus was my wedding, like that of Attis or Protesilaus, interrupted and broken up".

Attidis uel Protesilai: "quelle érudition déplacée dans la bouche d'une amante au désespoir", Bétolaud exclaimed. He did not read *Attidis*, but *At(h)racidis*, a clever conjecture of Beroaldus' (also preferred by Oudendorp, Hildebrand, Eyssenhardt and Gaselee).

Atracis is a woman from Atrax, a place in Thessaly, viz. Hippodameia. Cf. Ov. *Am.* I, 4,7 f. *desine mirari, posito quod candida uino, / Atracis ambiguos traxit in arma uiros.* Also at *Ep.* 17, 250 Hippodameia has the epithet *Atracis*. Oudendorp thinks that Apuleius meant to write *Peirithoi*, not *Protesilai*, but made a mistake. Today scholars are convinced that *Attidis vel Protesilai* is the correct reading. Bursian, *SBAW*, München 1881, p. 128 quoted Paus. 7, 17, 9 ff. and Arn. 5, 5 ff. who mention a wedding between Attis and the daughter of the king of Pessinus (in Arnobius: Midas), prevented at the last moment by a jealous Agdistis. See H. Hepding, *Attis, seine Mythen und sein Kult*, Giessen 1903, pp. 100 ff.; H. W. Obbink, *Cybele, Isis, Mithras*, Haarlem 1965, pp. 18 f.; M. J. Vermaseren, *The legend of Attis in Greek and Roman Art*, Leiden 1966, pp. 31 f.

The conjecture *Atyis* (Kiessling) is also rejected by Hepding p. 115, n. 17: "In der Atysnovelle bei Herodot spielt der Umstand, dass Atys νεόγαμος ist, eine so nebensächliche Rolle, dass ich es nicht für wahrscheinlich halte, dass an unserer Stelle eine Anspielung auf ihn verständlich sein konnte. Dagegen ein Vergleich mit dem unglücklichen Ausgang der Hochzeit des Attis und der Königstochter (Timotheus) oder seine Liebe zu der Nymphe (Ovid) oder auch zu Kybele (Diodor) ist hier völlig am Platz".

Protesilaus departed for Troy with forty ships even before the arrangements for his marriage to Laodamia had been completed. On arrival he fell — the first Greek to do so — at Hector's hand. His young wife was so inconsolable that Hermes brought Protesilaus up from the underworld for one day, at the end of which Laodamia departed for Hades with her husband. One may see an anticipation of Charite's suicide in the present comparison with Protesilaus' fate.

Concerning the treatment of the myth in classical authors, see G. Herzog-Hauser, *Die literarische Ausgestaltung der Protesilaos-mythe* in

199

Mélanges E. Boisacq, Bruxelles 1937, pp. 471-478. For later uses made of the myth see Hunger *s.v.* Protesilaos. Add to that E. Cecchi, *Borzetto per una Laodamia* (in the collection of short stories *Et in Arcadia ego*, 1936); Martinus Nijhoff, *Een idylle* (1940). Charite's considerable knowledge of mythology appears from 6, 29 (151, 7 ff.) as well: *credemus exemplo tuae ueritatis et Frixum arieti supernatasse et Arionem delphinum gubernasse et Europam tauro supercubasse*. Concerning mythology in the *Met.* see Bernhard pp. 208 f.; Neuenschwander p. 56 ff.; Feldbrugge pp. 119 ff.

dispectae: the old conjecture *dispestae* (from *dispesco*) recurs up to and including vdVliet and is defended by Médan p. 162. Editors however no longer doubt the correctness of F's *dispectae* (from *dispeciscor*, a verb that occurs nowhere else; Médan p. 183 assigns it to the "langue familière" notwithstanding!). See F. Leo, *Analecta Plautina II*, Gottingae 1898, p. 33.

Summers, p. 177, remarks that the marriage is not valid since there has been no *deductio in domum mariti*. See also E. Levy, *Der Hergang der römischen Ehescheidung*, Weimar 1925, pp. 68-75. For the days suitable for a wedding, see Marquardt p. 43; Balsdon, *Roman Women*, pp. 180 f. (with literature in note 34, p. 313).

CHAPTER XXVII

A terrible dream; the old woman tells a story to comfort the girl.

Sed ecce saeuissimo somnio mihi nunc etiam redintegratur, 95, 16-18
immo uero cumulatur infortunium meum: "But, see, in a fright-
ful nightmare my misery has now been renewed, or rather brought to a
climax".

sed ecce: for conjunctions with *ecce* see Callebat, *S.C.*, p. 424. Heine p.
174 points out that *ecce* often introduces an unpleasant, unhappy episode.

saeuissimo: Oudendorp preferred to read *scaeuissimo*, but Hildebrand
is right in explaining *saeua somnia* as "quae res terribiles indicant".
Note the sigmatism.

immo uero: Callebat, *S.C.*, p. 328 notes the influence of oratorical style.

infortunium: in Plautus and Terence (Médan p. 168), but also once in
Livy (1, 50, 9) the word occurs in the sense of a flogging, whipping.
According to E. Wölfflin, *Substantiva mit in privativum, ALL* 4(1887),
p. 409 and S. G. Stacey, *Die Entwicklung des livianischen Stils, ALL* 10
(1898), p. 56 the word is a poeticism but Ogilvie *ad loc.* terms it "collo-
quial language of archaic times". Cf. ThLL *s.v.* "in sermone non tam
poetico quam cotidiano". Here the meaning is "misery", a sense in which
it occurs before Apuleius only in Plautus (once: *Mer.* 165) and Horace
(*Ars* 103).

nam uisa sum mihi de domo, de thalamo, de cubiculo, de 95, 18-21
toro denique ipso uiolenter extracta per solitudines auias
infortunatissimi mariti nomen inuocare: "I dreamt that I had
been violently dragged from house, apartment, bedroom, from my very
bed, and was roaming in distant wastes, calling the name of my luckless
husband".[1]

Weyman (*SBAW* 1893, p. 335) and, following his lead, vdVliet, Helm
I/II and Vitali delete *de cubiculo* since they regard it as a gloss on *de
thalamo*. The expression may be defended on stylistic grounds: it pro-
duces a fine crescendo ("Wachsende Glieder") and it is noteworthy that
while the number of syllables increases, the space described decreases in
size. See also Bernhard p. 183, note 26.

Concerning *de* (instead of *e*) see Callebat, *S.C.*, p. 200.

inuocare: in all other cases in the *Met. inuocare* has as its object one or
more divinities (amongst whom Caesar at 3, 29 (73, 16) must be included).
The word gives a very clear indication of the relationship between Charite

---

[1] One is inclined to add "helplessly" before "calling". See the note on *inuocare*.

and Tlepolemus, witness 8, 7 (182, 12 ff.) *imagines defuncti, quas ad habitum dei Liberi formauerat, adfixo seruitio diuinis percolens honoribus ipso se solacio cruciabat*. In this situation, therefore, the echoes of the husband's name (though we have not yet heard it, or the girl's) have a note both tragic and ironic.

95, 21-23 eumque, ut primum meis amplexibus uiduatus est, adhuc ungentis madidum, coronis floridum consequi uestigio me pedibus fugientem alienis: "while he, as soon as he was bereft of my embraces, still drenched in perfume, still crowned with garlands, followed in my tracks as I fled on feet that did not belong to me".

The accusative and infinitive construction must be regarded as an anacoluthon, notwithstanding Bernhard p. 94 who recognizes only one instance (92, 13-20), but see comm. on 77, 6. Judging from their punctuation (after *inuocare*) Oudendorp and Hildebrand appear to have recognized the difficulty.

ungentis madidum, coronis floridum: note the parallelism. F's spelling *ungentis* is justifiably followed by Helm, Giarratano-Frassinetti, Robertson, Terzaghi and Brandt-Ehlers; the remaining editors read *unguentis* with φ. F spells without *u* also at 10, 21 (253, 11), where oddly enough Helm and Brandt-Ehlers do not accept it; at 11, 9 (273, 4) the spelling once again is the usual *unguentis*.

Perfumes and garlands were fixed attributes of various festivities in antiquity, including weddings. For the use of these things among the Greeks compare the scholion on Ar. *Av.* 161 νυμφίων βίον· ὅτι οἱ γαμοῦντες στεφανοῦνται, cf. Eur. *IA* 905 f.: σοὶ καταστέψασ' ἐγώ νιν ἦγον ὡς γαμουμένην / νῦν δ'ἐπὶ σφαγὰς κομίζω.

According to Fest. 56 L (= 63 M) (*s.v. corolla*) the Roman bride fashioned her own wreath: *corollam noua nupta de floribus, uerbenis herbisque a se lectis sub amiculo ferebat* (she wore the wreath, then, under the *flammeum*, a red veil). Not only the bride and groom (cf. Tert. *Cor.* 13, 4 *coronant et nuptiae sponsos*) but the guests also had wreaths. (See K. Baus, *Kranz*, pp. 93-98, who discusses the various interpretations of the wreath at weddings.) Tertullian adds to the words just cited: *et ideo non nubemus ethnicis, ne nos ad idololatriam usque deducant, a qua apud illos nuptiae incipiunt*; Clement of Alexandria also opposes the use of wreaths and ointments (*Paed.* 2, 8). στεφάνων δὲ ἡμῖν καὶ μύρων χρῆσις οὐκ ἀναγκαία. Cf. Min. Fel. 38, 2. J. Schrijnen, *La couronne nuptiale dans l'antiquité chrétienne (Collectanea Schrijnen*, Nijmegen - Utrecht 1939, pp. 268 ff.) draws the conclusion from these and other instances that during the first two centuries Christians did not use wreaths, but apparently he confuses principle and practice. See Baus' criticism (p. 99).

me pedibus fugientem alienis: Bétolaud translates "pendant que je m'éloignais, d'une fuite, hélas! involontaire", probably remembering the horatian expression *malis ridere alienis* (*S.* 2, 3, 72). Possibly ThLL *s.v. alienus* intends the same when adding "sc. *per somnium*": Charite flees malgré soi. Carlesi and Vitali explain more directly: "cioè con quelli di un cavallo". Plin. *Nat.* 29, 8, 19 offers a parallel *alienis pedibus ambulamus* (i.e. in a sedan chair) which favours the latter interpretation.

Utque clamore percito formonsae raptum uxoris conquerens 95, 24-25
populi testatur auxilium: "When with anxious cries he bewailed the capture of his lovely wife and claimed the help of the people".

In view of the *solitudines auiae* there will not have been a great deal of *populus*, but perhaps the young man's status as *filius publicus* is relevant to his cry for help.

percito: Helm's "und wie er ein Geschrei erhob" shows he emphasizes the verbal element in *percitus*. ThLL *s.v. clamor* regards the word as an adjective, which seems preferable. For the meaning cf. vdP. p. 156.

formonsae: unlike *pulcher* the word *formonsus* usually refers to beauty of a person in the *Met.* See Callebat, *S.C.*, p. 383; for the orthography *ibid.* n. 33 (with literature). It is remarkable that Charite, even in a dream, has her *maritus* refer to her own beauty.

raptum: the noun *raptus* occurs in Apuleius in our passage only.

quidam de latronibus importunae persecutionis indigna- 95,25-96,3
tione permotus saxo grandi pro pedibus adrepto misellum
iuuenem maritum meum percussum interemit: "one of the robbers, infuriated by his importunate pursuit, hit my poor husband over the head with a huge stone he had picked up from the ground, and killed him".

First the alliteration of *p* and *r* points to the robber's anger, next the repetition of *m* to the girl-narrator's grief.

quidam: see comm. on 76, 6; *de* has partitive value as at 88, 21 f. *siqui de familia*; cf. on the other hand *quidam seruulum* (88, 28).

persecutionis: at 10, 27 (258, 17) the word is used in a different sense (continuation). Médan pp. 148 f. sees in the use of words in their etymological meaning a "preuve d'une sûre érudition". Whether or not that is true, neither Charite nor her creator, lacks erudition.

grandi: see comm. on 76, 8.

adrepto: Giarratano, Terzaghi and Scazzoso prefer F's spelling *abrepto*, the other editors write with ς *adrepto* (or *arrepto*), an obvious correction. See Helm Praef. *Fl.* p. XLVII, vdP. pp. 59 f.; comm. on 76, 9.

Talis aspectus atrocitate perterrita somno funesto pauens 96, 3-4
excussa sum: "Aghast at this dreadful sight, I started in a panic out of my ominous dream, trembling all over".

What is the meaning of this dream? According to Perry (1923, p. 203) and Merkelbach (*Roman*, p. 75, n. 4) the dream points ahead to 8, 1 ff., where Charite's husband dies in fact. Junghanns (p. 144, n. 45) remarks

that the content of the dream in no way tallies with 8,1 ff.; moreover
"entkräftet die Alte den Traum sofort durch die Erklärung zur Traum-
deutungslehre (96, 6-14), die Apul. kaum anbringen würde, wenn er sie
für falsch hielte", a somewhat naive argument, since irony is an obvious
possibility.

This is not the only time that Tlepolemus appears in a dream of
Charite's. The second (and last) time is narrated at 8, 8 (183, 8 ff.):
*tunc inter moras umbra illa misere trucidati Tlepolemi sanie cruentam et
pallore deformem attollens faciem quietem pudicam interpellat uxoris.*
There we are dealing with a topos: the appearance of the dead lover with
all his wounds; see H. R. Steiner, *Der Traum in der Aeneis*, Bern 1952,
p. 26, n. 5, who discusses the best known instance in Latin literature:
Sychaeus' appearance in Dido's dream (Verg. *A*. 1, 353 ff). If 183, 8 ff.
contains a reminiscence of Virgil, the same may be the case with the
present dream. Compare Dido's dream at *A*. 4, 465 ff.: *agit ipse furentem/
in somnis ferus Aeneas; semperque relinqui/ sola sibi, semper longam in-
comitata uidetur/ ire uiam et Tyrios deserta quaerere terra.* Pease *ad loc.*
notes the sound symbolism, Steiner p. 49 remarks: "Die Stimmung der
trostlosen Einsamkeit könnte nicht besser wiedergegeben werden als
durch diese Traumlandschaft, die Wüste, und durch die einsame Reise
auf der langen Strasse, die — wir ahnen es — in die Unterwelt führen
wird. Es handelt sich um Traumsymbole, die von zeitloser Gültigkeit
sind und deren Deutung nicht schwer fällt". In a footnote Steiner com-
pares Hermann Hesse, *Narziss und Goldmund*, 1930 p. 171 and 95, 18
ff. above. If we apply his remark to our passage, it means that not only
Tlepolemus' death but also Charite's own is "predicted". In that case the
expression *somno funesto* is particularly apt.

96, 5-7 Tunc fletibus eius adsuspirans anus sic incipit: "bono
animo esto, mi erilis, nec uanis somniorum figmentis
terreare: "Then the old woman, joining her sighs to the girl's tears,
spoke: "Be of good heart, my lady; do not be frightened by the empty
figments of (your) dreams"."

adsuspirans: see comm. on 94,5.

esto: see Médan p. 22 for the use of this imperative in the *Met.* Im-
perative side by side with subj. (adhortative or prohibitive) is not an
unknown phenomenon in Apuleius; see the evidence collected by Callebat,
S.C., p. 101; also vdP p. 116.

mi erilis: *mi* once again for *mea* as at 94, 17; *erilis*, according to Calle-
bat, *S.C.*, p. 482 (see also p. 124) an archaic word, is used in the sense
of *era* by Apuleius alone. It may seem strange that the old woman
addresses the girl by this title, but Helm in his *app. crit.* compares 9, 16
(214, 22) where an old procuress addresses the baker's wife as *mi erilis*.
Domina, too, is often used "pro mero titulo et in honorifica allocutione"
(ThLL). See 2, 20 (42, 5); 2, 24 (44, 24); 2, 26 (46, 21); 5, 2 (104, 23). For
nec with subj. see Médan p. 21; vdP p. 42.

Nam praeter quod diurnae quietis imagines falsae perhi-
bentur, tunc etiam nocturnae uisiones contrarios euentus
nonnumquam pronuntiant: "Whereas the images presented by
day-time dreams are simply fake, night-time dreams often announce
events actually opposite to the truth". The anus' words indicate that
Charite's dream was nocturnal rather than one during the day; see comm.
on 92, 13 f.

praeter quod = praeterquam quod: the combination does not occur
before Apuleius (LHSz p. 244). Apuleius employs it, not for the first time
in the *Met.* (thus Callebat, *S.C.*, p. 339) but earlier[1] in *Apol.* 16 (19, 17 f.)
praeter quod non sum iurgiosus; this sense should be distinguished from
that of *praeter id quod*; see Waszink p. 453.

The old woman's first statement is contradicted by antiquity's great
authority in this field, Artemidorus Daldianus, *Onirocriticon* I, 7: ἔτι
πᾶσι τοῖς πρόδηλον αἰτίαν ἐκφεύγουσι προσέχειν χρή, ἐάν τε νυκτὸς ἐάν τε
ἡμέρας ὁραθῇ, μηδὲν διαφέρειν νυμίζοντας εἰς πρόγνωσιν τὴν νύκτα τῆς
ἡμέρας μηδὲ τὴν δείλην ἑσπέραν τῆς δείλης πρωίας, ἐὰν συμμέτρως |τις ἔχων
[τῆς] τροφῆς καθεύδῃ· ἐπεὶ αἵ γε ἄμετροι τροφαὶ οὐδὲ πρὸς αὐτῇ τῇ ἕῳ παρέ-
χουσιν ἰδεῖν τὸ ἀληθές. (for this last remark cf. *Met.* I, 18!). Artemidorus'
statement, however, appears to contain a polemic element, and it is quite
possible that the old woman voices current theories. The second part of
the statement is confirmed in Artem. *Onir.* 2, 60: δακρύειν καὶ ὀδύρεσθαι καὶ
ἐπὶ νεκρῷ καὶ ἐπὶ ἄλλῳ ᾧτινιοῦν καὶ αὐτὸ τὸ λυπεῖσθαι χαρὰν ἐπί τινι καὶ
ἡδονὴν ἐπὶ κατορθώματι ἐσομένην προαγορεύει ὀρθῶς καὶ κατὰ λόγον. Cf.
also Plin. *Ep.* I, 18, 2: *Refert tamen euentura soleas an contraria somniare.*
*Mihi reputanti somnium meum istud, quod times tu, egregiam actionem
portendere uidetur.*

Denique flere et uapulare et nonnumquam iugulari lucro-
sum prosperumque prouentum nuntiant: "So tears and beatings
and even sometimes getting killed foretell a profitable and favourable
outcome".

The usual sense of *ergo, igitur* appears the correct one for *denique*,
better in any case than Helm's "Kurz"; Callebat, *S.C.*, p. 325 wants
"for instance".

Salmasius and later vdVliet understandably deleted *nonnumquam*;
however, the word may be defended with a reference to Bernhard pp.
153 ff., who lists repetitions of words within a short distance where no
rhetorical effect is intended. One may be inclined to see in this repetition
an expression of the emotion of the *anus*, who is hastily looking for
comforting words; in that case there is a sophisticated contrast with the
stylized tricolon. There is, on the other hand, variation in *prouentum
nuntiant* vis à vis *euentus...pronuntiant*, though it be only *variatio in*

---

[1] We think with most scholars (e.g. Walsh pp. 249-251) that the Apology was
written before the *Met.*

repetitione. For the thought cf. Artemidorus as quoted above; add Querolus, ed. Ranstrand p. 24, 26 ff.: *Talia egomet et iam manifesta malo quam tua somnia. Funus ad laetitiam spectat, lacrimae ad risum pertinent et mortuum nos ferebamus: manifestum est gaudium.* Concerning this theory of contraries in dreams, see J. Veremans, *Pompeius' Droom*, (Lucanus, *Pharsalia VII*, 7-44) in *Handelingen van het drieëndertigste Nederlands Filologencongres* (1974), Amsterdam 1975, pp. 158-164.

96, 11-14   contra ridere et mellitis dulciolis uentrem saginare uel in uoluptatem ueneriam conuenire tristitie animi, languore corporis damnisque ceteris uexatum iri praedicabant: "whereas laughter and stuffing your tummy with sweeties and erotic encounters have been known to foretell that one is going to be bothered by sadness of heart, sickness of body and other problems".

The sentence offers a number of textual problems:

1. With Eyssenhardt, Helm III (and Helm-Krenkel) and vThiel we maintain the reading of F: *praedicabant*, which may have an iterative sense (thus also Helm in his Add. et Corr. to the Praef. *Fl.* p. 49). The present *praedicant* is found in φ and preferred by Hildebrand, vdVliet, Gaselee, Giarratano-Frassinetti, Terzaghi and Scazzoso. The future was first thought of by ç, not Helm; Helm defends it with a reference to Blase, *Hist. Gramm. der lat. Spr.* III 1, p. 121 (Leipzig 1903), treating of the future containing a general rule. For this gnomic future see now LHSz p. 310. It is printed by Helm in his earlier editions, by Robertson, Brandt-Ehlers and Vitali. The verb *praedicere* is not required here (cod. Dorv., Oudendorp): see vdP. p. 27.

2. The final infinitive presents us with more difficulties. F has *uel axatum iri*, F² *uel anxiatum iri*; neither makes sense and some surgery is needed — with certain consequences for the preceding nouns which have been transmitted as *tristitie animi languori corporis damnique ceteris*.

a. If we delete *uel* in F² we have a choice either to follow Hildebrand, who wished to link *anxiatum iri* with genitives: *tristitiae animi, languoris corporis damnique ceteri anxiatum iri* (for this genitive construction there are no parallels, however), or, with most editors, to opt for ablatives: *tristitie animi, languore corporis damnisque ceteris anxiatum iri* (Tert. *Paen.* 10 provides a parallel).

b. Of the many conjectures, Helm's *uela datum iri* (Helm-Krenkel) is at first sight the most attractive, but for such a use no useful parallels are to be found. The same in fact goes for his earlier conjecture *uiam datum iri*, since 273, 17, quoted in the *app. crit.*, differs in meaning. With Robertson, Brandt-Ehlers and vThiel we have chosen Beroaldus' conjecture *uexatum* (Robertson ingeniously defended its likelihood in his *app. crit.*:

a possible explanation of the corruption is *uêxatum, la* being caused by the preceding word *languore*). This choice, of course, necessitates *tristitie* (ç), *languore* (Colvius) and *damnisque* (ç).

We may note that in this series *ridere* is contrasted on the one hand with *flere*, on the other with *tristitie animi*; *uapulare* and *iugulari* have no counterparts; *languor corporis* is contrasted with *uentrem saginare*, but *in uoluptatem ueneriam conuenire* (repetition of *u*-sound) has no clear contrast in *damnis ceteris uexatum iri* (note the sigmatism!).

The diminutive *dulciola* occurs in Apuleius only (Médan p. 134). Note the variation in the use of conjunctions: *et...et, et...uel*, asyndeton, *...que*.

Sed ego te narrationibus lepidis anilibusque fabulis pro- 96, 14-15
tinus auocabo: "Come, I shall straightaway distract you with lovely fairy-tales and an old woman's stories".

For the juxtaposition of *ego* and *te* see Callebat, *S.C.*, p. 95; *narrationibus* is an old correction (ς) for *tener rationibus* (F); Bernhard p. 32 provides further instances of chiasmus in which the nouns surround the adjectives. Apart from feminine charms *lepidus* in the *Met.* is used only to describe narratives within the novel. See Heine p. 172, n. 1 and ibid. pp. 224-226 concerning the combination with *fabula*.

APPENDIX I

Military terms in the robber episode.

Opinions differ concerning the interpretation of the military terms in the robber episode. One opinion takes these terms as metaphorical, the other interprets them as literal. Hildebrand[1] and Bernhard[2] hold the first opinion, the second is that of Neuenschwander[3]. Médan occupies an intermediate position[4].

The phenomenon of brigandage in antiquity has been studied in its historical aspect by e.g. McMullen[5] and Flam-Zuckermann[6], who show that it used to create great problems for the Roman authorities. "Brigands, being endemic in the ancient world, naturally made a place for themselves in its culture (...) supplying incidents to several books of Apuleius' Metamorphoses"[7]. Brigandage sometimes occurred on so large a scale that cities were besieged or large tracts of territory were dominated by robbers[8]. With a reference to MacKay[9] McMullen subsequently remarks that robbers are favourite characters in the Hellenistic novel. In the novel too the robbers are by no means afraid of large scale operations. In the *Ephesiaca* of Xenophon of Ephesus the journey of Hippothoos and his band of robbers is described as follows: ἐνέπρησαν δὲ καὶ κώμας καὶ ἄνδρας ἀπέσφαξαν πολλούς; Hippothoos' band grows: ἦν δὲ αὐτοῖς καὶ τὸ ληστήριον ἀνθρώπων πεντακοσίων; a further undertaking: Οὐ γὰρ ἐδόκει τῷ Ἱπποθόῳ αὔταρκες εἶναι ληστεύειν κατ' ἄνδρα, εἰ μὴ καὶ κώμαις καὶ πόλεσιν ἐπιβάλον[10].

Data derived from both history and the novel, then, show that large bands of robbers existed and doubtless needed efficient organization. It is most likely that they will have found the model for their organization

---

[1] On 82, 27: "De more militiae, quacum latrocinium ubique comparatur."
[2] p. 195: "Eine Fülle von Ausdrücken des Kriegshandwerks wird auf das Räuberhandwerk übertragen..."
[3] p. 68: "Nach Art eines Heeres haben sich die Räuber organisiert..."
[4] *uexillarius, antesignanus, tirocinium* and the like are listed under 'métaphores diverses" (p. 255); *denso conglobatoque cuneo* under "termes de la langue militaire employés au sens propre" (p. 256).
[5] R. McMullen, *Enemies of the Roman Order*, Cambridge (Mass.) 1966, in particular Appendix B: *Brigandage* (pp. 255-268) with literature.
[6] Léa Flam-Zuckermann, *A propos d'une inscription de Suisse* (CIL, XIII, 5010): *étude du phénomène du brigandage dans l'empire romain*, Latomus 29 (1970), pp. 451-473 with literature.
[7] McMullen p. 256.
[8] McMullen pp. 263 f.
[9] P. A. MacKay, *Klephtika. The Tradition of the Tales of Banditry in Apuleius*, *G&R* 10 (1963), pp. 147-152.
[10] Xen. *Eph.* 4, 1, 1; 4, 1, 5; 5, 2, 2.

in the Roman army. This supposition is supported by the fact that the bands of robbers were often made up of deserters[11].

In the light of the above a literal interpretation of the military terms in the robber episode of the *Metamorphoses* seems the more attractive. Within the novel the terminology is used by several characters; and the robber society is seen as a military organization from several points of view.

The first robber: *castra nostra* (80, 20), *expugnare* (80, 18), *dux* (80, 22).

The second robber: *expugnare* (81, 71), *munire* (81, 12; 81, 20), *pugnam contemnere* (81, 22), *potiri* (81, 23), *uexillarius* (82, 2), *dux* (82, 8), *antesignanus* (82, 18), *sacramentum*[12] (82, 27; 86, 1; 90, 15), *dextera Martis* (82, 27), *commilito* (82, 28; 88, 15; 90, 5), *militia*[13] (86, 1); *contubernalis* (86, 26)[14], *excubare noctes* (87, 21), *cohors* (88, 5), *conferta manus* (88, 14)[15], *agminatim* (89, 24).

The third robber: *diripere* (154, 12), *castra* (154, 14) and when his words are quoted by the ass *commilito* (157, 2), *itinera pacare* (157, 4), *indutias seruare* (157, 5), *tirocinium* (157, 6), *Martia cohors* (157, 7).

Haemus: *Marti clientes* (158, 4), *manipulus* (158, 14), *stipendium* (158, 24), *mucrones Martii* (160, 8), *castellum* (162, 8).

Charite: *densus conglobatusque cuneus* (95, 11).

The ass: *speculatores sorte ducti excubabant* (79, 11), Mars (91, 11)[16] *castra commouent* (92, 3), *proelium conficere* (147, 6), *lorica* (152, 12). Moreover certain words and expressions obtain an extra dimension if we start from a literal interpretation of the military terminology, thus e.g. at 82, 22 *raptim reportamus*[17].

The argument so far does not intend to suggest, however, that all military terms should be taken literally. *Cinctum atque obsessum* (90, 2) of course must be taken in a transferred sense, so also *causariam missionem* (77, 19) and *commilito* (78, 8)[18].

We are, then, in complete agreement with Neuenschwander[19] when he says that Apuleius presents us with a group of robbers who have organised themselves entirely on army lines.

---

[11] McMullen pp. 264 ff.; Flam-Zuckermann p. 462.
[12] See comm. *ad loc.*; cf. Xen. *Eph.* 2, 14, 4 (Hippothoos and Habrocomes) ὅρκους ποιοῦσι συνεργήσειν τε καὶ συλλήψεσθαι.
[13] See comm. *ad loc.*
[14] See comm. *ad loc.*
[15] See comm. *ad loc.*
[16] Cf. Xen. *Eph.* 2, 13, 1 Οἱ δὲ περὶ τὸν Ἱππόθοον τὸν λῃστὴν ἐκείνης μὲν τῆς νυκτὸς ἔμειναν εὐωχούμενοι, τῇ δὲ ἑξῆς περὶ τὴν θυσίαν ἐγίνοντο. Παρεσκευάζετο δὲ πάντα καὶ ἀγάλματα τοῦ Ἄρεος καὶ ξύλα καὶ στεφανώματα.
[17] See comm. *ad loc.*
[18] One might think that the ass feels he is now part of the robbers' organization. This, however, seems rather unlikely; cf. e.g. 9, 13 (212, 11) *de meo iumentario contubernio* (no robbers in the neighbourhood either!)
[19] See note 3.

APPENDIX II

87, 10: *Fraglantia* or *flagrantia?*

F's orthography is *fraglantia* also at 6, 12 (137, 10) *solis fraglantia,* but (forms of) *flagrantia* are found at 4, 1 (74, 9); 4, 14 (85, 11); 4, 31 (99, 21) and 6, 32 (153, 21).

According to ThLL (which does not mention *Met.* 137, 10) *fraglantia* is found elsewhere only at Arn. 5, 6 and Ambr. *Is.* 8, 73; in Arnobius both Reifferscheid (CSEL) and Marchesi (CSLP) adopt the correction *flagrantia* of the *editio princeps,* but in Ambrosius Schenkl (CSEL) retains the orthography of the best manuscripts (UNT however have *flagrantia*).

The orthography of the verb in its various forms must obviously be taken into account. In the *Met.* the situation is as follows:

   1. Forms of *flagrare = ardere* are found at 8, 22 (194, 5) *flagrabat;* 10, 2 (238, 4) *flagrantem;* 10, 25 (256, 20) *flagrantissimis.*

   2. Forms of *fraglare = ardere* are found at 4, 31 (99, 7 f.) *fraglantissimo,* but φ *flagrantissimo;* 5, 9 (109, 20) *fraglantes,* but ς *flagrantes;* 5, 23 (121, 6) *fraglans* but φ *flagrans.*[1]

   3. *Flagrare = olere* at 6, 11 (136, 6) *flagrans,* but Helm and others with vdVliet *fraglans,* Barthius *fragrans;* 10, 21 (253, 11) *flagrantissimo,* but Helm and others with vdVliet *fraglantissimo* (before vdVliet forms of *fragrare* were preferred, apparently because prescribed by Beroaldus).

   4. *Fraglare = olere* at 2, 8 (32, 5) *fraglans,* but φ *flagrans;* 4, 2 (76, 1) *fraglantis;* 10, 34 (265, 5) *fraglante.* Probably 3, 19 (67, 1) *fraglantibus papillis* (but φ *flagrantibus*) is to be mentioned here, too; see vdP. *ad loc.* (here, too, before vdVliet *fragrare* was preferred).

The ancient grammarians distinguished between two verbs; cf. Nonius p. 438, 16: *flagrare est ignescere, incendi et ardere, fragrare uero olere; et in plurimis inuenitur ista decretio;* Servius on Verg. *A.* 1, 436: *quotiens incendium significatur, quod flatu alitur, per "l" dicimus, quotiens odor... per "r".*

Helm, who admits the distinction 1) and 2) among the groups mentioned above, therefore emends 3) to 4); he bases his opinion on a paper by Wölfflin in *ALL* 4 (1887), pp. 8-10. Wölfflin distinguishes between the same two verbs as the ancient grammarians, but notes two developments: *fragrare* becomes *fraglare* (dissimilation, see also Sommer p. 212), but by an interchange of *l* and *r flagrare* also becomes *fraglare* in popular language. This metathesis is not found in literature for a long time. "Von

---

[1] ThLL mentions the following passages (outside the *Met.*) Manil. 2, 880; *id.* 5, 745; Curt. 6, 6, 16; Stat. *Silv.* 4, 4, 27; Juv. 13, 182; Suet. *Nero* 22, 1; Flor. *epit.* 3, 5, 3; Tert. *Nat.* 2, 9, 13; *Tract. in Luc.* 1, 25; Paul. Nol. *Epist.* 23, 33.

Fronto an dagegen zeigen die massgebenden Handschriften eine solche Bevorzugung der Metathesis, dass wir notwendig auch an eine veränderte Taktik der Schriftsteller glauben müssen" (p. 8).

This theory is strongly opposed by Paratore in the introduction to his edition of Amor and Psyche (Firenze ²1960). The variants *flagrare* and *fraglare* are according to Paratore (p. 27) an "incertezza grafica dei copisti, ma non quella di un litterato, come Apuleio, educato nelle scuole di retorica". A similar judgment occurs in the ThLL (W. "scriptoribus dat quae librariorum sunt"), slightly softened by Grimal (ed. A&Ps, pp. 58 f.) and Callebat, *S.C.*, p. 129.

Such a statement cannot be checked, is not falsifiable and therefore does not belong to scholarship. We cannot reach beyond our first witness, viz. ms. F. If we accept with Helm the variants *flagrare/fraglare* for *ardere*, we must also do so for the sense *olere*. See also Bonnet, p. 175.

APPENDIX III

A textual problem.

91, 15-17 F: *ego ů nūquã* (*nū* added by a second hand) *alias hordeo* (*eo* possibly by a second hand instead of *eu*) *cibatus* (*ciba* added by a second hand) *sũ minutatĩ & diutina cogitatione iurulentũ sẽp es-serĩ* (- added by a second hand)

φ: *ego uero nūquã* (*nū* added by a second hand) *alias ordeum* (*um*: altered by a second hand, originally *o*) *tũṣ* (‾ by a second hand) *sũ minutatĩ et diutina cogitatione iurulentũ sẽp esse*

Oudendorp A (1786)	*ego vero nunquam alias hordeo cibatus, tunsum nî minutatim et diutina coquitatione iurulentum semper essem*
Oudendorp B	*ego vero numquam alias hordeum nisi tunsum minutatim et diutina coquitatione iurulentum semper essem.*
Hildebrand (1842)	*ego mero numquam alias ordeo cibatus, cum minutatum et diutina coquitatione iurulentum semper eserim*
Eyssenhardt (1869)	*ego uero numquam alias ordeum cibatus ni minutatum et diutina coquitatione iurulentum* [*semper eserim*]
vdVliet (1897)	*ego uero nunquam alias hordeum* ⟨*nisi*⟩ *tunsum minutatim et diutina coquitatione iurulentum semper esse* ⟨*solitus*⟩
Helm I/II 1907-1913	*ego vero, ut qui alias hordeum praeter tussum minutatim et diutina coquitatione iurulentum semper* ⟨*spr*⟩*everim*
Gaselee (1915)	*ego vero, qui numquam alias hordeum cibatus ni minutatum et diutina coquitatione iurulentum semper eserim*
Giarratano (1929)	*ego uero, ut qui alias hordeum contusum minutatim et diutina coquitatione iurulentum semper essem*
Helm III (1931)	*ego uero, numquam alias hordeo crudo cibatus* ⟨*sed tu*⟩*sum minutatim et diutina coquitatione iurulentum semper esse* ⟨*solitus, inte*⟩*rim*
Robertson (1940)	*ego uero, numquam alias hordeum* ⟨*crudum sed*⟩ *tunsum minutatim et diutina coquitatione iurulentum semper* ⟨*solitus*⟩ *esse,* [*rim*]
Terzaghi (1954)	= Giarratano
Helm (Akad. Verl.) (1956)	(= Helm-Krenkel): *ego vero, numquam alias hordeum* ⟨*crudum sed*⟩ *tunsum minutatim et diutina coquitatione iurulentum semper esse* ⟨*solitus, inte*⟩*rim*

Brandt-Ehlers (1958)	= vdVliet
Frassinetti (1960)	ego uero, numquam alias hordeo cibatus nisi tun⟨sum⟩ minutatim et diutina coquitatione iurulentum semper esse⟨t⟩, [rim]
Vitali (1960)	ego vero, ut qui alias hordeum praecontusum minutatim et diutina coquitatione iurulentum semper essem
Scazzoso (1971)	ego vero, ut ⟨qui⟩ numquam alias hordeum crudum sed tunsum minutatim, et diutina coquitatione iurulentum semper ⟨solitus esse⟩
vThiel (1972)	ego vero, numquam alias hordeum cibatus [sum] ⟨nisi⟩ minutatum et diutina coquitatione iurulentum [semper esserim]

Further proposals:

Lütjohann (1873)	ego vero numquam alias hordeo ⟨crudo pransus, cum adhuc⟩ tunsum minutatim et diutina coquitatione iurulentum semper essem
Novák (1904)	ego vero qui numquam alias hordeo cibatus sum ⟨integro, sed tunsum⟩ minutatim et diutina coquitatione iurulentum semper esse ⟨consueram⟩
Leo (1907)	ego vero numquam alias hordeum nisi tus(s)um minutatim et diutina coquitatione iurulentum expertus, sero
Armini (1928)	ego vero nun⟨c⟩, quam⟨quam⟩ alias hordeu⟨m⟩ cibatu⟨i tu⟩ssum minutatim et diutina coq⟨u⟩itatione iurulentum semper e[s]serim
Castiglioni (1929)	ego vero, ⟨qui⟩ numquam alias hordeum nisi contusum minutatim et diutina coquitatione iurulentum semper esse ⟨consue⟩rim

Among all these proposals Hildebrand's certainly is the most economical. His *mero* is a happy stroke, though probably unnecessary.

APPENDIX IV

Apuleian influences in *Gil Blas* by Le Sage.

"It is tempting to hazard that Apuleius was in Le Sage's mind when he composed the early scene set in the cavern of the brigands." Thus Walsh (p. 241), rather more carefully than E. H. Haight[1], characterizes the influence *Met.* IV may have had on the first book of *Gil Blas* (published 1715). Whether the influence was direct or indirect (by way of Espinel), there are in any case obvious similarities between the two, as the following fragments may show.

Fr. I   Gil Blas is captured by two men and taken to a subterranean cave (I 4).
Quand nous eûmes fait environ deux cents pas en tournant et en descendant toujours, nous entrâmes dans une écurie qu'éclairoient deux grosses lampes de fer pendues à la voûte. Il y avoit une bonne provision de paille, et plusieurs tonneaux remplis d'orge. Vingt chevaux y pouvoient être à l'aise, mais il n'y avoit alors que les deux qui venoient d'arriver... Nous sortîmes de l'écurie, et, à la triste lueur de quelques autres lampes qui sembloient n'éclairer ces lieux que pour en montrer l'horreur, nous parvînmes à une cuisine où une vieille femme faisoit rôtir des viandes sur des brasiers et préparoit le souper. La cuisine étoit ornée des ustensiles nécessaires, et tout auprès on voyoit une office pourvue de toutes sortes de provisions. La cuisinière (il faut que j'en fasse le portrait) étoit une personne de soixante et quelques années. Elle avoit eu dans sa jeunesse les cheveux d'un blond très-ardent; car le temps ne les avoit pas si bien blanchis qu'ils n'eussent encore quelques nuances de leur première couleur. Outre un teint olivâtre, elle avoit un menton pointu et relevé, avec des lèvres fort enfoncées.

Fr. II   After some time a second group of robbers arrives at the cave. The old "kitchenmaid", called Leonarde, enlists Gil Blas to assist her in her duties (I 5).
Je cédai à la nécessité, puisque mon mauvais sort le vouloit ainsi, et, dévorant ma douleur, je me préparai à servir ces honnêtes gens.[2]...
Un grand plat de rôt, servi peu de temps après les ragoûts, vint achever

---

[1] Cf. E. H. Haight, *Apuleius and his influence*, New York 1963 (repr.), pp. 114/115: "Gil Blas' experiences in the robbers' cave... take from Apuleius... the cave setting, the old hag cook, the narration of their life histories by three robber chieftains, and the capture of the lady, who tells her own thrilling love story."
[2] Walsh, p. 241, n. 3 notes the Apuleian element in the use of the ironic adjective. A similar Apuleian element may be seen in "mon mauvais sort" (*saeua Fortuna*!).

de rassasier les voleurs, qui, buvant à proportion qu'ils mangeaient, furent bientôt de belle humeur, et firent un beau bruit. Les voilà qui parlent tous à la fois. L'un commence une histoire, l'autre rapporte un bon mot; un autre crie, un autre chante: ils ne s'entendent point[1].

Desperate complaints of Gil Blas (I 6). They recall Charite's despairing   Fr. III
cries in the *Met.* (4, 24 f.).
O ciel! dis-je, est-il une destinée aussi affreuse que la mienne? On veut que je renonce à la vue du soleil; et comme si ce n'était pas assez d'être enterré tout vif à dix-huit ans, il faut encore que je sois reduit à servir des voleurs, à passer le jour avec des brigands, et la nuit avec des morts! Ces pensées qui me semblaient très-mortifiantes, et qui l'étaient en effet, me faisaient pleurer amèrement.

Led by their chief Rolando the robbers fire at a travelling carriage and   Fr. IV
capture it (I 9, 10).
Le seigneur Rolando courut d'abord à la portière du carrosse. Il y avoit dedans une dame de vingt-quatre ans, qui lui parut très-belle, malgré le triste état où il la voyoit. Elle s'étoit évanouie pendant le combat, et son évanouissement duroit encore. Tandis qu'il s'occupoit à la considérer, nous songeâmes, nous autres, au butin... On prit, par ordre du capitaine, la dame, qui n'avoit point encore rappelé ses esprits, et on la mit à cheval, entre les mains d'un voleur des plus robustes et des mieux montés. Puis, laissant sur le grand chemin le carrosse et les morts dépouillés, nous emmenâmes avec nous la dame, les mules et les chevaux... Mais quand elle eût repris l'usage de ses sens, et qu'elle se vit entre les bras de plusieurs hommes qui lui étaient inconnus, elle sentit son malheur. Elle en frémit... Puis, cédant tout à coup à ces images épouvantables, elle retombe en défaillance; sa paupière se referme, et les voleurs s'imaginent que la mort va leur enlever leur proie[2].

---

[1] Cf. *Met.* 4, 8 (80, 14 f.) *clamore ludunt, strepitu cantilant, conuiciis iocantur.*
[2] Cf. *Met.* 4, 25 (94, 11 ff.) *"nimirum", inquit, "tanto compendio tuae redemptionis defraudare iuuenes meos destinas?"*

INDEX OF WORDS

216

lucerna 89, 6-7
luculentus 93, 22-94, 3
lusitare 79, 17-20
lymphaticus 94, 1

M
maceratus 85, 10-13
machina 84, 23-25
madidus 75, 20-24
malum 94, 9-11
manducare 92, 5-7
mansio 78, 10-12
manus 84, 21-22
Mars 91, 10-12
matronatus 92, 14-20
mehercules 92, 14-20
memoria 81, 1-5
mens 78, 18-20
mentiri 77, 24-26
meridies 77, 7-9
merito 80, 21-24; 91, 4-6
meta 89, 14-17
-met(suffix) 77, 9-15
Metus 85, 8-10
mi(= mea) 94, 16-18; 96, 5-6
militia 85, 25-86, 1
mineus 75, 10
ministerium 82, 1
ministerium facere 80, 10-12
minutatim 91, 15-92, 1
mirabundus 87, 2-3
miscere 89, 21-24
miseratio 76, 14-17
Misericordia 85, 8-10
missio 77, 17-19
modus 76, 20-23
momentum capere 88, 7-10
mortales 88, 3-5
mugitus 90, 12-18
multi numero 76, 20-23; 79, 15; 89,24-
    90, 3
multiiugus 84, 19-21
mutuo 94, 25-26

N
namque 88, 27-28
naufragium 85, 13-14
nauiter 83, 14-16
ne 77, 26-78, 1-2
ne...quidem 81, 25-26; 90, 12-18
nec 74, 17-18; 85, 8-10; 90, 7; 96, 5-6
nec mora cum 77, 7-9; 81, 24-25
nec...quidem 83, 14-16
nec secus 89, 9-11; 90, 8-12
nec tamen 89, 20-21; 90, 7
nec...uel 92, 5-7
nemo quisquam 90, 20-22

nidor 76, 25-77, 6
nil quicquam 79, 21
nimio uelocitatis 75, 15-18; 76, 12
nimirum 94, 11-13
nimium 78, 23-27
nisi 90, 22-24
nitor 75, 12-15
nocte promota 92, 3-5
noctis initio 81, 24-25
nos 82, 15-18
nostri (= mei) 90, 7-8
noualia 87, 7-9
nudatus 85, 21-22
numerosus 81, 8-10
nummularius 81, 16-19
nuncupatus 94, 26-95, 2

O
ob id 78, 23-27
obdere 88, 22-26
oblatus 85, 5-8
obnixus 82, 6-7; 89, 1-4; 90, 12-18
obstinatus (with inf.) 77, 15-17
obtundere 76, 5-11
officium 95, 2-4
offigere 82, 6-7
optio 86, 8
ora 86, 10-12
ordeum 91, 12-13
ornare 95, 5-8
osculum ingerere 95, 5-8
ouilis 79, 4-8

P
pactum iugale 94, 26-95, 2
pannosus 83, 19-20
parens 94, 16-18
parricidium 83, 1-4
partim 92, 3-5
partus 85, 5-8
patibulum 82, 9-10
paupertinus 83, 19-20
pellere 87, 1-2
per fidem sacramenti 82, 26-28
per-(prefix) 78, 23-27
percitus 76, 18-20; 95, 24-25
perditus 84, 21-22
perobliquus 78, 23-27
persecutio 95, 25-96, 3
petere 84, 13-14
pignerare 94, 25-26
pigre 90, 22-24
plane 74, 19-75, 1
plangor 76, 14-17
plures numero 79, 15; 80, 6-8
porrectus 75, 24-76, 3
postliminium 94, 9-11

postuma spes 78, 3
prae ceteris 86, 8
praeceps 78, 6-8; 84, 4-7
praeclarus 75, 18-20
praesens 90, 12-18
praestare (with inf.) 74, 11-13
praestinare 86, 15-17
praestolari 81, 24-25
praeter 80, 17-21
praeter quod 96, 7-9
praeualere 85, 19-21
pressus 94, 9-11
primarius 84, 17
primitiae 86, 22-23
principalis 94, 21-23
procul dubio 76, 20-23
proditus 86, 19-21
prolixus 74, 11-13
promicare 75, 10
pronus 79, 1-2
propter 77, 9-15; 88, 7-10
prorsus/prorsum 77, 17-19
prospicere 83, 19
Protesilaus 95, 15-16
prouentus 87, 6-7
Prouidentia 85, 8-10
publicus 89, 20-21
pulmenta 79, 24-80, 2
pulpa 85, 25-86, 1
puluereus 78, 16-17
punicans 75, 24-76, 3
putor 76, 25-77, 6

Q
qua(= ubi) 79, 4-8
quam 76, 25-77, 6
quamquam + adj. 92, 24-93, 3
quamquam + subj. 89, 14-17
quamuis 74, 11-13; 90, 20-22
quid(in the sense of cur) 83, 19-20
quidam   76, 5-11;   76, 25-77, 6;   77,
      9-15; 79, 13-16; 80, 6-8; 84, 7-12;
      90, 22-24; 91, 10-12; 95, 25-96, 3
quidem 81, 1-5; 91, 13-15
quidni 93, 5
Quies 85, 8-10
quis (= quibus) 87, 29-88, 3
quo 76, 23-25; 79, 11-12; 91, 15-92, 1
quod 74, 13-15; 81, 13-16

R
raptus 95, 24-25
rasura 85, 24
receptaculum 85, 19-21; 87, 29-88, 3
recondere 86, 9-10
reddere 90, 12-18
redemptio 92, 24-93, 3

refectio 79, 17-20
reficere 75, 15-18
reformare 92, 3-5
refricare 94, 9-11
religio 82, 22-24
reluctare 89, 14-17
repandere 88, 10-13
repentinus et inopinatus 84, 5
reportare 82, 18-22; 87, 7-9
rescula 83, 19
sibi reseruare 90, 12-18
resistere 88, 18-20
respiratus 86, 14-15
retrorsus 76, 23-25
Riualitas 85, 8-10
roridus 87, 14-16
rosarius 76, 3-5
rumigare 92, 9-10
rurester/rurestris 75, 24-76, 3
rursum (pleonastic) 88, 14-18

S
sacramentum 85, 25-86, 1
sagaciter 84, 1; 88, 10-13
sagina 84, 23-25
saginare 75, 1-2
salubre consilium 88, 26-27
sanguis 92, 24-93, 3
sarcimen 86, 10-13
sarcina 85, 19-21; 91, 1-4; 92, 14-20
saucius 92, 2
scaena 89, 17-19; 94, 20
scaeuitas 75, 18-20
scaeuus 75, 18-20; 88, 26-27
schema 89, 17-19
scilicet 82, 5-6; 83, 13-14; 83, 17; 92,
      24-93, 3
scrutariam facere 81, 1-5
sebacius 89, 6-7
secretus 74, 13-15
secta 88, 3-5; 92, 22-24; 93, 6-8
secum 78, 3; 78, 10-12
securus + gen. 92, 22-24; 93, 12-19
secus 89, 9-11
sed 75, 18-20; 76, 5-11; 77, 22-23
semitectus 85, 14; 87, 29-88, 3
semiuiuus 85, 13-14
sensim 82, 3-5; 89, 11-14
sensus 78, 18-20
serenus 86, 9-10
sermo 80, 3-6
sermonis terminus 91, 9-10
seruare 88, 3-5
seruiliter 93, 12-19
seruire 78, 3-5
sessio 85, 10-13
seta 86, 10-12

sic 79, 17-20; 93, 8-11
sicubi 75, 2-4
singula rerum 75, 18; 82, 5-6; 83,
    13-14; 88, 20
Sobrietas 85, 8-10
solus 82, 29-30
solitarius 81, 19-21
sollers species 86, 6-7
sollicite 85, 5-8
Sollicitudo 85, 8-10
Sors 77, 22-23
sorte ducere 80, 10-12
sospitator 79, 24-80, 2
spem...propagare 95, 5-8
spiritus 90, 12-18
spontalis 83, 1-4
stagnare 79, 2-4
stipatus 79, 2-4; 79, 13-16
stridere 79, 23
subire effigiem 86, 3-6
sublicius 84, 23-25
sublimis 82, 1-3
subsistere 94, 16-18
subtrahere 88, 10-13
sueta 93, 6-8
summas 92, 14-20
super (instead of de) 84, 15-16
suppellectilis 85, 2-3
suppetiatum 82, 14-15
suscipere 81, 6-8
se suspendere 84, 1
suus 81, 1-5; 83, 1-4; 83, 16

T
tabulae 94, 26-95, 2
taeda 89, 6-7; 95, 4-5
tam magnus 79, 17-20
tantillum 95, 12-15
tempestiuus 87, 19-23
termini 91, 1-4
terrere ad 82, 22-24
Terror 85, 8-10
timidule 81, 1-5
tolerare 82, 6-7; 95, 5-8
torus 83, 14-16
tot numero 79, 13-16

toti (= omnes) 77, 24-26; 91, 6-8
trames 79, 4-8
tremens 79, 23
trepidus + gen. 82, 22-24
tribuere 92, 22-24
Tristities 85, 8-10
tu quidem 92, 22-24
tuguriolum 83, 10-11
tumultuarius 79, 24-80, 2
tunc 81, 2-3; 85, 14-17
tune 81, 6-8
turbela 90, 3-6
tutus 80, 17-21

U
uadimonium 88, 5-7
ualefacere 87, 27-29
ualuae 81, 26
uel 89, 14-17; 94, 7-8
uenaticus 89, 9-11
uenatio 84, 23-25
uenator 84, 21-22
uenenum 76, 3-5
ueneratus 83, 4-6
uespera 86, 23-25; 88, 10-13
uestis stragula 83, 17
uexillarius 82, 1-3
uidelicet 76, 14-17
uigilare 82, 5-6
uinum merum 91, 9-10
uisitatus 88, 22-26
ultra 92, 13-14
undique 79, 4-8
unus 85, 19-21
unus quisque 82, 14-15
uocabulum 75, 24-76, 3
uocula 79, 23
usque 90, 20-22
usquequaque 75, 12-15
utcumque 81, 1-5; 85, 3-4; 89, 1-4

V
Venus 75, 12-15
Veritas 85, 8-10
Voluptas 85, 8-10

INDEX OF GRAMMAR AND STYLE

223

INDEX OF OTHER SUBJECTS

INDEX OF PASSAGES FROM THE METAMORPHOSES

228

INDEX OF PASSAGES FROM
GREEK AND LATIN AUTHORS

Gel.		Hor.	
3, 14, 10	81, 1-5	*Ars*	
5, 14, 7	84, 26-85, 1	15	83, 19-20
6, 22, 4	76, 20-23	103	95, 15-16
9, 13, 8	88, 28-89, 1	165	82, 1-3
10, 13	92, 3-5	*Carm.*	
12, 13, 4	88, 26-27	1, 19, 14 f.	91, 9-10
13, 21, 12	78, 12-13	1, 24, 7	85, 8-10
14, 6	75, 12-15	1, 37, 2 ff.	91, 13-15
14, 6, 3	82, 3-5	2, 1, 6	86, 9
16, 5, 2	79, 8-9	3, 21, 21 f.	75, 12-15
17, 10, 4	81, 10-13	4, 13, 4	79, 17-20
Grat.		*Ep.*	
Cyn. 1, 269	89, 9-11	1, 2, 65	89, 9-11
Greg. M.		1, 10, 23	83, 19-20
Epist. 7, 75	74, 15-17	1, 14, 37	85, 8-10
Greg. Nyss.		1, 18, 84	82, 11-14
De hom. opif. 26, 1	84, 23-25	2, 2, 199	85, 14-17
Greg. Tur.		*S.*	
Franc.		1, 1, 117	82, 30-83, 1
		1, 9, 56	74, 11-13
2, 23	86, 6-7	2, 2, 20	79, 24-80, 2
5, 2	94, 16-18	2, 3, 27	90, 22-24
Heges.		2, 3, 72	95, 21-23
5, 31	94, 9-11	2, 3, 118	83, 17
Hdt.		2, 6, 103	75, 2-4
1, 85 ff.	79, 17-20	2, 8, 58 f.	93, 5
2, 121 β	82, 18-22	Hyginus	
8, 50	91, 1-4	*Fab.* 275, 4	81, 13-16
Hesychius		*praef.* 17 (Rose)	85, 8-10
s.v. σάλος	75, 9	*Inscr. Dessau*	
Hier.		2354	88, 21-22
Ep.		6824	88, 21-22
22, 6, 2	92, 13-14	Isid.	
58, 2	79, 17-20	*Etym.* 17, 7, 54	75, 24-76, 3
112, 5	83, 10-11	*Orig.*	
120, 11	87, 27-29	11, 1, 81	85, 25-86, 1
Hil.		19, 26, 1	83, 17
in Matth. 5, 14	76, 20-23	St. John	
Hippocr.		19, 24	80, 10-12
progn. 5	86, 14-15	Josephus	
Hist. Apoll. r.T.	92, 24-93, 3	*B.J.* 7, 5, 5	84, 23-25
c. 33		Jul. Val.	
Hom.		1, 7	92, 14-20
Il.		1, 13	80, 14-16
2, 504	91, 1-4	2, 32	89, 14-17
4, 406	81, 13-16	2, 34	76, 14-17
5, 338	75, 12-15	3, 3	80, 16-17
23, 186	75, 12-15	3, 24	87, 14-16
Od.		Justin.	
8, 364	75, 12-15	1, 10 pr.	94, 23-25
11, 263	81, 13-16	9, 4, 4	84, 11-12
		12, 2, 15	84, 11-12
h.Ven. 61	75, 12-15	23, 1, 9	89, 9-11
		32, 3, 16	80, 10-12

240

44, I, I   91, 1-4

Juv.
6, 78 f.   95, 4-5
10, 107   78, 6-8
13, 26 f.   81, 13-16
13, 182   Appendix II
14, 81   85, 1-2

Lact.
Opif. 8   75, 4-7
Phoen. 9   87, 14-16

Liv.
1, 4, 4   88, 28-89, 1
1, 16, 3   79, 24-80, 2
1, 50, 9   95, 16-18
2, 15, 5   77, 15-17
3, 6, 9   86, 6-7
3, 55, 1   74, 17-18
4, 4, 30   90, 8-12
4, 41, 8   85, 8-10
4, 49, 11   94, 9-11
4, 59, 6   89, 17-19
5, 12, 5   74, 17-18
6, 6, 14   77, 17-19
8, 33, 16   86, 8
9, 6, 8   93, 6-8
9, 44, 11   90, 20-22
10, 32, 6   90, 20-22
22, 17, 6   88, 22-26
22, 23, 3   75, 15-18
24, 18, 10   75, 15-18
26, 11, 10   76, 23-25
28, 24, 6   93, 6-8
31, 12, 6   93, 12-19
38, 40, 2   91, 1-4
42, 34, 3   94, 21-23

Liv. Andr.
com. 4   75, 1-2

Luc.
Phars.
1, 601   88, 3-5
4, 781 f.   79, 13-16
5, 442   79, 2-4
7, 7-44   96, 9-11
9, 106 f.   94, 7-8
9, 804   76, 20-23

Lucian.
v.h. II 46   82, 10
Symp. 45   80, 14-16

Lucil.
765 f. (Krenkel)   79, 17-20

Lucius Ampelius
29, 1   79, 13-16

Lucr.
2, 817 ff.   75, 12-15
3, 293   86, 9-10
5, 104   81, 10-13
5, 679   83, 9-10
5, 761   83, 12-13
5, 1033   86, 23-25
6, 987   76, 25-77, 6
6, 1232   76, 3-5
6, 1263   80, 12-14

St. Luke
23, 34   80, 10-12

Macer
De re militari 2   77, 17-19

Macr.
1, 1, 4   80, 14-16
1, 6, 9   85, 8-10
3, 18, 11   76, 5-11
7, 3, 20   76, 5-11

Mamert.
St. An. 138, 5   83, 9-10

Manil.
2, 880   Appendix II
4, 739   84, 26-85, 1
5, 190   84, 26-85, 1
5, 745   Appendix II

St. Mark
15, 24   80, 10-12

Mart.
1, 25, 8   90, 7-8
1, 102   91, 10-12
3, 77, 6   85, 25-86, 1
3, 93, 23   79, 17-20
8, 33, 3   84, 23-25
10, 90, 2   79, 17-20
12, 57, 7 f.   81, 16-19
14, 40   89, 6-7
14, 41   89, 6-7
14, 42   89, 6-7
14, 61   89, 6-7
14, 62   89, 6-7

Mela
3, 54   80, 16-17

Men.
Men. 816 (Jaekel)   82, 5-6

Methodius
Res. 1, 20, 4-5   84, 23-25

Min. Fel.
30, 6   85, 25-86, 1
37, 11   75, 15-18
38, 2   95, 21-23

Naev.
Lyc. 31   89, 17-19
  (33 f. Warm.)

242

29, 821 F	84, 18
Poll.	
5, 57	89, 9-11
Plb.	
6, 35, 11	80, 10-12
Pompon.	
Atell.	
33	84, 21-22
166	91, 15-92, 1
Porph.	
on Hor. *Ep.*	
1, 1, 14	84, 21-22
1, 18, 49	89, 9-11
2, 1, 81	84, 21-22
Prop.	
1, 15, 13	90, 20-22
1, 16, 27	79, 23
2, 18, 24	75, 12-15
2, 30b, 26	87, 14-16
3, 5, 43 f.	89, 14-17
4, 4, 48	87, 14-16
4, 8, 25	84, 23-25
Prud.	
Cath. 3, 101	75, 10
Ham. 278	75, 9
Perist. 10, 363	75, 20-24
Psych.	
244	85, 8-10
775	89, 9-11
Ps. Acro	
on Hor. *Carm.*	
1, 37, 2 ff.	91, 13-15
Ps. Long.	
De subl. 3, 2	85, 1-2
Publ. Syr.	
R 7	85, 8-10
Querolus	
ed. Ranstrand	
p. 24, 26 ff.	96, 9-11
Quint.	
Decl.	
339 (p. 340, 14)	85, 25-86, 1
Inst.	
5, 10, 97	86, 8
6, 3, 88	84, 1
7, 8, 4	86, 8
8, 3, 13	94, 9-11
10, 1, 2	81, 19-21
10, 1, 102	94, 9-11
12, 2, 2	88, 3-5
Rhet. Her.	
3, 3	80, 17-21

Rufin.	
patr. 1, 2 col. 302	90, 12-18
B(Migne 21)	
Sal.	
Cat.	
5, 9	78, 18-20
14, 1	84, 3, f.
58, 12	89, 14-17
60, 6	88, 14
Jug.	
6, 1	85, 4-5
17, 1	78, 18-20
88, 4	74, 17-18
95, 2	78, 18-20
106, 3	84, 15-16
108, 3	74, 17-18
Or. Lep. 5 p. 148, 19	
Kurfess	88, 26-27
Or. Phil. 3	82, 3-5
Sappho	
fr. 2, 6	75, 12-15
Schol.	
Juv. 2, 147	77, 26
Pers. 5, 185	92, 3-5
Soph. El. 505	84, 15-16
Stat. Theb.	
3, 198	81, 13-16
7, 252	81, 13-16
Script. Hist. Aug.	
Ael. Spart.	
Pesc. Nig. 7, 1	88, 26-27
Fl. Vopisc.	
Aurel. 34, 6	85, 8-10
Treb. Poll. *Gall.* 9,4	85, 8-10
Sen.	
Con. 1,5 *passim*	86, 8
Ben.	
2, 34, 1-2	89, 9-11
4, 3, 2	79, 17-20
4, 13, 1	75, 1-2
4, 34, 1	86, 6-7
7, 31, 5	82, 22-24
De Ira	
2, 16, 1	85, 1-2
3, 15, 4	94, 7-8
De Prov. 2, 10	90, 24-91, 1
Dial. 6, 2, 5	81, 1-5
Ep.	
12, 10	94, 7-8
15, 2	83, 23-25
24, 16	79, 23
37, 1 f.	90, 15
48, 8	76, 23-25

245

AUG 1 3 1982